WOMEN'S ACTIVIST
ORGANIZING
IN US HISTORY

WOMEN, GENDER, AND SEXUALITY IN AMERICAN HISTORY

Editorial Advisors:
Susan K. Cahn
Wanda A. Hendricks
Deborah Gray White
Anne Firor Scott, Founding Editor Emerita

A list of books in the series appears at the end of this book.

WOMEN'S ACTIVIST

ORGANIZING

IN US HISTORY

A
**UNIVERSITY OF
ILLINOIS PRESS**
ANTHOLOGY

COMPILED BY
DAWN DURANTE

INTRODUCTION BY
DEBORAH GRAY WHITE

**UNIVERSITY OF
ILLINOIS PRESS**
Urbana, Chicago, and Springfield

This anthology was compiled with the assistance of Laura Rocco,
Eleanor Hinton, and Alison Syring.

Library of Congress Cataloging-in-Publication Data
Names: Durante, Dawn, editor.
Title: Women's activist organizing in US history : a University
    of Illinois Press anthology / compiled by Dawn Durante ;
    introduction by Deborah Gray White.
Description: Urbana : University of Illinois Press, [2022] | Series:
    Women, gender, and sexuality in American history | Includes
    bibliographical references and index.
Identifiers: LCCN 2021035829 (print) | LCCN 2021035830 (ebook) |
    ISBN 9780252044342 (cloth ; alk. paper) | ISBN 9780252086410
    (paperback ; alk. paper) | ISBN 9780252053337 (ebook)
Subjects: LCSH: Women—Political activity—United States—
    History—Sources. | Women in the labor movement—United
    States—History—Scources. | Feminism—United States—
    History—Sources.
Classification: LCC HQ1236.5.U6 W6695 2022 (print) | LCC
    HQ1236.5.U6 (ebook) | DDC 320.082/0973—dc23
LC record available at https://lccn.loc.gov/2021035829
LC ebook record available at https://lccn.loc.gov/2021035830

Dedicated to Anne Firor Scott
a founding series editor
(1921–2019)
and to all the other past and present editors of the series

Mari Jo Buhle
Jacqueline Dowd Hall
Nancy Hewitt
Stephanie Shaw
Susan Armitage
Susan Cahn
Deborah Gray White
Wanda Hendricks

CONTENTS

Preface   ix

Introduction: The Difference that Difference Makes   1
Deborah Gray White

1   "To Cast Our Mite on the Altar of Benevolence:
Women Begin to Organize" (Excerpt)   13
Anne Firor Scott

2   "'There Sho' Was a Sight of Us':
Enslaved Family and Community Rituals"   33
Daina Ramey Berry

3   "The Daily Labor of Our Own Hands"   60
Lara Vapnek

4   "Latin Women from Exiles to Immigrants"   86
Nancy A. Hewitt

5   "Performing and Politicizing 'Ladyhood':
Black Washington Women and New Negro Suffrage Activism"   111
Treva B. Lindsey

6   "'It Was the Women Who Made the Union':
Organizing the Brotherhood"   138
Melinda Chateauvert

7   "Nurse or Soldier? White Male Nurses and World War II" (Excerpt)   158
    Charissa J. Threat

8   "'Black Beauticians Were Very Important': Southern Beauty Activists
    and the Modern Black Freedom Struggle"   180
    Tiffany M. Gill

9   "Organizing for Reproductive Control"   205
    Anne M. Valk

10 "Things Fall Apart; the LGBT Center Holds" (Excerpt)   235
    Deborah Gray White

    List of Original Publications   251

    Contributors   253

    Index   255

PREFACE

In 1987 a new series was formed at the University of Illinois Press. Dedicated to telling the histories of women in the United States, the inaugural year of the Women in American History series saw two books published: *Women Doctors in Gilded-Age Washington: Race Gender, and Professionalization* by Gloria Moldow and *Friends and Sisters: Letters between Lucy Stone and Antionette Brown Blackwell, 1946–93* edited by Carol Lasser and Marlene Deahl Merrill. While the first books in the series speak to some of the commitments embedded in the conception of the series, more recent books in the series also signal change. The series has grown to be more diverse in authors and topic (with much more work still to be done), revealing the ongoing evolution of women's studies as a discipline. In that vein, the name of the series has changed as well. To reflect the changing standards and commitments of the series, the name of the series was expanded to Women, Gender, and Sexuality in American History as a result of a series planning session at the 2014 Berkshire Conference of Women Historians with the series under the leadership of Susan Cahn, Wanda Hendricks, and Deborah Gray White.

This anthology is a celebration of thirty-five years (and counting) of exemplary scholarship in the Women, Gender, and Sexuality in American History series that honors the breadth of the publishing commitments of the series from its early books, many of its most popular chapters, and some of its award winners. There have been several drafts of this manuscript, each iteration shorter than the last after difficult decisions made in service of the need to keep the anthology a reasonable length. The biggest task in creating this book became deciding how to curate and organize decades' worth of impactful scholarship into a single volume: organize. This emerged as the theme of the volume itself, as books in the series delved into the labor, activist, and community organizing at work across the history of women and their gender and sexuality in the United States. Chapters and excerpts grapple chronologically with these histories. No organizational structure could have allowed for each book in the series to be represented due to the constraints of publishing realities, but those books and chapters remain very much available to readers in other ways.

The Women, Gender, and Sexuality in American History series is near and dear to my heart. It was, in fact, the very first series I oversaw as an acquiring editor. While my institutional affiliation changed near the end of compiling this volume, I am no less passionate about the work I did with the series and am pleased to be able to complete this project. As an acquisitions editor, I tell the authors I work with that their book will be a series of collaborations, and this anthology has been no different. There was much work done researching, coordinating, securing permissions, and countless other tasks, and this book would not be complete without the help of many extraordinary women. Laura Rocco helped to build the very foundation of this volume during a practicum at University of Illinois Press when she was a graduate student in the University of Illinois at Urbana-Champaign's School of Information Sciences. Assistant acquisitions editor Eleanor Hinton took on a great deal of work on the project after I left the University of Illinois Press and, like everything she touches, the volume is better for it. I have endless gratitude to Alison Syring for all the work we've done together, but especially for her years of support in keeping this project moving forward and for taking on the role of acquiring editor of the volume in its homestretch. From the moment I pitched the idea to the series editors, there was complete support and enthusiasm. They will always have my deep appreciation for their willingness to be involved, with particular thanks to Deborah Gray White. As a series author herself, she was the perfect choice to write this anthology's introduction, and, she has done a tremendous job in drawing out the connections between these pieces on women's organizing.

Organizing, reforming, resisting: the need for these energies are still felt urgently as a broken political system, misogyny, homophobia, racism, and myriad structural inequities persist. May the histories collected in this these pages and the dozens of books published in the Women, Gender, and Sexuality in American History series help to give us tools and insights into how we can continue to do more to organize against these systems through our labor, our activism, and our community building.

WOMEN'S ACTIVIST
ORGANIZING
IN US HISTORY

INTRODUCTION

THE DIFFERENCE THAT DIFFERENCE MAKES

DEBORAH GRAY WHITE

> . . . if I am interested in pebbles as pebbles, then I best not be distracted by the flatness
> of some or the roundness of others, the beige of one or the rosiness of another. For it
> is their pebbleness I said I was interested in, not their shape or their color.
>
> —Elizabeth V. Spelman, *Inessential Woman:*
> *Problems of Exclusion in Feminist Thought*

Obviously, this anthology is not about pebbles. It is a collection of essays about organizing in America. But just as the philosopher Elizabeth Spelman found it appropriate to begin her book about feminist thought with musings about the meaning and significance of the similarities and differences of pebbles, pebbles seems an appropriate analogy for the subject at hand.[1] For as most of these essays make apparent, in the 19th and 20th century, American women organized *as women* apart from men because they had different needs, skills, and concerns, or, to put it another way, an essential "pebbleness" that compelled them to organize. But just as significant as women's understanding of themselves *as women* was the fact that their strategies and methods differed according to their race, class, sexuality, and ethnicity. In other words, like pebbles, women's various identities differentiated them such that in analyzing their organizing it is difficult, to near impossible, to focus on their sameness without also recognizing their differences.

This collection emphasizes both of these ideas. One of its organizing principles is women's historic need to accentuate their gender identity apart from men and organize around issues they deem important. On the other hand, these essays show that, historically, the degree to which they did so, and how they did it, had every-thing to do with how they were different from each other. *Women's Activist Organizing in US History* also has another overarching theme. These essays demonstrate that the multiple identities of members of any organization make it difficult to decide on common goals and to sustain organizational activity. In other words, speaking metaphorically, taken singularly, individual pebbles are simpler than they are in aggregate, for when put together they present some unresolvable dilemmas.

———

From the beginning of the American nation, women organized apart from men not only because gender was a basic organizing principle of the new nation, but because women thought they had something to contribute *as women.* In Anne Scott's essay we learn that in both black and white women's organizations, women were able to establish identities separate from the men in their families. In tandem with establishing organizations that helped the indigent, they helped themselves carve out a place for women as the caregivers of the new nation and thus laid the foundation for later claims to citizenship and, as Treva Lindsey's essay shows, for the vote. Organizational work provided friendship networks outside the family and helped literate black and white women demonstrate their skills and their intelligence in a world that discriminated against them because they were women.

Almost all of these essays show gender to have been a metalanguage in American history. Just as historian Evelyn Brooks Higginbotham has called attention to the role of race as a metalanguage, these essays show that gender has a "powerful all-encompassing effect on the construction and representation of other social and power relations. . . ."[2] For example, in Daina Ramey Berry's essay on enslaved African Americans in Georgia we learn that gender governed the way owners organized work. Though both men and women did drudgingly heavy monotonous work, much non-field plantation work was organized around gender difference such that women were made cooks and seamstresses, and men did work that took them off of the plantation, thus giving men more mobility than women. In a world made bleak by oppression, men still initiated courtship and gained the highly valued asset of mobility by being allowed to travel to waiting wives on other plantations.

Throughout the nineteenth and twentieth centuries, women earned less money than men. Women organized around equality in the workplace not just because they believed themselves to be as deserving as men but because workplace inequities left women dependent on husbands, brothers, and fathers for their very subsistence and thus vulnerable to men's struggles, irresponsibility, whimsicalness, meanness, and downright violence. Lara Vapnek's chapter, "The Daily Labor of Our Own Hands," argues that, both before and after the Civil War, white women who lived together in the Massachusetts textile mills and worked in the garment industry organized for women's independence and self-sufficiency. They supported Garden Homesteads that would have made women proprietors of their own eastern homes instead of wives of western male settlers. In showing a preference for factory work, and even prostitution, over domestic service, they claimed agency over their bodies, an agency they would have had to surrender if they became household servants.

These white women were not unlike Nancy Hewitt's Latin women who *as women* fought for the vote and skilled factory positions as a way to represent their own economic interest; or Anne Valk's late-twentieth-century women who fought for the exclusive right to determine when and if they had children. When opposed by men, or government agencies, or union officials who argued that women's "natural" place was in the home as caretakers and mothers, women like those in these essays resisted essentialist representations which held women to be unfit for anything else.

But as Charissa Threat's essay indicates, women could be, and were, protective of their caretaker role when it served them. They not only used it, as Anne Scott shows, to justify their otherwise prohibited public activism, but they used it to police the boundaries of the nursing profession. In "Nurse or Soldier? White Male Nurses and World War II" Threat demonstrates how, for most of the twentieth century, the American Nurses' Association put all kinds of limitations on male nurses. She also shows how during World War II the Army and Navy would not enlist men as male nurses despite the severe shortage of medical personnel. Had female nurses been more supportive of the men in their profession, they might have benefitted from the military ranks that men could command. Instead, they discriminated against men as they held steadfastly—both during and after the war—to the idea that nursing was "a quintessentially female profession."

Just as the women of the American Nurses Association used the "woman as caretaker" role to maintain their advantage in the nursing profession, throughout history men have policed their identity as protectors, breadwinners, and warriors. This is made clear in Scott's work on women's benevolence work, which she demonstrates was undertaken because it did not directly threaten men or masculinize women. Hewitt's essay on Latin women in the cigar-making industry and Vapnek's piece on women in the textile and garment industry also demonstrate how easily men were threatened by assertive women who either competed with them for skilled employment or demanded the vote as a means of bettering their own economic condition. Melinda Chateauvert's work in "'It Was the Women Who Made the Union': Organizing the Brotherhood" further illustrates how protective men were of their masculine prerogatives. The Brotherhood of Sleeping Car Porters and Maids, the first all-black labor union, founded in 1925, survived and was successful in part because of the money raised by the women of its Women's Economic Councils. The wives and female relatives of the porters also ran interference between the union and the spies the railroad company used to break the union. Even though women—who were employed Pullman maids, wives of Pullman porters, and just unconnected union supporters—kept the union financially solvent, the men of the Brotherhood stressed black manhood rights and cultivated what Chateauvert calls an "alienating masculine culture."

Chateauvert's essay throws light not only on the predicament of the black women in the Brotherhood of Sleeping Car Porters and Maids but also on the difference that difference makes. In the all-black setting of the union, black women organized apart from men, but in the General Federation of Women's Clubs (the national organization that brought together local women's clubs) black women organized apart from white women. Similarly, in the union they were marginalized because they were women; in the latter they were discriminated against because they were black. Class made for another element of difference as the working-class women of the union and the middle-class women of the black women's club movement, both literally and figuratively did not "take tea." Union women found club women haughty and dictatorial, and middle-class women found union women uncultured. To complicate the story further, while some female supporters chose to organize by adopting tactics that were indistinguishable from union men, others were "unwilling to challenge the traditional division of union labor, maintaining that women should provide the conventional feminine support that complemented their husbands' quest for manhood." This latter choice highlighted the way sexuality circumscribed black women. Not wanting to appear too masculine, some women stayed away from speaking in public, collecting dues, and meeting in gender-integrated settings while they took up fund raising in their local churches and charity organizations. In short, though women organized *as women*, different groups of women organized separately because society's hierarchies of race, class, and sexuality positioned them such that their experiences of womanhood were radically different. As most of these essays show, women's organizing was aimed at expanding women's opportunities and opening all avenues of life. But women could not embrace the needs, ideals, ideologies, and tactics of all women, only those they felt an affinity with, and this had everything to do with race, class, and sexuality—the other metalanguages that structured their lives. Returning to Elizabeth Spelman's metaphorical pebbles, it is impossible to make sense of these essays without being distracted (or enriched) by the different shape or size (or race, class, or sexuality) of the pebbles (women) under analysis.

In fact, all of the essays deal with the difference that difference made in women's organizing. In the 1830s, women were not *supposed* to speak in public or gather with men in gender-integrated settings. Women's property was given over to their husbands upon marriage, and women could not sue for divorce. And, of course, they could not vote. Women were not *supposed* to work outside the home, wear pants, have sexual desire, or initiate courtship. They were not *supposed* to compete with men, either for supremacy or equality in private gender relationships, or in the public spheres of politics and entrepreneurship, or even on the factory floor. All women were subject to these disabilities and the laws and customs that under-girded them, but their race, class, and sexuality determined how they could and did organize to resist.

For example, historically, white and black American women were perceived differently. From the nation's inception through the twentieth century, white na-tive-born women were perceived to embody piety, purity, submissiveness, and domesticity.[3] As historian Mary Beth Norton tells us, they were "keepers of the nation's conscience, the only citizens specifically charged with maintaining the traditional republican commitment to the good of the entire community."[4] White women often used the representations of their womanhood to justify their or-ganizational activity. As argued by historian Linda Kerber, "domestic behavior had a direct political function in the republic." Since republics were thought to be fragile, the republican mother was theorized (mostly by women) as the family member who was the bulwark against autocracy. As mothers socialized their sons and daughters to be moral and virtuous citizens, they strengthened the nation, and simultaneously "justified women's absorption and participation in the civic culture." Republican motherhood redefined women as more than helpmates to their husbands, and the formulation became the foundation of the argument for women's education. Throughout the nineteenth and into the twentieth century, women, in the name of moral motherhood, fought not only for their educational advancement but against slavery, alcohol, and prostitution. They justified their fight for the vote on the grounds that as mothers and wives they were guardians of the family and nation. Facing fewer restrictions in the home than elsewhere, women, says historian Carl Degler, expanded their influence and power by transforming the world into one large home.[5] White women gained more rights in the twentieth century and they increasingly expressed their agency outside of the metaphor of the home. Nevertheless, their behavior was used to take the moral pulse of the nation.

By contrast, black women were thought to embody immorality. They were never perceived to represent the moral conscience of the American nation, nor were they ever taken to be a model of Republican motherhood. Beginning with the importa-tion of Africans as slaves, black women were worked in the fields and taxed as if they were men. By definition they were considered "mannish" women and thus unfeminine. Unlike native-born white women, who were perceived to be "naturally" demure, domestic, and pious, the black woman was perceived as either a mammy, an overweight black woman who loved her whites more than her blacks; a Jezebel, a woman who never refused a man's sexual advances; or a Sapphire, a woman who usurped the black man's power in the home and community. Because the enslaved status of the overwhelming majority of black women for nearly 250 years allowed them to be exploited for both their productive and reproductive labor, black women were thought to be abnormal, despite the fact that like white women they were subject to laws that circumscribed women's agency. Like Sojourner Truth, who was made to bear her breast before an anti-slavery audience because male attendees did not believe that she was a woman, black women carried the burden of proving that they were not perversions of femaleness. One way free black women did this was to create a cult of respectability designed to show that they were just as maternal, sexually pure, and domestically inclined as white women. Necessarily coded heterosexual, the cult of respectability helped shore up the public character of black men as well as women, but, though it prevailed as an anti-racist strategy throughout the nineteenth and twentieth century among the black striving classes, it was unable to counter the perception of black women as perpetually angry and dissatisfied.[6]

Of course, just as these representations, or tropes of womanhood, have sexuality and definitions of femininity and masculinity embedded in them, they also speak to class. Historian Dorothy Sue Cobble reminds us that "class differences have always affected the lives of women" and that "their views of what reforms were desirable and possible have been shaped in a class crucible."[7] Though American racial structure sometimes obscures and almost always complicates a class analysis, the essays in this anthology clearly demonstrate that wage-earning women who worked in the public sphere organized differently than middle-class, native-born women. While the latter entered the public sphere under the cover of domesticity, women who worked for a living had no such shield. Men found them threatening and limited their advancement and the money they could make. Ethnicity and/or immigrant status only complicates class analyses, for it is a fact that, for most of the nineteenth and twentieth century, immigrant women who were not socially constructed as "white" were not privy to the privileges and/or status that whiteness conferred.[8] Irish women, for example, were often perceived within the idiom of blackness, and thus like black women were thought to be biologically prone to deviant behavior. Historian Danielle Taylor Phillips reminds us that unlike domestic workers who were considered white, such as native-born Anglo-American, English, French, German, and Swedish women, Irish and black women were thought to embody racial inferiority and were considered biologically incapable of performing skilled wage labor. Both were described as "immoral, unintelligent, uncouth, dirty, lazy, and hostile."[9] According to historian Donna Gabaccia, we should not study race, class, nationality, and culture in isolation, for doing so makes it impossible to discern the way these identity variables intersect to create human identity or influence behavior.[10] In short, we learn a lot more about women's organizing (pebbles) when we search for the difference that difference makes.

These essays help us do just that. For example, the essays by Scott and Lindsey show that even though black and white women organized *as women* to aid the poor and gain the vote, they did so from their own separate racial corners using tactics they respectively judged proper for their race and class. Mindful of the racist practices that imposed poverty on African Americans and the racist beliefs that judged them to be deficient women, black women were less judgmental than white women while they were also careful to model respectability. In their benevolence work they did not differentiate between the worthy and unworthy poor. In fighting for suffrage they did not and could not engage in spectacle as white women did. While white women saw ladyhood as constraining and designed tactics meant to show themselves beyond its confining boundaries, black women had to present themselves as ladies in order to do the political work necessary to uplift the race *and* the social/psychological work necessary to support black men.

By themselves, these two essays demonstrate the dilemmas posed by what legal scholar Kimberlé Crenshaw has brilliantly demonstrated to be the multiple dimensions of identity. In her discussion of "political intersectionality," Crenshaw observes that "women of color are situated within at least two subordinated groups that frequently pursue conflicting political agendas. The need to split one's political energies between two sometimes opposing groups is a dimension of intersectional disempowerment that men of color and white women seldom confront."[11] In other words, gender causes black men and women to experience racism differently, and racism causes white and black women to experience sexism differently. This places black women in the untenable and often irreconcilable position of having to take sides against themselves.[12]

This phenomenon is reflected in several of the essays in this volume. Confronted with the realities of race and gender and the racism and sexism that flowed from each, either separately or in combination with each other, black women made conscious and unconscious choices. Daina Ramey Berry's essay, for example, confirmed my findings that enslaved men and women did not experience slavery the same way, and that "within the institution of racial slavery there were two systems, one for women, the other for men."[13] The greater mobility that Berry shows belonged to men had consequences for the resistance strategies used by men and women respectively. Looking at the racism and classism that divided black women from white and black middle-class women, Chateauvert shows how identity variables prevented women from joining hands *as women*. Black women union supporters separated themselves from black middle-class women while they also did not join hands with white working-class women. She also shows the influence of sexuality by demonstrating how those who challenged union men by stepping outside of the boundaries of acceptable female behavior risked being perceived as too masculine and often endured rebuke when they did.[14]

Chateauvert allows us to see that the metalanguages of class and sexuality impose the same kind of intersectional dilemmas as race and gender. Even when the latter are held constant, class and sexuality make for radically different intragroup life experiences, often forcing women to make conscious and unconscious choices in order to reconcile their various identities. For example, the working-class white women in Vapnek's essay and the Latin women in Hewitt's essay demonstrate the kinds of decisions made by women who had to reconcile class, race, and gender. White women who worked in the textile industry joined hands with men in their trade unions, and the Latin women who worked in the cigar-making industry found common cause with men who organized for better working conditions and higher wages and who helped their communities in mutual aid societies. In essence, their ties to the men of their class and ethnicity were often stronger than the bonds of womanhood. Neither group of women felt that native-born, white, middle-class women understood the needs of the working class well enough to either join with them in their struggles against men or allow these women to speak on their behalf. And both groups found it politically expedient to sometimes distance themselves from blacks, whether they were working-class or not or whether they shared a common ethnicity.

All of this difference speaks to the difficulty embedded within all organizing: the difficulty of building alliances across identities such that both the reason for organizing and the needs of those organizing can be addressed simultaneously. History has demonstrated how difficult a chore this has been. We need only look at organizing for women's suffrage. Could mid-nineteenth-century black women as a group really align with white women who opposed the Fifteenth Amendment because it denied the vote to women while it granted it to black men? Could they join hands with white women who were former slaveholders or who employed them as domestic servants? What do we make of white women who abandoned black women and aligned with white racists in their quest for the suffrage? Organizing among working-class women raised some of the same issues. Could black working-class women really joins hands with their white counterparts who, as Vapnek demonstrates, used the metaphor of white slavery to unite working class women?[15]

While all of the essays in this anthology demonstrate, sometimes obliquely, the organizing dilemmas posed by intersectionality, Anne Valk's essay, "Organizing for Reproductive Control," and my essay, "Things Fall Apart: The LGBT Center Holds," address the problems quite directly. Both of these essays show that alliances across identities are necessarily short-lived and more beneficial to those who are dominant in the hierarchy of race, class, and gender. Valk, for example, shows the different ways that Washington, D.C.'s middle-class white women and working-class and poor black women approached the issue of reproductive freedom. White women's race and class caused them to see reproduction rights in the context of abortion rights, which they saw as a means to women's liberation. The poor, mostly black, women who they allied with posed reproductive rights differently—as the freedom to choose when to have children free from poverty without the fear of sterilization. While they came together for a short period *as women* united for reproductive rights, their differences created a wedge that could be bridged only temporarily. Similarly, in "Things Fall Apart," though sexual minorities were able to unite and march together—for same-sex marriage, adoption rights, equality in the military, privacy rights, and anti-discrimination laws—white middle-class lesbians, gays, bisexuals, and transsexuals who identified themselves as "normal" ultimately benefitted the most. In this multicultured, economically layered, and racially and sexually diverse community, not everyone experienced or served the community the same way and thus the needs of all LGBTs could not be met all at once by the same organization.

Although this introduction has emphasized difference, Tiffany Gill's work on black women in the beauty industry shows us what happens when identity variables remain relatively constant and black women lead and set their own agendas outside of the influence of black men or white women. Gill shows us how the beauty shop became a safe empowering female space, and how economically autonomous black beauticians were able to bridge even the class divide and become community activists during the modern civil rights movement. To put it another way, Gill's essay shows us women (pebbles) and shows us how to analyze women (pebbles) whose differences were minimal and who could organize and be effective because of their sameness.

———

When Elizabeth Spelman wrote *Inessential Woman* back in 1988 and used the metaphor of pebbles to interrogate the problem of difference in feminist thought, she could legitimately quarrel with the way feminist scholarship was being written. She argued that "the focus on woman 'as woman' has addressed only one group of women—namely, white middle-class women of Western industrialized countries." She complained that scholars did not talk about what women had in common *as women*, rather that they conflated the condition of one group of women with the condition of all women, and treated the differences of white middle-class women from all other women as if they were not differences.[16] Hence, her discussion of pebbles and the necessity of understanding the dilemmas presented by their sameness and difference.

This anthology represents the distance that scholarship has come since the last quarter of the twentieth century. White middle-class women are no longer the starting point of all feminist scholarship and we now consider how various variables intersect and overlap to influence identity. Though readers can try, as I have done, to discern what it is that women have in common with each other, what separates them, and how their sameness and difference has determined their organizing goals and strategies, taken in aggregate these essays do not even try to present a tidy picture. They present women and their organizing in all their multiplicity and glorious complexity. And for all kinds of reasons, this is something to celebrate.

Notes

1. Spelman uses Uncle Theo, a character in Iris Murdoch's *The Nice and the Good,* who is perplexed and disturbed by the untidiness of pebbles on a beach to begin her exploration about the differences and sameness of women. Her point is to show that, ultimately, there is so much difference among women that whatever sameness exist is made almost irrelevant by difference. See *Inessential Woman: Problems of Exclusion in Feminist Thought* (Boston: Beacon Press, 1988), 1–17.

2. Evelyn Brooks Higginbotham, "African-American Women's History and the Metalanguage of Race," in *Signs* 17, no. 2 (Winter 1992): 252

3. Barbara Welter, "The Cult of True Womanhood: 1820–1860," *American Quarterly* (Summer 1966) Vol. 18, No. 2 Part 1, 152.

4. Mary Beth Norton, "The Evolution of White Women's Experience in Early America," *The American Historical Review* 89, no. 3 (1984): 617.

5. Linda Kerber, "The Republican Mother," in *Women's America: Refocusing the Past,* eds. Linda Kerber and Jane Sherron De Hart, 3rd ed. (New York: Oxford University Press, 1991), 87–95; Carl N. Degler, *At Odds: Women and the Family in America from the Revolution to the Present* (New York: Oxford University Press, 1980), 298–327.

6. For a discussion of these issues, see the following: Hazel Carby, *Reconstructing Womanhood: The Emergence of the Afro-American Women Novelist* (New York: Oxford University Press, 1987), 89–94; Hazel Carby, *Race Men* (Cambridge, MA: Harvard University Press, 1998), 9–41; Kevin Gaines, *Uplifting the Race: Black Leadership, Politics and Culture in the Twentieth Century* (Chapel Hill, NC: University of North Carolina Press, 1996), 67–99; Willard B. Gatewood, *Aristocrats of Color: The Black Elite 1880–1920* (Bloomington, IN: Indiana University Press, 1990), 332–348; Evelyn Brooks Higginbotham, *Righteous Discontent: The Woman's Movement in the Black Baptist Church, 1880–1920* (Cambridge, MA: Harvard University Press, 1993), especially 185–230; Martha Jones, *All Bound Up Together: The Woman Question in African American Public Culture, 1830–1900* (Chapel Hill, NC: University of North Carolina Press, 2007), 127–28; Wahneema Lubiano's discussion of Anita Hill and the representations of black women in "Black Ladies, Welfare Queens, and State Minstrels: Ideological War by Narrative Means," in Morrison, ed., *Race-ing Justice, En-gendering Power: Essays on Anita Hill, Clarence Thomas, and the Construction of Social Reality* (New York: Random House, 1992), 323–61; and Deborah Gray White, *Too Heavy a Load: Black Women in Defense of Themselves, 1894–1994* (New York: W. W. Norton, 1999), 56–109.

7. Dorothy Sue Cobble, *The Other Women's Movement: Workplace Justice and Social Rights in Modern America* (Princeton, NJ: Princeton University Press, 2004), 1.

8. See for example the work of David Roediger: *The Wages of Whiteness: Race and the Making of the American Working Class* (New York: Verso Books, 1999) and *Working Toward*

Whiteness: How America's Immigrants Became White, The Strange Journey from Ellis Island to the Suburbs (New York: Basic Books, 2005).

9. Danielle Taylor Phillips, "Moving with the Women: Tracing Racialization, Migration, and Domestic Workers in the Archive," in *Signs* 38, no. 2 (Winter 2013): 383.

10. Donna Gabaccia, "Immigrant Women: Nowhere at Home?" in *Journal of American Ethnic History* 10, no. 4 (Summer 1991): 68.

11. Kimberlé Crenshaw, "Mapping the Margins: Intersectionality, Identity Politics and Violence against Women of Color," *Stanford Law Review* 43, no. 6 (July 1991): 1252.

12. For an example see White, *Too Heavy a Load*, 13–20.

13. Deborah Gray White, *Ar'n't I A Woman? Female Slaves in the Plantation South* (New York: W. W. Norton, 1985), 62.

14. See White, *Too Heavy a Load*, 160–75.

15. See also Dana Frank, "White Working-Class Women and the Race Question," in *International Labor and Working-Class History* no. 54 (Fall 1998).

16. Spelman, *Inessential Woman*, 3.

CHAPTER 1

TO CAST OUR MITE ON THE ALTAR OF BENEVOLENCE

Women Begin to Organize
(Excerpt)

ANNE FIROR SCOTT

Benevolence: Disposition to do good, desire to promote the
happiness of others, generosity, charitable feeling.
—*Oxford English Dictionary*

In the last quarter of the eighteenth century, as the song had it, the world turned upside down. The whole complex of events and experiences encompassed in the Revolution and the formation of the Constitution created a sense of ferment, of new opportunities, but also of fear that the new experiment might fail if citizens were not up to the challenge. Women sensed new possibilities. John Adams was more prescient than he knew when he joked, in response to Abigail's exhortation that he and his colleagues should "remember the ladies" when they wrote a new constitution, "We have been told that our Struggle has loosened the bands of Government every where. That Children and Apprentices were disobedient—that schools and Colledges were grown turbulent . . . But your Letter was the first Intimation that another Tribe more numerous and powerfull than all the rest were grown discontented. . . ."[1]

By the 1790s, as President Washington, departing from office, was advising his fellow citizens to cherish virtue, education, and the new federal government, and Judith Sergeant Murray was announcing that young women were about to "form a new era in our history," the first female benevolent societies began to appear.[2] They were the first step toward what Linda Kerber has called "a synthesis . . . that

would facilitate women's entry into politics without denying women's commitment to domesticity."[3] Their self-imposed task was to fill at least part of the gap
as the numbers of people in need increased and local government aid did not.[4]

While economic development had brought a rapid increase in the number of
poor people, it also increased the number of business and professional men and
skilled artisans who could support their families without relying on the full-time
economic production of wives and daughters; such women were in the vanguard
of benevolent organization. In 1800 even very prosperous families still relied on
women for plenty of productive work, but as some goods once made at home began
to be available in the market there was a margin of time that could be devoted to
the kinds of collective enterprises hitherto the domain of men.[5]

There were precedents. Men had created voluntary associations for many
years and women had occasionally made their own experiments, though none had
lasted long.[6] In Boston in 1778, for example, young Hannah Mather had organized
a "woman's lodge" for the purpose of "improving the mind, that by *Strength* and
Wisdom, we might beautifully adorn the female character, . . ." but it disappeared
when members married and began to have children.[7] During the Revolution some
women (probably more than were recorded) banded together to raise money, provide amenities to the soldiers, and support the movement for independence. These
groups dissolved when the war was over, but memory of their accomplishments
lingered.[8]

Women were also accustomed to the idea of benevolence; it meant a quality
that good Christians were expected to exhibit, especially those whom God had
favored with health, wealth, and standing in the community. Taking care of the
less fortunate was not only a Christian duty, it might also insure one a place in
heaven, and certainly enhanced the reputation of one's family. Individual women
had engaged in charity as far back as the record ran; now they proposed to join
together for greater effectiveness.

The women set out to provide help for people in trouble: poor people, particularly those recognized as "worthy," and especially women and children. The
desire to do good was a powerful motivation, but it was not the only one. From
the beginning, benevolent women—still under the influence of the challenges
of the revolutionary age—were intent on their own spiritual and intellectual
improvement An increasing number of women were acquiring some education and developing a desire for more. While young women would soon begin
flocking to female seminaries, their mothers and married sisters tried to make
benevolent societies educational institutions for themselves.[9] Here and there a
female "reading circle" or a literary society appeared—groups, usually of young,
single women, intended entirely for self-education—but for the most part adult

women seemed to feel more at ease seeking to improve themselves in a context of carrying out significant community responsibilities. Murray's "new era in female history" was underway.

While development took place at different times in different places, over the first two decades of the nineteenth century most settled parts of the United States experienced rapid growth and increased interaction with the rest of the country. Voluntary associations of all kinds proliferated, to supplement the old institutional structures of family, church, and local government.[10]

The first "female societies" appeared in coastal cities from Savannah to Boston, but within two decades women in towns and villages all over the country, usually led by wives and daughters of the most visible and respected families, had begun to follow suit. In the rapidly growing cities poverty was increasingly visible, but in many prosperous towns and villages it was not yet a pressing problem; something more than simple need attracted women to collective activity. Though the swift rise of the benevolent society is often described as a response to the Second Great Awakening, the impulse to organize was not limited to places where the revival spirit had struck. Many women felt, however vaguely, that in the new age now coming into being a new kind of participation in community life was expected of them.

Societies took various forms and various names. In Philadelphia there was a Female Association for the Relief of Women and Children in Reduced Circumstances; in New York one group, inclined to specificity, called itself the Female Association for the Relief of the Sick Poor, and for the Education of Such Female Children as Do Not Belong To, or Are Not Provided For, by Any Religious Society; the Female Benevolent Society of St. Thomas and the Daughters of Africa were only two of many groups of free black women; in Savannah, Boston, and Petersburg, Virginia, white women combined to establish and administer asylums for female orphans, and in Baltimore to create a charity school for girls. Mite societies, cent societies, missionary societies, mutual aid, charitable and sewing societies were all variations on the same central idea. Whatever they called themselves, their essential activities were similar. Missionary societies began by raising money to send young men to preach in foreign parts or in the West, but very shortly many of them were engaging in local charity as well. Sunday school societies set out to provide a modicum of education for laboring children, but soon found that clothing and shoes were a necessary prerequisite to learning. Charitable societies distributed Bibles and preached temperance. Some groups were affiliated with a particular church, others were ecumenical, based on neighborhoods, kinship, or class.[11] Protestant groups were most numerous, but Catholic and Jewish women set up their own associations.

No matter where they were, who the members were, or what they called themselves, organizational forms were remarkably similar. Written constitutions were universal: every society established rules about meetings, the uses of money, and qualifications for potential recipients of charity.[12]

Free black women in New England and Pennsylvania were among the first to organize. Their motivation was in many ways quite different from that of their white contemporaries. Limited on all sides by prejudice and poverty, they began to establish societies for mutual aid and self-education. Despite the meagerness of their resources, they undertook to help one another and those even less fortunate. In 1809, for example, when the men in the African Benevolent Society of Newport, Rhode Island, though welcoming women's labor, would not permit them to vote or hold office, the women set up a separate association. In 1818 the Colored Female Religious and Moral Society of Salem (Massachusetts) drew up a forthright constitution which could be distinguished from those of its white neighbors in Boston or Cambridge by its plain speaking and its focus on mutual aid and self-help. Article 4, for example: "We promise not to ridicule or divulge the supposed or apparent infirmities of any fellow member, but to keep secret all things relating to the Society, the discovery of which might tend to do hurt to the Society or any individual." Or article 5: "We resolve to be charitably watchful over each other, to advise, caution and admonish where we may judge there is occasion, and that it may be useful; and we promise not to resent, but kindly and thankfully receive such friendly advice or reproof from any one of our members."

The society announced that it was formed for the benefit of sick and destitute *members*, and that if any member committed a "scandalous sin, or walk unruly, and after proper reproof continue manifestly impenitent, she shall be excluded from us, until she give evidence of her repentance."[13]

These strenuous requirements for self-monitoring and self-improvement reflected black women's conviction that the behavior of one affected the image of all. For them, mutual aid was to be psychological as well as material.

While they read and talked, women knitted, sewed, or made palm-leaf hats to supply the needs of the poor, either directly or by selling their handiwork for cash. They solicited money and goods from sympathetic men and used the money to organize schools, orphans' homes, homes for elderly women, soup kitchens, and employment services. For the most part members ran these institutions themselves, or hired needy women of their own social group to do so. "Managers" were assigned to visit people who needed help, and "prudential committees" allocated goods and money between meetings. A few societies experimented with work relief.[14]

White women's societies nearly always made a distinction between the "worthy" and the "unworthy" poor. The first group was made up of what might be called the working poor: people they considered respectable and self-respecting but who had met with unemployment or illness or the common misfortune of having too many children. Once-prosperous widows who had fallen on hard times or were too old to work were viewed with special sympathy. On the other hand, people who seemed unembarrassed by their poverty, who loved rum, or were thought to be ingenious beggars who were able to take advantage of their benefactors, were deemed unworthy.[15] Foreigners were often viewed with suspicion. In cities like Boston and New York, women worried lest they mistakenly help professional beggars or people who would sell their gifts to buy liquor. In small towns where most people knew each other, identifying people was easier. Occasionally some maverick member would raise the issue: Do we really *know* what "worthiness" is and who possesses it? But usually the concept was taken for granted and required no justification. Black women, by contrast, made few such distinctions; from their perspective virtually all African Americans who needed help were worthy of it.

Benevolent women brought their domestic habits into the public arena. Not only did they sew and knit for the poor just as they did for their own families, they also behaved as good mothers were supposed to: rewarding virtue, attempting to cure bad habits, and concentrating special attention upon children and old women, precisely as they did in their homes. They visited people in need, and liked to believe that warm relationships were established. Deaths of long-term clients were noted in the same words as those of longtime members.

Depending very much upon the capability of local leaders, societies varied in effectiveness and degree of sophistication. For example, one of the earliest—the New York Widows' Society as it came to be called—was a well-run and wide-ranging operation from the start. Isabella Graham, the founder, a highly educated, self-confident Scottish woman, had considerable experience as a teacher, and had herself been a self-supporting widow. An intensely religious person who was never happier than when writing on theological issues, she was also an astute politician who gained support for her enterprise from powerful men in the government of New York.

The Widows' Society was a prolific creator of long-lasting welfare institutions: schools, orphanages, workrooms for indigent women, for example.[16] The intensity of members' commitment might be measured by the fact that so many risked their lives by remaining in the city to provide aid to their clients during successive epidemics of yellow fever.[17]

A generation later Sarah Josepha Hale offered similarly creative leadership to the Boston Seaman's Aid Society. Graham and Hale were well-known women; many others, never heard of beyond the boundaries of their own communities, demonstrated administrative skills and imagination in the pursuit of their goals. When no natural leaders emerged, societies formed in an initial burst of enthusiasm often dwindled and died. Thousands, however, survived, in old communities and new ones, in cities and country towns—anywhere there were women. In the frontier settlements charitable societies appeared almost as swiftly as town government. Simple as these early collective efforts may seem on the surface, when they are viewed as a widespread social phenomenon, puzzles appear: Why were many so similar, despite wide differences in geographic location and original purpose? Why did they appear in places where poverty was only barely visible as well as in rapidly growing cities where it was an obvious problem? Were they, as some historians believe, one of the ways an increasingly self-conscious elite, black as well as white, began to define itself as separate and different from "the poor"?[18] Did women use benevolence as some men did philanthropy to consolidate their positions as community leaders?[19] Why did some women belong to two, three, or four such societies—spreading themselves and their resources thin, rather than concentrating both? Why did benevolent women feel free to invade the privacy of those they sought to help in ways that they would have found most offensive had they been the subjects of such invasion?[20] Most of all, one would like to see the benevolent societies through the eyes of those they presumed to help—but alas, no recipient seems to have left her reflections. It is not possible to find complete answers to these questions, but the surviving records of individual societies reveal something about the consciousness of the women themselves, a sensibility so different from our own that only a strenuous effort of historical imagination enables us to begin to see the world as they saw it. As benevolent-society members met and talked and wrote minutes and went about helping and exhorting their poorer neighbors, they revealed the values that pushed them on. In language that owed something to sermons and the King James Bible, and something as well to sentimental novels, they offered their perception of the world outside their own social class. We can see limitations and possibilities revealed and anxieties expressed.

Now and then, through the veil of sentimental language, it is possible to detect a skeptic who questioned the way things were being done, or who preferred blunt speech to euphemism, but for the most part benevolent women, particularly those who were white, spoke and thought like the characters in *Little Women*. Marmee and Meg existed by the thousand; only an occasional Jo, an occasional Amy, added variety to the landscape.

Black women, perhaps because the language of oppression had made euphemism anathema to them, spoke more plainly. Their situation was different from that of white benevolent women in fundamental ways. "Worthy" and "unworthy" were not so much part of their vocabulary: the fact that they shared with their poorer sisters all the indignities of racial prejudice and the stigma attached to black women gave a different tone to their statements and to their work.

Variations in the spirit and activity of benevolent societies across the country tell us something about the variety of American communities and of American women.

The Cambridge (Massachusetts) Female Humane Society was founded in 1814 in the setting of a small, semirural, homogeneous village.[21] It began with a concern "for the relief of the Indigent sick, particularly Females residing in Cambridge and the Port." Any woman who cared to join was welcome and the society denied vehemently that it intended to represent any one social group or religious view. Class lines were fluid; members were entitled to ask for assistance from the society. Recognizing sickness as a great threat to people whose income depended upon being able to work daily, the society decided to pay for doctors and apothecaries as necessary. In summer when wood was cheap the women bought a large supply in order to sell small quantities at cost when cold weather had driven the price up.

Frequent comments on the general good health and comfortable circumstances of most Cantabridgians suggest that no perception of pressing need had called this group into existence. The women had simply caught the prevailing contagion for organizing. Unlike many of their sister societies, this one put no special emphasis upon doing God's work or on the good that members were doing their own souls. They were not much concerned with the issue of worthiness. The president urged members not to worry too much about being imposed upon, but to give freely when need was perceived since it was better occasionally to help someone who was not much in need than to overlook someone who was. The Humane Society assumed that able-bodied people of either sex would work to support themselves; their aid was for those unable to work. In 1842, when the Washingtonian temperance revival was in full swing, the minutes recorded "a great improvement in the habits of many of the suffering poor."

Just to the south, Rhode Island women were intent on education as the sovereign remedy for poverty. In Providence a Female Society for Relief of Indigent Women and Children had begun in 1801 with education, a school for children, and a plan for work relief as the first order of business.[22] In 1811 in the small town of Bristol, eighty-eight women had joined together announcing that a third of whatever money they raised would be used for the education of children.[23] Further west, in Shrewsbury, Massachusetts, in 1832, about one in five of the town's adult women, wives of ministers, merchants, professional men, and substantial farmers, joined the Shrewsbury Charitable Society.[24] Their constitution forbade gossip, and serious subjects for discussion were assigned for each meeting.[25] The society met in homes (always designated as "*Mr.* So-and-So's house" though only women were present); tea was served, but the rule was that it should be kept simple. Occasionally a "dear sister of the society" was in need and was promptly helped. The typical client was a widow, or the wife of an alcoholic or disabled breadwinner. A third needed help only once; another third received help twice; the final third were regulars.

Not far away, in Hopkinton, New Hampshire, the Chesterfield Female Benevolent Society, which began with such enthusiasm that it met weekly, represented a somewhat different version of the familiar story.[26] The society decided to set up a library for the use of the community, dividing the books between the north end of town and the south—presumably so that they were within walking distance of all the inhabitants. Hopkinton women increased their resources by trading some of their handicrafts for palm leaf which they made into hats to sell. In so doing they were—though there is no mention of this fact in the record—competing with young single women for whom such hatmaking was a principal means of self-support. For a while the society flourished; then enthusiasm began to lag, and finally—after four years—the minutes ended on a sad note: "Met at Mr. Cook's, agreeable to adjournment, three in number, finished three hats, no appointments made." Perhaps there were simply not enough poor people in Hopkinton to keep the flame of benevolence alive, or perhaps sustained leadership never emerged.

In Lynn, the center of boot and shoe manufacture in Massachusetts, two societies competed for philanthropic resources: the Female Benevolent Society, founded in 1814 when the town had four thousand inhabitants, and the Lynn Fragment Society, which first met six years later.[27] Their constitutions were identical and there was a striking similarity of names between members and recipients. Most mysterious of all is the fact that a considerable number of women belonged to both societies.

The constitution of the Lynn Fragment Society suggests something about ideology as well as about practicality. The women announced that they wanted to exert their feeble efforts to "alleviate the distresses of the indigent, to cast our mite on the altar of benevolence—and though our means may be small, yet we think by proper economy in our domestic concerns, and by gathering up the fragments, and applying them to objects of need, the blessing of the poor may rest upon us, and the rich bounty of Heaven reward our philanthropy."

Article 6 authorized the treasurer to receive money and donations and required her to exhibit an *accurate* account with *proper vouchers* at every annual meeting.

In Morristown, New Jersey, another town of fewer than four thousand inhabitants, seventeen Presbyterian women founded the Female Charitable Society in 1813. There is no record that the society ever helped a man. Recipients were classified as: 1) Irish, 2) colored, and 3) "our own people." The historian of this society notes that from 1813 until 1870 there was "very little change in the scope of its work, or in its structure, standards and procedure. Many of the early members remained active for as long as two or three decades."[28]

In Salem, Massachusetts, the Female Charitable Society began early to place female orphans and children of disabled parents in foster homes for training. Though they used the existing laws of apprenticeship to "bind" these young girls for a fixed period of labor, in the early days the women made an effort to supervise the treatment the children received. In the 1830s a serious economic decline was too much for this system, and the practice of binding out was abandoned.[29]

The Daughters of Africa in Philadelphia was made up, Dorothy Sterling tells us, of nearly two hundred working-class women who banded together in 1821 to help each other. Their minutes may be epitomized by such entries as: "November the 15th 1822, Mary Brown borrowed of committee the sume of 4 wich she is to pay in 3 month to th Society for the Burial of her child" or "Sarah Pratte ten dollar for the lost of hir housband." The Female Benevolent Society of St. Thomas, also in Philadelphia but enrolling members of better-off black families, differed principally in its ability to help people beyond its own members. "Visited Mrs. Jones with the Committee and gave her 50 cts worth of groceries. She had been confined 10 days. [signed] Grace Douglass."[30] Unlike white women, these black women had very few wealthy patrons and no hope of receiving help from the government.[31]

Benevolent societies abounded in New England, New York state, the Western Reserve, and the Middle Atlantic states. In the South, too, despite its thinly spread population and comparatively small number of urban areas, the first society had appeared in 1801 when women in Savannah organized and administered a home for orphan girls.[32] The entire Board of Managers was female. Records survive of benevolent societies in Baltimore, Richmond, Raleigh, Nashville, Augusta, Petersburg, Charleston, and New Orleans. An obscure note in a local history tells us that in 1819 women from three Protestant churches met in Clarke County, Georgia—here there was no town of any size—to form a Female Mite Society.[33]

Southern towns produced benevolent societies that were indistinguishable from those in the North or the Middle West. In Petersburg, Virginia, in 1811 women undertook to raise money, organize, and manage an orphan asylum for girls. Securing a corporate charter from the state allowed them, in Suzanne Lebsock's phrase, to open "a large loophole in the common-law doctrine of civil death for married women," for under the common law, married women could not own property.[34] From that point forward, Petersburg women, black and white, multiplied associations: benevolent, missionary, and educational. Each church had a cluster of women's societies, though only the black Baptist church recognized this fact in its formal records. As elsewhere Petersburg churches depended heavily on women's societies to raise money, and the characteristic dense network of kin relationships prevailed.

In Charleston, Barbara Bellows discovered records of a vigorous and hardworking Ladies Benevolent Society, founded in 1813, made up of elite women who were not reluctant to visit lepers or to rescue children from houses of prostitution; they "typically encouraged the poor to become self-sufficient rather than fostering dependence. . . ."[35] In another coastal town, Wilmington, North Carolina, the

Female Benevolent Society in 1817 secured a charter for a school "for poor children and destitute orphans" which was later described as the beginning of a common school system in that area.[36]

The Female Bible and Charitable Society of Nashville, organized in 1817, had a secretary who had read law with her father. Surmounting the challenge of the 1819 depression, by the 1830s Nashville women were in full swing, as they established an orphan school, a house of industry, and other such institutions.[37]

By the 1820s the Raleigh (North Carolina) Female Benevolent Society had established an important place for itself in that small state capital. In addition to the usual commitment to aged widows and other distressed females, the Raleigh society was determined to provide employment for women who wanted to work, and education for destitute children. Younger members were expected to teach in the society's school, which enrolled twenty-six children on weekdays and more on Sundays. Managers took turns visiting each week to examine the pupils on their scholastic and religious progress. The women believed that education would rescue the children from poverty and "render them useful and respectable in the sphere to which it has pleased God to place them." Apparently they did not consider it necessary or inevitable that the children remain in that sphere, since they asserted that children who had "received the first rudiments of education from charity" might go on to become "shining lights in the world both for talents and for piety."

In 1821 the annual report noted the "great utility of providing work for females" and recorded that the society had supervised the manufacture of 195 pounds of donated cotton into cloth. The women who had spun and woven had together earned $141.78, and "thus in some degree obviated the necessity for private charity." Unfortunately the record does not show whether the society paid better wages than commercial establishments. The Raleigh women were among those who expressed qualms about their own ability to discern who was "worthy" and who was not. "It has been observed of this society," they noted, "that the managers ought to discriminate so as to bestow the largest portion of their favor on the most deserving. To this they can only answer that the most deserving may not be the most necessitous and though evil may have previously been committed, who shall say what has been resisted?"

They clinched the argument by quoting the Bible: "There is more joy in Heaven over one sinner that repenteth than over ninety and nine just persons."[38]

People moving west took the habit of benevolence with them. By 1829 Cincinnati had its network of women's organizations. Settlers had barely arrived in Cleveland when the women began to organize. In Chicago, where the first lot were platted in 1832, there was a Dorcas Society by 1835, followed by the Ladies Benevolent Society in 1843, and the Chicago Orphan Asylum in 1849. In 1858 came the Home for the Friendless. In the latter two institutions members of the board did the day-to-day work. Like many of their counterparts elsewhere the earliest institutions of this sort were characterized by limited funds, informal organization, and intense personal involvement.[39]

In Detroit the first recorded benevolent society was established by Catholic women in 1834 to oversee the poorhouse and establish an orphanage. In 1836 Protestant women set up an orphanage of their own.[40] Seven years later black women organized a Colored Ladies Benevolent Society which met in the Colored Methodist Church.[41]

Bearing witness to the nearly universal assumption that women were responsible for community welfare, when the Mormons set about establishing what they thought would be a permanent community in Nauvoo, Illinois, Joseph Smith took care to organize the women into a Relief Society. In addition to the usual benevolent functions, the society accepted responsibility for reinforcing the tenets of the evolving faith of the Church of Jesus Christ of Latter-day Saints and for providing help in the building of a temple. After Brigham Young led the Saints to Utah, the Relief Society was revived and became one of the most significant institutions in the carefully structured Mormon hierarchy.[42]

In San Francisco, four years after the gold rush began, it was clear that many "unprotected" women had followed husbands, brothers, and lovers to the gold fields, only to find that the men had died or disappeared.[43] The polyglot California population was heavily male, and a single woman was thought to be at considerable risk. Though by 1853 there were eighteen churches, several orphanages, and an almshouse, as well as some "secret and racial benevolent societies," a group of well-to-do women thought something else was needed. In August of that year they formed an association to "render protection and assistance to strangers, to sick and dependent women and children." The first challenge was to find employment for women whose male breadwinners had disappeared, and in a very short time the Ladies' Protection and Relief Society had put up a building as a refuge for such women. The second president (who remained in office for thirty years) was a Vermonter married to a lawyer-turned-tract-distributor who had gone to California to represent an undertaking firm. After her own demanding trip across the Isthmus of Panama during which she knew not what might have happened to her husband, Mrs. Gray had had no trouble imagining the situation of other women. Building on by now half a century of eastern experience, the San Francisco society immediately asked the legislature for five thousand dollars to carry on its work. The petitioners came back with three thousand dollars and promptly set out to raise the rest—members were firmly instructed to collect no less than two hundred dollars apiece, which they proceeded to do. When a local businessman gave the society a full city block in an undeveloped part of San Francisco, the women enthusiastically undertook to be managers of property as well as benefactors of the poor.

Perhaps because the lone women who first aroused concern found an extensive choice of husbands, the society's charitable focus quickly shifted to children.

Members took orphans into their homes and tried to raise them to be clean-living, right-thinking, and hardworking. The society welcomed children of any ethnic group and did not hold them responsible for their parents' failings.[44] Nor did they insist that the boys, at least, stay in "the station to which God has appointed them." On the contrary, they begged local businessmen to provide opportunities for their young charges: "A boy who would be a laggard at the plough, might become a brilliant inventor . . ." if only he had a chance. "Remember your hopes and fears and aspirations . . . remember the strong preference that stirred within you for one occupation or craft more than another, so that you felt it easy and joyful to earn your bread in one way, and repulsive or well-nigh impossible in another."

The women made no such plea for the girls, who were taught housewifery and, presumably, prepared for marriage. Given the early California sex ratio, this was doubtless realistic, but it showed some myopia on the part of these energetic and effective women who had themselves found it "easy and joyful" to engage in a very active life away from housewifery.

The 1906 earthquake tested the organizational resilience of the society. With energy and imagination the women moved large numbers of children to places of safety despite the chaos around them, and nursed those who fell victim to the post-earthquake epidemics. Only two children in their care died.

Fashions in welfare changed, foster homes became the accepted mode of dealing with orphans, and by the 1920s the San Francisco society was again concentrating on the needs of women, especially old women. Symbolic of continuity, and despite changing fashions, three members of the Board of Managers in 1953 were descended from members or associates of the first society in 1853.

These examples are a tiny but representative fraction of nineteenth-century benevolent societies. The patterns they established in the early nineteenth century have lived on. On 2 March 1983, the weekly newsletter of the First Methodist Church in Athens, Georgia, carried the following announcement:

> Circle 9 enables us to grow in three ways as Christian women through: study that fosters our spiritual and intellectual growth, service projects that express our concern for others, and fellowship that binds us together as friends.
>
> Our monthly programs have been quite varied, on Isaiah, worship, the Nestlé boycott, computers, and the interior spiritual life. . . .
>
> Our annual bake sale has provided the funds for making linens for the Ethel Harpst Home and gifts for its children, and for sending an underprivileged child to summer camp.[45]

Except for the Nestlé boycott and the computers, this notice might have appeared in almost any town in any year since 1812.

How did women's benevolence, expressed through their voluntary associations, compare with that of men? The material for a detailed comparison would have to be drawn from widely disparate sources, but there is enough evidence to support some impressions. First, some men were more likely than women to operate as individuals. Robert Dalzell's description of Amos Lawrence, one of the Boston Associates, shows him to be a one-man benevolent society who spoke and acted much as the women's groups did. Similarly, one Alexander Henry, an Irish immigrant merchant in Philadelphia and one of the early enthusiasts for Sunday schools, made it a practice to buy wood in large quantities for needy citizens and to pay for the education of young men training for the ministry.[46] Other men tended to make large gifts to institutions, particularly those that might bear their names. When men undertook to organize charitable associations the differences at first glance seem minor. In New York, for example, in 1787 a group of professional and business leaders had established a Society for the Relief of Distressed Debtors to provide food and clothing for men in debtors' prison. Because wives and children of those imprisoned for debt were sometimes permitted to share the erstwhile breadwinner's cell, such aid might feed a whole family. Gradually members of the society expanded their concerns to include vice, immorality, and drunkenness in the jails, and in 1791, in concert with the Medical Society of New York, they set up the New York Dispensary to serve the medical needs of the indigent. It is not clear how long this society persisted.

In another case, a group of New York men, declaring themselves tired of amelioration, set out to identify and then prevent the causes of pauperism. They wound up with much the same diagnosis as their compatriot women, which is to say they decided poverty was caused by intemperance, gambling, and lack of character. Indeed their whole effort was astonishingly revealing of the difficulty comfortable people had in analyzing the structural causes of poverty, and of the dismay they felt when "solving" the problem turned out to be a mirage. After a few years of effort the Society for the Prevention of Pauperism tacitly recognized defeat and resolved itself into a less ambitious Society for the Reformation of Juvenile Delinquents, which established, in 1824, a refuge to which juveniles could be committed by the courts.[47]

The only serious effort on the part of a historian to compare male and female associations in the antebellum years is found in Suzanne Lebsock's *Free Women of Petersburg*. Asking whether the organizational lives of men and women were indeed separate, and whether women's collective behavior differed from that of men, Lebsock answers yes to both questions. Women, acting collectively, were, she suggests, more apt to be highly personal and to direct their efforts toward other women. However, she also discovered in examining local records that after years during which poor relief had been accepted as women's responsibility, by the 1850s mixed associations began to take over responsibilities once carried by all-women groups. When this happened women constituted themselves as auxiliary to male societies.[48] A similar shift in Cleveland in the same decade suggests that some change in prevailing perceptions of responsibility was taking place, but whether the initiative came from men or women—or both—is not recorded.[49]

The most significant difference between male and female benevolence was this: for men, philanthropy or benevolence, whether conducted individually or in associations, was generally only part of a larger career. Much time was devoted to making the money of which they would then give some to worthy causes. Benevolence figured in the building of a man's career, both as a means of forming associations with other men and as a means of promoting a favorable public image, but it was rarely his central concern or source of identity. Women's benevolent societies by contrast *were* their "careers," an accepted extension of their defined role as wives and mothers.

Like some simple lifeforms that persist for millennia while more complex forms appear and disappear, the benevolent society has survived for nearly two centuries, through tumultuous change, and despite the proliferation of many more complex women's associations and the growth of the welfare state. The forms of organization invented by the founders of the benevolent societies shaped the future of voluntary associations of the most diverse kinds.

Although the founding of many early societies reflected the religious enthusiasm of the early nineteenth century, once they came into existence these groups took on a complex life that met both personal and collective needs beyond religious or spiritual ones. For individuals there was sociability with women of their own class or cast of mind and reassurance that as dispensers of benevolence they were important people in the community. Some women enjoyed the craftsmanship they practiced on behalf of the poor. Working together, black women found the kind of support white society denied them, and that they did not always receive from black men. And although their search for respectability was of a different order from that of white women, for them, too, the voluntary association provided a measure of status.

Visiting the needy offered a protected way to look across class boundaries and obtain a wider experience of life without risking one's own position. Some felt their souls benefited from exposure to the vicissitudes of life among the working classes; others, no doubt, simply enjoyed the sentiment of pity, the assurance, by contrast, of their own good fortune. In the early days the teaching or preaching which went along with charity allowed women to do things not otherwise permitted. A few— very few as far as the record goes—began to ponder the reasons for the extreme poverty they sometimes encountered and to make their own, often naive, social analysis. At the same time their encounters with clients increased awareness of class differences on both sides.

Over the years benevolent societies rarely stirred significant community opposition.[50] They have tended to fulfill the basic cultural expectation that women should be compassionate and nurturing; they have provided women with a public way to practice these virtues without calling their fundamental womanliness into question in any way. Perhaps this is one secret of their persistence.[51]

The concrete accomplishments of nineteenth-century societies were considerable. At a time when poverty was spreading and municipal governments felt hard-pressed to meet minimum needs, food, clothing, and medical care were very important to people who did not have these things. For at least the first half of the nineteenth century municipalities were often quite unable to keep up with multiplying demands for aid, and women's associations strove to fill the gap. At the most elemental level a child with shoes is better off than a child without shoes, no matter what complex motivation provided the gift.

From the beginning, women's societies created community institutions. First came orphan asylums, then schools, employment services, homes for wayward girls, libraries, old ladies' homes, and the like. These institutions were run on limited resources and depended heavily on the day-to-day work of benevolent women. Paid staff members were generally members of the societies who needed to earn their keep. Providing a setting for a dignified old age for even a minority of aged widows and spinsters and caring for orphan children met pressing community needs.

In the beginning, benevolent women thought vice led to poverty; in time they reversed the order: poverty might lead to vice, and their favorite cure was education.

What do the records of benevolent societies tell us about the women who built them? Clearly by the end of the eighteenth century numbers of women had acquired some education despite the scarcity of formal schools. The handwriting of members and subscribers, the skillful minutes, the carefully constructed constitutions, the precise records and accounts, the willingness to handle money—all suggest that the kind of female education Benjamin Rush had declared to be necessary for the new nation was already taking place.[52]

There is also evidence that many married women had some money of their own; furthermore, they seem to have had few qualms about asking men, in their families and out, for money to carry on charitable endeavors. From the earliest days women not only handled money in significant amounts but even in small communities they invested resources in local business enterprise.

From the beginning, white women's associations had a political dimension. Isabella Graham went to the legislature for a charter for the New York Widows' Society in the 1790s, and other societies did likewise. In time the New York legislature permitted a public lottery for the benefit of the Widows' Society. Incorporation was one way to reduce the normal limitations on women's legal right to act, and permitted them to do things otherwise forbidden to married women such as acquiring, holding, and conveying property.[53] The speed with which the San Francisco society asked for state money as well as a state charter suggests that by mid-century both had come to be standard procedure for benevolent societies.[54]

It has become a truism that organizational experience played a significant part in the changing self-concepts of the women involved. Nancy Cott, in *Bonds of Womanhood*, suggested that on the one hand benevolent societies reinforced the prevailing cultural definition of womanly behavior, but on the other hand helped make women conscious of themselves as women—a necessary first step, she argued, to the development of what would many years later be labeled a feminist consciousness. Nancy Hewitt took issue with this view saying that, at least among the elite charitable societies in Rochester, class and kin relations were far more likely to be reinforced than feelings of sisterhood. These observations are not mutually exclusive, nor do they encompass all the possibilities.[55] Members of benevolent societies might empathize particularly with women—thus establishing bonds of sisterhood—while at the same time exhibiting the class prejudices common to both sexes among their own friends and family. They certainly saw poor women as more vulnerable than poor men, and concentrated their resources on helping them.

And in any case, whether feeling bonds of sisterhood or those of class, active benevolent society members were inevitably changing themselves. Especially for the leaders, the voluntary association offered a chance to establish an identity independent of husbands and a chance to exercise competence or achieve ambition. When these things happened, even if only to a handful of women in a given place, but multiplied by hundreds and hundreds of communities, the aggregate effect was surely to begin to change the social definition of women's roles.

[...]

Notes

1. L. H. Butterfield, ed., *Adams Family Correspondence* (Cambridge, 1963), 1:370.

2. Historians have used the term "benevolent society" to designate a variety of types of association. I use it here as the women did themselves—to mean the spontaneous local groups, including missionary and mutual aid societies, which began to appear in the 1790s and a version of which can be found in many communities today. The term has also been used to describe national organizations such as the American Tract Society, the American Bible Society, the American Sunday School Society—the so-called "benevolent empire." These organizations included women but were run by men, and the historians who have written about them have focused on men. See for example, Clifford S. Griffin, *Their Brothers' Keepers: Moral Stewardship in the United States, 1800–1865* (New York, 1960), which ignores women. See also Charles I. Foster, *Errand of Mercy: The Evangelical United Front 1790–1837* (Chapel Hill, 1960).

3. Linda K. Kerber, *Women of the Republic: Intellect and Ideology in Revolutionary America* (Chapel Hill, 1980), xii.

4. Joan Jensen, *Loosening the Bonds: Mid-Atlantic Farm Women, 1750–1850* (New Haven, 1986), discusses this decline in public aid for dependent groups; see chapter 4, "The Social Geography of Dependency."

5. There have been a good many undocumented assumptions about the "leisure" available to middle-class women in the antebellum years. Perhaps a few very wealthy women did have time on their hands, but generally the wives of professional and business men worked hard. See, for example, Susan Hopper Emerson, ed., *Life of Abby Hopper Gibbons Told Chiefly through her Correspondence*, 2 vols. (New York, 1896, 1897), or Anna Davis Hallowell, ed., *Life and Letters of James and Lucretia Mott* (Boston, 1884), for the extremely demanding daily lives of two women married to intermittantly prosperous Quaker merchants. Or see Harriet Beecher Stowe's hilarious description of writing her books with a baby on her knee and the household swirling about her, in Annie Fields, ed., *Life and Letters of Harriet Beecher Stowe* (Boston, 1897), chapter 5, especially 125–33. Another Beecher sister believed that only a woman in the best of health could survive the labor required of a minister's wife. See the revealing correspondence in Jeanne Boydston, Mary Kelley, and Anne Margolis, *The Limits of Sisterhood: The Beecher Sisters on Women Rights and Woman's Sphere* (Chapel Hill, 1988), 339–40.

6. Frank Warren Crow, "The Age of Promise: Societies for Social and Economic Improvement in the United States, 1783–1815" (Ph.D. diss., University of Wisconsin, 1952).

7. Janet Wilson James, "Hannah Mather Crocker," in Edward James, Janet James, and Paul S. Boyer, eds., *Notable American Women* (Cambridge, Mass., 1971), 1:406–7. It is at least symbolically significant that Hannah Mather was a great-granddaughter of Cotton Mather, who in his day had promoted the formation of male associations for self-improvement. Hannah had ten children and cared for her aged parents. At sixty-six she published *Observations on the Real Rights of Women* and a book on Freemasonry in which she wished that "some respectable ladies would join in a society . . . [to] promote Science and Literature." It is recorded that she was a Federalist who took a lively interest in public affairs. Edward James kindly supplied these details from Janet James's notes.

8. Mary Beth Norton, *Liberty's Daughters* (Boston, 1980), 179–88, especially 185.

9. Linda K. Kerber, "Daughters of Columbia: Educating Women for the Republic, 1787–1805," in Stanley Elkins and Eric McKitrick, eds., *The Hofstader Aegis: A Memorial* (New York, 1974), 36–59.

10. An excellent discussion of this phenomenon is Richard D. Brown. "The Emergence of Urban Society in Rural Massachusetts, 1760–1820," *Journal of American History* 61, no. 1 June 1974): 29–51. Brown's explanation for the increase in the number of voluntary associations is "the interaction between the Revolution, the Second Great Awakening and its secular counterpart, the flowering of a romantic view of progress, and commercial development and population growth. Together these events brought much of urban society to country villages, making their old cultural isolation obsolete" (45).

11. It is important to note that even groups attached to a particular church were usually created by women, not by the church hierarchy.

12. Communication among members of widespread kin networks promoted this similarity. See for example, Lucretia Mott, writing to her mother-in-law on 2 Feb. 1820: "A few members of this district have in contemplation to form a society for the relief of the poor. . . . if it is not asking too much, I should like to have a copy of your constitution . . ." Hallowell, ed., *Life and Letters*, 71.

13. Dorothy Sterling, *We Are Your Sisters: Black Women in the Nineteenth Century*. (New York, 1984), 105–18.

14. Mary Bosworth Treudley, "'The Benevolent Fair': A Study of Charitable Organization among American Women in the First Third of the Nineteenth Century," *Social Service Review* 14 (Sept. 1940): 509–22, has a thoughtful discussion of the problems that work relief has always presented. She used the records of a number of early-nineteenth-century benevolent societies.

15. This distinction between worthy and unworthy poor is one of the strongest themes running through all the records of white benevolent societies. The idea is embedded in the history of charity. Gertrude Himmelfarb, *The Idea of Poverty* (New York, 1984), has an illuminating discussion of the distinction as it developed in England.

16. See *New York Times*, 6 Dec. 1959, 91, for an article about the 153-year history of the Graham School, successor to the Widows Society orphanage.

17. Joanna Bethune, ed., *The Power of Faith Exemplified in the Life and Writings of the Late Mrs. Isabella Graham* (New York, 1843).

18. See especially Mary P. Ryan, *Cradle of the Middle Class: The Family in Oneida County, N.Y., 1790–1865* (Cambridge, 1981), chapter 3, and Christine Stansell, *City of Women: Sex and Class in New York, 1789–1860* (New York, 1986), chapter 2 and passim.

19. See Robert Dalzell, Jr., *Enterprising Elite: The Boston Associates and the World They Made* (Cambridge, Mass., 1987), chapter 5, for an illuminating discussion of this issue. Also M.J. Heale, "The New York Society for the Prevention of Pauperism, 1817–1823," *New-York Historical Society Quarterly* 55, no. 2 (Apr. 1971): 153–76.

20. As the colonial historians make ever more fine-grained studies of seventeenth-century village life, it is clear that most villagers watched over each other's behavior without shame. It is not clear when it became uncommon for the "better sort" to be thus observed. The poorer people continued to be subject to such oversight; indeed they still are.

21. Records of the Cambridge Female Humane Society, Arthur and Elizabeth Schlesinger Library of the History of Women in America, Radcliffe College, Cambridge, Mass.

22. Constitution in Sophia Smith Collection, Smith College, Northampton, Mass.

23. Constitution of the Bristol R.I. Female Charitable Society, Sophia Smith Collection, Smith College, Northampton, Mass.

24. Jack Larkin, "An Extended Link in the Great Chain of Benevolence: The Shrewsbury Charitable Society," essay written for the Community in Change Project, Old Sturbridge Village, Mass., Oct. 1979. It is regrettable that this splendid essay, a model of its kind, has never been published.

25. The prohibition of gossip was common and perhaps with good reason. Only a month after Lucretia Mott had asked advice of her mother-in-law about the procedure for establishing a charitable society, James Mott was writing his parents that she was very much discouraged because "most of the conversation at the several meetings . . . has not been very interesting, or instructive; being too much of what is called gossip . . ." Hallowell, ed., *Life and Letters*, 72–73.

26. Minutes of the Chesterfield Benevolent Society in Hopkinton, New Hampshire, Schlesinger Library, Radcliffe College, Cambridge, Mass.

27. Records of these societies are in the Lynn Historical Society, Lynn, Mass.

28. Mary F. Kihlstrom, "The Morristown Female Charitable Society," *Journal of Presbyterian History* 50 (Fall 1980): 255–72.

29. Carol Lasser, "A 'Pleasingly Oppressive Burden': The Transformation of Domestic Service and Female Charity in Salem, 1800–1840," *Essex Institute Historical Collections* 116, no. 3 (Apr. 1980): 156–75.

30. Dorothy Sterling, *We Are Your Sisters*.

31. Anne M. Boylan, "Women and Politics in the Era Before Seneca Falls," *Journal of the Early Republic* 10 (Fall 1990): 365–85, shows how early white benevolent societies were able to get some money from city governments on the grounds that they were bearing part of the welfare burden of the community.

32. Savannah in 1800, with a population of 6,000 about equally divided between white and black, had only 204 white female children under age ten, yet apparently enough of them were orphans to call forth this pioneering effort.

The records of southern women's benevolent societies are indistinguishable from those in other parts of the country, and it is clear that societies existed even in small communities. Evidently these groups were a response to something more than simply industrialization or "modernization." There is no case to be made for southern exceptionalism from the voluntary association evidence.

33. Augustus Longstreet Hull, *Annals of Athens* (Athens, Ga., 1906).

34. Suzanne Lebsock, *The Free Women of Petersburg: Status and Culture in a Southern Town, 1784–1860* (New York, 1984), 197.

35. Barbara Bellows, "'My Children, Gentlemen, Are My Own': Poor Women, the Urban Elite, and the Bonds of Obligation in Antebellum Charleston," in Walter J. Fraser, Jr., et al., eds., *The Web of Southern Social Relations: Women, Family, and Education* (Athens, Ga. 1985), 51–71. See also Jane H. Pease and William H. Pease, *Ladies, Women and Wenches: Choice and Constraint in Charleston and Boston* (Chapel Hill, 1990), chapter 6.

36. "Beginnings of Common School System in the South," *U.S. Bureau of Education Report, 1896–97* (Washington, 1898), chapter 29, 1394–97.

37. Anita S. Goodstein, *Nashville, 1780–1860: From Frontier to City* (Gainesville, Fla., 1989), 59–61.

38. All of the preceding quotations about the society are from the Revised Constitution and By-Laws of the Raleigh Female Benevolent Society with Reports of the Society from Its Commencement (Raleigh, N.C., 1823).

39. Keith Melder, "Ladies Bountiful: Organized Women's Benevolence in Early Nineteenth Century America," *New York History* 65 (1967): 240; Mrs. W. A. Ingham, *Women of Cleveland* (Cleveland, 1893), 139; and Kathleen D. McCarthy, *Noblesse Oblige* (Chicago, 1985).

40. Alice Tarbell Crathern, *In Detroit Courage Was the Fashion: The Contributions of Women to the Development of Detroit from 1701 to 1951* (Detroit, 1953), 20–26.

41. Darlene Clark Hine, "Black Women in the Middle West: The Michigan Experience" (1988 Burton Lecture presented at the 114th Meeting and State History Conference of the Historical Society of Michigan).

42. Anne Firor Scott, "Mormon Women, Other Women," *Journal of Mormon History* (1987): 2–49.

43. Rowena Beans, *"Inasmuch..." The One-Hundred-Year History of the San Francisco Ladies' Protection and Relief Society* (San Francisco, 1953). All quotations in this and the next paragraph are from this study, pp. 28, 29.

44. This is in contrast to some self-righteous benevolent societies which refused to care for children whose mothers were prostitutes.

45. *The Steeple* 26, no. 9, published weekly except Christmas by the First United Methodist Church, Athens, Georgia. Close to home I find the following note in the *Newsletter* of the Inter-Faith Council for Social Service in Chapel Hill, N.C., Mar. 1988, vol. 8, no.1 [looking back fifteen years]: "The initial impulse for calling this organization into being was to meet some very pressing needs . . . the moving spirits were the Chapel Hill church women. . . ."

46. Edwin W. Rice, *The Sunday School Movement and the American Sunday School Union* (Philadelphia, 1917), 57.

47. Heale, "The New York Society for the Prevention of Pauperism."

48. Lebsock, *Free Women*, chapter 7. The whole of this chapter is relevant to my discussion here. See also Hallowell, ed., *Life and Letters*, 136, for evidence that the last national women's antislavery convention was held in 1839 because "some of the abolitionists made the discovery that men and women could do more efficient work together than alone. . . ."

49. Michael J. McTighe, "'True Philanthropy and the Limits of the Female Sphere': Poor Relief and Labor Organizations in Antebellum Cleveland," *Labor History* 2 (Spring 1986): 227–56.

50. It is recorded, however, that the women who organized the New York Widows Society met with "the ridicule of many, and . . . the opposition of not a few. The men could not allow our sex the steadiness and perseverance necessary to establish such an undertaking. . . ." See Bethune, *The Power of Faith*. Nancy Hewitt found evidence that the Guilford, Connecticut, church women failed to establish a charitable society in 1806 because of the opposition of a Presbyterian minister, the Reverend Mr. Elliott. Letter from Mary Stone to Mabel Hand Ward, 20 Aug. 1806, ms in the Presbyterian Historical Society, Philadelphia, Pa.

51. See Lori Ginsberg, *Women and the Work of Benevolence: Morality and Politics in the Northeastern United States, 1820–1885* (New Haven, 1990), for some thoughtful speculations along the line that men only objected to women as being "out of their sphere" when their activities threatened the established order, which benevolence, for the most part, did not seem to do.

52. See Benjamin Rush, "Thoughts Upon Female Education," in his *Essays: Literary, Moral and Philosophical* (1787), in which he argues that in a new country women needed to be educated for a broad range of responsibilities. He prescribed a curriculum that included reading, writing, grammar, arithmetic, bookkeeping, geography, history, astronomy, chemistry, and natural philosophy. He predicted great results from a higher level of education for women.

53. Lebsock, *Free Women*, 201.

54. Anne Boylan has examined this issue in detail in "Women and Politics."

55. Nancy F. Cott, *The Bonds of Womanhood: Woman's Sphere in New England, 1780–1835* (New Haven, 1975); Nancy Hewitt, *Women's Activism and Social Change: Rochester, New York, 1856–1872* (Ithaca, 1984), chapter 2.

From
*"Swing the Sickle for the Harvest is Ripe": Gender and Slavery
in Antebellum Georgia,*
by Daina Ramey Berry (2007)

CHAPTER 2

"THERE SHO' WAS A SIGHT OF US"

Enslaved Family and Community Rituals

DAINA RAMEY BERRY

God sets the lonely in families . . .
—Psalms 68:6 NIV

On 26 November 1840, William Barnett of Wilkes County placed an ad listing "TEN or TWELVE likely NEGROES" for sale in a local newspaper. This group of individuals included three skilled bondpeople described as "a good wagoner and first-rate field hand; a first-rate Cook, Washer and Ironer; another good Cook and field-hand; and some very likely boys, girls, and children." Following the detailed reference to the slaves' skills, Barnett concluded, "The above Negroes are of *good families,* and can be well recommended by all persons who know them."[1] Assuring potential buyers that these laborers came from "good families"—whether the family of the former owners or the enslaved—served as an additional incentive for purchasing them besides their apparent labor skills.

Slavery as a whole negatively affected the development and maintenance of families. Since slavery was inextricably linked to work, it is almost impossible to develop a solid understanding of enslaved families without acknowledging the backdrop of labor in which families and communities evolved and interacted. Long hours of backbreaking labor in agricultural and nonagricultural settings restricted the time bondpeople had to spend with each other. This chapter discusses family and community life among the enslaved. Although studies of enslaved families have devoted considerable attention to the structural analysis which is useful and included here, the primary objective of this chapter is to define and explore the opportunities for the creation and maintenance of families and communities in antebellum Georgia.[2] To maintain family and social bonds, bondpeople interacted in work-related environments such as working socials, and in non-work-related environments such as religious services (in interracial settings) and holiday festivals (within the enslaved community). Of course, it is difficult to think of anyone enslaved as having an ideal family situation when the reality of their experience involved the constant fear of separation and sale.

Defining Slave Families and Communities

Enslaved Africans interacted within particular types of relationships that represented "family" and, in a broader sense, "community." Loosely defined, family units might be labeled "cohesive or functional families" because they included a mix of biological, extended, and fictive connections that all operated as a family unit. "Fictive kin" represent family connections not related by blood. In contemporary society, some people refer to these relatives as "play cousins" or "play aunts and uncles." As in Louisiana, South Carolina, and Virginia communities, these families were complex, adaptive, and ever-changing—constantly living with the loss and gain of their members.[3] Enslaved women, men, and children relied on their adaptive abilities to develop familial connections in order to cope with the daily hardships and challenges of enslavement.

Enslaved communities in antebellum Georgia were diverse, close-knit, and sometimes geographically removed from each other. Considering communities as any group of people living together in a particular place or local area with certain commonalities such as race, religion, social position, etc., this chapter suggests that bondpeople in upcountry and lowcounty Georgia functioned in communities that developed patterns of interaction based on the plantation size and attitudes of their slaveholders. In the lowcounty, enslaved women and men lived on large plantations with multiple communities on one plantation. There were communities of field hands, communities of seamstresses, communities of ginners, as well as boatmen, blacksmiths, and sawyers. Many of these individuals lived on plantations with fictive and blood kin, so their families were often intact. Upcountry bondpeople lived in an enslaved community that was broad and incorporated people from neighboring counties. Thus family and community life in the upcountry was not confined to a single plantation. In order to develop a solid understanding of family and community life, one must first explore the parameters of the social environment.

One way to comprehend life in the quarters is by delving deeper into the personal relationships of the enslaved, taking concepts beyond determining whether bondpeople developed nuclear, simple, or complex family structures. To fully understand the family and community structure within enslavement and the environment that was available for family development, one must enter the enslaved quarters, witness their courting and marriage rituals, join them at the dinner table, and participate in their holidays and religious services.

Social Environment

The social environment shaped the options available for bondpeople to form relationships. Although men usually initiated courtship, demographic constraints, such as age and gender distributions, influenced mate selection in significant ways.[4] Depending on the size of the plantation, the open or closed nature of the system, the demands of the crop, the access to geographic mobility, the visitation patterns established, and the disposition of the slaveholder, bondmen and bondwomen elected to or were forced to partner with each other.

In the upcountry, mate selection often transcended plantation boundaries because most slaveholding units contained fewer than fifteen slaves. On small farms and plantations, like those common in Wilkes County, bondwomen and bondmen looked to other holdings for prospective partners because mate availability on their home plantation was extremely low. Small slaveholders supported the practice because owners of females profited from the offspring of these unions. Slaveholders of males also benefited because they could use visitation privileges as a measure of control. Wilkes County bondpeople often found their mates on adjoining plantations by necessity, and sometimes by choice, which explains the preponderance of less stable, abroad marriages in this community.

In the lowcountry, large slaveholdings fostered environments conducive to the development of families that were cohesive and more stable. Plantations in Glynn County were larger and usually contained balanced sex ratios, creating an environment that increased bondpeoples' chances of finding a mate on the same plantation.[5] Spousal selection was almost always limited to one plantation. Planters rarely allowed their laborers to associate with those on other estates, and bondwomen and bondmen were pressured to find spouses on their respective plantations. This practice continued simply because bondpeople had no other options. Therefore, when an enslaved male found a prospective partner, he began the courting process.

Courting Rituals

Enslaved family and community life began with courtship. Initially, "[t]he man would go to the cabin of the woman whom he desired, would roast some peanuts in the ashes, place them on a stool between her and himself, and while eating, propose marriage. If the man was accepted, the couple repaired to his cabin immediately, and they were regarded as man and wife."[6] As enslaved men and women searched for companions on their home plantation or on neighboring estates, they participated in a series of flirtatious games in order to win the affections of a potential spouse.[7] Former Wilkes County bondman Marshal Butler outlined the evolution of this process in the following song:

> If you want to go a courtin', I sho' you where to go,
> Right down yonder in de house below,
> Clothes all dirty an' ain't got no broom,
> Ole dirty clothes all hangin' in de room.
> Ask'd me to table, thought I'd take a seat,
> First thing I saw was big chunk o' meat.
> Big as my head, hard as a maul;
> Ash-cake, corn bread, bran an' all.[8]

Although he received tough meat, cake, and corn bread, Butler seemed overjoyed by the invitation to share a meal with his companion.

For young slaves, male and female alike, "courtship was both a diversion and a delight" because love interests distracted some from the reality of their oppression. It also represented an "intensely romantic" ritual that often led to marriage.[9] From the female perspective, Mariah Callaway, a Wilkes County bondwoman, noted that she enjoyed being courted by bondmen from neighboring plantations. She testified that "often in the evenings, boys from the other plantations would come over to see the girls . . . they would stand in large groups around the trees, laughing and talking."[10] Although men initiated the courting process by flirting with females in the fields, at dances, during religious ceremonies, or in the quarters, women controlled the pace through their responses to their male suitors.[11]

While courting, bondmen had to receive permission to spend time with potential mates; obtaining a pass represented one requirement for regular visitation. This mandate held true for large social activities as well; one ex-slave noted during an interview that "dances, corn-shuckings, picnics and all kinds of old time affairs . . . were attended by slaves for some distance around, *but they had to have passes.*"[12] Some bondmen, however, did not have the patience to wait for a pass, and they paid severe consequences for their disobedience. Marshal Butler's testimony serves as an example of the life-threatening risks enslaved males took to spend time with their female partners:

> I'se left home one Thursday to see a gal on the Palmer plantation—five miles away. Some gal! No, I didn't get a pass—de boss was so busy! Everything was fine until my return trip. I wuz two miles out an' three miles to go. There come de "Paddle-Rollers" I wuz not scared—only I couldn't move. They give me thirty licks—I ran the rest of the way home. There was belt buckles all over me. I ate my victuals off de porch railing. Some gal! Um-m-h. Was worth that paddlin' to see that gal—would do it over again to see [M]ary de next night . . . Um-m-mh—Some gal![13]

Slaveholders' attempts to control and monitor relationships were largely ignored by the enslaved because many, like Butler, did not feel obligated to wait for permission to visit loved ones.

In addition to clandestine and approved visits, courtship rituals involved the informal practice of giving gifts. Some bondpeople disliked the idea of giving presents to their prospective spouses. Butler critically noted, "Sometimes some fool nigger would bring a gal a present—like 'pulled-candy' . . . I had no time for sich foolishness."[14] His dissatisfaction with presents perhaps reflects that he had few, if any, material possessions to offer his female companion. One could assume, therefore, that those fortunate ones who had something to offer a partner probably had better chances of wooing their affections. Some women welcomed the addition of material items because hardly any bondpeople owned anything. Yet not all enslaved females sought partners with material possessions. Women like Adeline Willis of Wilkes County understood this and often preferred their mates' love instead of material items. "Lewis," she explained, "never bought me any presents 'cus he didn't have no money to buy them with, but he was good to me and that was what counted."[15] Clearly, love and affection took precedence over gifts for this enslaved woman. If the courtship was successful, marriage solidified the union.

Marriage Ceremonies

Marriage was one of the obvious outcomes and goals of courting. Although it was not legally sanctioned, enslaved partners viewed their unions with solemnity and pride and lived with the constant fear of being separated. Despite the obstacles, some sealed their unions through formal ceremonies involving biblical scriptures and witnesses, while others became husband and wife during private, informal moments. The presence of a member of the planter class did not ensure formality; therefore, some marriages were not acknowledged by their slaveholders. However, in most cases, enslaved couples had to obtain consent from their owners and, if present, their parent(s) as well. On a small farm in Hancock County, Georgia, which was originally part of Wilkes County, Mary and Starobin were married during a ceremony that their owners witnessed. Farmer Benton Miller described this event in his journal. "Hill Reeves married them," he explained, and "there was a great many negroes here" to attend this ceremony.[16] It is likely that the presence of so many bondpeople reinforced the union and possibly added new members to this enslaved community.

Enslaved couples who had formal ceremonies were often the property of a judge, justice of the peace, or preacher, or their owners were friends and relatives of such persons. "My Marster wuz a Jedge so he married all his niggers whut got married," explained Manuel Johnson. "He married lots ov y 'uther couples too," he continued, "I'members dat day use ter cum fer him ter marry dem."[17] Bondpeople who sought Johnson's owner had to obtain permission from their slaveholders as well. Clearly, some couples traveled to other parts of the county or across county lines to formalize their relationships. Most enslaved couples, however, recognized that their relationships had no legal sanction, and many legalized their unions after emancipation. "Dey ain marry den duh way dey do now," one slave explained. She stated that "attuh slabery dey hadduy remarry."[18]

Enslaved couples took marriage seriously because it was an important part of their culture. For some, it was the focus of their existence as well as a significant unifying moment when the entire community came together. When bondpeople found love, former slave Mariah Callaway explained, "a *real* marriage ceremony was performed from the Bible."[19] Interestingly, some associated "biblical" weddings with formality even though a large majority of enslaved persons were illiterate. Perhaps they recognized the importance of biblical instruction because they attended interracial prayer meetings and witnessed the sacred treatment of scriptures at these services. Benton Miller's enslaved workers left the plantation every Sunday to attend prayer meetings and wedding ceremonies all across the county.[20] Other enslaved individuals, such as Willis Cofer, had vivid recollections of the weddings on his plantation: "When slaves got married, de man had to ax de gal's ma and pa for her and den he had to ax de white folkses to 'low 'em to git married. De white preacher married 'em. Dey hold right hands and de preacher ax de man: 'Do you take dis gal to de bes' you kin for her?' and if he say yes, den day had to change hands and jump over de broomstick and dey wuz married. Our white folkses wuz all church folkses and didn't 'low no dancin' at weddins but dey give 'em big suppers when deir slaves got married."[21] Although the "formality" of "biblical weddings" raises questions about slave religion and the role of Christianity within the enslaved community, it appears that slave nuptials included informal rituals such as "jumping the broom," receiving verbal permission, or simply recognition from other members of the plantation community.

Less formal wedding ceremonies gave couples another avenue to solidify their relationships. On Hampton Point Plantation, Frances Kemble questioned "old House Molly" about the marital bonds in the enslaved quarters. Molly assured her that couples bound themselves "not much formally" because their overseer ignored such relationships. Likewise, in Wilkes County Adeline Willis claimed, "We didn't have no preacher when we married. My Master and Mistress said they didn't care, and Lewis's Master and Mistress said they didn't care, so they all met up at my white folks' house and had us come in and told us they didn't mind our marryin'." Shortly after that her owner sanctioned the union by stating that "there ain't no objections so go on and jump over the broom stick together and you is married."[22] Upon receiving verbal permission, Adeline and Lewis became husband and wife and solidified their union by "jumping the broom." This tradition was fairly common among slaves, as indicated in several narratives. Emma Hurley recalled "being told to 'step over the broom stick,'" and those enslaved in other southern states had similar recollections.[23]

Matrimony did not guarantee that enslaved couples could live with their spouses, so there was a preponderance of abroad marriages. Enslaved husbands with passes visited their wives once or twice per week on Wednesdays and/or Saturdays.[24] Male geographic mobility for the purpose of visitation shows that slaveholders supported a sharp gender division in terms of off-plantation travel. Adeline Willis, for example, married Lewis, who resided on an "adjoining planta-tion," but she proudly testified that he "came to see me any time 'cause his Marster ... give *him* a pass."[25] Their relationship depended upon how often their respective owners granted visitation passes. Adeline and Lewis continued to "court" after their marriage. "I lived on with my white folks," she asserted, "and he lived on with his and kept comin' to see me jest like he had done when he was a courtin'."[26] Others experienced more flexible visitation patterns. Jane Mickens and Wheeler Gresham both remembered that fathers could "come and go as [they] pleased."[27] Apparently, some owners supplied passes more readily than others, but enslaved partners often felt two weekly visits were not enough to maintain cohesive families. Reflecting on the relationship of his parents, Marshal Butler testified: "Mammy was a Frank Coller niggah and her man was of the tribe of Ben Butler, some miles down de road. Et was one of dem trial marriages—they'se tried so hard to see each other but old Ben Butler says two passes a week war enuff to see my mammy on de Collar plantation."[28] If it had been Butler's decision, he seemed to prefer that his parents see one another more than twice a week. In neighboring Oglethorpe County, originally part of Wilkes County, the pass system evolved in a fluid man-ner as bondmen "enjoyed [a] considerable freedom of movement." These visitation patterns marked regional trends that were customary to the Georgia upcountry.[29]

Abroad marriages were rare in the lowcountry. Only the narrative of Ryna John-son of St. Simons Island noted that her "huzbun . . . [was] frum Sapelo," a neigh-boring island.[30] It is likely that work patterns and the policy of enforced isolation discouraged abroad relationships in this region or that records indicating otherwise did not survive.

Bondwomen and men had mixed opinions about abroad marriages because of the advantages and disadvantages of these unions. The husband/father had greater freedom of movement than men with partners on the same plantation. Geographic mobility provided these men with new experiences and exposed them to places unfamiliar to most slaves. They often shared travel adventures with their wives and children; these stories gave them the hope to one day travel together as a fam-ily during freedom. In addition, abroad marriages provided family members with "emotional" or "social distance," protecting them from witnessing their loved one's abuse, exploitation, or overwork. Most scholars agree that "emotional distance" was a survival mechanism for enslaved families, which created "choices" unknown to couples with partners on the same plantation.[31] Negative aspects of these unions included limited time for familial nurturing and greater vulnerability to their owners' punishment and whims. Men had to be on their best behavior because their owners could revoke their visitation privileges at any moment. Finally, because a couple and family in an abroad partnership lived apart from one another, they had higher risks of permanent separation than those residing on the same estate.[32] Despite such challenges, bondwomen and bondmen did everything in their power to maintain and preserve their familial and communal connections. Some found that working socials represented an opportune time for strengthening their bonds.

Working Socials

During periods of decreased labor, bondpeople socialized with one another at inter-plantation events such as corn shucking, log rolling, syrup making, roof mending, quilting, regional cotton-picking competitions, and harvest festivals, events that all involved work. Slaveowners sought to capitalize on their investment through group activities and communal labor.[33] Multiple-plantation working socials gave planters an additional way to increase their capital by exploiting slaves' social activities in which enslaved men and women socialized, courted, danced, and ultimately married. The enslaved men and women created a space to express themselves and used these gatherings to escape the monotony of their daily lives.

Wilkes County bondpeople lived in an open community where opportunities for working socials occurred frequently. The owners of some small slaveholdings, because of their low populations, were forced to grant their bondwomen and bondmen permission to attend and participate in these types of activities. Thus, bondpeople sustained familial relations and met the obligations of marriage and parenting not only from their own efforts, but also because of the opportunities of interplantation contact approved by their owners.[34] Slaveholders who permitted their laborers to attend multiple-plantation socials gave them an occasion to mingle with enslaved laborers on neighboring farms and plantations. Many of these joint social activities involved kin-connected planter households, which convinced owners that their human chattels were under trustworthy supervision. Such practices granted bondpeople geographic mobility and social interaction while at the same time furnishing them with additional options to select a spouse and, ultimately, create a family. For example, on Benton Miller's farm in Hancock County, just south of Wilkes County, an enslaved female named Mary found her husband on the farm of her owner's brother-in-law.[35]

Working socials usually occurred around harvest time. Ex-slaves across five upcountry counties including Oglethorpe, Clarke, Green, Lincoln, and Wilkes testified about cooperative labor ventures.[36] Corn shuckings seemed to be the most memorable of these activities. Historian Eugene D. Genovese found that most "ex-slaves remembered corn-shuckings as their only good time," and others said "they were the best."[37] Bondpeople regarded such festivities positively because they were social events that involved working for themselves. Some of their testimonies reflect the festive atmosphere as many recalled singing to the music of a fiddle and eating food such as fresh meat and pound cake.[38]

Since work was central to most of these events, the social activities occurred after the completion of a particular task. Harvest festivals, for example, represented one type of working social that slaves looked forward to because of their celebratory nature. These festivals existed to return "thanks to the gods for having protected the crop" throughout the year.[39] Former bondwoman Catherine Wing remembered that they "use tuh hab big times duh fus hahves, and duh fus ting wut growed we take tuh duh church so as ebrybody could hab a piece ub it. We pray obuh it an shout."[40] Social activities in the lowcountry involved events restricted to slaves' home plantation, but upcountry bondwomen and men interacted with people on estates throughout the region and often across county lines.

"Peoples use ter be so good 'bout helpin' one 'nother," explained former Wilkes County bondman Henry Rogers. "When a neighbor's house needed covering," he continued, "he got the shingles and called in his neighbors and friends, who came along with their wives. While the men worked atop the house the women were cooking a delicious dinner down in the kitchen."[41] Rogers implicitly identifies a sexual division of labor at this particular working social. Some enslaved women, once outside of their owners' supervision, functioned in traditional or stereotypical familial roles by completing tasks such cleaning, cooking, and sewing. Historian Deborah Gray White explains that such strictly defined roles appealed to female field hands after a long day of back-breaking labor because they created a designated time to spend with other women. These interactions served as a social space for bondwomen to talk to each other about pregnancy, birth, and childrearing.[42] Even though these occasions involved "long hours of extra work," bondpeople enjoyed working socials because of the "community life they called forth."[43] Despite the sorrow many bondpeople experienced, they found time for "happy hours" often focusing on religion and celebrations.[44]

Religion and Holidays

Group interaction among the enslaved did not always involve labor. Outside of work responsibilities, bondwomen and bondmen interacted with their families and larger communities at church, at mealtimes, and at plantation social events. Holidays such as Christmas, Easter, and the Fourth of July enabled communities of people to celebrate during leisure activities without the pressure of an overseer or driver monitoring their behavior. Such holiday festivities gave relief from work and the opportunity to socialize with extended family and friends from nearby and distant plantations. Emily Burke witnessed Sunday festivities and made the following remarks: "The slaves had finished the tasks that had been assigned them in the morning and were now enjoying holiday recreations. Some were trundling the hoop, some were playing ball, some dancing at the sound of the fiddle, some grinding their own corn at the mill, while others were just returning from fishing or hunting excursions."[45]

It is clear that bondpeople used Sundays for a variety of activities. However, some bondpeople expressed little understanding of the underlying religious or national significance of these holidays. "Us didn't know nuffin' 'bout what dey wuz celebratin' on Fourth of July, 'cept a big dinner and a good time," explained Willis Cofer.[46] Easter marked a special holiday for those residing on the Cofer plantation in Wilkes County because "dat was de onlies day in de year a Nigger could do 'zactly what he pleased."[47] Only a few Glynn and Wilkes bondpeople testified that Santa Claus visited their cabins during Christmas, while some celebrated other holidays.[48] Emma Hurley noted, "I never heard of a Santa Claus when I wuz a child."[49] Christmas, for those who celebrated it, was a special holiday for enslaved people. It was a time for relaxation and jubilee because there was a respite from labor that on some plantations lasted as long as two weeks. The Christmas season served as the "climax of the year's work" and was celebrated by adults as well as children. Bondpeople enjoyed this holiday because they had a large feast; some couples even married during holiday social events. On St. Simons Island, laborers spent Christmas Eve at the "Praise House or little Church" anticipating the second coming of Christ.[50] On the Butler estate, a black preacher named London, the head cooper, delivered the sermon. Around the island, London was revered as "an excellent and pious man" who delivered sermons in his cabin on most Sundays to local bondpeople who did not attend worship services elsewhere.[51] Every year the Christmas Eve sermon revisited the story of Christ's birth, and the service ended with songs of praise and worship. Bondwomen and men enjoyed the following song at Christmastime:

King Jesus he tell you
Fur to fetch 'im a hoss an' a mule;
He tek up Mary behine 'im,
King Jesus he went marching' befo'.

      CHORUS.—

Christ was bon on Chris'mus day;
Mary was in pain.

Christ was born on Chris'mus day,
King Jesus was his name.[52]

The reference to a horse and a mule enabled bondwomen and bondmen to draw connections between their experience and that of "King Jesus."

Some members of the slaveholding class in Georgia, like those in other states, could not ignore religion among their bondpeople because, as one noted, there was "an immensely strong devotional feeling among these poor people."[53] This religious fervor was so apparent in Glynn County that those slaves belonging to Major Pierce Butler "petition[ed] very vehemently that he would build a church for them on the island" so that they could hold separate worship services and hear the word of God from slave preachers like London. But there was great concern over this request because "such a privilege might not be thought well of by the neighboring planters."[54]

When enslaved preachers and respected religious figures used their spiritual authority to influence their fellow laborers, planters feared the worst. On the Butler estate, a bondwoman named Sinda was revered as a prophetess with exceptional spiritual discernment, power, and authority over her peers. Bondwomen and men relied on her insight to help them cope with their lot, but in January 1839, Mr. King, the plantation overseer, felt that Sinda had taken her powers too far. When she predicted that the "world would come to an end at a certain time," all the enslaved laborers refused to work in the rice and cotton fields. This strike angered Mr. King, but he was even more furious with Sinda because of her influence over the other bondpeople. King threatened to punish her severely if her prediction proved false, and when the "day of judgment" came, he carried out his threat and quelled Sinda's "spirit of false prophesy" and returned the "faith of her people . . . from her to the omnipotent lash again."[55] The story of Sinda and her followers represents one reason that planters throughout the South feared the religious instruction of the enslaved. They knew that if an individual bondwoman or bondman gained influence or power over others, the results could be serious. One way to address this fear was to allow the enslaved to attend the religious services of the planter class.

Some Glynn County bondwomen and bondmen participated in Baptist and Methodist church services at their owners' congregations on the island and in Darien, a small town in neighboring McIntosh County. Lowcountry physician Dr. James Holmes, known in the area as "Dr. Bullie," remembered that "the colored people of the island were all Baptists, but our beloved Bishop always collected them together on the Sunday afternoons of his visitations and preached to them with understanding."[56] Those fortunate enough to have permission to travel to Darien could only attend services there once a month because slaveholders feared that frequent visits to other areas provided "opportunities for meeting between the Negroes of the different estates" that often led to "objectionable practices of various kinds."[57]

Members of the slaveholding class who were not so comfortable with slaves having separate worship services or accompanying their owners to service found ways to satisfy their religious conscience through private instruction. In March 1839, Frances Kemble found herself anxious about whether slaves on her husband's plantation would "come to prayers" in "the sitting room at eleven o'clock" one Sunday where she intended to "read prayers to them." She was pleasantly surprised when several came to this informal ceremony, especially since they came with "very decided efforts at cleanliness and decorum of attire." Boastfully, Kemble stated, "I was very much affected and impressed myself by what I was doing."[58] During this makeshift church service, Kemble struggled to contain her emotions when she read the scriptures to her enslaved "congregation." "It is an extremely solemn thing to me to read the Scriptures aloud to anyone," she expressed, "and there was something in my relation to the poor people by whom I was surrounded that touched me so deeply while thus attempting to share with them the best of my possessions, that I found it difficult to command my voice, and had to stop several times in order to do so." Clearly moved, Kemble dismissed the congregation of bondwomen and bondmen, feeling that they equally appreciated one another and respected one another's religious feelings.[59] Upcountry slaveholding women like Harriet Cumming of Wilkes County witnessed similar interactions with slaves on Sundays as her mother "taught them the Commandments, hymns, and a simple Catechism" in their family dining room.[60]

Despite religious instruction from members of the slaveholding class, some St. Simons Island bondpeople testified that they never participated in organized church activities. "Dey ain hab no church in doze days," explained former bondman Ben Sullivan, "an wen day wannuh pray, dey git behine duh house aw hide someweah an make a great prayuh. Dey ain suppose tuh call on duh Lawd; dey hadduh call on duh massuh an ef dey ain do dat, dey git nine an tutty."[61] Clearly, slaveholders tried to control the religious activities of their slaves, as this owner wanted slaves to pray to *him* rather than to "duh Lawd."

Religious activities represented a sacred time for family and community gatherings. Upcountry bondwomen like Arrie Binns of Wilkes County testified that her entire family worshipped together in a white church. She recalled being instructed to keep good manners during the sermon; there was "no lookin' to the right or the left." But this proved difficult the day a goat found its way into the church and disrupted the sermon so many times that Binns could hardly contain herself as she and her siblings struggled to suppress laughter. "We couldn't laugh a bit," Binns recalled, but " . . . I almost busted, I wanted ter laugh so bad."[62] She knew they would suffer from her parents' wrath if they did not mind their manners. Even though the Binns family interacted as a unit during services with whites, they also held their own private prayer meetings. "I 'members de meetins us use ter have down in our cabin," she recollected, "an' how everybody would pray an' sing."[63] Obviously some enslaved families made it a point to hold their own services and prayer meetings outside their owners' supervision. They nurtured their spirituality by using the time away from their owners to worship with one another.

Religious activities on Jane Mickens Toombs's Wilkes County plantation represented communal activities in which *all* bondwomen and men participated. Toombs testified that "Everybody went to Church, de grown folks white and black, went to de preachin' an' den all de little niggers wuz called in an de Bible red an' 'splained ter dem."[64] Like Arrie Binns, Toombs recalled segregated services "down in de Quarters, but dat wuz at night an' wuz led by de colored preachers."[65] During the summer months, Toombs also remembered that her Uncle George Gullatt "use ter preach ter de slaves out under de trees."[66]

Whether held in the yard or at a "Praise House," religious services among the enslaved were sacred events. Some were so sacred that members of the slaveholding class commented on them in their journals. "I wish I was an artist so that I could draw a picture of the scene," exclaimed Eliza Andrews about the Praise House on her father's Wilkes County plantation. "The women, when they get excited with the singing, shut their eyes and rock themselves back and forth, clapping their hands" to songs such as this:

Mary an' Marthy, feed my lambs,
Feed my lambs, feed my lambs;
Mary an' Marthy, feed my lambs,
Settin' on de golden altar.
I weep, I moan; what mek I moan so slow?
I won'er ef a Zion traveler have gone along befo;
Paul de' postle, feed my lambs,
Feed my lambs, feed my lambs. . . .[67]

Witnessing such a scene was a privilege for whites. As Andrews noted, "they won't give way to their wildest gesticulations or engage in their sacred dances before white people, for fear of being laughed at." The day she visited the Praise House, several slaves had gone to the river bank and she "did not get a full choir," however "whenever the 'sperrit' of the song moved them very much, [they] would pat their feet and flap their arms and go through a number of motions."[68] Slave spirituals so impressed Frances Butler Leigh, daughter of Glynn County plantation owner Pierce Butler, that she marveled with envy at the skill and character of them.

I often wish that I were a first-rate musician, that I might be able to collect, preserve, and harmonise some of their tunes. There is really nothing in the words, which if written down apart from the music, seem mere nonsense, but it is the way they sing the words, the natural seconds they take, and the antiphonal mode they unconsciously adopt. Also the remarkable minors that many of their songs are sung in, which it is almost impossible to imitate.[69]

Leigh not only noticed the rhythm, as bondpeople "always keep most exquisite time and tune," but she also found it remarkable that "no words seem too hard for them to adapt to their tunes, so that they could sing a long metre hymn to a short metre tune without any sensible difficulty." She also complimented those whose "voices have a peculiar quality that nothing can imitate; and their intonations and delicate variations cannot be reproduced on paper."[70]

Once the enslaved preacher stepped into the pulpit or makeshift pulpit under a tree, he greeted his "congregation" with joy in celebration of their gathering. Gender divisions were evident as the role of the preacher was reserved for males, even though enslaved women had active roles within the congregation. One woman testified that she was called to preach well after the abolition of slavery.[71] Attending church was an event, and women showed up in their best clothes.[72] Robert Shepard, an upcountry bondman, remembered that "[s]lave women had new calico dresses what they wore with hoop skirts they made out of grapevines." He also noted that they wore "poke bonnets with ruffles on 'em, and if the weather was sort of cool, they wore shawls."[73] As the preacher began his sermon, members of the audience responded by clapping, shouting, and singing praises.

Neal Upson, another former bondman, remembered his older sisters telling him stories about slave sermons. "There weren't many slaves what could read, so they jus' talked 'bout what they done heard the white preachers say on Sunday," he shared. "One of the favorite texts was the third chapter from John," he continued, "and most of 'em just 'membered a line or two from that." In addition to sermons and scripture readings, "there was sure a lot of good prayin' and testifyin'" at these meetings.[74] When the preacher moved his audience, bondwomen and men responded with call-and-response songs like the following:

What make the Preacher preach so hard,	O yes now.
The Prettiest thing I ever saw,	O yes now.
They study of religion while you're young,	O Yes now.
I lean in the Rock and never fall,	O yes now.
O march with the members,	Bound to go.
Aint you a member,	Bound to go.
Aint you a member,	Bound to go.
Believer fare you well.[75]	

This song represented the congregation opening the doors of the church, seeking those who had not officially joined the fellowship to answer the call. "When a nigger joined the church," former upcountry bondwoman Fannie Hughes recalled, "there so' was a lot of shoutin' and singin'. Wish you could heard it."[76] Once a person joined the church, "a colored preacher did the baptizing," usually in a local river; thus the slave was now part of a church family.[77] Ben Sullivan, a former bondman from St. Simons Island, noted, "Dey hab big baptizing in duh ribbah . . . an dey dip em on duh ebb tuh was duh sins away an dud preachuh he make a great prayuh tuh duh ribbuh."[78] Besides church services, baptisms, Sunday school, and other types of religious gatherings represented settings where courtship rituals, marriage ceremonies, and social interaction occurred. After prayer, worship, and the sermon, they concluded their religious celebrations with a dance.

Several bondwomen and bondmen had positive recollections about sacred and secular plantation dances. They testified about moving to the beat of a drum, swaying to the music of a fiddle, and other specially crafted instruments. Dr. Bullie commented on the fiddler at Raymond Demere's estate during one of his visits to St. Simons Island. "We met there a character by the name of Hickey," he explained, "who could play to perfection the country jigs popular in those days."[79] Apparently, "Hickey" was so skilled with the fiddle that Dr. Bullie could not resist taking a "turn on the grass plat before the door."[80] Similarly, ex-slave Ryna Johnson explained that "[w]en we is young, we use tuh hab big frolic an dance in a ring an shout tuh drum. Sometime we hab rattle made out uh dry goad [gourd] an we rattle em an make good music."[81] Several others remembered performing a dance called the "Buzzard Lope" that imitated the actions of different animals, particularly birds.[82] As the participants hastened the pace, they also changed the rhythm of the dance.

Regardless of whether they worked or played, communal events such as working socials, religious ceremonies, and dances provided a designated time and place for the enslaved to interact with one another and to participate in courtship rituals. At dances, bondwomen and men expressed themselves spiritually, musically, and socially. Saturday nights "were always the time for dancing and frolicking," explained one Wilkes County enslaved male.[83] Another testified, "We sure frolicked Saturday nights. Dat wuz our day to howl and we howled."[84] Reflecting on one of these events, Jane Harmon boasted about her dancing skills: "I allus could dance, I cuts fancy steps now sometimes when I feels good. At one o' dem big ole country breakdowns (dances), one night when I wuz young, I danced down seben [7] mens, dey thought dey wuz sumpin'! Huh, I danced eb'ry one down!"[85] Enslaved males readily admitted that their women partners had impressive dancing skills. "Our gals sure could dance," stated Butler, "and when we wuz thirsty[,] we had lemonade and whiskey . . . de gals all liked it."[86] It appears that planters sanctioned these dances, which is not surprising considering the open nature of the upcountry enslaved community; however, it is difficult to determine how often these events occurred. Some slaveholders participated in or witnessed the festivities. In fact, planters had such vivid recollections of enslaved dances that they wrote about them in their journals, diaries, and letters. One Wilkes County planter even recalled the lyrics to a song titled "The Negro Caller," and kept the lyrics in his personal scrapbook:

Get yo' pardners, first Kioatilliou!
Stomp yo' feet, an' raise 'Em high;
Sure is, "Oh, dat water—milliou!
Gwine to git a houre lively."

S' lute yo' pardners! scrape politely;
Don't be bumpim' give the res'
Balance all! now step out rightly
Alluz dance yo' level bes.

Fo' ward, foak! Whoop up niggers!
Back agin! Don't be so slow;
Swing Comahs! Min' de figgers;
When I hollers, den yo' go

Hands around! hol' up yo' faces;
Don't be lookin' at yo' feet;
Swing yo' pardners to yo' places!
Dats de way—dat's hard to beat

Sides forward! where you's ready
Make a bow as low's yo' kin;
Swing against wid opsit lady!
Now we'll let yo' swap agin

Ladies Change! Shet up dat talkin';
Do yo' talkn' after while;
Right and lef'! don't want no walkn';
Make yo' steps, an' show yo' style.[87]

Given the title, it appears that this song is reflective of a dance (cotillion) orchestrated by a "Negro Caller" who used an authoritative tone to shout directives that controlled the pace and movement of the dance. Considering that this record appeared loose in a planter's scrapbook, it is likely that someone in the slaveholding family witnessed this ritual and documented what they saw. Even though the author and origin remain lost to history, it is clear that someone witnessed bondpeople dancing to the commands of a person referred to as the "Negro Caller," and they deemed it interesting enough to keep in their family scrapbook.

Although dances were fairly common in Wilkes County, some enslaved parents did not permit their children to participate in such events. Emma Hurley testified that she "ain't never danced a step nor sung a reel in my life. My Ma allus said we shouldn't do them things an' we didn't, she said if we went to the devil it wouldn't be 'cause she give us her 'mission!'"[88] Enslaved mothers and fathers had their own sets of rules and regulations for the rearing of their children despite owners' desire to control the physical and social activities of their "property." Resisting their slaveholders' authority gave enslaved parents like the Hurleys space to enforce *their* own ideals and morals. For others, dances became sites for courting and for the maintenance and development of functional families regardless of demographic constraints.

Family Structure

Creating a family was important to the enslaved because relatives served as outlets necessary for their survival. Whether in abroad marriages or in home plantation relationships, extended familial connections were extremely important even after the abolition of slavery in 1865. Former Wilkes County bondwomen and men reunited with their relatives after Emancipation because they were accustomed to geographic mobility and the multiplantation interaction they had had during slavery. Abroad spouses and family members often lived in neighboring counties, yet searching for them was not as challenging as it was for those who had to look out of state. For example, forty-one families from Wilkes County appear in the records of the Freedman's Savings and Trust Company from 1870 to 1872.[89] These former bondwomen and bondmen applied for bank accounts in Augusta, the primary urban center of the Georgia upcountry. Their applications included biographical sketches of their extended families, marital status, children, occupation, age, and complexion.

Many of these individuals had substantial kin networks and complex families. The family of Julie Ann Truett serves as a good example. Truett was fifty-nine years old when she filed for an application in 1871. She and her deceased husband Alligan had only one child, named John, but she had seven siblings, of whom two were listed as "dead." Her brother Toby was "carried off to Alabama," and the whereabouts of her father Sandy were unknown. Truett said he "was carried off many years ago when I was small."[90] Her mother Molly appears in the record as "dead." Truett lived in Wilkes County, "7 miles from Washington" all of her life and she worked as a cook, which is probably the same work she did during slavery.

The former bondwomen and men in these records had large kin networks and a variety of occupations; several were "taken to Texas" while others were "carried off to Alabama," and a significant proportion of their siblings had died. The females of childbearing age had at least one child, while one woman, "Mat Basket," was expecting because her file listed her second child as "Baby not born."[91] Thirty-five knew both parents' names (sometime surnames), two knew of only one parent, three had white fathers, and one had no knowledge of his parental ties.[92] More than one-half of those that filed for bank accounts (twenty-one) listed a spouse. Louisa Kane, for example, was forty-nine years old when she submitted her application in 1872. She worked as an agricultural laborer ("farmer") in Washington during bondage and was in a relationship with a white man named "Robert," whom she "never married." It is difficult to determine whether "Robert" was Louisa's former owner or a man she met after slavery, but the fact that she listed him in the column marked "Husband" signifies evidence of miscegenation and suggests that Louisa believed she and Robert were husband and wife even though they "never married."[93]

Extended families were crucial to Glynn County slave family stability as well; relatives in this region often lived together for many years. Enslaved Africans on St. Simons Island made references to aunts, uncles, cousins, and grandparents. Charles, for example, recalled "Muh gran, she name Louise an come frum Bahama Ilun."[94] Likewise Charles's wife Emma had some memories of her grandmother: "gran Betty she wuz African."[95] In addition to matrifocal and extended family patterns, Glynn County bondpeople established conjugal relationships with or without their owners' permission. Nuclear family structures represented one outcome of such relationships. Enslaved families in this region expanded across two and sometimes three generations.

When J. D. Legare visited Glynn County in 1832, he said that Hopeton Plantation, operated by James Hamilton Couper (J. H. Couper), "is decidedly the best regulated plantation we have ever visited, and we doubt whether it can be equaled (certainly not surpassed) in the Southern States."[96] Hopeton contained 4,500 acres of land and was the home of as many as 600 enslaved laborers during the antebellum period.[97] Situated on the south side of the Altamaha River "about five miles from [the town of] Darien, [and] fourteen miles from the sea," Hopeton produced rice, cotton, sugar, Irish potatoes, cow-peas, turnips, and rye.[98] On 14 March 1830, 390 slaves lived in 110 family groupings at Hopeton. This population had 199 females, 159 males, and 32 illegible names.[99]

The family structures at Hopeton included nuclear, single-parent, couples without children, and extended connections. Nearly half the families represented (fifty) belonged to nuclear households, and thirty-two families included extended kin connections. Eighteen couples appear without children, like "Old Dick" and "Camba" who were sixty and sixty-one years old, respectively. Of the other family structures, thirteen included mothers and their offspring, and three fathers appear with offspring. Several couples had six children living with them on this estate—much different than the family structure in the Georgia upcountry, where it is difficult to trace paternal ties. Other estates in Glynn County contained significant family connections.[100]

Families at Retreat Plantation had few disruptions to their connections because the King family rarely sold their Retreat slaves. Thirty bondwomen and men appeared on both the 1827 and 1859 lists and by the latter date contributed to seventeen nuclear families, which indicates some stability on this plantation. The enslaved population exceeded 100 slaves during the antebellum period, consisting of 140 in 1827, 112 in 1850, 129 in 1859, and 142 in 1860.[101] Between the years 1827 and 1860, the population did not change much. In 1827, for example, females represented 47 percent of the population while males made up 53 percent of the workforce.[102] Thirty-two years later, the population decreased by 8 percent from 140 to 129. Of this later population, women totaled 55 percent while men represented 45 percent of the labor force. These statistics suggest a relatively balanced slave population; however, age distributions allow additional conclusions to surface.

The age distribution among enslaved men and women at Retreat was conducive to the formation of families except in 1859. The number of available males between the ages of ten and nineteen was significantly lower than the number of females. Women in this age group (ten through nineteen) made up 17 percent of the total enslaved population while men represented only 6 percent. Thus, by 1859, teenage women may have had trouble finding a mate at Retreat because they outnumbered men nearly three to one. For those men and women in their twenties, the age distribution was even, with ten men and ten women, which probably created a good chance for finding a mate at that age. Single men in their thirties outnumbered women 1.4 to 1.

Anna Page King identified seventeen nuclear families among the 142 enslaved men and women listed at the time of her death, which included 68 percent of the slave population.[103] Such high percentages indicate that the majority of Retreat slaves lived on a plantation with relatives present. Thus, individuals such as Alfred and Liddy grew up, married, had children, and lived together at Retreat for more than thirty years. This couple, like several others, appeared on the 1827 list as infants, but by 1860 they had given birth to two children, Frederick and Adalette. When considering these statistics, particularly in settings where demographic conditions provide a climate conducive for monogamy and nuclear families, enslaved couples often selected their spouse "based on a complex combination of reasons."[104] Some slaves preferred not to marry to avoid becoming attached to a partner only to witness their abuse or sale, while others did all they could to find a partner for support. Many of the reasons enslaved couples chose one another are still unknown to contemporary scholars.

Family and Community Interaction

Despite physical distance between family members, enslaved parents nurtured and disciplined their offspring, creating family interaction that was intimate and personal. Wives socialized with their husbands in small log cabins approximately sixteen by twenty feet, containing one or two rooms depending on the size of the family.[105]

Enslaved families utilized all possible avenues to maintain cohesive family units. As a child, Henry Rogers testified that "the fust thing I 'members is follerin' my Mother er 'round . . . everywhere she went I wuz at her heels."[106] Others also expressed deep love and affection for their mothers. "The first thing I recollect is my love for my mother," explained Adeline Willis. "I loved her so," she continued, "and would cry when I couldn't be with her." Even after Adeline married and had children of her own, she continued to love her mother "jest that-away."[107] Maternal bonds marked the strength of family unity and were reinforced through legal codes. The connection between mother and child became legally sanctioned through the Georgia Slave Code of 1755, which read in part that "slaves shall follow the condition of the mother and shall be deemed in law to be chattels personal in the hands of their owners and possessors."[108] In addition to this mandatory legislation, slaveholders reinforced female-headed families by assigning cabins, food rations, clothing, and land (i.e., garden plots) to enslaved mothers.[109] These practices and the Georgia Slave Code explain why some slaveholders preferred more women over men—a woman's capacity to bear children represented a constant source of additional labors. Birth lists rarely denoted the "father" of a particular child because of this practice of identifying slaves through maternal lineage. For example, when Hugh Fraser Grant of Elizafield Plantation noted the enslaved births and the distribution of supplies such as blankets and tools, he only listed the mother's name.[110]

By ignoring the father-child association through this legal stipulation, enslaved families developed matrifocally, leaving many of the parental obligations solely to enslaved mothers. The challenge to maintain stable families increased; such laws hardly considered the father after the birth of new slave progeny. Although owners encouraged women to give birth, they made few promises regarding the maintenance of paternal bonds. In spite of the legal recognition of the mother-child connection, enslaved fathers found ways to raise their children. Jane Mickens's father, for example, lived on a different plantation but she recognized his authority despite his absence. "My Pa didn't 'low his chillun ter go 'roun" she explained. "No'm, he kep' us home keerful lak."[111] Clearly, her father was able to keep his fifteen children from visiting other slaves, even though he did not live at the same "home." Thus, distance and time did not stop fathers from parenting.[112] Despite parentage, many understood that in reality, "all de chilluns b'longed to de gal's white folkes."[113]

Mealtimes provided periodic contact among enslaved families and the larger community because they created a space that was sometimes outside their owner's presence. On estates with large workforces, a plantation cook, usually an older woman, prepared all the meals.[114] Marshal Butler of Wilkes County recollected that they ate breakfast at dark, lunch in the fields, and dinner in the slave cabins; the first two meals were for the entire plantation community, the last was shared with individual family members.[115] Butler's memory of breakfast "at dark" suggests that this first meal was served before dawn, prior to entering the fields. Bondwomen and bondmen started their day with a 4:00 a.m. wake-up horn and they had to be in the fields forty-five minutes later, so this meal had to be a quick one. Likewise, lunch was probably rushed as well since it took place in the fields and overseers kept their workers on a rigid schedule during daylight hours. Dinner in the cabins was most likely the best meal for family socialization; one can speculate about the types of conversations that they participated in during this "family time"—seeing how each member made it through another monotonous day of agricultural or nonagricultural labor, or they might have talked about recent runaways, upcoming religious or working social events, or the marriage of a new couple. It is also feasible that they discussed plans to put an end to their enslaved status.

Willis Cofer of Wilkes County described communal mealtimes on his master's plantation: "Dere wuz so many chilluns dey fed us in a trough. Dey jes poured de peas on de chuncks of cornbread what de had crumbled in de trough, and us had to mussel 'em out. . . . De only spoons us had wuz mussel shells what us got out of de branches [creeks]. A little Nigger could put peas and cornbread away mighty fast wid a mussel shell. . . . When a boy got to be a man enough to wear pants, he drawed rations and quit eatin' out of de trough."[116] Mealtimes for Cofer functioned more like a survival-of-the fittest competition. There was little time for socialization (i.e., conversation) during his meals; instead, Cofer and the other adolescents struggled to eat with much haste because they did not have the appropriate utensils. Clearly, eating was a communal event. Although Wilkes County bondwoman Jane Harmon's mealtimes differed in location from Cofer's, she also ate from a trough. Harmon explained that the bondpeople on her plantation, "et in de white folks' kitchen out' n er big tray whut wuz lak a trough."[117] Regardless of where enslaved women, men, and children ate their meals, the demands of labor forced them to eat according to their owner's preference.

Summary

Bondwomen and men created, maintained, and interacted with their families and communities despite spending most of their time working for their slaveholders. Bondpeople nurtured familial and communal connections during working socials and during periods of rest (i.e., holidays, religious services, weddings, and dances). They had fond recollections of these interactions because relatives helped them deal with the hardships of their condition. They used this space to express love for one another, to hope for a better day, and to dream of freedom. On small holdings in Wilkes County, the opportunities to create families differed from those on large plantations because bondpeople had to select a mate from another farm or estate. Enslaved men and women on small holdings were often involved in abroad relationships and were at the mercy of their owners for visitation. Large holdings were conducive to stable family formation on the home estate. Once slaves found partners, either on or off their home plantation, they married and usually had children. Families enjoyed participation in communal activities, but the reality of their enslaved status was always present.

Notes

1. *The News and Planter's Gazette,* 26 November 1840, emphasis added.

2. Larry E. Hudson, Wilma King, and Philip D. Morgan are exceptions in that their studies emphasized labor as a central part of the slave familial experience. See Larry E. Hudson Jr., *To Have and to Hold: Slave Work and Family Life in Antebellum South Carolina* (Athens: University of Georgia Press, 1997); Philip D. Morgan, *Slave Counterpoint: Black Culture in the Eighteenth-Century Chesapeake and Lowcountry* (Chapel Hill: University of North Carolina Press, 1998); and Wilma King, *Stolen Childhood: Slave Youth in Nineteenth-Century America* (Bloomington: Indiana University Press, 1995). For other work relating to enslaved family and community life, see John Blassingame, *The Slave Community: Plantation Life in the Antebellum South* (New York: Oxford University Press, 1972); Stephanie M. H. Camp, *Closer to Freedom: Enslaved Women and Everyday Resistance in the Plantation South* (Chapel Hill: University of North Carolina Press, 2004); Eugene D. Genovese, *Roll Jordan Roll: The World the Slaves Made* (New York: Vintage Books, 1974, 473–75); Brenda E. Stevenson, *Life in Black and White: Family and Community in the Slave South* (New York: Oxford University Press, 1996); and Deborah Gray White, *Ar'n't I a Woman? Female Slaves in the Plantation South* (New York: W. W. Norton and Company, 1985).

3. See Ann Patton Malone, *Sweet Chariot: Slave Family and Household Structure in Nineteenth-Century Louisiana* (Chapel Hill: University of North Carolina Press, 1992); Emily West, *Chains of Love: Slave Couples in Antebellum South Carolina* (Urbana: University of Illinois Press, 2004); and Brenda E. Stevenson, *Life in Black and White: Family and Community in the Slave South* (New York: Oxford University Press, 1996).

4. Blassingame, *The Slave Community.*

5. Balanced sex ratios did not guarantee the presence of cohesive families since age differentials played a significant role in mate availability. See Daina L. Ramey, "A Place of Our Own: Labor, Family and Community among Female Slaves in Piedmont and Tidewater Georgia, 1820–1860," Ph.D. dissertation, University of California, Los Angeles, 1998; and Daina L. Ramey, "'A Heap of Us Slaves': Family and Community Life among Slave Women in Georgia." *Atlanta History: A Journal of Georgia and the South* 44, no. 3 (Fall 2000): 21–38.

6. Ralph B. Flanders, *Plantation Slavery in Georgia* (Chapel Hill: University of North Carolina Press, 1933), 173.

7. For a vivid description of the courting process, see Blassingame, *The Slave Community*, 156–61.

8. George P. Rawick, ed., *The American Slave: A Composite Autobiography* (Westport, Conn.: Greenwood Press, 1977) (hereafter *AS*), vol. 13, pt. 4, 166.

9. Jacqueline Jones, *Labor of Love, Labor of Sorrow: Black Women, Work, and the Family, From Slavery to the Present* (New York: Vintage Books, 1985), 33.

10. Rawick, *AS*, vol. 12, pt. 1, 175.

11. Blassingame, *The Slave Community*, 159.

12. Rawick, *AS*, vol. 12, pt. 2, 69 (emphasis added).

13. Ibid., vol. 12, pt, 1, 162.

14. Ibid., vol. 12, pt. 1, 164.

15. Ibid., vol. 13, pt. 4, 165.

16. "The Farm Journal of Benton Miller," 10 October 1858, Georgia Archives, Morrow, Georgia (microfilm).

17. Rawick, *AS*, vol. 12, pt. 2, 341.

18. Ibid., 180.

19. Ibid., vol. 12, pt. 1, 175 (emphasis added).

20. "The Farm Journal of Benton Miller," Georgia Archives, Morrow, Georgia.

21. Rawick, *AS*, vol. 12, pt. 1, 207.

22. Ibid., vol. 13, pt. 3, 165.

23. Ibid., vol. 12, pt. 2, 176. For evidence in South Carolina, see Hudson, *To Have and to Hold*, 159; for Virginia, see Stevenson, *Life in Black and White*, 228–30; and for Louisiana, see Ann Patton Malone, *Sweet Chariot: Slave Family and Household Structure in Nineteenth-Century Louisiana* (Chapel Hill: University of North Carolina Press, 1992), 224.

24. This visitation pattern was fairly common throughout the South as slaves in Louisiana, South Carolina, and Virginia testified to similar options. See, for example, Stevenson, *Life in Black and White*, 208–12, and 230–34. For evidence on abroad marriages in Louisiana and South Carolina, see Malone, *Sweet Chariot*, 166–68, 227–28, 262, and 269, and Hudson, *To Have and to Hold*, 142–49, and 160.

25. Rawick, *AS*, vol. 13, pt. 4, 16, 165 (emphasis added).

26. Ibid., vol. 13, pt. 4, 165.

27. Ibid., vol. 13, pt. 3, 30, and vol. 12, pt. 1, 67.

28. Ibid., vol. 12, pt. 1, 160.

29. Clarence L. Mohr, "Slavery in Oglethorpe County, Georgia 1773–1865," *Phylon* 32, no. 1 (Spring 1972): 4–21, quote on 7. For commentary on the Wilkes County pass system, see Charles Danforth Saggus, "A Social and Economic History of the Danburg Community in Wilkes County, Georgia" (M.A. thesis, University of Georgia, 1951), 128.

30. Georgia Writers' Project, *Drums and Shadows*, 176. Perhaps lowcountry slaves offered no testimony on courtship and marriage because they spent the majority of their time working on their home plantations.

31. See Genovese, *Roll Jordan Roll*, 473–75; Hudson, *To Have and to Hold*, 141–45; Stevenson, *Life in Black and White*, 230–33; and White, *Ar'n't I a Woman?* 153–55.

32. Genovese, *Roll Jordan Roll,* 472–73.

33. Carole Elaine Merritt, "Slave Family and Household Arrangements in Piedmont Georgia" (Ph.D. diss., Emory University, 1986), 173.

34. Ibid., 129.

35. Mary married Starobin on 10 October 1858. See "Journal of Benton Miller," Georgia Archives, Morrow, Georgia.

36. Carole Elaine Merritt, "Slave Family and Household Arrangements in Piedmont Georgia" (Ph.D. diss., Emory University, 1986), 173.

37. Genovese, *Roll Jordan Roll,* 315 and 319. See also Weiner, *Mistresses and Slaves,* 22.

38. Rawick, *AS,* vol. 12, pt. 2, 69–70. For an extensive study of corn shuckings and other aspects of plantation culture, see Roger D. Abrahams, *Singing the Master: The Emergence of African American Culture in the Plantation South* (New York: Pantheon Books, 1992). See also Burke, *Pleasure and Pain,* 40–41.

39. Georgia Writers' Project, *Drums and Shadows: Survival Studies among the Georgia Coastal Negroes,* Malcolm Bell, Jr, ed. (Athens: Georgia University Press, 1986), 222.

40. Georgia Writers' Project, *Drums and Shadows,* 174.

41. Rawick, *AS,* vol. 13, pt. 3, 223–24.

42. See White, *Ar'n't I a Woman?,* 119–41, especially 119, and Genovese, *Roll Jordan Roll,* 319.

43. Genovese, *Roll Jordan Roll,* 316–17.

44. Emily Burke, *Pleasure and Pain: Reminiscences of Georgia in the 1840s* (Savannah, Ga.: Beehive Press, 1978, originally published in 1850), 41, and Camp, *Closer to Freedom,* 60–92.

45. Burke, *Pleasure and Pain,* 49–50.

46. Rawick, *AS,* vol. 12, pt. 1, 206.

47. Ibid., vol. 12, pt. 1, 205.

48. Ibid., vol. 12, pt. 1, 76, and vol. 12, pt. 2, 69.

49. Ibid., vol. 12, pt. 2, 2.

50. See Margaret Davis Cate, "Christmas and Other Holidays," typescript in Margaret Davis Cate Collection, University of Georgia.

51. Frances Anne Kemble, *Journal of a Residence on a Georgian Plantation in 1838–1839* (Athens: University of Georgia Press, 1984), 92. See also "Inventory and Appraisement of the Estate of Capt. John Butler, dec'd"; and McIntosh County Court of Ordinary, 21 February 1859, "Division of slaves belonging to the Estate of John Butler, dec'd," Butler Collection, HSP.

52. Eliza Frances Andrews, *The War-Time Journal of a Georgia Girl, 1864–1865* (1908, reprint. Lincoln: University of Nebraska Press, 1997), 90–91.

53. Kemble, *Journal of a Residence,* 106.

54. Ibid., 125–26, quote on 186. See also Charles C. Jones, *Religious Instruction of the Negroes in the United States* (Savannah, Ga.: T. Purse, 1842).

55. Kemble, *Journal of a Residence,* 118–19.

56. James Holmes, *"Dr. Bullie's" Notes: Reminiscences of Early Georgia and of Philadelphia and New Haven in the 1800s* (Atlanta: Cherokee Publishing Company, 1976), 194–96.

57. Kemble, *Journal of a Residence,* 261–62.

58. Ibid., 262.

59. Ibid., 261–63.

60. Marion Alexander Boggs, ed., *The Alexander Letters, 1787–1900: The Moving and Absorbing Saga of a Georgia Family* (Athens: University of Georgia Press, 1980), 106. I wish to thank Dale Couch of the Georgia Archives for identifying this source and the University of Georgia Press for lending me this out-of-print book.

61. Georgia Writers' Project, *Drums and Shadows,* 180.

62. Rawick, *AS,* vol. 12, pt. 1, 77.

63. Ibid., vol. 12, pt. 1, 77.

64. Ibid., vol. 13, pt. 4, 33. Benton Miller's three slaves regularly attended church on Sundays. See the Benton Miller Farm Journal, Georgia Archives, Morrow, Georgia.

65. Rawick, *AS,* vol. 13, pt. 4, 33.

66. Ibid., vol. 13, pt. 4, 33.

67. Eliza Frances Andrews, *The War-Time Journal of a Georgia Girl, 1864–1865* (1908, reprint. Lincoln: University of Nebraska Press, 1997), quote on 101, song on 90.

68. Ibid., 89.

69. Frances Butler Leigh, *Ten Years on a Georgia Plantation since the War, 1866–1876* (1883, reprint, Savannah, Ga.: Beehive Press, 1992), 147. Leigh was equally impressed with "boat songs."

70. Ibid., 147.

71. Andrew Waters, ed., *On Jordan's Stormy Banks: Personal Accounts of Slavery in Georgia* (Winston-Salem, N.C.: John F. Blair, 2000), 22–25.

72. Daina Ramey Berry, "'We Sho Was Dressed Up': Slave Women, Material Culture and Decorative Arts in Wilkes County, Georgia," in *The Savannah River Valley up to 1865: Fine Arts, Architecture, and Decorative Arts,* ed. Ashley Callahan (Athens: Georgia Museum of Art, 2003).

73. Waters, *On Jordan's Stormy Banks,* 129.

74. Ibid., 9–10. Other slaves such as Alice Bradley expressed great pride in the fact that her family owned a Bible. Bradley proudly testified that she knew her parents' birth and death dates because of the list printed in her family Bible. "I knows dem years is right" she explained after reciting the exact dates to her interviewer in the 1930s, "'cause I got 'em from dat old fambly Bible." Rawick, *AS,* vol. 12, pt. 1, 118.

75. Frances Butler Leigh, *Ten Years on a Georgia Plantation since the War, 1866–1876* (1883, reprint, Savannah, Ga.: Beehive Press, 1992), 148.

76. Waters, *On Jordan's Stormy Banks,* 114.

77. Ibid.

78. Georgia Writers' Project, *Drums and Shadows,* 180.

79. Holmes, *"Dr. Bullie's" Notes,* 133.

80. Ibid.

81. Johnson's reference to being young indicates that her memories of slavery occurred during childhood. Johnson shared her recollections in the 1930s as part of a federally sponsored project. See Georgia Writer's Project, *Drums and Shadows,* 176. See similar testimony by Floyd White, 182.

82. See Sterling Stuckey, *Slave Culture: Nationalist Theory and the Foundations of Black America* (New York: Oxford University Press, 1987), 12–17; and the Georgia Writers' Project, *Drums and Shadows*, 208.

83. Rawick, *AS*, vol. 12, pt. 2, 197.

84. Ibid., vol. 12, pt. 1, 163.

85. Ibid., vol. 12, pt. 2, 99.

86. Ibid., vol. 12, pt. 1, 163.

87. "The Negroe Caller," Dubose Family Papers, MS 1738, Hargrett Library, University of Georgia.

88. Rawick, *AS*, vol. 12, pt. 2, 279.

89. Alice O. Walker, ed., *Registers of Signatures of Depositors in the Augusta, Georgia, Branch of the Freedman's Savings and Trust Company*, vol. 1 (Augusta, Ga.: Richmond County Public Library, 1998). Hereafter cited as FS&T.

90. Ibid., 123.

91. Ibid., 282.

92. Ibid., passim.

93. Ibid., 469.

94. Georgia Writers' Project, *Drums and Shadows*, 177.

95. Ibid., 178.

96. J. D. Legare, "Account of an Agricultural Excursion Made into the South of Georgia in the Winter of 1832," Southern Agriculturist 6 (June–August 1833), 359.

97. T. Reed Ferguson, *The John Couper Family at Cannon's Point* (Macon, Ga.: Mercer University Press, 1994), 159.

98. Legare, "Account of an Agricultural Excursion," 360–65.

99. "An Inventory of the Goods and Chattels at Hopeton Plantation," Glynn County Court of Ordinary, Estate Records, Book D 1810–1843, Georgia Archives, Morrow, Georgia (microfilm).

100. See, for example, Elizafield Plantation where Hugh Fraser Grant identified the following twenty couples: Driver John and wife [Fortune], Old Harry and L Dinah, March and Amaretta, Emperor and Haigar, Stephen and Hannah, Caesar and Biney, Abraham and Nancy, April and Phillis, Brister and Lear, London and Sary, Prince and Nancy, M John and Matilla, Scipio and Dido, Andrew and Mira, Alec and Flora, Harry and Catherine, Nat and Betty, John Stake and Bess, Jack and Cumsey, and Ben and Nann. For the original journal, see "Elizafield Plantation Journal, 1838–1861," *Southern Historical Collection* #3213-z, Wilson Library, University of North Carolina, Chapel Hill. A microfilmed copy of the original journal is available through the *Records of Ante-Bellum Southern Plantations From the Revolution Through the Civil War*. See series J, pt. 4, reel 21.

101. William Page Will, 6 February 1827, *Margaret Davis Cate Collection*, courtesy of the Georgia Historical Society, Savannah, Georgia; "Inventory of the Personal Property & Estate of William Page, 1827," Glynn County Ordinary Estate Records, Inventories and Appraisals, Book D (Georgia Archives, Morrow, Ga.); U.S. Department of Commerce, Bureau of the Census, Federal Manuscript Census, Glynn County, Georgia, 1850–1860 (microfilm); Anna Page King Will, 7 March 1859, Court of Ordinary, Glynn County Or-

dinary Estate Records, Inventories and Appraisals, Book E (Georgia Archives, Morrow, Ga.); "Inventory of the Estate of Mrs. Anna Matilda King, 1860," William Audley Couper Papers #3687, *Southern Historical Collection,* Wilson Library, University of North Carolina, Chapel Hill; and Pavich-Lindsay, ed., *Anna: The Letters of a St. Simons Island Plantation Mistress,* Appendix 2.

102. The total enslaved population in 1827 was 140. Of this group, 66 were female and 74 were male.

103. Of the 142 bondpeople in the population, 125 of them belonged to family units. The remaining seventeen bondwomen and bondmen appear on the lists without designated family members. Enslaved families at Retreat are easily reconstructed by analysis of slave lists from 1827, 1859, and 1860. In addition to the order in which the master and/ or mistress placed slaves, personal letters of Anna Page King reveal family groupings as well. Other sources used to derive the seventeen families came from wills and estate inventories.

104. Stevenson, *Life in Black and White,* 234.

105. Flanders, *Plantation Slavery in Georgia,* 152–54.

106. Rawick, *AS,* vol. 13, pt. 3, 220.

107. Ibid., vol. 13, pt. 4, 162.

108. *The Digest of the Laws of the State of Georgia* (Philadelphia: R. Aitken, 1801), and Betty Wood, *Slavery in Colonial Georgia, 1730–1775* (Athens: University of Georgia Press, 1984).

109. He explained that enslaved fathers contributed to their families by supplying additional meats and fish. Otto, *Cannon's Point Plantation,* 44–45. Also see Merritt, "Slave Family and Household Arrangements," 160–61.

110. Albert Virgil House, ed., *Planter Management and Capitalism in Ante-Bellum Georgia: The Journal of Hugh Fraser Grant, Ricegrower* (New York: Columbia University Press, 1954), 255.

111. Rawick, *AS,* vol. 13, 33–36.

112. Wilma King explains that although slave parents spent the majority of their time laboring, "many never stopped trying to foster positive relationships" with their children. King, *Stolen Childhood,* 69–90, and passim. Also see King, "'Raise Your Children Up Rite': Parental Guidance and Child Rearing Practices Among Slaves in the Nineteenth Century South," in Hudson, *Working toward Freedom,* 143–62.

113. Rawick, *AS,* vol. 12, pt. 1, 207.

114. Roswell King Jr., "On the Management of the Butler Estate," *Southern Agriculturist* (December 1828): 523–29, especially 526.

115. Rawick, *AS,* vol. 12, pt. 1, 162–63.

116. Ibid., vol. 12, pt. 2, 202–3.

117. Based on this statement, one can assume that Harmon lived on a small plantation. Ibid., vol. 12, pt. 2, 97–102. Former slave Emma Hurly also recalled eating "pig-fashion in the kitchen." Ibid., vol. 12, pt. 2, 275.

From
Breadwinners: Working Women and Economic Independence, 1865–1920,
by Lara Vapnek (2009)

3

THE DAILY LABOR OF OUR OWN HANDS

LARA VAPNEK

In 1842, fourteen-year-old Jennie Collins set off from her home in Amoskeag, New Hampshire, to find a job in the textile mills of Lawrence, Massachusetts. Orphaned at the age of three, Collins had been raised by her Quaker grandmother, who gave her an unusual degree of liberty but left her with a limited education and no property. Like most girls, Collins must have learned basic domestic skills, such as sewing and cooking, in the expectation that she would marry and have a family of her own. When family support failed, however, Collins's domestic training had little market value. Like many girls and young women in New England, she made her way to the mills to take a position as a machine operative.[1]

When she reached Lawrence, Collins felt her loss of family protection, and she quickly realized that the popular sentimental view of young, white women stopped at the factory gate. In seeking out the employment agent, she was "treated neither with politeness nor consideration." She faced him on her own, and made "her own bargain with him." Earning "her own money," she was left to "hire her own board, buy her own clothes." She received no deference as a woman, and she knew that she "must work as hard and do her task as well as a man, or . . . be discharged, without ceremony or apology." Indeed, her sex entailed a burden, rather than a privilege; Collins earned only half of a man's wages and none of his "perquisites." She could never become eligible for a skilled position, since these were reserved for men.[2] Collins found herself outside the bounds of domesticity, yet compromised in her ability to negotiate the labor market.

By working in the mills, Collins violated middle-class ideas about the "separate spheres" of men and women. In the 1830s and 1840s, a flood of sermons, novels, and magazines popularized a new domestic ideal: girls and women would fulfill the dictates of God and nature by remaining at home, leaving men to negotiate the moral dangers of the marketplace. During this period, "home" took on a new cultural meaning as a repository of virtues under assault by the market revolution. This new ideology not only erased middle-class women's unpaid domestic labor as mothers, daughters, and housewives, but also excluded working-class women from the dominant, decorative feminine ideal.[3] African American women, the vast majority of whom were enslaved in the South, also stood outside the boundaries of domestic femininity, despite their performance of domestic labor for their own families and for their masters.[4]

As a young woman "cast on her own resources," Collins's situation anticipated that of hundreds of thousands of northern women forced to become self-supporting after the Civil War. Not only did many women lose sons, husbands, fathers, brothers, and prospects for marriage, but the intensification of industrialization after the war strained the viability of family farms and artisan workshops, increasing pressure on daughters and wives to find ways to earn money. By the early 1870s, daughters of farmers and craftsmen flooded into the labor force, joining orphaned girls and widowed mothers seeking employment in order to contribute to their family economy, or to support themselves if their families had dissolved. Finding few opportunities in the countryside, or in the prospect of westward migration, these women flocked to cities, where they formed an increasingly visible and impoverished class.

During the second half of the nineteenth century, the United States, imagined by its founders as a nation of property-owning men with dependent wives and children, became a nation of wage-earning men and women. Would this transformation lead to an upheaval in gender relations? If so, would the changes wrought by women's increasing presence in the labor force be positive, enabling women to develop new aspirations as individuals, or would they be negative, undermining family stability? The answers to these questions depended on whom you asked, and the stake he or she had in either preserving or transforming patriarchal gender and family relations. As the biography of Jennie Collins and hundreds of thousands of other women made clear, in many instances, the ideal that men supported women did not apply. Jennie Collins spoke for a small but growing number of women who used their new status as wage earners to claim formal and informal rights long denied to women, including wages sufficient for self-support, access to a wider range of occupations, and full political rights.

In Lawrence and in Lowell, where she soon moved, Collins became part of a group of factory operatives who saw themselves in collective terms. Like her, these women were young, white migrants from the New England countryside. They not only worked together, they lived together in company boardinghouses and spent their free time together, whether attending church, going to hear a lecture, or reading aloud to each other in the evenings as they did their mending. Collins found that the women she worked with subscribed to "as many papers, and ha[d] as much interest in public affairs as any of the men who work[ed] beside her."[5] Despite the exhaustion of standing for twelve or thirteen hours and the pressure of keeping "pace with belts, drums, and cylinders, and other parts of the machinery," the girls and women Collins met in Lawrence and Lowell "retain[ed] their vivacity and spirit of independence" through their political engagement and their mutual concern.[6]

In Lowell, that spirit of independence manifested itself most clearly in the ten-hour movement, led by Sarah Bagley, the charismatic founder of the Lowell Female Labor Reform Association. In 1845 and 1846, thousands of workers from all over Massachusetts signed petitions demanding that the state legislature limit working hours in publicly chartered corporations to ten hours per day, to provide workers time for study, worship, and self-improvement.[7] As early as the 1840s, a link was forged between social investigation and social reform. In this instance, however, the legislature investigated but refused to take action, urging the women of Lowell to rely on the benevolence of their employers rather than on state intervention.[8] Members of the Lowell Female Labor Reform Association condemned the legislators for their sympathy with employers and their "lack of independence, honesty, and humanity."[9] As wages dropped, hours lengthened, and conditions worsened, single, native-born women like Collins began moving to larger cities in search of better work.[10]

Collins arrived in Boston in 1850. Possessing few transferable skills and lacking a family of her own to live with, she took a job as a domestic servant. In Boston, as in other large cities, such as Philadelphia and New York, 60 percent of female wage workers found positions in domestic service. Another 30 percent were employed in the garment industry, and the remaining 10 percent worked in the few trades open to women, including printing, bookbinding, and clerking at dry goods stores.[11] Educated women might find jobs as teachers, but they, too, earned only half of what men did. Depending on whether or not they had husbands present, children, or aging parents to care for, urban women engaged in a range of more casual forms of labor to generate income, such as taking in boarders, laundry, or sewing, or going out to work for the day scrubbing or washing. In difficult times, some women turned to prostitution to supplement their earnings.[12] Collins may have worked as a general household servant before finding a position as a nurse in the family of John Lowell, an attorney, whose grandfather, Francis Cabot Lowell, had become extremely wealthy by establishing the textile mills in the town that bore his name.[13] While no direct record of Collins's work for the Lowell family survives, her time spent in this privileged household, which owed much of its wealth to the textile mill where she had once worked, may have sharpened her belief that workers were poor because they were deprived of a just share of the value they produced. Her time in the Lowell household also convinced her that "American girls" who valued their independence could not tolerate domestic service for long. While Collins had experienced the fast-paced labor and tight regulations of the Lowell mills as oppressive, she found the new limitations on her leisure time intolerable. Servants were not even allowed to "go out and buy a spool of thread until their appointed afternoon or evening."[14] Like other former servants, Collins complained of "incompetent mistresses" who knew nothing of housekeeping, but were determined to wring as much work as possible out of their household help.[15] To explain native-born white women's increasing rejection of domestic service, Collins quoted Patrick Henry's famous motto, "Give me liberty or give me death!"[16] By invoking Henry, Collins cast women's rejection of service in revolutionary terms.

Collins's critique of domestic service was widely shared. An 1869 investigation of the conditions of sewing women in Boston by the New England Women's Club revealed a strong animosity toward domestic service among the entire working-class community. Investigators reported that "poor girls" struggled "under a weight of debt and poverty" rather than work as servants. Native-born white women spoke with pride of the fact that they had "never had to live out yet." More shocking still, some chose prostitution rather than domestic service as a means of preserving their independence.[17] While middle-class women's labor reformers used the prostitute to symbolize the dangers of women's dependence on men, some working-class women used the trade to gain higher wages than they could earn from either service or sewing, and to free themselves from what they considered to be the oppressive conditions of living in someone else's household and being at their beck and call twenty-four hours a day. On a purely practical basis, prostitution offered women relatively high pay and flexible hours, making it an option for women with children or other dependent relatives who required their care.[18] For single women, who complained of their sexual vulnerability as live-in servants, sex work in boardinghouses or brothels offered some measure of control over the terms of their sexual encounters.[19] Some women judged prostitution preferable to living in as a domestic servant.[20]

The Lowell family's ability to find a white, native-born woman like Collins to work for them during the 1850s reflected their wealth and status. By that time, middle-class families with one "maid of all work" were far more likely to hire an Irish immigrant for the job. Young Irish women fleeing the potato famine (which began in 1845) often migrated alone, leaving behind parents and siblings in desperate poverty. The assurance of steady work, combined with employers' provision of room and board, appealed to Irish women who felt a strong obligation to save money to send back home. Acknowledging that many working women went hungry, Collins calculated the sole benefit of domestic service as having enough to eat. The promise of adequate food and shelter may have been enough to rec-ommend the occupation to women who had faced starvation during the famine.[21] Some German women entered service, too, but those who did not speak English were considered less desirable household workers. German women were more likely to migrate with their families, which made them less likely to work as ser-vants.[22] For mistresses seeking pliant household workers, however, the fix from immigrant labor proved temporary. As Catharine Beecher, a leading purveyor of domestic advice, complained in 1869, "the Irish and the German servants . . . become more or less infected with the spirit of democracy" and soon became as difficult to manage as native-born Americans.[23]

Radical members of the working class associated the growing demand for ser-vants with the growth of a pretentious, parasitic managerial class that snubbed its nose at manual labor. Collins and other working-class labor reformers accused employers of skimping on food and wages for their domestic employees. A song titled "The Bell Goes A-ringing for Sai-rah," published in the *American Workman,* a Boston labor reform paper, recounted overwork, low pay, and stingy rations. The singer introduces herself as "the general slave round the corner," with a wage of "a hundred a year." While her employer, a man who worked in a downtown office, earned "a thousand," the servant found her "own sugar and beer." Sarah described herself as "lady's maid, housemaid, and cook," explaining, "I do everything, honor, no joking; I scarcely have time to draw a breath, For she'll ring if the fire wants poking."[24]

Although Collins bristled at the subservience expected of domestic servants, she must have used her time in the Lowell household to gain the connections she needed to secure more satisfying employment. The Lowell family moved to an estate in Chestnut Hill in 1858. By 1860, Collins was working as a garment maker for a downtown Boston firm, and by 1861 she had gained a skilled position as a vest-maker at Macular, Williams & Parker, a Washington Street merchant known for its high-quality work.[25] Like many working women, she had difficulty securing lodging, but she appreciated her time off from work, spending some of it taking a class on English history at a Unitarian church.[26]

Within ten years of arriving in Boston, Collins had worked her way into a rela-tively secure position in the female labor market. Her ability to make this transition rested not just on her determination and ability, but on the fact that single, native-born white women had the widest degree of choice in the narrow field of female labor. By 1860 just one-third of native-born white women worked as servants, in contrast to 78 percent of foreign-born white women, most of whom were Irish, and 87 percent of African American women.[27] While Irish women took domestic jobs because they wanted to save money to send back home, African American women took domestic jobs because they could obtain no other work. While African

Americans constituted only 1 percent of the population of Boston in 1860, their extremely constrained opportunities for earning a living reveal the racial segregation that structured the northern labor market.[28] As "A Colored Woman" explained in a letter to the *Philadelphia Morning Post* in 1871: "When respectable women of color answer an advertisement for a dressmaker . . . they are invariably refused, or offered a place to cook or scrub, or do housework; and when application is made at manufactories immediately after having seen an advertisement for operators or finishers, they meet with the same reply." Black women who refused to work as domestics were left to "eke out a scanty livelihood sewing at home."[29] An African American woman from Rhode Island complained that "colored females" were "compelled to accept the meanest drudgeries or starve," being excluded from places where native-born white women could find work, such as "the milliner, the dressmaker, tailor, or dry good store."[30]

Although the Civil War ended slavery, it did not fundamentally change the racial segregation of the labor market in the industrializing cities of the Northeast and Midwest. While white female workers became more class-conscious during the war, this consciousness did not extend to addressing racial inequality. The substitution of white working-class women for slave women in labor reform discourses invoked the degradation of women of color, only to erase them as real people with their own experiences of exploitation and resistance. African American women existed on the margins of labor reform as symbols of degraded womanhood, rather than as participants in postwar efforts to improve, or even transform, women's economic conditions.

Collins's hatred of slavery fueled her support for the Union cause. When the war broke out, she found new opportunities for action: organizing her fellow workers at Macular, Williams & Parker to make keepsakes to send to Union soldiers, volunteering in a Boston military hospital, and forming a soldiers' relief association.[31] Like the hundreds of thousands of other women who volunteered to sew, knit, or wrap bandages, Collins gained a new sense of the patriotic value of her labor during the war. Like many middle-class volunteers who went on to form women's clubs and organizations, she acquired significant organizational experience.[32]

Collins's perceptions of the war were strongly colored by her social class. Wealthy men's ability to buy their way out of the draft for $300 made many working-class men and women see the federal government as willing to spill a "poor man's blood for a rich man's money." These sentiments helped spark draft riots in New York City in 1863.[33] From returning soldiers, Collins heard stories of "everywhere the same great gulf between the rich and the poor." Together on the battlefield and in military hospitals, these soldiers from modest backgrounds "felt how much more they had to pay for their liberty than did the law-protected man of wealth, who sat in his home and smoked his cigar, while a hired substitute fought his battles."[34]

Collins herself had been unprotected from the harshness of the labor market as a fourteen-year-old girl, but the situation was far worse for young men, who were exposed to mortal danger. Although she supported the fight against slavery, the war heightened Collins's sense that the government acted to protect corporations and property owners at the expense of workers. The war gave Collins a new sense of belonging to a national working class. Many workers around the country shared her new sense of class consciousness.

Numerous strikes flared during the war. Labor activity peaked in 1865 and continued at a high level until the depression of 1873. Workers' protest was concentrated in the industrializing towns and cities east of the Mississippi and north of the Ohio River and the Mason-Dixon Line, which contained three-quarters of the nation's factory workers and produced 70 percent of its manufactured goods through the early twentieth century.[35] The labor movement encompassed a diverse group of trade unions, working men's and women's associations, and leagues devoted to single issues, such as land reform or the eight-hour day (a continuation of the struggle for the ten-hour day). In addition to conducting strikes and promoting boycotts to raise wages and improve working conditions, these groups worked together to support other initiatives, such as establishing cooperatives of consumers and producers. Some sought political leverage to press for public distribution of land in the West.[36]

Like many former abolitionists, Collins saw the labor question as the next major political issue facing the nation. She first took the stage as a public speaker in 1868, when she was asked to present a working woman's point of view on the labor question during public debates at Washington Hall. The next year, she appeared at an Eight-Hour convention where, according to one contemporary, "she entered into leading political and social questions of the day in a remarkably intelligent manner, and from that time her reputation was made as a public speaker."[37] Collins soon joined the New England Labor Reform League, a mixed group of trade unionists, former abolitionists, and advocates of the eight-hour day led by Ezra Heywood, an anarchist who later became notorious for his advocacy of free love. Despite its dismissal by one historian as a motley group of "sentimental reformers," the New England Labor Reform League not only made room for women, it actively sought their participation and included them as officers.[38]

Organized in mixed, city-wide assemblies, the labor movement in Boston as in other industrializing cities articulated a strong sense of class identity. The Civil War had accelerated the development of national networks of transportation, production, and distribution, leading to the growth of large cities and speeding the integration of all Americans into a national market. The federal government had vastly, although temporarily, expanded its power by waging a successful war against the Confederacy, emancipating slaves, and embarking on Reconstruction. William

H. Sylvis, a former iron molder, seized on these conditions to establish the National Labor Union, which embraced a broad ideal of worker solidarity. Espousing a viewpoint similar to that adopted later by the Knights of Labor in the 1880s, Sylvis envisioned a grand alliance of "producers" who would push the government to serve the needs of the majority by establishing an eight-hour day, supporting workers' cooperatives, and ensuring the wide distribution of land. These ideas received a limited implementation with the passage of the Homestead Act and the introduction of an eight-hour day for federal employees. Activists like Collins, however, saw far more to be accomplished for the United States to fulfill its promise of democracy.[39]

In April 1869 Jennie Collins joined Aurora Phelps and Elizabeth Daniels, whom she had met in the New England Labor Reform League, in establishing the Boston Working Women's League. Phelps, who had been a hospital nurse during the war, was known for her advocacy of free land for working women. Although her life had been "laborious," including stints as a servant and an outworker, she had attended college at Oberlin before moving to Boston. Phelps presented herself as having been briefly married in England, where she had borne a child. Daniels was married to a laborer but had no children; she had worked as a sewing machine operator and an artist before becoming a leader of Boston's eight-hour movement.[40]

Although the League lasted only a year, it provides a rare glimpse into working-class women's self-conceptions and political aspirations. The group presented themselves as "working women," claiming entitlement to participate in public debates on the basis of their status as self-supporting, productive citizens. They advocated homesteads for working women, higher wages for needlework, and establishment of a nonprofit employment bureau.[41] While supported by the larger movement for labor reform and receptive to alliances with elite women devoted to women's rights, members of the Boston Working Women's League expressed a determination to speak for themselves that reflected an independence of thought and action that many found surprising.

Aurora Phelps proposed the idea for Garden Homesteads in 1864, two years after the Homestead Act promised 160 acres of public land to any adult citizen who could pay a small registration fee and live on the land continuously for five years. While the offer of free land was supposed to ensure America's republican future by enabling men to leave wage work and become farmers, the costs of establishing homesteads were beyond the means of most working-class families, and even more out of reach for families without a male breadwinner. By establishing homesteads close to Boston, Phelps hoped to give women the means to become independent proprietors, while enabling them to remain closely connected to their families and their communities. Like most people at the time, Phelps believed that wages were governed by supply and demand, meaning that urban women's rates of pay would increase if a significant number of female workers left the city. Her advocacy of land reform reflected a long tradition of British, American, and Irish labor activists demanding rights to land as a means of restoring the independence lost through the deskilling of labor and the introduction of machinery. While most proponents of land reform associated the redistribution of land with the restoration of family values under threat from the pressures of industrialization, Phelps viewed Garden Homesteads as creating new opportunities for female independence.[42]

In the spring of 1869, the Boston Working Women's League circulated Phelps' petition for Garden Homesteads. The petition described everything women needed to become homesteaders, including "rations, tools, seeds and instruction in gardening, until such time as the women would be able to raise their own food, or otherwise become self-supporting." No rent would be due for the first three years. After that, each woman's rent would be applied to purchasing her plot, which could be passed along to her female heirs upon her death. Inspired perhaps by state homestead exemption laws, they asked that their property be protected from seizure for debt. The petitioners identified themselves as impoverished, overworked Boston women, "dependent for our daily bread upon the daily labor of our own hands." The petition rhetorically cast the legislature as the protector of last resort for working women, pleading: "you should think for us, and take counsel from your own kind ears to do for us better than we know how to ask."[43]

Although the tone of the petition played off familiar narratives of female dependence, it mixed these more traditional appeals with a new consciousness of citizenship gained by patriotic sacrifice during the Civil War. Not only had many Boston working women lost fathers, brothers, and husbands in the conflict, thousands had worked "on contract army shirts at eight cents each, from dawn to midnight." Given their sacrifice of love and labor, Phelps believed, the commonwealth and "the nation" owed these women "a debt it [could] never pay."[44] From this perspective, a demand for state provision of land and simple homes might not seem so radical, especially when the federal government was giving away large tracts out West, not only to homesteaders but to railroad corporations.

In discussing her proposal for Garden Homesteads at a labor reform convention, Phelps argued that working women had a "righteous claim" on the government for relief. If, indeed, democratic government was instituted "for the people," then it should aid in "protecting all [of its] . . . citizens in the enjoyment of life, liberty, and happiness."[45] Virginia Penny, a former teacher who addressed women's limited options for earning a living in her popular book *Think and Act* (1869), insisted the government play a more active role in addressing the problem of women's economic inequality. Penny advocated laws mandating equal pay for men and women doing equal work; taxing unmarried men to support single women; and providing support for "worthy industrious" women unable to support themselves.[46]

In demanding Garden Homesteads, women who signed the petition rejected the popular advice that eastern workers improve their conditions by heading west. Since the 1850s Horace Greeley, the editor of the *New York Tribune,* had been exhorting, "Go west, young man, go west." After the Civil War, Mary Livermore, a leading advocate of suffrage and temperance, used her Chicago paper, the *Agitator,* to encourage women to join the migration. In a letter to a Boston labor paper, she promised "a very great demand in the West for the labor of women, especially on farming settlements and in smaller towns."[47] Virginia Penny, who had sought opportunity as a teacher by moving from Kentucky to Ohio, advised women in the "crowded thoroughfares of the eastern United States, who by their hard labor scarce earn a pittance, that they might do much better by going into the plenteous West, and engaging in the capacity of seamstresses in families, dairy maids, and similar offices."[48] While Penny focused on women's prospects for self-support, other commentators suggested that the "excess" women of the East would have an easier time finding husbands if they headed west. Jennie Collins responded with annoyance to the suggestion that Boston working girls migrate to improve their prospects for marriage, noting that she had yet to meet a New England working woman "who would forego the dignity of self-support . . . for allurements so invitingly set forth to them in the West."[49] When someone suggested western migration to Elizabeth Daniels, she retorted that working-class women from Boston might just as easily "go to the moon, with scarcely a penny, or even clothing sufficient to keep them warm."[50]

Equally bold as these women's request for land was their demand that they be allowed to speak for themselves. Rebelling against elite assumptions that working-class women needed "thinking women" to act on their behalf, the Working Women's League asked in its petition that "no one will be allowed, except at our own express desire, to speak before your committee in our name."[51] The petition called for independence for working-class women on several levels. By living in homes that they owned, on land where they could grow food to support themselves, these women would fulfill the Jeffersonian dream of a republic populated by independent proprietors. By owning this property themselves, women would upend republican ideology, which posited women, like children, as dependent on men. They would escape their dependency on employers for an insecure livelihood, and they would no longer have to seek charity or take recourse to prostitution, each of which implied a morally compromising dependence.[52] Through their petition, these women claimed political independence, including the right to think and to speak for themselves and to make new claims as citizens.[53]

Collins, Phelps, and Daniels called a meeting to discuss the petition for Garden Homesteads and to introduce the Boston Working Women's League to the public on Wednesday, 21 April 1869. Parker Pillsbury, who attended the convention and wrote about it for the *Revolution,* Elizabeth Cady Stanton and Susan B. Anthony's women's suffrage newspaper, considered the gathering in "every way peculiar." Not only was it called by "working women, in the severest sense of the word," it was called primarily *for* working women.[54] An equally surprised correspondent from the *American Workman,* a Boston labor paper, noted that the meeting was managed by the working women themselves, "and the gentlemen or [ladies] other than working-women were not allowed to take up time, except by their permission." The journalist found it "quite amusing to see how some of the old stagers among the men were snubbed by the application of this rule so opposed to ordinary usage."[55] He did not comment on the "ladies." They may have been reticent to voice their opinions in a public meeting of men and women, preferring to limit their discussions to private forums, such as the New England Women's Club.[56]

The working women's meeting, held in a basement room, began in the morning with about twenty-five people. By noon, the crowd reached a hundred, and in the evening, when women were released from work, it rose to three hundred. Adopting the novel idea of using social investigation as a platform for social reform, the morning session focused on "eliciting facts," while the evening session focused on plans for "organization and future action." The organizers estimated the average of wages of Boston's 40,000 women with full-time, weekly employment at about three dollars per week, "out of which they had to board, clothe, and lodge themselves," and often support "dependent children." About half of these women worked in the needle trades, where wages varied greatly. While skilled women with steady positions in custom shops, like Jennie Collins, could make a decent living, women who sewed at home for clothing contractors fared much worse. The meeting included testimony from outworkers, who reported "that they had recently worked on nice shirts at two shillings a piece." The organizers estimated that at least 2,000 needle-women in Boston earned no more than twenty-five or thirty cents a day.[57]

Collins, Phelps, Daniels, and other women who worked in the garment industry described the increasing subdivision of labor under the "Boston system." As Aurora Phelps recalled, when she was younger, "girls were taught full trades." Their labor had a progression: "They made pants, coats, overcoats, and then they learned to cut." Now, however, "one stitches the seam, another makes the buttonholes, and another puts the buttons on." Collins accused employers of preventing women from learning skilled trades. When work for these "half-skilled" women slacked, they tramped from shop to shop, often waiting for weeks until they could find a new position. Meanwhile, they subsisted "for a week on a 5-cent loaf of bread." At times, Phelps admitted, she herself had been so poor she was unable to afford the soap and fuel necessary to wash her clothes. In these conditions, she remarked, working women would be "less than human" if they did not "feel the difference between their condition and that of the rich, well-dressed ladies who pass them."[58]

The meeting concluded with several resolutions. First, the women described the system of "divided labor" and the increasing use of machinery as monotonous and degrading to both the minds and bodies of female workers. However, they admitted that a return to household or artisan forms of production was both "impossible and undesirable." Instead, poor working women should be given Garden Homesteads, land and "houses of which they themselves are mistresses, where they may regain their natural health of soul and body." They acknowledged that not all working women wished to move out of Boston and leave the paid labor force, explaining, "those of us who are skilled workwomen, in the receipt of good wages, and therefore in the enjoyment of a high degree of independence" are "not discontented with our present condition and not desirous of settling on the land." However, they endorsed Garden Homesteads as a good option for women unable to make ends meet in the city, especially those supporting dependents.

Collins had been an ardent abolitionist since childhood, and she and the other leaders of the Working Women's League used metaphors of wage slavery to critique the labor conditions of northern white working women.[59] They identified the plight of "the white women and girls who, today, in Massachusetts give a fair day's work for thirty cents earnings" with that of "the negro slave women of South Carolina" before the Civil War. They used the language of wage slavery to present white working-class women as the "objects of enlightened philanthropic sympathy," just as southern slave women had been.[60] Given the success of abolition, identifying working women with southern slaves may have seemed like a good strategy. Virginia Penny recommended that the abolitionist motto "Am I not a woman and a sister?" be applied to working-class women.[61] In her 1871 novel *Work,* Louisa May Alcott described the new movement on behalf of women's labor reform as offering "the chance" to "help lay the foundation of a new emancipation."[62] This identification of wage workers with slaves stretched back to the 1830s, when American and British labor leaders charged the "lords of the loom" and the "lords of the lash" with enriching themselves by stealing the value that their workers produced. The power of the idea of wage slavery lay in its seemingly self-evident contradictions: northern white women should not be slaves, especially in a nation that had just waged a bloody war to abolish the "peculiar institution."[63] Although they opened their new organization to all self-supporting women, the Boston Working Women's League's language of wage slavery identified their movement as white.

The New England Women's Club also investigated the conditions of the city's needlewomen. Drawing from city records and from personal interviews, the group's privately printed report was a landmark in social investigation. Like the Boston Working Women's League, they noted the increasing subdivision of labor, low wages, high prices for board, and dangers of prostitution. Their solutions to these problems reflected their own class position. They called urgently for something to be "done to dignify domestic service," bemoaning that so many women "have been slaves to the unproductive needle all their lives, because they never had any opportunity to learn the work for which they were best fitted by nature!"[64] Ironically, this group of elite women devoted to social progress and determined to forge lives that reached beyond the domestic sphere prescribed domestic service as the best solution to working women's poverty. While the working-class women who proposed Garden Homesteads hoped to turn pieceworkers into independent proprietors organized within a collective, the elite women of the NEWC hoped to turn these predominantly native-born women into servants. United in their mutual concern for the conditions of Boston's poorest wage-earning women, they proposed dramatically different solutions, although Lucy Stone, a radical member of the NEWC, offered her support for Garden Homesteads.

The idea of Garden Homesteads gained enough public attention to be granted an immediate hearing before the state legislative committee on the hours of labor. About a hundred women attended, half working women "in the technical sense of the phrase" and half "ladies of culture and wealth with a liberal representation from the New England Women's Club." The hearing opened with Aurora Phelps presenting her petition. She noted that many of the women who signed it "were deterred from coming by threat of employers; some were persuaded to keep away by increase of pay; many who came were too timid to take a part." Phelps discussed women's limited options for earning a living, noting the declining value of skill and the low rates paid for piecework. To make matters worse, outworkers could not find steady employment, but paid weekly for their board. During slack periods, those without families to fall back on turned to "soup-houses." Phelps saw charity as negative, warning that women who depended on it "feel degraded, lose self-respect, and, by and by go *down.*" Phelps presented Garden Homesteads as providing women with the chance to become economically independent. She recommended tracts of land just outside the city, in Medford, Dorchester, and Swampscott, as good places to try the experiment, estimating that "five thousand women would avail themselves of this plan at once, if it could be inaugurated."

The legislators asked Phelps why poor women did not try housework. She explained that women who entered domestic service were "treated as strangers and aliens," adding that she knew of cases "where the very food was grudged to them and hunger was kept off by buying outside, and this in aristocratic circles." She knew what she was talking about, having "tried it herself, both as domestic and as nurse." She might have added that domestic jobs were available only to women without children or other dependent relatives to care for, while her scheme allowed working-class women room for families of their own. Imagine the class tensions in the room as Phelps revealed the conditions of working women in Boston, not just in the needle trades but also in the households of the elite statesmen and clubwomen who attended the hearing; a "hushed and muffled silence brooded over the room."[65]

The Boston Working Women's League embraced a broad agenda. As Elizabeth Daniels wrote in a letter to the *Revolution*: "The organization . . . will accept for woman nothing less than the ballot, and the right to hold any office."[66] While members of the group worked to build alliances with suffragists like Stanton, Anthony, and Stone, they also asserted their own authority on the problems of working women. At an early meeting held at the house of Mrs. Daniels, the women described themselves as "the natural counselors of their less skillful sisters, to the almost utter exclusion of men, and to the absolute exclusion of ladies of refined leisure." Given the interest expressed in working women by the NEWC, this statement can be read as a polite, but firm suggestion that affluent female reformers concerned with the conditions of working women mind their own business. Indeed, this declaration of class difference and organizational independence denied the possibility of class bridging so important to the self-conceptions of Boston's female reformers.[67]

Even Louisa May Alcott, who attended NEWC meetings with her aunt, Abby May, saw female reformers' attempt to connect with working women as awkward. In *Work*, Alcott's protagonist, Christy, watches as erudite reformers recite European statistics, tell stories of women in antiquity, and describe an "Ideal Republic." Meanwhile, "anxious seamstresses, type-setters, and shop-girls" whisper together, wondering how any of these "pretty" ideas will increase their wages.[68] Clearly, good intentions could not bridge the gulf of class that separated these women, especially since so many working-class women had worked as servants.

Members of the Boston Working Women's League hoped to intervene in the market for women's labor by establishing their own employment agency. They criticized existing agencies, run for profit, as preying on women who needed work and misleading both employers and employees. Their non-profit bureau, run by the women themselves, would "be established on entirely new principles," seeking to match potential employers and employees. Again, they warned of the interference of middle-class and wealthy women in this enterprise; elite women were liable to create an agency "dangerous to the independence of the women who earn their daily bread by the daily labor of their own hands, since it could easily be transformed into an institution (professedly philanthropic) where the working women would be put off, without substantial or efficient aid, with the empty forms of condescending charity." Significantly, the employment bureau they envisioned would place women in "all legitimate industrial avocations, other than that of household service."[69]

Although they had appealed to the language of white slavery at their opening convention, the women made no distinctions of race, ethnicity, or skill in membership. "Any working-woman of Boston, dependent upon the daily labor of her own hands for her daily bread" was invited to join, and there was no admission fee. While committed, above all, to independence, these women were nonetheless dependent on contributions from citizens of "wealth and standing," since working-class women were too poor to pay dues. The organization established an advisory board that included the mayor of Boston and received a significant contribution from Post Fifteen of the Grand Army of the Republic: free use of a building at 815 Washington Street. Collins was well known for her work among soldiers and veterans, and the building may have been given to her fledgling organization out of appreciation. Possession of free space enabled the organization to envision a program of public meeting and debates two or three evenings a week, which employers and "ladies of all classes" would be invited to attend.[70] Middle-class women would not be excluded, but they would be put in the position of students rather than teachers regarding the problems of women's work.

In addition to her leadership of the Boston Working Women's League, Collins advanced the cause of working women around the state as a speaker for the New England Labor Reform League. In July 1869 she was invited to address the first convention of the Daughters of Saint Crispin, a new organization of women who worked in shoe manufacturing. Collins praised the women for their independence and their success in organizing.[71]

In the fall of 1869 Collins traveled to Dover, New Hampshire, where the 800 employees of the Cocheco Cotton Manufacturing Company struck to protest a 12 percent wage cut.[72] The operatives Collins met in Dover resented the company's decision to boost its profits by increasing the number of looms a woman tended from two to six and by raising the prices workers paid the company boardinghouse from $2.25 to $6.00 a week. The ground for this struggle may have been laid by the Ladies Female Reform Association, which had a branch in Dover in the 1840s.[73] Collins built support for the strike in Lowell, where she "rallied the factory women and girls" who "gathered by the thousands in Huntington Hall, one of the largest in New England, to listen to Jennie's appeal for her sisters in Dover."[74]

In the course of the strike, Jennie Collins articulated a new consciousness of female wage workers as consumers. The Cocheco Company manufactured cal-ico, inexpensive printed cloth that factory operatives and farm women made into dresses. Collins felt certain that once women around the country "understood the facts, [they] would allow the Cocheco goods to rot on the shelves before they would purchase them."[75] She embraced the use of the boycott, which became a significant technique for the Knights of Labor in the 1880s and for middle-class women who formed consumers' leagues in the 1890s. The striking women at Dover held out for several months, but were ultimately defeated by the company, which warned the women to return to work or be blacklisted. In a letter to the *Revolution* reflecting on the strike, Collins admitted defeat "for the noble but oppressed women" who took part in the strike, but predicted an eventual victory, declaring: "We working women will wear fig-leaf dresses before we will patronize the Cocheco Company."[76]

Collins's leadership in Dover and her correspondence with the *Revolution* brought her into contact with leaders of the women's suffrage movement, who invited her to address the National Woman Suffrage Association at its annual meeting in Washington, D.C. Leaders of the movement described Collins in sentimental terms, claiming that her speech describing working women's exploitation at the hands of factory owners moved delegates to tears.[77] Paulina Davis described Collins as slight of build, "all brain and soul." Davis noted that Collins told "her touching stories with such a tender, natural pathos that few eyes are dry during her speeches."[78] The earliest historians of the women's rights movement tended to reduce working women to stock characters, rather than acknowledge them as formulators of political ideas. At the Union League, Collins held the audience in her sway "for two full hours." Her success earned her "a purse, and the offer of a free passage to California and back," with the understanding that she would lecture on the conditions of working women along the way.[79]

Collins accepted the offer, and she seemed poised to take her place on the national lecture circuit. However, she felt the need to find more concrete ways to address the problems her speeches described. She transformed the Working Women's Hall at 815 Washington Street into "Boffin's Bower," a new center for working women named after a location in Charles Dickens's novel, *Our Mutual Friend.* In addition to providing a free employment agency, an industrial training program, and free lunches, Boffin's Bower offered working women a parlor for relaxation, complete with carpet, potted plants, a piano, and two canaries. One visitor noted a reading room with "all the Boston Dailies on file, besides quite a good collection of books and pamphlets." Collins managed to acquire a library of "four hundred volumes of well-selected reading matter."[80] The Bower sponsored a full program of music and lectures. A reporter from the Belfast, Maine, *Republican,* described Collins as "a democratic little body, with more nervous energy in her make-up than a dozen women ought to have . . . she talks and walks quickly, plans constantly, and executes as rapidly."[81] Collins subsequently added temporary lodgings for working women and moved the center to 1031 Washington Street, a few blocks away from the original location.[82]

Collins continued to earn money by lecturing, and in 1871 she published a book titled *Nature's Aristocracy,* whose proceeds she contributed to Boffin's Bower. As a speaker, Collins was known for her wit, her common sense, and her use of anecdote.[83] Her book displayed all these qualities, using individual stories of working women's hardscrabble lives to advocate the agenda of the New England Labor Reform League: an eight-hour day, the establishment of workers' cooperatives, and full political rights for women. Collins framed her project as the restoration of American democracy, a system that seemed to be going awry due to the dangerous growth of monopolies of "railroad, land, ship, and telegraph companies" that "threaten to overturn our whole system of government." Like William Sylvis, the recently deceased leader of the National Labor Union, she believed that workers had to organize to gain greater political power. After all, workers were in the majority, and in a democracy, "the *majority will rule.*" As her book's title suggested, Collins saw democracy not as a leveling of all distinctions, but as the removal of the artificial barriers against individuals exercising their full range of talents. She called for restoration of the people's political power, better public education, and a broader field of employment for women.[84] Women's rights advocates such as Susan B. Anthony and Elizabeth Cady Stanton also called for the admission of women to all trades and professions, reflecting their recognition of women's limited choices of occupation as a central element of women's inequality with men.[85]

While Collins advocated women's rights, she did so from a distinctively working-class perspective. Unlike elite and middle-class advocates of women's rights, who embraced a universal vision of "woman" to be freed from the fetters of unjust laws and outdated conventions, Collins saw her sex as sharply divided by class, arguing that there could be no single conception of "woman's rights" since "there are not certain wrongs that apply to the whole sex." In her opinion, working-class women, who generally lacked male protection, felt "the power of the law" most strongly and needed political rights most urgently. For example, Civil War widows who struggled to make a living and pay their taxes had no voice in influencing how their children were to be educated: "In short, they were obliged to do a man's work, and all of a mother's; under the double disadvantage of being physically weak and of possessing no political influence that would entitle them to respect." As a result of their political powerlessness, they were often unfairly denied pensions, or taken advantage of in business. Meanwhile, younger women, pushed into factories due to the failure of male support, gained "contact with the world and . . . experience in affairs of business," which gave them "an independence of character and a knowledge of [their] rights, which under present circumstances, serves only to aggravate [their] discontent." Given rights to vote and hold office, working women could push for a government more responsive to their needs, including an eight-hour day and equal pay for equal work.[86]

Collins made working women's struggles for independence a major theme of her book. While Aurora Phelps had pursued independence in terms of proprietorship, Jennie Collins envisioned working women gaining independence through skilled, respected, fairly compensated wage labor. Surveying the narrow and poorly paid field of women's employment, Collins admitted that while women who worked in "the store, the tailor's shop, the printing-office, and binderies" might be "very far indeed from being independent," they enjoyed "a far greater degree of latitude in mental and physical action than" women who worked in "the kitchen or chambers of a modern mansion." While Collins doubted that any woman under the present economic and political system could be "wholly independent," she urged her female readers to "adopt the next best course, and be as independent as they can."[87]

Collins took a dim view of charity, warning in *Nature's Aristocracy* that it led to dependence in its recipients and a false sense of superiority in its dispensers. Drawing, perhaps, on her experiences as a servant in the household of John Lowell, she painted the following scenario: "It often happens that while the mistress of a house is visiting the poor or attending the board meetings of some charitable institution, there are servant-girls at her home washing the clothes and ceilings, taking up the carpets, or cooking the dinner, with whom she has had a long and exciting debate over the twenty-five cents per week which the servant wished to have added to her wages." Most likely, Collins continued, the mistress had refused her servant, while donating ten dollars to a fund to aid former servant-girls, "who would not have been the wrecks she saw had they received decent compensation for their work." Likewise, the textile magnate who cut wages could be counted on to contribute money to aid fallen women, failing to appreciate that women's low wages forced them to turn to prostitution "to avoid more acute suffering."[88]

Collins continued to comment on the state of women's labor through a series of annual reports she issued from Boffin's Bower, which mixed anecdotes from her work at the center with observations gathered from visits to "work-shops, boarding-houses, lodging-houses, dancing-halls, prayer meetings, the markets, Saturday nights, theatres, libraries, reading-rooms, the tombs in station-houses, the pawnbrokers, and other places including the various public charity and reformatory institutions."[89] Her determination to seek out knowledge of poverty reflected a transatlantic interest in gathering labor statistics in order to pressure the state to take greater responsibility for the conditions of the working class.[90] The Labor Commissioner of the Imperial Council of Berlin requested copies of her reports, as did the U.S. Department of State. Like other members of the New England Labor Reform League, Collins advocated the creation of a state bureau of labor statistics and applauded its establishment in 1869. Benjamin Sanborn, a newspaper editor and a founder of the American Social Science Association, described Collins as "a detective and registrar of charity" who had "more curious and exact knowledge about one class of the Boston poor than I ever found in any other person."[91]

Collins's knowledge of poverty proved especially useful in hard times. The great fire in Boston in 1872 threw large numbers of shop girls and sewing women out of work; Collins assisted the women in getting relief and securing the back wages they were owed.[92] The severe economic depression that began in 1873 reversed the gains made by organized labor after the Civil War and increased the burden of

Collins's work in providing aid for the needy. In 1874 Massachusetts passed a law limiting hours in factories to ten hours per day. However, the law applied exclusively to women and children, separating their struggles from those of working men and implying that women, like children, were especially imperiled by industrial labor.[93]

In 1875 Azel Ames, a thirty-year-old sanitary engineer who gathered labor statistics for the commonwealth of Massachusetts, took this argument a step further. His popular book, *Sex in Industry,* condemned women who took jobs outside of domestic service for imperiling their health and threatening the future of the race.[94] Collins countered these allegations with facts: more than three-quarters of the 9,119 women treated at the Boston City Hospital during the past nine years worked as servants, cooks, or housekeepers, while just 7.5 percent of the hospital's female patients worked as seamstresses and 3 percent as shop girls.[95] Despite his lack of proof, Ames's argument continued to hold common-sense appeal. By the mid-1870s a backlash against working women's claims for independence developed as part of a broader cultural shift toward invoking the "natural" differences of gender, race, and class that had come under attack during Reconstruction.[96]

As the postwar movement for labor reform crumbled, Collins became something of a lone crusader for the rights of working women. While strident in her defense of the poor, she became less pointed in her attacks on the privileged. When depression returned during the harsh winter of 1877–78, she provided over 8,000 free dinners, saving many women from starvation. As the director of a charitable institution—even one far more egalitarian than others in the city—she relied on merchants, manufacturers, and wealthy individuals whom she could not afford to alienate. Major donors included her former employer, Macular, Parker & Williams; the labor reformer Wendell Phillips; and the suffragist Mary Livermore, who served as a conduit for donations from women around the country.[97] A profile in the *Chicago Tribune* celebrated Collins's new moderation, noting that many moderates found the theories Collins advanced in *Nature's Aristocracy* "a little bit 'cracked,'" but that she now focused her energies on helping the poor rather than advancing questionable social theories.[98] The speed and distance she traveled may be measured by her 1873 proposal to open a training school for domestic servants, representing a capitulation to popular ideas about women's proper place in the labor market, which she had earlier rejected in no uncertain terms.[99] Collins's trajectory from a militant labor organizer to the director of a charitable institution suggests how quickly hopes for radical social reconstruction faded after the Civil War and how intractable the problem of working-class women's limited occupations and low wages remained.[100]

Collins's friend Aurora Phelps continued to work for Garden Homesteads, celebrating the tenth anniversary of the Women's Homestead League in 1874. Collins, who attended the celebration, endorsed Garden Homesteads "as a means of practical relief to many friendless, but worthy and industrious women."[101] Although the legislature had refused the Boston working women's petition for free land in 1869, two years later they incorporated the "Women's Garden Homestead League" with Aurora Phelps as the director. With the support of a thousand subscribers, Phelps purchased a 60-acre tract of wooded land in Woburn, Massachusetts, adjacent to the Boston & Lowell railroad. She drew up plans for a female community, which she named after herself. In "Aurora," she hoped to realize her vision for Garden Homesteads and to provide residents with an additional source of income by establishing a cooperative laundry. She may have gotten the idea from a cooperative laundry established a few years earlier by unionized female workers in Troy, New York. Like most workers' cooperatives, both ventures would be short-lived.[102]

In October 1873 Phelps held a ceremony to dedicate the Bethesda Laundry. Despite a storm, "a large number of ladies and gentlemen from the surrounding villages" attended, along with several labor reformers. Evidently not a supporter of temperance despite her Baptist faith, Phelps christened the building by throwing a bottle of whiskey at the wood frame. She missed, but the celebration continued with speeches and songs. Reporters who attended noted that several women had already begun digging the cellars for their houses. Despite this optimistic beginning, the plan failed. Three years later, Phelps died destitute in Woburn, possessing little more than "a dilapidated bedstead, ragged bedclothes, two or three rickety chairs, and a few books." Her estate was too small to cover her funeral expenses, leaving them to be borne by the town.[103] Unlike Collins, who was remembered after her death in 1887 with glowing obituaries in the daily papers of Boston, New York, and Chicago, and in women's and labor periodicals, Phelps's demise received barely any public notice. By the end of her life, mainstream publications such as the *New York Times* and the *Saturday Evening Post* had dismissed her as a utopian reformer, and the radical movement she had once been part of had crumbled.

While it is tempting to dismiss Phelps's plan for Garden Homesteads as a quaint protest against the inevitable course of industrialization, the support the idea received among working women should alert us to their strong desires for independence during the 1860s and the 1870s. Ideally, Garden Homesteads would have established working-class women as the heads of their own households and allowed them to gain a fair return on their labor by farming, or working in the cooperative laundry. The plan would have given women a degree of economic independence rarely achieved in families, where men continued to hold most rights to property, or in the labor market, where women continued to earn only half of what men did. The plan reveals women's continued linkage of economic independence with political rights. In Aurora, women would have voted and held office, making it a bold experiment in women's self-governance. Its failure revealed the strength of the very limitations it sought to transcend.

In the turbulent decades that followed the Civil War a small, but significant group of women in Boston came together to claim a new social identity as "working women" who depended "upon the daily labor of our own hands for our daily bread."[104] Their self-definition posed a working-class alternative to the middle-class norm of dependent women, who confined their labor to the unpaid work of caring for their own families.

These working women used their self-support, eked out through long hours at menial jobs in the garment industry or in domestic service, to make new claims as productive citizens. Like former slaves who demanded "forty acres and a mule," these women believed that they had yet to receive fair compensation for their labor. They hoped to enlist the state government in a variety of measures designed to increase their independence, from granting them land for farming, to guaranteeing an eight-hour day, to supporting cooperatives that would offer them a just compensation for their labor. Determined to represent themselves politically, they demanded rights to vote and hold office, recognizing that their political incapacity hindered their ability to make the government respond to their needs. Conservatives denied women's need for individual rights, arguing that women were protected and represented by their fathers and husbands. Women's growing presence as wage workers revealed the fallacy of this assumption. In the breakdown of family support that followed the Civil War, these women seized on a new possibility: independence. Their ability to make good on this claim would be challenged not just by employers but also by their erstwhile allies: working men eager to define women, like children, as properly dependent upon men; and reform-minded middle-class women concerned with their difficulty finding "good help" and determined to put their stamp on social policy by claiming to represent the best interests of working-class women.

Notes

1. Helen L. Sumner, *History of Women in Industry in the U.S.* (Washington, D.C.: Government Printing Office, 1910), 31; Thomas Dublin, *Transforming Women's Work: New England Lives in the Industrial Revolution* (Ithaca, N.Y.: Cornell University Press, 1994), 77–85.

2. Jennie Collins, *Nature's Aristocracy; or, Battles and Wounds in Time of Peace* (Boston: Lee and Shepard, 1871), 313–14; Anne Phillips and Barbara Taylor, "Sex and Skill: Notes toward a Feminist Economics," *Feminist Review* 6 (1980): 79–88.

3. Barbara Welter, "The Cult of True Womanhood: 1820–1860," *American Quarterly* 18, no. 2 (Summer 1966): 151–74; Jeanne Boydston, *Home and Work: Housework, Wages, and the Ideology of Labor in the Early Republic* (New York: Oxford University Press, 1990).

4. Jacqueline Jones, *Labor of Love, Labor of Sorrow: Black Women, Work, and the Family from Slavery to the Present* (New York: Vintage, 1986).

5. Collins, *Nature's Aristocracy,* 314, 180–81.

6. Quoted in Sumner, *Women in Industry,* 111; Collins, *Nature's Aristocracy,* 181.

7. Teresa Anne Murphy, "Bagley, Sarah George," *ANB Online* (February 2000); Murphy, *Ten Hours Labor: Religion, Reform and Gender in Early New England* (Ithaca, N.Y.: Cornell University Press, 1992).

8. Dublin, *Women's Work,* 125.

9. Resolutions Denouncing Mass. Legislative Report, *Voice of Industry,* 9 January 1846, 3, reprinted in *Women and Social Movements in the United States, 1600–2000,* ed. Kathryn Kish Sklar and Thomas Dublin (Alexandria, Va.: Alexander Street Press, 2007).

10. Jennie Collins, "New England Factories," *The Revolution,* 31 January 1870; Paul R. Dauphinais, "Être à l'Ouvrage ou Être Maîtresse de Maison: French-Canadian Women and Work in Late Nineteenth-Century Massachusetts," in *Women of the Commonwealth: Work, Family and Social Change in Nineteenth-Century Massachusetts,* ed. Susan L. Porter (Amherst: University of Massachusetts Press, 1996), 63–83.

11. Dublin, *Women's Work,* 155–58, 187.

12. Marilynn Wood Hill, *Their Sisters' Keepers: Prostitution in New York City, 1830–1870* (Berkeley: University of California Press, 1992), 64–65; Barbara Meil Hobson, *Uneasy Virtue: The Politics of Prostitution and the American Reform Traditions* (New York: Basic Books, 1987), 92–93.

13. Collins Obituary, *Boston Evening Transcript,* 21 July 1887; "John Lowell," *Dictionary of American Biography,* Base Set, American Council of Learned Societies, 1928–1936. Reproduced in Biography Resource Center (Farmington Hills, Mich.: Thomson Gale, 2006).

14. Collins, *Nature's Aristocracy,* 103–4; Sumner, *Women in Industry,* 183.

15. "Good Servants," *Workman's Advocate,* 19 June 1869; Jennie Collins, "Why Women Avoid Housework," clipping from *The Woman's Journal* 3, issue 10 (n.d.), 74, The Gerritsen Collection of Aletta H. Jacobs (ProQuest, Chadwyck-Healey, 2002–2009).

16. Collins, *Nature's Aristocracy,* 105.

17. NEWC, *Report of the Committee on Needlewomen* (Boston: John Wilson and Son, 1869), 19.

18. Hobson, *Uneasy Virtue,* 96–97; Hill, *Sister's Keeper,* 84.

19. Ruth Rosen, *Lost Sisterhood: Prostitution in America, 1900–1918* (Baltimore: Johns Hopkins University Press, 1982).

20. Timothy Gilfoyle, *City of Eros: New York City, Prostitution, and the Commercialization of Sex, 1790–1920* (New York: W. W. Norton, 1992), 287.

21. Hasia R. Diner, *Erin's Daughters in America: Irish Immigrant Women in the Nineteenth Century* (Baltimore: Johns Hopkins University Press, 1983), xiv, 71, 81, 90, 93, 94; Carol Lasser, "The Domestic Balance of Power: Relations between Mistress and Maid in Nineteenth-Century New England," in *History of Women in the U.S.: Historical Articles on Women's Lives and Activities,* ed. Nancy F. Cott, (Munich; New York: K.G. Saur, 1992–1993), 20 volumes, vol. 4, 123–24; Diane M. Hotten-Somers, "Relinquishing and Reclaiming Independence: Irish Domestic Servants, American Middle-Class Mistresses, and Assimilation, 1850–1920," *Éire-Ireland* 36, nos. 1–2 (Spring–Summer 2001): 185–201.

22. Stanley Nadel, *Little Germany: Ethnicity, Religion, and Class in New York City, 1845–1880* (Urbana: University of Illinois Press, 1990), 76, 192n60.

23. Quoted in Lasser, "Mistress and Maid," 125.

24. "The Bell Goes A-ringing for Sai-rah," *American Workman,* 5 June 1869.

25. Christine Stansell, *City of Women: Sex and Class in New York, 1789–1860* (Urbana: University of Illinois Press, 1987), 111.

26. Report of the Working-women's Convention of 21 April 1869, *American Workman,* May 1869; Wendy Gamber, "Tarnished Labor: The Home, the Market, and the Boardinghouse in Antebellum America," *Journal of the Early Republic* 22, no. 2 (Summer 2002): 184, 195–96; "The Death of a Noble Woman," *Journal of United Labor,* 30 July 1887.

27. Dublin, *Women's Work,* 158–59.

28. *New York Times,* 2 March 1869, reprinted in *The Black Worker: A Documentary History from Colonial Times to the Present,* ed. Philip S. Foner and Ronald L. Lewis, vol. 2 (Philadelphia: Temple University Press, 1978), 360–61; Brown, "The Negro Woman Worker," in *Black Women in White America: A Documentary History,* ed. Gerda Lerner (New York: Vintage, 1972), 251; Leon F. Litwack, *North of Slavery: The Negro in the Free States, 1790–1860* (Chicago: University of Chicago Press, 1961), 155.

29. *National Standard,* 11 November 1871, reprinted in *The Black Worker,* ed. Foner and Lewis, 2:281.

30. Quoted in Paula Giddings, *When and Where I Enter: The Impact of Black Women on Race and Sex in America* (New York: Bantam, 1985), 69.

31. Elizabeth F. Hoxie, "Collins, Jennie," in *Notable American Women: A Biographical Dictionary,* ed., Edward T. James, (Cambridge, Mass.: Belknap Press of Harvard University Press, 1971), 3 volumes, 1:362–63; Catherine Clinton, *The Other Civil War: American Women in the Nineteenth Century* (New York: Hill and Wang, 1999), 81.

32. Jeanie Attie, "Warwork and the Crisis of Domesticity in the North," in *Divided Houses: Gender and the Civil War,* ed. Catherine Clinton and Nina Silber (New York: Oxford University Press, 1992), 243–59.

33. Jonathan Grossman, *William Sylvis, Pioneer of American Labor* (New York: Columbia University Press, 1945), 49–50.

34. Collins, *Nature's Aristocracy,* 285–86.

35. Daniel T. Rodgers, *The Work Ethic in Industrial America, 1850–1920* (Chicago: University of Chicago Press, 1979), xiii–xiv.

36. Norman J. Ware, *The Labor Movement in the United States, 1860–1895: A Study in Democracy* (1929; reprint, Gloucester, Mass.: Peter Smith, 1959), 1–2, 4–5.

37. "Death of a Noble Woman."

38. David Montgomery, *Beyond Equality: Labor and the Radical Republicans, 1862–1872* (1967; reprint, Urbana: University of Illinois Press, 1981), 136, 412–14; Martin Henry Blatt, "Heywood, Ezra Hervey," *ANB Online* (February 2000); "Working Men's and Women's Labor Reform Convention," *American Workman,* 21 August 1869.

39. Grossman, *Sylvis,* 191, 222, 224, 227, 229, 238.

40. "My Laundress," *American Workman,* 1 May 1869.

41. Sumner, *Women in Industry,* 31.

42. Jamie L. Bronstein, *Land Reform and Working-Class Experience in Britain and the United States, 1800–1862* (Stanford, Calif.: Stanford University Press, 1999), 2–6, 8, 78–81, 173–85.

43. "The Wail of the Women," *Workingman's Advocate,* 24 April 1869, 1; Paul Goodman, "The Emergence of the Homestead Exemption in the United States: Accommodations and Resistance to the Market Revolution, 1840–1880," *Journal of American History* 80, no. 2 (September 1993): 470–98; Alice Kessler-Harris, *Out to Work: A History of Wage-Earning Women in the United States* (Oxford: Oxford University Press, 1982), 80–81.

44. "The Homestead Question—What and Why?" *American Workman,* May 1869.

45. "The Work-woman," *American Workman,* 26 June 1869.

46. Virginia Penny, *Think and Act; A Series of Articles Pertaining to Men and Women, Work and Wages* (Philadelphia: Claxton, Remsen, and Haffelfinger, 1869), 29, 83, 98, 189.

47. Robert E. Reigel, "Livermore, Mary," in *NAW,* 2:410–13; Letter from Mary Livermore, *American Workman,* May 1869.

48. Penny, *Think and Act,* 29.

49. "Go West, Young Girl," *Boston Daily Globe,* 24 March 1875, 3, *ProQuest Historical Newspapers.*

50. "White Slaves of New England," *Workingman's Advocate* 5, no. 4 (8 May 1869).

51. "Wail of the Women."

52. "Homestead Question—What and Why?"

53. "The Working-Women's League," *American Workman* 2, no. 4 (May 1869).

54. Parker Pillsbury, "How the Working Women Live," *The Revolution,* 13 May 1869; William Leach, *True Love and Perfect Union: The Feminist Reform of Sex and Society* (Middletown, Conn.: Wesleyan University Press, 1989), 134–36.

55. "The Working Women in Council," *American Workman,* May 1869.

56. Monday, 12 April 1869, "N.E.W.C. Meetings, 1868–1870," New England Women's Club Records, Schlesinger Library, Radcliffe Institute, Harvard University, Folder 40.

57. "Working Women in Council."

58. *Workingman's Advocate* 5, no. 41 (8 May 1869); Rosalyn Baxandall, Linda Gordon, and Susan Reverby, "Boston Working Women Protest, 1869," *Signs* 1, no. 3 (1976): 803–8.

59. "Death of a Noble Woman."

60. "Working Women in Council"; Sumner, *Women in Industry,* 149.

61. Penny, *Think and Act,* 197. For discussion of antebellum uses of this motto, see Karen Sánchez-Eppler, *Touching Liberty: Abolition, Feminism, and the Politics of the Body* (Berkeley: University of California Press, 1993); and Jean Fagan Yellin, *Women and Sisters: The Antislavery Feminists in American Culture* (New Haven, Conn.: Yale University Press, 1989).

62. Louisa May Alcott, *Work: A Story of Experience,* ed. Joy S. Kasson (1873; reprint, New York: Penguin, 1994), 336–41.

63. David R. Roediger, *The Wages of Whiteness: Race and the Making of the American Working Class* (London: Verso, 1993); Gunther Peck, "White Slavery and Whiteness: A Transnational View of the Sources of Working-Class Radicalism and Racism," *Labor* 1, no. 2 (June 2004): 41–63. Scholarly study of "whiteness" has recently come under critical scrutiny. See Eric Arnesen, "Whiteness and the Historian's Imagination," and responses by James Barrett, David Brody, Barbara Fields, Eric Foner, Victoria Hattam, and Adolph Reed; Peter Kolchin, *International Labor and Working-Class History* 60 (October 2001): 3–92; Peter Kolchin, "Whiteness Studies: The New History of Race in America," *JAH* 89, no. 1 (June 2002):

154–73. However, Roediger's insights remain useful for understanding the intersections of race and class.

64. NEWC, *Report of the Committee on Needlewomen*, 19–20.

65. "Working Women in Council."

66. "Working Women Again," *The Revolution*, May 1869.

67. Sarah Deutsch, "Learning to Talk More Like a Man: Boston Women's Class-Bridging Organizations, 1870–1940," *American Historical Review* 97 (April 1992): 379–404.

68. Alcott, *Work*, 330–31.

69. "The Working Women's League," *American Workman* 2, no.4 (May 1869).

70. "The Boston Workingwoman," *American Workman*, 21 August 1869.

71. Mary H. Blewett, *Men, Women and Work: Class, Gender and Protest in the New England Shoe Industry, 1780–1910* (Urbana: University of Illinois Press, 1990), 167–70.

72. Collins, *Nature's Aristocracy*, 196–97.

73. Thomas Dublin, *Women at Work: The Transformation of Work and Community in Lowell, Massachusetts, 1826–1860* (New York: Columbia University Press, 1979), 120.

74. "Jennie Collins and the Dover Strike," *The Revolution*, 30 December 1869.

75. "Jennie Collins and the Dover Strike," *The Revolution*, 30 December 1869.

76. Jennie Collins, "New England Factories," *The Revolution*, 13 January 1870.

77. Hoxie, "Collins, Jennie," in *NAW*, 362–63.

78. Paulina W. Davis, *A History of the National Woman's Rights Movement for Twenty Years* (New York: Journeymen Printers' Co-Operative Association, 1871), 30.

79. "Jennie Collins in Washington," *The Revolution*, 10 February 1870; "Death of a Noble Woman."

80. Margaret Andrews Allen, "Jennie Collins and Her Boffin's Bower," *Charities Review* 2 (December 1892): 106.

81. "Boffin's Bower," *Woman's Journal*, 25 March 1871.

82. Allen, "Jennie Collins and Her Boffin's Bower," 105.

83. Lilian Whiting, "Jennie Collins," *Chautauquan* 8, no. 3 (December 1887), 159.

84. Collins, *Nature's Aristocracy*, 296–97, 300.

85. Blewett, *Men, Women, and Work*, 173; Ellen Carol DuBois, *Feminism and Suffrage: The Emergence of an Independent Women's Movement in America, 1848–1869* (Ithaca, N.Y.: Cornell University Press, 1978), 121–24.

86. Collins, *Nature's Aristocracy*, 304–5, 306, 309–10, 314.

87. Ibid., 103–4.

88. Ibid., 222.

89. Quoted in Allen, "Jennie Collins and Her Boffin's Bower," 111.

90. Daniel T. Rodgers, *Atlantic Crossings: Social Politics in a Progressive Age* (Cambridge, Mass.: Harvard University Press, 1998).

91. Quoted in Allen, "Jennie Collins and Her Boffin's Bower," 115.

92. Mary A. Livermore, "Jennie Collins' Work," *Boston Daily Globe*, 31 July 1887, 5, *PQHN*.

93. Mary H. Blewett, *Constant Turmoil: The Politics of Industrial Life in Nineteenth-Century New England* (Amherst: University of Massachusetts Press, 2000), 102–3.

94. Azel Ames, *Sex in Industry: A Plea for the Working Girl* (Boston: Osgood, 1875), 20. For further discussion, see Lara Vapnek, "The Politics of Women's Work in the United States, 1865–1909," (Ph.D. diss, Columbia University, 2000), 89–93.

95. Collins, *Sixth Annual Report of Boffin's Bower,* 11–13.

96. Richard Hofstadter, *Social Darwinism in American Thought,* with a new introduction by Eric Foner (Boston: Beacon, 1992), 31–35.

97. Mary Livermore, "Jennie Collins," *Woman's Journal,* 6 August 1887; Collins, *Sixth Annual Report of Boffin's Bower,* 16–17; "Boffin's Bower: Miss Jennie Collins' Report for the Past Year—The Bower in Prosperous Condition," *Boston Daily Globe,* 18 June 1873, 8, *PQHN.*

98. "Jennie Collins and Boffin's Bower—What the Newspaper-Men Think of Her," *Chicago Daily Tribune,* 19 December 1875, 10, *PQHN.*

99. "School for Housekeepers: Jennie Collins' Latest Project for the Education of the Working Girls," *Boston Daily Globe,* 3 February 1873, 8, *PQHN.*

100. Hoxie, "Collins, Jennie," in *NAW,*1:362–63; "[History of the] Work Committee," 1938, 3–4, NEWC Records, SL, folder 95; Eric Foner, *The Story of American Freedom* (New York: W. W. Norton, 1998), 113–20.

101. "Local Miscellany," *Boston Daily Globe,* 23 May 1874, *PQHN.*

102. Carole Turbin, *Working Women of Collar City: Gender, Class, and Community in Troy, New York, 1864–1886* (Urbana: University of Illinois Press, 1992), 163–164.

103. "Aurora," *New York Times,* 28 October 1873, 4, *PQHN;* "Suburban Notes," *Boston Daily Globe,* 27 November 1873, 5, *PQHN;* "A Community of Women Only," *Saturday Evening Post* 53, no. 21 (20 December 1873), 8 "Death of Noted Character," *Boston Daily Globe,* 6 January 1876, 5.

104. "The Working-Women's League," *American Workman* 2, no. 4 (May 1869).

From
Southern Discomfort: Women's Activism in Tampa, Florida, 1880s–1920s,
by Nancy A. Hewitt (2001)

4

LATIN WOMEN FROM EXILES TO IMMIGRANTS

NANCY A. HEWITT

Though some elite Latin women followed the lead of their Anglo neighbors and formed social organizations among themselves, far more were active in ethnic clubs that provided mutual aid for the community at large. In this sense, Latin women often functioned more like their African American counterparts, joining organizations with men and alongside neighbors of varying economic circumstances as well as single-sex and class-specific organizations. For Latins, however, mutual aid societies rather than churches and schools served as the foundation for cross-class and mixed-sex efforts at collective advancement. Of course, Latin activists faced some of the same barriers that other Tampa activists did, including Jim Crow laws that inhibited the formation of interracial alliances in the immigrant enclaves. Yet racial divisions, whether rooted in Florida segregation laws or cultural legacies carried from home, were overcome in certain circumstances. The strength of the cigar unions, which remained havens of mixed-sex and interracial organizing, shaped Latin women's activism just as strongly as did participation in mutual aid societies. Both institutions brought women and men into joint public ventures, although with different emphases. The unions sustained working-class agendas and limited the ability of elite Latins to inculcate middle-class values among the immigrant masses. At the same time, ethnic solidarity was reinforced and class differences mitigated by the participation of immigrant families, across the economic spectrum, in mutual aid societies and ethnic social clubs.

Mutual aid societies—El Centro Español, El Centro Asturiano, El Círculo Cubano, La Unión Martí-Maceo, and L'Unione Italiana—served as important arenas of Latin civic life in the early twentieth century. They had all been founded between 1891 and 1902, with Spaniards organizing the first. Forming a small but well-to-do minority in Tampa's ethnic enclave in the 1890s, Spanish elites, led by the cigar manufacturers Ignacio Haya and Enrique Pendas, founded El Centro Español in 1891. Spaniards from Asturias formed the second club, followed by Cubans and Italians, each creating organizations to provide social and cultural sustenance, emergency aid, health care, and burial services to their members. Though men organized and ran the clubs and were most likely to be found there in the evenings and on weekends playing dominoes, sipping *café con leche*, drinking, and debating, women and children enjoyed use of the medical services and participated in social and cultural events. Modeled on voluntary associations in Spain, Italy, Cuba, and Key West, those in Tampa were a response as much to the unsanitary and malarial conditions of Ybor City and West Tampa as to the cultural isolation of exile and immigration. Functioning like modern health maintenance organizations, the clubs offered families inexpensive medical care and prescriptions, along with burial insurance, for a small weekly fee.[1] Several clubs bought land for cemeteries, and El Centro Asturiano built a hospital, which opened in 1905, to serve not only its own members but the larger Latin community as well.

Each ethnic club built its own clubhouse. Some were more extravagant in size and decor than others, but all had libraries, theaters, banquet halls, ballrooms, and cantinas. El Centro Asturiano built an elaborate new clubhouse in 1914, after its former building burned to the ground. Reporting on its opening on May 15, the *Tampa Morning Tribune* called it "the most beautiful building in the South." Three days of celebration, including the presentation of original operatic scores, balls, and banquets, introduced the $110,000 edifice to the community. The structure included a 1,200-seat theater, chairs graced with mahogany backs and red velvet cushions, a 27-by-80-foot stage, modern lighting fixtures, a cantina and ballroom, and a library well stocked with Spanish-language classics. More than three thousand members took advantage of the services offered by El Centro Asturiano, and another two to three thousand participated in the picnics the club hosted at nearby Sulphur Springs. The picnics in summer 1911 were so large that the Tampa Electric Company had to press all of its cars into service to meet the demand from Spanish, Cuban, and Italian guests.[2]

In most clubs, families held memberships, which were listed under the male head of household. Early club records rarely even mention women's names, though it is clear from newspaper coverage and oral histories that women participated actively in the organization's events.[3] Only La Unión Martí-Maceo provided a counterweight to men's domination of early mutual aid societies. When Afro-Cubans held a "grand assembly" in June 1902 to approve the club's establishment, the men offered special thanks to the women for honoring the club by their participation.

Like the other clubs, La Unión Martí-Maceo adopted the practice of listing men's names in the registers of membership and dues, but a few women appear independent of husbands or fathers among the pioneer members. More important, La Unión Martí-Maceo established a *comité de damas* (a women's committee) to organize social functions, keep records, and raise funds. After 1904, women were also put in charge of dispensing economic and unemployment benefits to club members.[4]

For most families and certainly for most women, economic benefits—especially medical and burial benefits—offered the greatest incentive for paying dues, particularly during hard times. But the dances, operas, plays, and picnics mutual aid societies held were important in drawing the larger community together. On these occasions, clubs were often thrown open to the public at large, attracting hundreds, sometimes thousands, of immigrants from the various national groups. Women often served informally as organizers of these events, and the tickets sold added to the societies' treasuries. The clubs with the largest auditoriums, such as El Círculo Cubano, also housed mass meetings of cigar workers during strikes and served as communication and distribution centers for information, food, and clothing, alongside the Ybor City Labor Temple. Like Black churches, these clubs attracted wealthy, middle-class, and working-class members, with cigar makers, housewives, the daughters of factory owners, foremen, and stemmers mingling in club corridors, meetings spaces, and ballrooms. Even though each club was racially and nationally distinct, the social events brought Latins together across these divides.

As the medical and social benefits of club membership multiplied and the clubhouses themselves grew larger and more elaborate, women outside La Unión Martí-Maceo also formed women's auxiliaries to formalize their efforts on the clubs' behalf. Often publicly portrayed in purely ornamental roles—as queen of the tobacco festival, singer in a musical production, or icon of an ethnic club in citywide parades and galas—women had long been critical to the practical benefits the mutual aid societies offered. As second-generation Latin women, reared and educated in the United States, came of age, they followed the lead of their Afro-Cuban sisters and institutionalized their contributions, thus ensuring greater visibility and recognition. In 1913, the women of El Centro Español—led by the wives of club leaders—organized La Sección de Damas de Protección y Auxilio. Under the direction of Mrs. Julia López, wife of a Spanish factory owner, the members organized theatrical performances, festivals, *verbenas*, picnics, and other events to celebrate national pride and raise funds. The first donations gathered by La Sección de Damas were used to construct a fence around El Centro Español cemetery.[5]

Women in other clubs soon followed suit, and eventually girls, young women, and *damas* formed separate associations in each club to direct health, recreational, and fund-raising projects. Within El Centro Español, the most affluent women continued to dominate such activities, and the club itself maintained its reputation as Ybor City's most elite institution. Its very elitism had been one of the factors that led more politically progressive Spaniards to form El Centro Asturiano in 1902. Here, women from less affluent families, even some who were themselves employed as cigar workers, sales clerks, or secretaries, formed a women's auxiliary with the express purpose of improving the club's medical facilities. The women of El Centro Español also raised substantial funds for their hospital and later provided money for an operating table and beds for surgical patients.[6]

The affluent and incontestably white women leaders in El Centro Español were those most likely to be invited to participate in Anglo women's civic organizations. For instance, Mrs. Jennie Díaz, an El Centro Español member, was active in the Hepzibah Rescue Home and the WCTU in the 1910s. Her sister-in-law and co-worker in La Sección de Damas, Mrs. Josefina Díaz, joined the Children's Home in the 1910s and in 1921 was appointed first vice-president of the board. Other Latin, mainly Spanish, women appeared as members and officers of Anglo-dominated missionary societies and on the entertainment and social committees of the Friday Morning Musicale. In this same period, the Tampa Yacht and Country Club, the city's most prestigious Anglo organization, invited a few Spanish families to join, while the Tampa Woman's Club opened its doors to select Latin women.[7]

Despite the efforts of well-to-do Latin women to both replicate and participate in the efforts of their Anglo neighbors, one critical difference was clear. In the ethnic enclaves of Ybor City and West Tampa, the working classes were powerful proponents of their own vision of a well-ordered society. Though appreciative of assistance from affluent countrywomen and men, women cigar workers rarely looked to them for leadership. Their own class-based organizations and class-inflected ideologies provided a buffer against the good intentions of both Anglo and Latin elites.

Even in the halls and amphitheaters of the clubs and mutual aid societies, Latin workers often set the agenda. This was particularly the case in El Círculo Cubano, La Unión Martí-Maceo, and L'Unione Italiana, where working men and women dominated the membership. There the women's auxiliaries offered laboring women and the wives of workers the greatest opportunity to wield skills learned on the shop floor to benefit the community at large. For these women, the medical care provided by the clubs—including midwifery, emergency medical care, and prescriptions—was the single most important benefit of club membership.[8] The community support for health care also provided jobs for a small circle of women professionals, particularly nurses and midwives. The business section of the city's directories regularly listed the names of two or three midwives with Italian or Spanish surnames.[9] For women, then, the mutual aid societies could provide employment as well as care. In addition, during strikes, clubhouses offered meeting spaces, emergency assistance, and communications centers for both sexes.

Wage earners, of course, also enjoyed the social benefits that ethnic clubs offered. They attended the dances, plays, and picnics in large numbers, used the libraries and cantinas, and took advantage of the operas, dance concerts, and theater productions to become some of Tampa's most culturally sophisticated citizens. Whereas affluent Anglo women formed societies to promote music, the arts, and reading among native-born white Tampans, working-class Latins were showered with opportunities to enjoy internationally celebrated singers, actors, dancers, and writers. They also participated in plays, vaudeville-style shows, and concerts in which Spanish, Cuban, and Italian traditions were sustained and intermingled.[10] The cultural vitality of the ethnic enclaves was both bred in and carried over from factory floors, where *lectores* read international news, political tracts, and socialist-realist and romantic novels to the workers. The plays, musicals, lectures, and libraries in the clubhouses were designed to appeal to this politically oriented audience. Famous opera companies, theater troupes, singers, and actors from Europe thus had to vie for attention with radical orators and organizers, such as Carlo Tresca, Big Bill Haywood, Elizabeth Gurley Flynn, and Luisa Capetillo.

Industrywide strikes provided exclamation points amid this rich and lively environment of political debate and cultural expression. In between and sometimes in the midst of these upheavals, Cuban and U.S.-based unions continued to compete for the loyalties of Tampa cigar workers. Following the 1901 strike, manifestos, weekly journals, speeches, wildcat strikes, and organizing campaigns littered the landscape of Ybor City and West Tampa. The Cigar Makers' International Union (CMIU) labored diligently to convince Latin workers of the benefits of "American-style" unionism, including the ability of a union man to support a family on his wage alone. In 1908, the organizer A. Sineriz called it "a disgrace to any community or craft" for women to be "in the factories working," while men spent their wives' and daughters' earnings in barrooms and worse places. Sineriz claimed that even if a "man take [*sic*] care of the children, his care is not the care of the mother, and the children grow up seeing the father as the tyrant of the family, and they cannot have respect for him but fear, and are prepared to accept any other kind of tyrant."[11] The organizer's own fears suggest that such role reversals were not unfamiliar in the Latin districts. To him, they reflected social chaos that could be set right only through increasing the man's wage.

Sineriz's analysis reveals two key concerns of CMIU organizers in Tampa: the unconventional role of women in the industry and the apparent power of radical and "tyrannical" male leaders. American union leaders were also uncertain about how to respond to Tampa's mixed-race labor force, since most locals throughout the United States remained segregated and limited to skilled workers. Only the most radical organizations, such as the Industrial Workers of the World (IWW), replicated the kind of inclusive industrial unionism that characterized Cuban labor organizations. The CMIU was especially concerned, then, when a 1908 visit from Big Bill Haywood, the acclaimed organizer of the IWW, reinvigorated "'the old dyed in the wool,' 'never say die' remnant of La Resistencia."[12]

The "never say die" remnant had actually reemerged almost as soon as the 1901 strike ended. In the years leading up to and following Big Bill Haywood's appearance, both women and men in this contingent made their presence known, but women were especially prominent. In January 1902, for instance, the *United States Tobacco Journal* reported that "the Resistencia Society, which caused so much trouble last year, is rapidly reorganizing. The woman, Luz Herrera, and several others who led the strikers have returned to the city, and frequent meetings are being held at the hall in Ybor City."[13] By the following April, Altagracia Martínez was appealing to her "tobacco stemmer comrades" to "reorganize as soon as possible" and to "overcome the wasting away of spirit caused by our lack of collective effort."[14] In November, a "popular committee" published the manifesto "Alerta!" urging workers to "prepare a defense against the enemy" that "furtively attempts to sow confusion in our ranks." The authors of the manifesto asked, "Will we be ignorant puppets and stupid playthings of the machinations of the manufacturers" or, referring to the CMIU organizers, prey to "the ambitious machinations of aspiring fools and the womanly passions of some lustful skirt chasers?"[15]

In 1903, *Justicia*, a local Spanish-language paper, published a special edition memorializing the heroines of the 1901 strike. Recalling the women's march on city hall, the editors proclaimed, "To your decision we owe the end of the abuses. Oh you women—you have served as the model of valor, abnegation, and energy, and in the future continue to serve as an example to the men."[16] Clearly, gender and class identities were still deeply entwined among Latin labor activists in Tampa.

Labor organizing in Cuba was also at a fever pitch in the early 1900s. Because of the ease of travel and communication between South Florida and the island, émigré workers followed events there closely. In June 1902, Cuban workers sent a telegram to their comrades in Florida announcing victory in a prolonged cigar strike. Immediately, a thousand Latin workers formed a parade, marching from Ybor City to West Tampa, where wild celebrations erupted.[17] The first labor walkout organized solely by women in Cuba occurred two years later among Havana laundry workers. The leaders were mostly Afro-Cubans, many of whom were arrested when police violently suppressed the strike.[18] Coverage of such events in Tampa kept workers receptive to organizers' calls for united action across lines of race, sex, skill, and workplace.

It was in this context that the CMIU launched its most effective organizing campaign ever among Tampa's Latin workers. George Perkins, president of the

CMIU, was less than enthusiastic, complaining about "the aversion" of this group "to our movement," the disruptive effect of "radicals" on their ongoing efforts, and the "rather formidable following" of the IWW in the city.[19] Still, since no union had gained recognition by factory owners after the defeat of La Resistencia, he approved the campaign. It began in 1909, and in July 1910, a lengthy strike erupted. The CMIU walked a fine and hazardous line between sustaining American-style unionism and gaining support among Latin workers. As much a lockout by employers as a walkout by workers, the 1910 strike involved some 10,000 men and 2,000 women in a battle for union recognition. Taking hold in an atmosphere charged with tension, the struggle quickly flared into violence and gained the attention of the national press in the United States and Cuba.

Early in the uprising, Tampa's Anglo union leaders supported their Latin counterparts. On July 12, Cuban and Italian workers staged a massive demonstration in a city park, with more than 10,000 people in attendance. The following day, a crowd of 4,000 marched from Ybor City to downtown Tampa, where they surrounded Court House Square and settled in to hear a series of speakers demanding workers' rights. Hernan Regener, a city councilman representing Ybor City, noted that most of the skilled occupations in Tampa were fully organized and claimed that recognition of the cigar makers' union would ease rather than intensify hostilities between workers and their bosses. A Mr. Johnson spoke for the CMIU, followed by the president of the local printers' union and then by several Spanish speakers, including José de la Campa, president of the joint committee of CMIU locals.[20]

The *Tampa Tribune*, concerned about the support shown by Anglo labor leaders, concluded that Latins were only "inspired to their defiance of the law" because they believed they were "backed" by "the other unions of this city, largely composed of Americans." In general, however, the Anglo press did not provide widespread coverage of the workers' rallies, which were reported in detail only in Spanish-language newspapers. Instead, English-language papers, including the *United States Tobacco Journal*, carried articles detailing the destitution visited on women and children by the machinations of radical labor agitators. Under the headline "Human Document of the Strike," *Tribune* editor Goode M. Guerry told the tale of a middle-aged tobacco stemmer, the wife of a cigar roller and the mother of six, who, with "hopelessness in her voice and the tragedy of want upon her face," described the intimidation and starvation imposed on her family by the "well-paid leaders of the cigarmakers."[21]

Disputing Guerry's melodramatic portraits, local members of the Socialist party denounced manufacturers who locked laborers out and city officials who refused to aid needy families. Though equally appalled by the depredations heaped on "helpless women and children," the Socialist writer S. Elliott expressed outrage at the remedies offered by such civic leaders as Guerry: "Seize their Fathers by Stealth! Kidnap their brothers and husbands! shrieks the Editor.... Deprive them of their natural protections and turn [them] over, naked and alone, to the tender mercies of... the Manufacturers Association and the American Tobacco Trust."[22]

Though Elliott blasted civic leaders for their hypocrisy, he joined them in relegating women to the category of helpless victim. However, given Anglo Tampans' historic use of vigilante violence against male strikers, it was the men caught in the conflict's cross fire who were far more vulnerable. In September, a bookkeeper, J. F. Easterling, was shot and gravely wounded as he walked from his car to work at the Bustillo Cigar Company in West Tampa. Though it was never clear who fired the shots or whether they were intentionally directed at the victim—who had himself fired at a group of strikers some weeks earlier—two Italian men, Angelo Albano and Castenge Ficarrotta, were arrested six days after the shooting. While being transferred from West Tampa to the county jail that night, the accused were spirited away; deputies claimed they were overpowered by a group of twenty to thirty men. The Italians were discovered a short time later, handcuffed together and hanging from a tree. A note tacked to Albano's shirt read: "Beware! Others take notice or go the same [w]ay. We know even more. We are watching you. If any more citizens are molested look out." Though there was no evidence that the lynch victims were directly connected to the strike, much less the shooting of Easterling, the *Tribune* proclaimed that "the corpses swinging in the moonlight" represented "the verdict that the people of this city will not tolerate... assassins for hire." When Easterling died of his wounds a few days later, many Anglos were no doubt satisfied that justice had been done.[23]

Arson, beatings, arrests, and armed confrontations in the street followed the lynching. In October, the *Tribune* reported that in the "interest of the weak—the wives and children of fanatics," "three hundred loyal citizens finally went forth to afford protection to those in danger." This new citizens' committee broke up gatherings of workers; attacked the offices of the union newspaper, *El Internacional*, and the Labor Temple; assisted in the arrests of union leaders; and closed down emergency soup kitchens. Landlords were induced to evict striking workers, and merchants in the ethnic enclaves were pressured to refuse them credit. The committee soon swelled to "nearly a thousand members," including the "backbone of the business community," and by late October, the *Tribune* looked eagerly toward a resumption of production.[24]

At the same time, the Cuban correspondent for *La Lucha*, a Havana-based paper, predicted that Anglo vigilantism would only lead to workers' more intense commitment to the strike. He proved accurate as attacks on the community served to heighten unity among Latin workers. The reporter noted the "great indignation" among Cuban and Italian immigrants throughout the community and, echoing José Martí in "Nuestra América," asked, "Do we live in the United States?... It seems like a lie to us that in the land of Washington, Lincoln and other shining figures of

American liberty, such degrading acts are committed that are not worthy of the culture...."[25] With the arrival of strikebreakers from other parts of Florida and the South, the situation only worsened.

As in 1901, when the men became subject to ever more brutal attacks, Cuban and Italian women took their place on the front lines. They were particularly aggressive in patrolling factories to keep out individuals who strayed from the union line. This time, Italians joined their Cuban sisters in supporting union demands. Stemmers told *La Lucha*'s correspondent that though they were only "unfortunate women [*infelices mujeres*],—[we] possess faultless credentials as honorable daughters of labor."[26] Their actions soon belied their self-deprecating descriptions.

Throwing off the dependency with which Anglo editors and Socialist sympathizers enshrouded them, a group of Italian women gathered near the Argüelles factory in November to keep strikebreakers from entering. Prowling citizen patrols arrested six, and they were each fined fifty dollars for disturbing the peace. Though Judge Ernest Drumright, who heard the case, was convinced that "you dependents were enticed to do what you did by someone behind you," he still chose to punish the women as he would "any other violator of the law." A *Tribune* reporter derided the women's actions as "ludicrous," claiming that the "deluded members of these unheralded minstrels" had tried to "scratch and bite" the "citizen police." But the *United States Tobacco Journal* took the incident more seriously, labeling the "mob of Italian women ... armed with clubs" as "*viragos.*"[27] *El Internacional* championed the "six ladies." The paper used the women's arrest to attack "the arbitrariety of that Trinity"—"manufacturers, citizens, and officers of the law"—which understood "only the terms of brute force." In the same paper, Adele Kossovsky, a Socialist organizer and wife of a local machinist, published a letter chiding "Judge Drumwrong" and the deputies for showing the "lack of natural respect" that women deserved. *La Lucha*, too, provided favorable coverage of the women's efforts. The Cuban paper viewed it as an inevitable and necessary act by heroines who were forced to defend workers' rights because if men did so, they would be subject to arrests and assaults.[28]

La Lucha kept workers in Cuba well informed of activities in Tampa between July 1910 and January 1911. They warned them to avoid taking work in South Florida, which would undermine strike efforts, and reported in great detail the shootings, beatings, and arrests as well as the lynching that punctuated the prolonged walkout. Presenting a far more sympathetic portrait of the strikers than their editorial counterparts among Anglo Tampans, the editors of *La Lucha* noted the widespread community support for the strike, the central role of Italians, the critical efforts of women stemmers and female community leaders, and the fund-raising activities of women and workers in Cuba who provided assistance to their comrades abroad.

Outside the coverage offered by Spanish-language reporters, Latin working-class women had few platforms, other than the streets, to voice their opinions.

A document expressing the views of Latin women in Key West did circulate, however, in the same week that Judge Drumright rendered his decision. Twenty-eight women, half Cuban and half Italian, published a manifesto "to the Workers of Tampa in general and in particular to our Comrades, the Women." Hoping to keep the cigar workers from losing heart, the authors assured them of continued support—material as well as moral. Calling on the legacies of the religious martyr Joan of Arc, the French communard Louise Michel, and the Spanish labor radicals Belén Sarraga, Teresa Claramunt, and Soledad Gustavo, the women proclaimed, "It is our duty to protest" against those "who degrade our sons," for degradation to them is "degradation to us."[29] Drawing on sacred as well as secular heroines and on historic as well as contemporary radicals, these Latin women wielded their "strength of soul" in an effort to sustain the strike.[30]

The authors of the women's manifesto picked their heroines well. Teresa Claramunt was a textile worker and anarcho-syndicalist organizer in Barcelona. In 1884, at age twenty-two, she cofounded the anarchist collective of Sabadell, which formed part of the Spanish Federation of Workers. She participated in a number of strikes, traveled through France and England, organized anarchist circles in several Spanish cities, founded the newspaper *El Productor*, and, in 1905, published *La Mujer: Consideraciones generales sobre su estado ante las prerrogativas del hombre* (Woman: Considerations about her condition in comparison with the privileges of man). Although persecuted by Spanish authorities—Claramunt was imprisoned three times during the 1890s and exiled to Málaga in 1903 and Zaragoza in 1909—she never wavered from "the ideal of human emancipation." Belén Sarraga, born in Spain in 1874, was active in anticlerical campaigns before traveling to the Americas in the early 1900s. There, she continued her battle against the conservative politics of the Catholic church. An eloquent speaker, she organized meetings and demonstrations in Chile before moving on to Mexico.[31] Louise Michel was an international hero among anarcho-syndicalists for her efforts during the 1871 Paris Commune. Joan of Arc, though perhaps an unlikely model for anticlerical Latin workers, had long been maligned by conservative church officials, most recently when progressive Catholics successfully agitated for her beatification in 1909. In recognizing the work of their compatriots in Europe, Latin America, and the Caribbean from the medieval period until the present, the Cuban and Italian women of Key West demonstrated both the breadth of their political education and their sense of deep and common Latin as well as gender bonds.

Despite the dedication of Tampa's Latin workers and the support of their comrades in Key West and Cuba, the strike was sustained for only two more months.

Arrests and evictions slowly depleted union ranks, financial resources dwindled, citizens' patrols squelched protest, and strikers finally drifted back to work. In January 1911, the CMIU declared the strike over, without gaining recognition from cigar factory owners and without winning over the mass of Latin workers to American-style unionism. The national leadership of the CMIU harbored deep resentments against Tampa's foreign-born laborers, convinced that it was their Latin temperament and their lack of discipline rather than the overwhelming power of Anglo authorities and the lack of financial resources that led to defeat.

Although Tampa cigar workers failed to gain recognition for their union, they did reach a sympathetic audience among workers across the country. As Latins returned to the factories, they were greeted by resolutions of support from an astonishing array of workers in cities from coast to coast. Union locals in New York City, Brooklyn, Philadelphia, and Syracuse, New York; St. Joseph, Michigan; Evansville, Indiana; York, Pennsylvania; Akron, Ohio; Seattle, Washington; and dozens of other cities protested the brutal treatment of Tampa strikers, the lynching of Ficarrotta and Albano, and the raid on the offices of *El Internacional*. In one of the many letters to President William Howard Taft and to the Department of Justice, native-born and immigrant workers characterized the actions of the Tampa citizens' committee, the police, and the Cigar Manufacturers Association as "unfair, unwarranted, unAmerican, unmanly, unlawful, and Brutal in the extreme." The cigar makers' delegation to the tenth annual convention of the Washington State Federation of Labor, meeting in Seattle, resolved to boycott the product of Tampa factories until the demands of the CMIU were met.[32]

Such national support should not be surprising. The concerns generated by large immigrant populations, growing industrial work forces, and women's place in both created upheavals in city after city during the 1910s, and laborers kept themselves apprised of movements elsewhere in hopes of gaining leverage in their own struggles. Middle- and upper-class Americans were just as concerned with the momentous changes in the nation's economic and demographic patterns. Congress funded several massive studies in the early twentieth century that were intended to provide the basis for a better-informed, more scientific approach to public policy. The Labor Department's *Woman and Child Wage-Earners in the United States* appeared in 1910. The Immigration Commission published its findings, *Immigrants in Industries*, in twenty-five parts in 1911. The Bureau of Labor Statistics presented its study, *Wages and Hours of Labor in the Clothing and Cigar Industries, 1911 to 1913*, in 1915. Dozens of local and state inquiries undertaken by settlement house leaders, social welfare workers, university professors, and various committees and commissions supplemented and sometimes challenged these federal reports.

Though the experts who descended on Tampa and other cities in pursuit of data brought many biases and preconceptions with them, they did provide some useful statistical snapshots of Latin women and men. The Bureau of Labor Statistics offered an especially detailed analysis of Cuban and Italian women's place in the cigar industry and the larger immigrant community. By 1913, Tampa was second only to New York City in the number of individuals employed in cigar factories, though the numbers recorded by the investigators—8,061 for Tampa and 22,416 for New York City—underestimated the total labor force by ignoring those, pre-dominantly women, employed in home-based work in both cities. The in-depth analysis of wages, hours, and conditions in Tampa focused on a subset of 3,128 factory workers employed in thirteen establishments and on 127 Latin households containing at least one cigar worker. While Tampa cigar workers often compared themselves with their counterparts in Cuba and Puerto Rico, this survey compared them with cigar workers in other U.S. cities.[33]

Embracing the biases of Tampa's Anglo civic leaders, the investigators portrayed the Cubans as easy-going, fun-loving, but unambitious individuals who "lack the stability and power to adapt themselves to innovations." Moreover, they were peri-odically led astray by militant radicals. The report claimed that it was the failure of Cubans to develop good relations with their employers over the years that opened the door for Italians to take over the industry.[34] Despite the unity Cubans and Ital-ians displayed during the 1910 strike, federal experts were certain that competition rather than cooperation characterized relations between the two Latin "races." The fate of other workers employed in the cigar industry—the sizable minority of Spanish men, who still held highly skilled or managerial positions, and a scatter-ing of Canadians, German Jews, English, Mexican, and African Americans, and a Scots, a Syrian, and a Magyar—was largely determined by the actions of Cubans and Italians. In these two groups, women formed a critical component of the labor force, with 803 Italian and 532 Cuban women sharing factory floors with 846 Italian and 3,013 Cuban men. These numbers, combined with the study's emphasis on the increased Italian presence, suggest that Cuban men were at risk of being replaced not just by Italians but specifically by Italian women. The confrontation between groups was potentially more fierce because the overall size of Tampa's cigar labor force was shrinking. Though accurate statistics are hard to find, in 1908, there were roughly 10,500 cigar workers in the city; in 1912, there were fewer than 9,000. Moreover, Italians, especially men, pursued numerous other occupations—owning bakeries, saloons, groceries, and truck farms and working in these businesses or as fruit and vegetable, milk and ice vendors—while few Cubans of either sex sought work outside the tobacco industry.[35]

Although increased competition for a declining number of jobs must have been the primary concern of most cigar workers, investigators were far more anxious about the overall health of the industry, the ability of workers to adapt to new technologies (which Cubans were seen as particularly resistant to or incapable of mastering), and the failure of Latins in general to purchase homes and apply for U.S. citizenship. Literacy in their native languages was high among Cubans and Italians, women and men; but literacy rates in English were substantially lower, again especially for Cubans, and this was seen as another measure of immigrants' failure to embrace American ways. Ignoring the distances involved, researchers also concluded that Italians were more committed to establishing themselves in the United States because they made far fewer visits back home than did their Cuban counterparts. Cuban men dominated the rolling benches and shared with Spaniards the most highly skilled and well-paid positions in the cigar industry, but the 1915 government report nonetheless portrayed them as lazy, proud, and excitable workers with little attachment to American values or the capitalist system.[36]

Though misguided in portraying the Cuban character and in suggesting the hopes of manufacturers lay with a more docile Italian work force, the investigators were right in one respect. Latin workers eagerly embraced a range of radical views that were considered "un-American" by Anglos. With the defeat of the CMIU and American-style unionism in 1910, radical ideas again found fertile ground in Ybor City and West Tampa. In 1912, as government agents surveyed the Latin enclaves, Latin workers welcomed Socialist and anarcho-syndicalist organizers into their midst to revitalize the community's revolutionary tradition.

For the next decade, local Socialists, including the labor leader José de la Campa and the self-styled critic and commentator Adele Kossovsky, competed with other radical organizers for the hearts and minds of Tampa's tobacco workers. They wrote letters to the editor, formed consumer cooperatives, and hosted picnics and rallies to mobilize both immigrant and native-born support for the Socialist cause. May Day festivals became an annual event in the 1910s, with parades, picnics, and the crowning of the May queen serving as the backdrop for the presentation of speeches and manifestos. On May 1, 1914, the Socialists hosted a huge dance at De Soto Park, following a march from Ybor City to the city courthouse. Representatives of both the Socialist party and the IWW gave speeches—in English, Spanish, and Italian. The featured speakers, Carlo Tresca and Elizabeth Gurley Flynn, received wild applause when introduced as leaders of the 1913 Patterson silk workers' strike. Following Flynn's impassioned address, several votes by acclamation of all present were taken in support of various labor causes around the country. Impressed with the militancy and solidarity of the Tampa workers, Flynn was nonetheless concerned that a number of Black women and men stood along the fence, apparently not welcome to enter the grounds. She and Tresca jumped the fence to speak with local African Americans about IWW organizing among Black workers in Philadelphia and Patterson. Openly critical of Jim Crow unions as well as segregation at large, the "rebel girl" made no mention of the Afro-Cubans in attendance at the cigar workers' picnic; she was apparently unaware of the racial complexities that allowed Afro-Cuban workers to participate in Ybor City-based events while African Americans remained outsiders.[37]

Tampa's mayor and other city officials appeared periodically at Socialist-sponsored events, perhaps viewing such efforts as a necessary antidote to anarcho-syndicalist activities in the émigré centers. For the most part, however, they opposed any form of radical activity and looked for reasons to disperse Latin workers' gatherings and arrest suspected agitators. In 1912–13, the city police, the Spanish and Mexican consuls, and the U.S. Department of Justice were deeply concerned with anarchist agitation in the ethnic enclaves. In addition to IWW leaders from the United States and Italy, anarchist organizers from Mexico, Spain, and Puerto Rico visited the city for extended periods. These included Jaime Vidal of the Maritime Workers Union; Manuel Salinas, who was involved in a plot to assassinate the Mexican president; Francisco Martines, who headed a plot against the president of Argentina; and Luisa Capetillo, the cross-dressing spokeswoman of the Puerto Rican tobacco workers' union. Some of these outside agitators considered settling in Ybor City or West Tampa. Salinas, for example, was an intimate of Manuel Pardenas, who had worked in Ybor City before assassinating the Spanish prime minister in 1912, and Capetillo accepted a job as a reader at a local factory. These radical organizers gathered around them a circle of young anarchists who met at coffeeshops and restaurants interspersed among the cigar factories. These included eighteen-year-old Maximiliano Olay, who had arrived in Tampa from Spain via Havana in 1908. When he and Salinas were arrested for vagrancy in 1913, Olay identified himself as a "Cigar Maker & Reader" and, according to police records, "admits being an anarchist."[38]

The decision of such workers as Olay to combine anarchist politics with employment as a *lector* fueled the fears of civic authorities and factory owners. In his autobiography, *Mirando al mundo*, Olay claimed that his own conversion to anarchism came from listening to readers during his first days as a cigar maker.[39] Because the institution of the *lector* held sway throughout the industry in South Florida and flourished in Cuba, Puerto Rico, and New York as well, Olay and his coworkers were introduced to a range of radical ideas and international perspectives on labor politics. Manufacturers had long been hostile to the institution of the reader, which allowed an individual to proselytize to workers on the shop floor. Yet cigar workers made it clear they would fight as vehemently for their right to employ readers as they did for higher wages, better working conditions, and union recognition.[40] By the 1910s, the institution had become both more entrenched and more threatening.

When Olay joined the ranks of readers in 1912–13, he was in good and diverse company. Local readers included not only white Cuban and Spanish men, representing a range of political ideologies and reading styles, but also Facundo Acción, president of La Unión Martí-Maceo, and the Puerto Rican labor organizer Luisa Capetillo. Capetillo shared Olay's anarchist ideals and had honed her speaking and organizing skills in Puerto Rico as a *lectora* to tobacco stemmers and a correspondent for *La Unión Obrera*, the official paper of La Federación Libre de los Trabajadores (FLT), the anarcho-syndicalist union of Puerto Rican cigar workers. Like La Resistencia, the FLT was an industrial union that recruited women and men, white and Afro-Puerto Ricans, and skilled and unskilled workers. At its annual convention in 1908, the FLT became the first organization of any kind in Puerto Rico to demand women's enfranchisement; and the organization regularly passed resolutions calling for improvements in women's education and legal and political rights.[41]

In 1907, Capetillo published her first book, *Ensayos libertarios* (Emancipating essays), which she dedicated to "the workers of both sexes with love and admiration for the producing class." She lectured and published widely over the next several years, advocating the abolition of church and state, the development of emancipatory models of education, the substitution of communal for private property, and the replacement of marriage with free unions based on love. Capetillo carried her vision and her organizing skills to the United States in 1911, collaborating first on the journal *Cultura obrera* (Workers' culture) in New York City and then publishing a collection of essays, *Mi Opinion sobre las libertades, derechos, y deberes de la mujer* (My opinion on the liberties, rights, and needs of women).[42]

In 1912, Capetillo moved again, this time to Tampa, where she worked as a *lectora* and journalist. Although immersed in the working-class life of Ybor City, she roomed with the family of a German machinist on Lamar Avenue, two blocks north of the Clara Frye Hospital in a section that bordered both Ybor City and Tampa's Black business district. She penned short sketches of Latin life and longer essays on political and social issues. Several of these essays were incorporated into a revised edition of *Mi opinión*, which was published in Ybor City in 1913 and was proudly displayed in the libraries of local ethnic clubs.[43] She also wrote articles that were published in her 1916 collection, *Influencias de las ideas modernas* (Influences of modern ideas), a volume that certainly benefited from her contact with the rich traditions of Spanish, Cuban, and Italian theater, opera, dance, and music in Ybor City.

If she followed her own dictates as a *lectora*, cigar workers must have heard her disquisitions on the benefits of vegetarianism and cold water baths, the dangers of religious orthodoxy, the transformative power of progressive education, the struggles of labor in Spain, France, and Puerto Rico, and the significance of modern drama, dress reform, and free love to workers' emancipation. A Puerto Rican Emma Goldman, Capetillo saw art, literature, drama, physical health, mental and spiritual well-being, labor solidarity, sexual emancipation, and anarcho-syndicalist politics as part of one grand agenda.[44] On one issue, however, Capetillo rejected the views of Goldman and many other anarchists. Instead of seeing woman suffrage as a means of seducing another contingent of workers into supporting an authoritarian and capitalist state, she viewed the vote as a crucial weapon in labor's arsenal. Following the FLT's logic, Capetillo embraced suffrage as absolutely necessary for working women and men to protect their rights and promote their interests in the face of a powerful state controlled by capitalists and large landowners.[45]

In the case of woman suffrage, Capetillo came closest to the views of Adele Kossovsky, who denounced men's power to "deprive me of the right to vote because I am a woman." Kossovsky equated her political disfranchisement with "the southern gallantry of Tampa Editors who refuse me space in the columns of their dailies because I demand justice for those who are the bread and salt of the earth. . . ."[46] Capetillo would have agreed with Kossovsky's views on voting rights for women, but she was far less concerned with Anglo editors' response to her pleas. Her audience, in Tampa as in Puerto Rico, New York, and later Havana, was the Latin working-class.

Tampa's émigré community clearly embraced Capetillo, enough to pay her weekly salary as a *lectora* and to keep her memory alive for later generations of Latin residents. Though few Latin men or women embraced her views on the suffrage—into the 1930s, Tampa's immigrants were less likely than their counterparts in northern and midwestern cities to gain U.S. citizenship—they shared her materialist and mutualist ethos.[47] Rejecting the church and the state as institutions on which workers could or should depend, Latins established the kinds of mutual aid societies, labor organizations, and kinship networks Capetillo favored for sustaining daily life and working-class culture. People lived on their porches and balconies, paraded the streets on Saturday nights and Sunday afternoons, and regularly gathered at coffeeshops, clubhouses, grocers, saloons, and the Labor Temple to exchange information and advice. Fishmongers and crab vendors hawked their goods, elaborate funeral processions incorporated brass bands in streets filled with mourners, and fruit and vegetable sellers went door-to-door delivering fresh produce. Restaurants and bakeries had tables and chairs set out on sidewalks, while individuals selling espresso, *café con leche*, and rolls invaded the factories on a daily basis.[48] The streets were so lively on the weekends that businesses in Ybor City refused to observe local laws against Sunday liquor sales, despite a 1911 municipal crusade to enforce the regulation.[49]

If the boundaries between the street and shop, home and workplace, secular and sacred were permeable in the Latin community, definitions of family were broadly inclusive. The novelist Jose Yglesias, who was reared in Ybor City, captured this sense of family in his autobiographical novel, *The Truth about Them*. His mother "was the last of the girls" at home, he wrote, "but Grandmother drew others to her—girls who had come from Cuba or Key West alone, others who were orphaned in adolescence, and nieces and nephews of Grandfather's." The family was shocked when one of the granddaughters, Adelaide, was fired from her job at a local factory because she left work to attend to a sick aunt. "'That's only allowed in cases involving the immediate family,' her supervisor said. *Immediate family*—that was the first time we had heard the phrase." Equally disconcerting was the attitude of more assimilated relatives. Uncle Cándido, for instance, "did not say Old Folks Home with the sad, pitying accent of Latins who believed only Americans [were] so callous as to rid themselves of the old."[50]

Considering the family as a wide array of relatives and pseudo-kin and looking at mutual aid societies as distinct from and superior to the institutional care offered to Anglos in need, Latin workers echoed the patterns of mutuality practiced in the African American community. In developing this labyrinth of care, they borrowed heavily from European socialists and syndicalists, creating worker and consumer cooperatives and recreational and educational clubs alongside the mutual aid societies. In 1907, anarchists organized El Círculo de Instrucción y Recreo to provide reading rooms, lecture halls, and music lessons for workers; donations from working men and women, factory owners, and anarcho-syndicalist circles in the city funded the project. A year later, Spanish and Italian grocers, who dominated the trade in Ybor City and West Tampa, organized the Tampa Retail Grocers. Perhaps in response to this owners' association, two hundred cigar workers established a food cooperative to get goods at cost and sell them to members more cheaply. The store, which opened in Ybor City, was named La Crécherie, in honor of a Paris venture that had inspired the Latin workers. In 1911, Italians in West Tampa met to form a consumers' cooperative in their neighborhood.[51]

As with African Americans, the ethos of mutuality among Latins was forged both in workplaces and the larger community, and workers expected others to abide by their sense of reciprocal obligations. When, for instance, bakery owners in Ybor City attempted to use strikebreakers during a 1915 walkout over wages, they earned the wrath of cigar workers. Families and boardinghouse keepers were called on to boycott those bakeries employing strikebreakers, and members of the cooks' local made sure that restaurants bought bread only from union shops. Cigar makers living in boardinghouses were asked to enforce compliance among landlords and landladies. As a result of this communitywide support, the strike was soon settled, and the bakers' wages were raised.[52]

Yet this incident also reflects some of the fissures in the city's ethnic enclaves. The bakery owners were primarily Italian, and their actions were incomprehensible to their Cuban counterparts who ran coffeeshops, restaurants, and other small businesses. Though Cuban and Italian workers stood together in 1910 and Cuban workers and small shopkeepers had long made common cause against wealthy capitalists, Italian entrepreneurs were still suspect when it came to issues of labor solidarity. Conflicts among immigrants—between Latin workers and Latin owners, between older Cuban and newer Italian residents, between Afro-Cubans and lighter-skinned Latins, and between women and men—indicated the difficulty of meeting mutualist ideals, just as conflicts over class, color, gender, and respectability fractured African American unity behind the veil of segregation. In Latin as in African American neighborhoods, distinctions of wealth became more visible in the early twentieth century with the rise of elite Spanish and Cuban pioneers and an influx of poorer Cuban and Italian immigrants.

Moreover, the attempt to create spaces for themselves in a racially bifurcated society created a host of problems both within the Latin community and between it and its native-born counterparts. Among Latin workers, the acceptance of Jim Crow outside the shop floor and union hall caused continual friction, reflected in the almost wholly separate cultural activities, educational institutions, and social organizations among Afro-Cubans and their whiter neighbors—Cuban, Italian, and Spanish. Exacerbating such tensions, affluent Latin civic leaders wanted to guarantee that they would not be lumped together with Blacks as objects of Anglo discrimination. In August 1915, for instance, the Cuban consul in Tampa, Ralph M. Ybor, protested the posting of a "No Cubans Allowed" sign at the entrance to Passe-á-Grille, a popular beach resort south of St. Petersburg on the Gulf of Mexico. The indignity was compounded when the editor of the *St. Petersburg Times* claimed that "the Cubans are driving the white people from Passe-á-Grille." When complaints to local authorities failed, Ybor took his case to Washington, D.C., arguing that the rights of Cubans were protected by federal statutes against depriving "any citizen of the United States of any rights or privileges granted or guaranteed by the Constitution, because of race or color." Drawing on Reconstruction-era legislation to ensure the rights of white Cubans, who themselves discriminated against Blacks, must have seemed ironic to local African Americans; but Ybor's argument eventually held sway, and the offending sign was removed.[53]

Those who sought to exclude Cubans from South Florida's beaches differentiated between "prominent Cubans," such as Ybor, whom they were happy to have as guests at Passe-á-Grille, and "the lower element," whom they sought to keep out. Consul Ybor refused to accept such invidious distinctions, though the *Tribune* urged him to accept the fact that there "are undesirables among every race of people." The editor urged Ybor to put aside his protest and "devote his energies instead to Americanizing his people, teaching them to read and write the English language, to learn to respect the social requirements—in general to make better citizens of them." A more sympathetic response came from "An American Girl," who published a letter in the *Tribune* claiming that "the Cuban man ranks first in Tampa" when it comes to "politeness, manners, and the courtesies that are to be extended to a lady." Moreover, she noted, "they do not exclude Americans from their parks and clubs." The letter writer's admission that she was from the North may have undercut the value of her opinion for many local whites.[54]

The incident, however, did raise, once again, questions about Cubans' place in the Jim Crow South and the divisions between "higher" and "lower" elements in the Cuban community. The fear that all Cubans might join African Americans on the dark side of the racial divide provoked immediate and adamant reactions from well-to-do and whiter Cuban leaders. At the same time, Anglo authorities suspected that Afro-Cubans happily passed themselves off as white whenever they could. In the midst of the beach controversy, a local priest, the Reverend William Tyrell, wrote his superiors that "it is well known here that very many Cubans [who pass as white] are colored."[55] His certainty that this was the case no doubt reflected the opinions of his parishioners and other civic leaders.

Anglo civic leaders' failure to sympathize with Cubans excluded from a St. Petersburg beach resort did not reflect their state of mind when it came to matters of labor. A challenge to the status of Afro-Cuban workers, introduced in 1915 by a proposed federal immigration law, led to united protests by the Cuban consul, the mayor, the president of the Board of Trade, and the local U.S. congressman. Claiming that a Senate amendment barring all persons of African descent from entering the United States, if written into the immigration act, would cause considerable harm to the South Florida cigar industry, local leaders called on the House of Representatives and President Woodrow Wilson to revise the final bill. La Unión Martí-Maceo organized a special meeting to discuss the matter, adding its concerns to those voiced by white politicians; and Ralph Ybor assured his Black compatriots that the American president would not allow any law to pass that would be prejudicial to Cuba, which could be considered "a little sister" of the United States. In this case, Anglo civic leaders rallied to the Cuban cause, agreeing that "the Cuban colored people are orderly and hard-working citizens, beneficial to the community."[56] Eager to maintain a full complement of cigar workers, of which Afro-Cubans constituted a significant minority, Anglos found common ground with Latins.

The activist identities that Latin women juggled in the early 1900s took shape amid the shifting configurations of interest and concern among Blacks and whites; workers and employers; skilled and unskilled laborers; Italians, Cubans, and Spaniards; and women and men. In the midst of strikes, for instance, class solidarity overcame differences of race, nationality, and sex, even as it heightened differences of wealth. In more peaceful periods, such ethnic clubs as La Unión Martí-Maceo, L'Unione Italiana, and El Círculo Cubano reinforced ethnic and racial bonds among Latin residents. Within their respective walls, members from different class backgrounds and, at least during social and cultural events, of both sexes interacted.

It was also during periods of labor peace that cigar workers and more affluent Latins reverted to sex-specific arenas—whether men's clubs and women's auxiliaries or packers' and stemmers' union locals. Although still living and socializing with working-class men, women stemmers, banders, and bunchers were less active in managing union affairs when their male comrades, free from harassment by employers and Anglo civic leaders, could assume control. Despite the shared commitment of Latin workers to labor solidarity and the traditions of men's leadership, tensions between working men and their female comrades over access to skilled jobs and the priorities of union demands erupted periodically. After 1915, these eruptions occurred more frequently and more publicly, spinning the kaleidoscope in ways few Latins had ever imagined.

Federal investigators provide a context, hidden in the dry language of charts and statistics, for the growing tensions between women and men in Tampa's cigar industry. Though the overall work force was shrinking, women were gaining access to once masculine domains, particularly the rolling benches. Initially relegated to positions as stemmers, banders, and bunchers, women constituted more than 10 percent of those hand-rolling cigars by 1912. Men, meanwhile had little interest in breaking into the ranks of women's jobs. The women who challenged men for seats at the rolling benches were most likely older Cuban and Italian women with years of experience in the industry and the union. They had provided support for men's organizing efforts, but they also drew on a rich fund of experience in building their own claims for equity. In addition, nearly a quarter of Cuban women in the industry were widows, who were as dependent on employment and adequate wages as any man. Among Italian women workers, far more were married, but they provided the economic security for their families while husbands and sons worked to establish truck farms and small businesses.[57]

By the early 1910s, then, the women who worked in Tampa's cigar factories were increasingly experienced, and their wages were increasingly critical to family support. They were also highly literate and, through work experience, Spanish-language papers, political speeches and rallies, and *lectores*, were familiar with the organizing efforts of laborers, including women, in Cuba, Spain, Puerto Rico, and other parts of the Latin world. Of the Cuban-born women surveyed by the Bureau of Labor Statistics in 1911–13, nearly 90 percent had worked in the cigar or tobacco industry at home before migrating to Tampa, and they were among the most effectively organized of all cigar workers. Only the CMIU locals of selectors and of packers and pickers could compete with the banders' local, composed exclusively of "Cuban women and girls," in organizational strength. Moreover, Latin women were far less likely than their male kin and coworkers to leave Tampa during labor uprisings. Women were thus able to gain leadership positions in the midst of strikes that were denied them in more peaceful moments. This also meant that some wives and daughters served as household heads and primary breadwinners in the absence of husbands and fathers.[58]

Transformations in the work force challenged men's dominance of the industry and offered new openings for women's activism. By the mid-1910s, the stirring sentiments offered by their sisters in Key West, the experience of young working-class women in Protestant missions, the single-sex organizations developed in African American and Anglo communities, and the presence of Luisa Capetillo inspired Latin women to embrace a more sex-specific and militant agenda. The emergence of "New Women," Latin style, coincided with similar developments among African American and Anglo Tampans, creating new initiatives in each community and a small but growing common ground from which the first sustained interracial and interethnic coalitions among women would emerge.

Notes

1. Gary R. Mormino and George E. Pozzetta, *The Immigrant World of Ybor City: Italians and Their Latin Neighbors in Tampa, 1885–1985* (Urbana: University of Illinois Press, 1987) chap. 6; Records of El Centro Español, El Centro Asturiano, La Unión Martí-Maceo, El Círculo Cubano, and L'Unione Italiana in Special Collections, University of South Florida Library.

2. Mormino and Pozzetta, *The Immigrant World of Ybor City*, 181–82; *El Centro Asturiano en Tampa* (Tampa: Centro Asturiano, n.d.), 13–19; *Tampa Morning Tribune*, May 15 and 17, 1914, and April 3 and September 23, 1911.

3. Mormino and Pozzetta, *The Immigrant World of Ybor City*, chap. 6.

4. Susan Greenbaum, *Afro-Cubans in Ybor City: A Centennial History* (Tampa Printing, 1986), esp. 7–8; Mirabal, "Telling Silences and Making Community," 49–69; La Unión Martí-Maceo, Minutes, 1900–1901, Records of La Unión Martí-Maceo. The women's committee apparently originated as early as 1901 with La Unión, one of the two Afro-Cuban clubs that later merged to form La Unión Martí-Maceo. See La Unión Martí-Maceo, Minutes, June 16, 1901.

5. *El Centro Español, Memorial Book, Fiftieth Anniversary, 1891–1941* (Tampa: Tampa Tribune, 1941), 98–99.

6. Paulina Browne Hazen, comp., *The Blue Book, Tampa, Florida, 1912–13* (Tampa: Tribune Publishing, 1912); Tampa City Directory, 1912, 1914, 1920, 1921; *El Centro Español, Memorial Book*, 99.

7. Hazen, *The Blue Book, Tampa, Florida, 1912–13*; Tampa Woman's Club, Minute Book, 1920–21, HCFWC Papers; *El Centro Español, Memorial Book*, 98–99.

8. Patiño Río interview, September 4, 1985; Dolores Patiño Río, interview by author, April 7, 1986, Tampa; Angelina Mazzarelli, interview by author, September 26, 1988, Tampa.

9. Only one African American midwife was ever listed, and no Anglo midwives were listed, which of course does not mean that they did not exist, but they were certainly not recognized openly.

10. Mormino and Pozzetta, *The Immigrant World of Ybor City*, chap. 6.

11. A. Sineriz, "Report from Tampa," in *Cigar Makers' Official Journal*, October 1908.

12. *Cigar Makers' Official Journal*, December 1909. The focus on a few despotic leaders, however, did not mean that the CMIU had faith in the bulk of workers. Visiting Tampa in 1909, George Perkins, the national president of the CMIU, deplored the "misguided and impatient demands of the masses," noting how rare was "the man who has the courage to stand for what he thinks." Quoted in George E. Pozzetta, "Italians and the General Strike of 1910," in *Pane e Lavoro: The Italian American Working Class*, ed. George E. Pozzetta (Toronto: Multicultural History Society of Ontario, 1980), 25. See also George Perkins to Samuel Gompers, June 27, 1910, reel 36, microfilm, American Federation of Labor Papers. Of course Perkins's remark assumes that the only man who truly stands for what he thinks is one who supports the CMIU.

13. *United States Tobacco Journal*, January 11, 1902. The hall in Ybor City was either the Labor Temple or El Círculo Cubano.

14. Her address was summarized, in Spanish, in *El Federal* (Ybor City), April 27, 1902.

15. "Alerta!" reel 1, *La Federación* and Labor Manifestos, Microfilm of *El Internacional* and Related Materials. It is not entirely clear what the reference to "lustful skirt chasers" means, but it suggests that CMIU organizers were suspect on personal and sexual as well as public and political grounds.

16. "Nuestras mujeres," special edition, *Justicia*, November 24, 1903, reel 1, *La Federación* and Labor Manifestos, Microfilm of *El International* and Related Materials.

17. *Tampa Morning Tribune*, July 1, 1902.

18. Pedro Luis Padrón, *La mujer trabajadoras* (Havana: n.p., 1972), quoted in Carmen E. Parrilla Cruz, "Coming into Being among the Cuban Women" (Ph.D. diss., New School for Social Research, 1984), 21.

19. Quoted in Pozzetta, "Italians and the General Strike of 1910," 35.

20. These events were covered in detail in the Havana-based paper La Lucha, July 10, 12, 14, and 19, 1910.

21. *Tampa Morning Tribune*, September 16 (first quote) and October 11, 1910 (second quote). Other headlines on the strike included "The Slaughter of the Innocents." See also *United States Tobacco Journal*, September 24, 1910.

22. S. Elliott to Editor, *El Internacional*, October 7, 1910 (original in English).

23. This rendition of the lynching is taken from Ingalls, *Urban Vigilantes in the New South*, 95–97. For discussions of violence perpetrated by both sides in the strike, see *La Lucha*, September 15 and 20, October 28, and November 8, 1910.

24. *Tampa Morning Tribune*, October 1 (first quote) and 18 (second quote), 1910.

25. *La Lucha*, November 8, 1910.

26. Ibid., November 2 (on Italians' general support for the strike) and September 13 (quote), 1910.

27. *Tampa Morning Tribune*, November 15 (Judge Drumright's opinion) and 16 (reporter's description), 1910; *United States Tobacco Journal*, November 19, 1910 (*viragos* quote). Virago is an archaic word for a noisy, domineering woman or an Amazon.

28. *El Internacional*, November 18, 1910 (original in English); *La Lucha*, November 13, 1910. Mrs. Kossovsky was an outspoken Socialist organizer who frequently published letters in the Latin press.

29. "A los trabajadores de Tampa" (1910), reel 1, *La Federación* and Labor Manifestos, Microfilm of *El Internacional* and Related Materials.

30. The phrase was used in a letter from Octavio J. Monteresy to Editor, *El Internacional*, November 18, 1910.

31. On Teresa Claramunt, see Isabel Segura, *Guía de mujeres de Barcelona* (Barcelona: Ajuntament de Barcelona, 1995), 151–53, 200–201. On Belén Sarraga, see obituary of Belén de Sarraga, spelled Zarraga, in *El Tarapaca* (Iquique, Chile), February 26, 1951.

32. On the massive influx of cigar workers at the end of strike, see *Tampa Morning Tribune*, March 5, 1911. During February 1911 alone, 1,568 people entered Tampa from foreign ports. The paper clearly believed that the vast majority of these were cigar workers returning to their jobs. On national support for Tampa workers, see "Cigarmakers, 1911," Department of Justice, RG 60, National Archives (quote from St. Joseph, Michigan, Cigarmakers' Local 457 to President Taft, January 11, 1911); and Washington State Federation of Labor, *Proceedings of the Tenth Annual Convention* (Seattle: Washington State Federation of Labor, 1911), 96. I thank Dana Frank for alerting me to the last document.

33. The analysis here and below is based on Bureau of Labor Statistics, *Wages and Hours of Labor in Clothing and Cigar Industries, 1911 to 1913* (Washington, D.C.: Government Printing Office, 1915), esp. 61–77, which contain comparative wage rates for the different groups of cigar workers in different cities; 189–253, on the 127 Latin households studied in Tampa; and 405–45, which contain the general statistical tables on Tampa cigar makers. Individual tables and pages will be cited where appropriate, but these pages form the general background for the following paragraphs.

34. Ibid., 203–4.

35. Ibid., 65, 204–6, table II on 75, and table 67 on 405.

36. Ibid., 241–44, tables on 423–25 on native language literacy, tables on 442–45 on English language literacy, 250–51, tables on 433–35 on visits abroad, table 109 on 439 on home ownership, and tables 111 and 112 on 441 on citizenship status.

37. On the May Day activities, see *Tampa Morning Tribune*, May 2, 1912, and May 2, 1914. See also Elizabeth Gurley Flynn, *Rebel Girl: An Autobiography, My First Life, 1906–1926* (New York: International Publishers, 1973), 184–85. It is also possible that in her memoirs Flynn confused her Tampa experience with other southern visits since she spent little time in the South and was always horrified by confrontations with Jim Crow there.

38. Constant Leroy [pseudonym for José Sánchez], *Los secretos del anarquismo: Ase-sinato de conelejas y el coso ferrer* (Mexico City: Renecimiento, 1913); Maximiliano Olay, *Mirando al mundo* (Buenos Aires: Impresos Americalee, 1941); Tampa Police Arrest Report, January 19, 1913, Miscellaneous files, #5606, Bureau of Investigation, Department of Justice, RG 60, National Archives.

39. Olay, *Mirando al mundo*, chaps. 1–3.

40. On readers, see Mormino and Pozzetta, "'The Reader Lights the Candle,'" 4–27; Pérez, "Reminiscences of a Lector," 443–49; and Castro, "Oír leer," 221–39.

41. On Luisa Capetillo's work with La Federación Libre de Trabajadores, see esp. Azize, *La mujer en la lucha*, chap. 3. See also N. Ferrer, *Luisa Capetillo*; and Ramos, *Amor y anarquía*.

42. Azize, *La mujer en la lucha*, 79–85.

43. The only city directory listing Luisa Capetillo as a resident gives her address as 1808 Lamar Avenue, where she roomed with Emil Reutimann, a machinist, and his wife, Ameile. The Clara Frye Hospital was located at 1615 Lamar Avenue. I thank Ana Varela-Lago for informing me that the 1913 edition of *Mi opinión* can still be found in El Centro Asturiano's library.

44. I can find no reference to Emma Goldman in Capetillo's work or visa versa. I thank Candace Falk, director of the Emma Goldman Papers Project at Berkeley, for allowing me to pour through the project's extensive international files.

45. Azize, *La mujer en la lucha*, chap 4.

46. A. Kossovsky to Editor, *El Internacional*, October 28, 1910.

47. On the failure of Tampa immigrants to gain citizenship, see Mormino and Pozzetta, *The Immigrant World of Ybor City*, 301. They note that in 1930, fewer than 25 percent of Tampa's foreign-born adults had acquired U.S. citizenship, compared with 58 percent of New York City's immigrants, 67 percent of Jacksonville's, and 71 percent of Atlanta's.

48. On daily life in Latin enclaves of Ybor City and West Tampa, see ibid., chaps. 6 and 8; Patiño Río interview, September 4, 1985; Mazzarelli interview; Delia Sánchez, interview by author, October 5, 1988, Tampa; Yglesias and Corro interview; and Saunders, *Bridging the Gap*, chap. 2.

49. On police efforts to enforce Sunday closings and their failure, see, for instance, *Tampa Morning Tribune*, July 25, 1911.

50. These portraits of family and community ideals are in Jose Yglesias, *The Truth about Them* (New York: World, 1971), 80, 164, 165. Though this is a novel, it is based on the author's experiences and those of his family and friends in Ybor City. His fictional accounts are corroborated by his personal recollections. Yglesias and Corro interview.

51. On cooperative efforts, see *Tampa Morning Tribune*, January 16 and July 6 and 8, 1908; "Antorcha," August 26, 1907, reel 1, *La Federación* and Labor Manifestos, Microfilm of *El Internacional* and Related Materials; and *El Internacional*, April 14 and 21, 1911. The late George Pozzetta generously shared his findings on Tampa's Latin cooperatives with me.

52. *El Internacional*, January 1, 12, 19, and 22, 1915.

53. *Tampa Morning Tribune*, August 25 (quotes on Ybor) and September 13, 1915 (quote from *St. Petersburg Times*).

54. *Tampa Morning Tribune*, September 13, 1915 (first quote); "Remarks by Reader," n.d., clipping in author's possession (second quote).

55. Rev. W. J. Tyrell to Rt. Rev. Bishop Carley, July 20, 1915, Letters, Clippings, Etc., 1895–1935, Records of the Catholic Church.

56. *Tampa Daily Times*, January 8, 1915.

57. Bureau of Labor Statistics, *Wages and Hours of Labor*, 244–47 (on conjugal condition of cigar workers), table II, 72–77 (on sexual division of labor in various jobs). According to the bureau's statistics, 48.0 percent of Cuban women workers were married, 22.9 percent widowed, and 29.1 percent single. No doubt some of the single women were also sole or significant contributors to family income. Among Italian women, the figures were

an astonishing 85.1 percent married, 5.5 percent widowed, and 9.4 percent single. The statistics on wage earning by married Italian women suggest that their employment was determined less by cultural dictates than by economic opportunities.

58. Ibid., table 73 on 409 (on previous occupations), tables 100, 101, and 102 on 424–25 and table 117 on 445 (on literacy), 227 (on the banders' union), and table 106 on 433–35 (on visits home). Over 98 percent of Cuban men and women could read Spanish, and over 96 percent of both groups could write in Spanish. For Italians, the comparable rates were over 87 percent in each category for men and over 70 percent for women. Literacy in English among workers was considerably less common but increased with years of residence in the United States; about one-third of Cuban women workers who had lived in the United States for ten or more years could speak English.

5

PERFORMING AND POLITICIZING "LADYHOOD"

Black Washington Women and New Negro Suffrage Activism

TREVA B. LINDSEY

The politics of appearance and bodily adornment flourishing among African American women in Washington in the late nineteenth and early twentieth centuries greatly contributed to the evolution of black women's political activism in the Jim Crow era. Suffrage activism was one the major hotbeds for established and new African American women activists.[1] In the context of Jim Crow and women's continued disenfranchisement, African American women began to re-imagine and implement new strategies anchored in strategic performances of black femininity in public acts of protest.[2] The black press in Washington acknowledged this new chapter of African American women's suffrage activism. On February 17, 1900, the *Colored American* published a column titled "Women's Case in Equity." With a triumphant tone the writer remarked,

> There is nothing about the woman suffragist today to remind one of the agitator of a quarter of a century ago. The mannishly attired, short skirted, short-haired woman, who, for so many years, was the butt of the satirist and the cartoonist, has been shoved off the board and in her place stands the cultured, womanly woman of the twentieth century. In her dress she keeps pace with fashion.[3]

The description connected the masculine physical appearance of the "agitator of a quarter of a century ago" with her political efficacy and viability. Agitator, in this article, reads as more derisive and undesirable, and, arguably, as masculine. According to the newspaper, the self-presentation of earlier activists marginalized them. Even the reference to short skirts suggested a lack of feminine propriety and a childish demeanor. Throughout the nineteenth century, women wore long skirts; young boys and girls wore short skirts. Perceived as comical, unattractive, and unfashionable, suffrage activism of African American women was something the *Colored American* seemingly devalued until the arrival of the "cultured, womanly woman of the twentieth century." This cultured woman did not have short hair, and she kept abreast of fashion's trends. The seriousness of African American women's political voices was linked to a politics of appearance and bodily aesthetics even by those in support of universal suffrage.

In this chapter, I examine the interplay of politics of appearance and bodily aesthetics to New Negro–era suffrage discourse and activism. The nation's capital played a particularly integral role in the national movement while also serving as a battleground for localized efforts for enfranchisement. Black women in Washington participated in suffrage organizations and clubs and protest activities, including elite and well-known Washington women such as Mary Church Terrell and Anna Julia Cooper.[4] Both Terrell and Cooper in their respective autobiographies gave voice to the necessity of equal rights for black women—specifically the right to vote. The voices of African American suffragists in Washington reached a fevered pitch during the early twentieth century, and yet this voice took shape in the performance of strategic quiet, feminine propriety, feminine artifice, and resistive equanimity.

The road to passing a constitutional amendment that secured the right to vote literally and figuratively ended in Washington. Only in the capital city would a constitutional amendment be ratified. Black women's suffrage activism did not have a singular approach.[5] Kate Masur maintains that black women valued the vote as a vehicle through which they could claim a space within public debates on their own terms.[6] Other scholars, notably Elsa Barkley Brown, emphasize that many freedwomen tended to view the enfranchisement of black men as a means of achieving communal goals.[7] In her "To Catch the Vision of Freedom: Reconstructing Southern Black Women's Political History, 1865–1880," Brown posits that the concept of family and community bound African Americans together in the postslavery world, not the pursuit of full personhood or citizenship as defined by the Constitution.

The notion of "shared responsibility" for communities and families extended to how these women viewed the enfranchisement of black men. Enfranchising black men thereby enfranchised the families and communities from which these black men came. Furthermore, the notion of freedom that thrived among these particular communities of African American women was that of a "collective freedom." Brown argues,

> Their sense of community, related to the collective character of their notion of freedom, had foundation in their understanding that freedom, in reality, would accrue

to each of them individually only when it was acquired by all of them collectively. It was this very sense of community rather than citizenship, of peoplehood rather than personhood, that was the basis for their activities.[8]

Combating racist "New Women" and sexist "New Negro" men, New Negro women created political agendas and developed performative strategies to address their status as third-class citizens.

Existing scholarship on black women's participation in the women's suffrage movement emphasizes the complexity of the relationships between black and white women suffragists.[9] Much of the scholarship also addresses the issue of suffrage from an intraracial perspective and details how black male political activists either supported or fought against women's suffrage.[10] Scholarship of black women's post-Reconstruction activism also details black women's engagement with the politics of respectability. Black women in Washington strategically invested in these politics for a New Negro womanhood vision that demanded respect for black women as political actors and full citizens. Several factors influenced the development of a new black women's political culture: the passage of the Fifteenth Amendment, which affected interracial and intraracial cooperation in the suffrage movement, the disenfranchisement of black men through state-authored legislation, the formation and re-energizing of local black women's organizations, and the configuration of political agendas that encompassed aestheticized approaches to African American women's suffrage activism. The combination of these factors sparked a new wave of suffrage activism among African American women.[11] Two of the periods often discussed in relation to post-Emancipation black women's suffrage activism are 1870 to 1896 and 1896 to 1935. These years are central to my temporal conceptualization of the New Negro era, as I demarcate the commencement of the era of the New Negro woman in 1893. This demarcation thereby engulfs the last few years of the first major period of post-Emancipation black women's suffrage activism. The interplay between black women's political aspirations during the early twentieth century in conjunction with African American women's bodily aesthetic discourses were foundational to New Negro women's political activism. Through a brief historical overview of the herstory of suffrage, with a particular focus on Washington, an examination of the fractures that occurred after the passing of the Fifteenth Amendment, and a critical consideration of how African American women in Washington configured their performative strategies for activism, using the Women's Suffrage March in Washington of 1913 as a specific site of inquiry, I rethink the disruptive possibilities of African American's women's politics of appearance and bodily aesthetics. More specifically, I show that African American women using feminine propriety were not merely adhering to existing gender norms and expectations but were remixing feminine propriety as an audacious practice for claiming space.

African American Suffrage and Suffrage Activism in the United States

As early as 1670 the North American colonies denied free black people the right to vote.[12] In the existing U.S. colonies, property was the preeminent qualification for suffrage.[13] Enslaved blacks could not vote in any colony or state. Formal legal restrictions, however, do not tell the whole story. Free black men voted in nearly every colony and state during the mid- to late eighteenth century.[14] After the American Revolution and in the early nineteenth century, state constitutions in Delaware, New Hampshire, New York, Pennsylvania, Massachusetts, and Maryland protected the voting rights of black men. Prior to the formation of the United States as a nation, the vote was not connected to citizenship or subjects; therefore, it was not expected that all subjects would vote. Neither was it expected, in the newly formed republic, that all citizens would vote. In the earliest incarnations of black voting rights in states such as North Carolina and New York, black women were excluded. Although only a small number of free black men could and did vote, free black women encountered the triple bind of inferior racial, class, and gender statuses as early as the eighteenth century.

In some cities, such as Baltimore, black voting in some elections outnumbered white voting.[15] Philadelphia attorney and legal historian John Hancock acknowledged that black and white male voters alike in numerous states ratified the proposed American Constitution. The number of eligible black voters increased when states such as Connecticut, Rhode Island, and Vermont abolished slavery in the post–Revolutionary War era. According to the state constitutions of Pennsylvania, Massachusetts, and New Hampshire, free black men in these early states also had the right to hold office. By 1820, the period of postrevolutionary abolition ended and even those areas that abolished slavery began to restrict the rights of free blacks. White women and propertyless white men were denied many legal rights, including the right to vote. Whiteness, however, guaranteed greater legal protections.[16] Although abolition became the leading political cause among free blacks during first half of the nineteenth century, many African American political activists embraced a broader political agenda that included universal suffrage. The political agendas of free blacks of the late eighteenth and early nineteenth centuries conveyed both the immorality of slavery and political aspirations for equality.

Historian Leon Litwack explains that demands for suffrage were often encompassed in the rhetoric of black abolitionists and that suffrage was thought of broadly and not in gender-specific ways.[17] In the city of Washington and the Territory of Columbia, many free blacks participated in local and national efforts for abolition and universal suffrage. This small but powerful community employed gender-neutral suffrage rhetoric in their struggles for political equality in the early nineteenth century. The 1800 U.S. Census reports that the total population of enslaved and free people of color in Washington was 4,037; 3,244 were identified as slaves and 793 as free blacks.[18] The Georgetown area in Northwest Washington had a significant population of black people, including 1,449 black slaves and 227 free blacks in 1800.[19] The population of enslaved blacks increased until the abolition of slavery in Washington and Georgetown in 1862. The free black population grew more gradually but encountered a notable surge immediately following the Civil War. Free blacks in Washington and the Territory of Columbia fighting for equal suffrage during the antebellum era produced a political landscape in which racial equality was defined more broadly.

The fight for universal suffrage among African Americans in Washington during this period was also largely led by religious institutions. As some of the few black institutions, early black churches became central to African American political activism in Washington. The Mount Zion United Methodist Church and the African Church were cornerstones in this political effort.[20] Congregants adamantly opposed slavery and advocated for universal suffrage and other rights from the pulpit and the pews.[21] Women were among the leaders in these fledgling congregations. As early as 1814 the leadership and congregants of the Mount Zion Methodist Church aligned themselves with progressive political agendas and attempted to address the religious, educational, and social needs of Washington's enslaved and free black communities.

The first Anti-Slavery Convention of American Women took place on May 9, 1837. This interracial gathering of women developed a far-reaching, progressive agenda: redefine women's roles both inside and outside the domestic sphere, to abolish slavery, and to end racial discrimination in non-slaveholding states.[22] The resolution they drafted proposed:

> That this convention do firmly believe that the existence of an unnatural prejudice against our colored population, is one of the chief pillars of American slavery— therefore, that the more we mingle with our oppressed brethren and sisters, the more deeply are we convinced of the sinfulness of that anti-Christian prejudice which is crushing them to the earth in our nominally Free States.[23]

The women at this convention denounced both slavery and racial inequality in non-slaveholding states. This denouncement was similar to that made by congregants and leaders of Mount Zion Methodist Church in Washington. While local institutions such as Mount Zion provided the foundation for local, universal suffrage activism, this convention initiated a national, interracial suffrage movement.

This interracial, mixed-gender movement cohered, though not without disagreements and differing approaches. The greatest test to this movement came after Emancipation and with the ratification of the Fifteenth Amendment, which granted African American men the right to vote. Tensions spilled over in the debates leading up the amendment's ratification and culminated with powerfully divergent standpoints on the meaning of enfranchising African American men. Nearly three years before the ratification in 1870, women's rights activist and racial equality advocate Sojourner Truth proclaimed, "There is a great stir about colored men getting their rights, but not a word about the colored women; and if colored men get their rights, and not colored women theirs, there will be a bad time about it. So I am keeping the thing going while things are stirring; because if we wait till it is still, it will take a great while to get it going again."[24] Alliances between black and white suffragists changed substantially during the late nineteenth century. Schisms along racial and gender lines created a context in which a new but continually evolving black women's political culture emerged.[25] African American women fighting for the vote faced the difficult conundrum of supporting universal suffrage or the more politically expedient and more probable enfranchisement of black men. Universal suffrage was the only path to black women's enfranchisement, but the chance of it becoming a reality in the late nineteenth century did not measure favorably against an amendment securing for black men the right to vote.

In debates leading up to the ratification, some prominent white women suffragists made powerful statements against black men being enfranchised before white women. White abolitionist-feminist movement figures such as Elizabeth Cady Stanton stated at the First Annual Meeting of the American Equal Rights Association that "there is a depth of degradation known to the slave women that man can never feel. To give the ballot to the black man is no security to the woman. Saxon men have the ballot, yet look at their women, crowded into a few half-paid employments. Look at the starving, degraded class in our 10,000 dens of infamy and vice if you would know how wisely and generously man legislates for woman."[26] This particular statement indicated Stanton's belief that black men could not understand the experience of black women. She used the example of white women's oppression as being a result of only white men being able to vote in order to insist upon fighting for universal suffrage. When pushed further, however, Stanton traversed more contentious territory in her privileging of education as a determinant for suffrage. Stanton explained,

> If we are to have further class legislation, . . . the wisest order of enfranchisement was to take the educated classes first. If women are still to be represented by men, then I say let only the highest type of manhood stand at the helm of State. But if all men are to vote, black and white, lettered and unlettered, washed and unwashed, the safety of the nation as well as the interests of woman demand that we outweigh this incoming tide of ignorance, poverty and vice, with the virtue, wealth and education of the women of the country. With the black man you will have no new force in government—it is manhood still; but with the enfranchisement of woman, you

have a new and essential element of life and power. Would Horace Greeley, Wendell Phillips, Gerrit Smith or Theodore Tilton be willing to stand aside and trust their individual interests, and the whole welfare of the nation to the lowest strata of manhood? If not, why ask educated women, who love their country, who desire to mould its institutions on the highest idea of justice and equality, who feel that their enfranchisement is of vital importance to this end, why ask them to stand aside while 2,000,000 ignorant men are ushered into the halls of legislation?"[27]

Calling African American men "2,000,000 ignorant men" alienated Stanton from many African American suffragists. She and Susan B. Anthony left the American Equal Rights Association in response to the group's endorsement of a suffrage amendment that enfranchised only black men. Founded in 1866 by abolitionist-feminists, the AERA's purpose was to fight for rights for both women and African Americans. Until the schism that occurred as a result of the ratification of the Fifteenth Amendment, the AERA served as a viable political vehicle for interracial cooperation and for addressing both racial and gender inequities. By 1868, however, Stanton and Anthony formed a partnership with antiblack Democrat George Train to finance their publication, *Revolution*.[28] The publication made "disparaging references . . . to black men, who frequently were depicted as being inferior and prone to commit criminal acts."[29] Stanton and Anthony's move to support "educated suffrage," coupled with the publication of such an inflammatory document, strained relationships between white women and African American suffragists.

The racist and sexist rhetoric of opposing factions situated black women in a complicated space, torn between elimination of racial restrictions on the vote and the affirmation of all women's exclusion from it. Even outspoken political activists such as Truth found it difficult to navigate this polarized, political terrain. As the contours of the new political landscape became more visible, Truth and several women from the abolitionist-feminist community attempted to sketch out a productive space within a contentious and increasingly volatile political climate.[30] In *Sojourner Truth: A Life, a Symbol*, Nell Irvin Painter discusses Truth's political shift toward "neutrality" in the aftermath of the ratification of the Fifteenth Amendment. Carol Faulkner's *Women's Radical Reconstruction* and Rosalyn Terborg-Penn's *African American Women in the Struggle for the Vote, 1850–1920* document in detail the transforming of the political climate for abolitionist-feminists as well as how black women navigated an increasingly divided suffrage-activist community during and post-Reconstruction. The shifts these scholars explore, I argue, resulted in the emergence of a New Negro suffragist. This particular era of suffrage activism by black women grew out of post-Reconstruction and Jim Crow realities.

As Darlene Clark Hine explains, many African American women "were outraged that women—of any race—should 'stand in the way' of obtaining the vote for black men."[31] Notable black women activists such as Frances Watkins Harper advocated acceptance of black men's enfranchisement and embodied the outrage Hine describes. This perspective cannot be reduced to the simplistic argument that race trumped gender for black women political activists; it also indicates a strategic intraracial alliance based on the belief that black men could better represent black women's political interests than white women. In most cases, these women also continued fighting for universal suffrage and for black women's political power in a more general sense.[32] Within the post-Reconstruction political climate, black women suffragists had to rethink how to approach the struggle for universal suffrage. An additional challenge surfaced on the agendas of African American women suffragists as Jim Crow laws and other state-authored policies and regulations re-disenfranchised black men across the nation in the late nineteenth century. With both black men and black women disenfranchised once again, black women recast their efforts for achieving racial and gender equality within the public political sphere. In 1890 the National American Woman Suffrage Association formed out of merging of two suffrage associations, mending previous relationships between white and black suffragists and proffering an "intergrationist" approach to political activism. During this period African American women suffragists made difficult choices that imparted lasting effects on their roles and voices within the national suffrage movement.[33]

Black women built on the tradition of using the public arena and established new networks and organizations to advance their own goals and their sense of themselves as free women of color. The multidimensional terrain of African American women's political activism during this period was particularly visible in Washington. The "victory" of black male suffrage, however, was short lived there. During the 1870s, as Kate Masur's work shows, Washington underwent significant political changes that altered how and who controlled the nation's capital.[34] In 1871 the president and a popularly elected House of Delegates appointed a governor and council to govern Washington.[35] Within this new territorial government, African Americans held fewer seats in the elected, legislative body. In the first incarnation of this new governing structure, President Ulysses S. Grant appointed three black men to the council. By 1873, however, financial mismanagement, deepening economic depression, and political corruption led Congress to reorganize Washington's government. Whites from both the Democratic and Republican Parties, seeking to explain economic and political hardships in Washington, identified black suffrage and the appointed black council members as the problem. In 1874 Congress disenfranchised all Washingtonians. While whites lost control of the local government, the disenfranchisement of black Washingtonians had more far-reaching consequences.

From both local and national perspectives, the political terrain upon which black women in Washington were acting required new alliances and strategies to address their disenfranchisement. In the nation's capital, however, the context for suffrage activism greatly differed from suffrage activism in other cities and states. African American women suffragists in Washington had to combat the disenfranchisement of all Washingtonians, efforts to circumvent the Fifteenth Amendment by local and state governments outside Washington, and staunch opposition to women's suffrage. Black women suffragists in Washington vehemently fought for enfranchising D.C. residents, in addition to fighting for women's suffrage and protecting black male suffrage.[36] They also had the additional obstacle of local disenfranchisement. Consequently, black women's suffrage activism in Washington paralleled yet diverged from the national African American and women's suffrage movements of the late nineteenth and early twentieth centuries. All Washingtonians, regardless of race or gender, were disempowered to an extent at the ballot, and that changed the political calculus. Local efforts for enfranchisement extended beyond any particular group; African American women political activists concerned themselves with the struggle for suffrage and political representation for Washingtonians at the local level and for African Americans at the national level.

The influx of thousands of blacks to Washington during the Civil War and Reconstruction also altered the political terrain for African Americans in the nation's capital, particularly for black women. Allan Johnston's *Surviving Freedom: The Black Community in Washington, D.C., 1860–1880* explores the effects of Civil War and Reconstruction on black migrations to Washington. Johnston, however, does not focus on the gender-specific ramifications of African American migrations to Washington during this period. Although acknowledging differences between the access black men and women had to property, his portrait of Washington primarily illuminates the struggles of black men, which becomes conflated with the struggles of black Washingtonians.[37] Greater access to educational institutions was one of the most significant changes for blacks. The establishment of schools increased the number of literate black Washingtonians, which fueled the circulation of black newspapers, political propaganda, and other activist ephemera. The circulation of such material also connected local struggles to an imagined, national racial community striving for greater equality. This connection informed black Washington women's activism in national suffrage movements. African American suffragists in Washington mobilized around a political goal that would not provide them with the right to vote because universal suffrage would not secure full representation for residents of the nation's capital. The vote was subordinated within a broader vision of full inclusion within the body politic. Black women in Washington based their activism in their unique circumstance of disenfranchisement. In the nation's capital, the face of the African American women's suffrage activism was Mary Church Terrell. Her voice and elite status placed Terrell at the center of a new wave of political activism in Washington.

New Negro Women's Suffrage Activism: Washington and Beyond

African American women in Washington capitalized on emerging Progressive Era ideals and the invention of new strategies for racial progress within African American communities. They founded organizations that attended to basic needs of African Americans as well as social issues such as temperance, the mainte-nance of the black family, and black female respectability. The majority of black newspapers in Washington focused on activism around issues such as lynching, economic disparities, and African American suffrage, efforts led by black men and supported by black women. The widespread, intraracial expectation for black wom-en's involvement in social and political movements for racial equality, neverthe-less, was not leadership.[38] Black women used their gender-specific organizations to promote African American political struggles for racial equality, to articulate new ideas about the future of African American women's political identities, and to situate advocacy for gender equality within a still-forming and multifaceted political consciousness.

African American women configured an intraracial, gender-specific politi-cal culture that strategically employed an array of tactics that included but was not limited to the politics of respectability, self-determination, and racial uplift. Cynthia Neverdon-Morton argues that "even though black women living in dif-ferent communities realized that there were some needs unique to their areas, they also understood that certain needs were common to all communities where African Americans lived."[39] The connection between the local, national, and, in some activist circles, international political struggles of peoples of African descent informed African American women's political culture. Nearly all black women believed that they should have the right to vote. Although not all black women were suffragists, Paula Giddings explicitly states in *When and Where I Enter: The Impact of Black Women on Race and Sex in America* that "one would be hard pressed to find any Black woman who did not advocate getting the vote."[40] Black women political leaders rallied around this widely held sentiment. In Washington, African American women participated in suffrage organizations and in discourses regard-ing the significance of enfranchising black men and women alike despite their local predicament, which deprived them of the possibility for full representation in the body politic for distinct reasons. The specific needs of African Americans in Washington did not preclude black women from actively engaging in a political movement that would not improve their unique status as a triply disenfranchised community. Black women in Washington fought for suffrage on three fronts: as blacks, as women, and as Washingtonians.

All roads to a constitutional amendment for women's or universal suffrage led to Washington. Cognizant of this, black women suffragists in Washington perceived their role in the voting rights movement as particularly significant. African American women in the District made the most of residing in one of the most cosmopolitan southern cities. They lived in a city with a more progressive politics regarding race and gender than other cities and towns to the south. Washington also had an established black community that provided financial resources and extensive networks for black women to build on as they forged new paths in African American political activism. The localized efforts of black Washington women worked in conjunction with national organizations such as the National Association of Colored Women, the Commission on Interracial Cooperation, and the National American Woman Suffrage Association. Additionally, prominent educational institutions in Washington such as M Street High School and Howard University produced an educated, politically savvy community of black women who recognized the importance of the politics of appearance for political efficacy in the early twentieth century. Although not limited to this elite group of women, black women suffrage activists in Washington invested in "political celebrities." How these women were styled in the images of them that circulated in black periodicals affected how receptive African Americans were to their political messages.[41] For black women political activists, their appearances often determined their political cachet and effectiveness. Skepticism, optimism, and disillusionment informed black women's political behavior as they entered into the public arena through both traditional and nontraditional political activities. Hope for fuller citizenship coexisted with what Kate Dossett identifies as ambivalence about participating in a women's movement that historically and continuously relegated black women to the margins.[42]

Black women's refusal to remain on the political periphery was particularly evident in Washington. Their political activism took center stage in African American political discourse in the local black press. Both the *Colored American* and the *Washington Bee* supported universal suffrage. The editorial staff of both periodicals published these pieces while maintaining their commitment to universal suffrage. These newspapers participated in the elevation of black women activists in Washington to "political celebrities," most notably Terrell. The *Colored American* column I cited earlier in the chapter, "Woman's Case in Equity," was paired with a line drawing of Mary Church Terrell and proclaimed,

Woman suffrage, once a subject for ridicule, has ceased to be a joke. It is one of the grave problems of the hour. The wonderful advancement of the feminine sex in business, in the professions, in the industries, and in the world of finance, is giving her an importance in the affairs of life which the sensible man must recognize, and subscribe to a change of laws and customs to accord with the higher conditions that have come about in consequence of woman's broadening influence.[43]

Noting the progress women had made in inserting themselves into spheres from which they were historically excluded, the *Colored American* called upon "sensible" men to respond to the increased presence and political necessity of women in the public sphere. Her 1898 address specifically tackled the racial and gender oppression black women confronted. The subheading of the article, "Gracefully and Forcefully Presented by Mary Church Terrell before the Brainiest of Equal Suffragists in America—The Premier Representative of Our Womanhood Makes the Hit of the Convention," conveyed a profound sense of pride in Terrell, specifically in her ability to engage with a group of women identified as among the "brainiest" in America.

The editorial detailed how black women were transforming political, cultural, and economic spheres. The article also focused on a speech Terrell delivered at a meeting of National American Woman Suffrage Association, where her message echoed an earlier speech she gave at NAWSA in 1898. Invited by suffragist and NAWSA leader Susan B. Anthony, Terrell delivered "The Progress and Problems of Colored Women." Her 1898 and 1900 addresses specifically tackled the racial and gender oppression black women confronted. By 1900, Terrell was a political activist of national repute. Widely recognized by blacks and whites alike as a spokeswoman for African American and women's rights, black Washington suffragists at Howard University as well as other prominent figures such as Nannie Helen Burroughs and Anna Julia Cooper interacted and exchanged ideas with Terrell on a regular basis. Terrell was uniquely positioned and privileged to articulate a black women's political agenda that was informed significantly by African American women's political discourse and activism in the nation's capital.

Terrell delivered "The Justice of Woman Suffrage," a keynote address for the February 1900 meeting of the NAWSA. The *Colored American* described her speech as "a masterpiece of argument, scholarly and logically put and was delivered with that ease and grace of bearing, that ineffable charm and magnetism of manner and dignity and force that are characteristic of all Mrs. Terrell does or says."[44] This glowing review mirrored the respect and admiration black women Washingtonians held for the founder and president of the National Association of Colored Women. Before presenting Terrell's own words to black Washington, the newspaper's editorial staff concluded that "by Mrs. Terrell's appearance at this convention both the cause of women in general and the Negro in particular has been incalculably benefited."[45] Unlike her prior speech to the NAWSA in 1898, in which she addressed the plight of black women, "The Justice of Woman Suffrage" positioned Terrell as a women's activist who spoke for all women, equally and publicly affirming the importance of gender as well as racial equality.

"The Justice of Woman Suffrage" is a foundational speech for New Negro women involved in the struggle for voting rights. Excerpts from her speech accompanied the *Colored American* story about Terrell and circulated among black suffragists in Washington. Terrell's words resonated with black women in Washington who were conversing with Terrell and developing and refashioning their political rhetoric to more accurately articulate the necessity of suffrage for black women locally, nationally, and internationally. In her speech, Terrell explained:

> The founders of this republic called heaven and earth to witness that it should be a government of the people, and by the people; and yet the elective franchise is withheld from one half of the citizens, many of whom are intelligent, cultured and virtuous, while it is unstintingly bestowed upon the other, some of whom are illiterate, debauched, and vicious, because the word "people," by an unparalleled exhibition of lexicographical acrobats, has been turned and twisted to mean all who are shrewd and wise. The argument that it is unnatural for women to vote is as old as the rock ribbed and ancient hills. . . . Nothing could be more unnatural than that a good woman should shirk her duty to the state, if it were possible for her to discharge it.[46]

Terrell touched on many significant points—including the founding principles of the United States, the denial of suffrage to intelligent and virtuous citizens, and the conflation of personhood with manhood. Terrell pointed to the founding principles of the United States to legitimate universal suffrage. Positioning universal suffrage in this way aligned it with broader political trends that called upon individuals to serve the interests of the state through personal and collective responsibility. Terrell's speech exemplified what Salamishah Tillet calls "critical patriotism."[47] Tillet commences her genealogy of critical patriotism with Frederick Douglass. Similar to Douglass's, Terrell's patriotism "enables [her] to become a model citizen, one who does not repudiate but reifies, does not dismantle but reengages the meta-discourse of American democracy."[48] Terrell calls out the hypocrisy of democracy while maintaining an investment in the possibility of a liberatory and just democracy.

What is most striking about Terrell's speech is her emphasis on class as the basis for her characterization of suffrage as both a right and a privilege that should be extended to blacks and women. Her statement aligns with a political agenda influenced by politics of black respectability. In her emphasis on illiteracy and debauchery, Terrell gestured toward widely held perceptions about low-income communities. "The Justice of Woman Suffrage" suggests that individuals of "questionable" moral character should not be enfranchised, if "respectable" women and blacks remain disenfranchised. Terrell's support for respectability in defining the suffrage, the body politic, and political culture was not unique among black Washingtonians. Washington's black newspapers contributed to political discourses that demonized poor people, regardless of race. Leading publications focused primarily on black women suffragists who adhered to a burgeoning politics of respectability that emerged out of the black clubwomen's movement.

In the "Woman's Case in Equity," the *Colored American* staff made a clear distinction between suffragists of the past and the modern suffragist. Placing the image of Terrell on the front page of the paper confirmed the arrival of this modern activist, which connected women's appearance and style to the content of their politics. "Woman's Case in Equity" articulated that the perception of suffragists as women falling outside of the parameters of respectability distinguished the earlier movement from the current one. The paper's coverage of Terrell provided a modern example of the ideal black suffragist. Terrell's sketch portrays a fully covered woman with long hair pinned up into a neatly coiffed bun. The only visible skin in the image of Terrell is one side of her face in profile and the very top of her neck. The newspaper's conception of a "woman suffragist of today" also exemplified a particular vision of femininity that fit the politics of respectability. For women like Terrell embracing this performance of femininity, hyperpropriety became a vehicle through which African American women could articulate the New Negro standpoints regarding equality for black women.

The connection between effective political activism and feminine fashion reveals how prevailing racial, sexual, and gender ideologies influenced New Negro women's political culture. The heightened visibility of black women's bodies in the public arena sparked discussions about the significance of black women's physical appearance to social and political movements for equality. Black women could not escape myths about their hypersexuality, depravity, uncontrollable anger, and impropriety, and they therefore fashioned and performed a distinct form of feminine propriety while engaging in political activism.[49] While black suffragists like Terrell embraced respectability as one of many political tools, white suffragists in the early 1900s began rethinking their strategies and how to reclaim the national spotlight for their political agenda through more stylized and theatrical political demonstrations.[50] Both black and white suffragists recognized the importance of performance and bodily aesthetics to women's political activism, but how this recognition affected their political acts differed.

The Suffrage Parade held on March 3, 1913, in Washington highlighted the differences, tensions, and points of divergence for black and white women suffragists in the modern suffrage movement. African American women used this historic event to bring national attention to a burgeoning African American women's political culture that would not be silenced by white suffragists or anti-suffragists. The white women organizers of the march also had a distinct political agenda that reflected a "New Woman" ethos and an emerging political culture.[51] The clash of these racialized political cultures had a history dating back several decades but was reignited in the planning stages of the parade. This convergence of political cultures exposed the fragility and fluidity of coalitions across the lines of race and gender that had shaped the national suffrage movement from its inception.

During the first decade of the twentieth century, the National American Woman Suffrage Association began exploring new political strategies. Despite progress at the state level, there was little movement toward a constitutional amendment. Members of NAWSA traveled annually to the nation's capital to petition for federal protection of women's suffrage. While largely symbolic, this regular political performance also reflected growing support for the movement. Each year, the number of signatories grew.[52] The act also solidified a potential political base composed primarily of women. Some African American suffragists took part in this process despite reservations about the commitment of NAWSA to a fully universal conception of suffrage that applied to women as well as blacks.[53] African American women's reservations were grounded in NAWSA's refusal to pass a resolution against Jim Crow at its 1899 convention and a consistent trend of racist argumentation at the annual conventions.[54] Despite warranted skepticism of NAWSA and its leadership, African American women in Washington continued to involve themselves in local and national actions for suffrage. A glimmer of hope in the struggle for women's voting rights appeared in 1912 with Theodore Roosevelt's Progressive Party, which pledged to secure equal suffrage for men and women. Roosevelt, however, lost the election to Woodrow Wilson, prompting renewed fervor and dedication to achieving national recognition of women's suffrage.

To garner greater attention for the suffrage cause, leaders at the 1912 NAWSA annual convention in Philadelphia decided to plan a suffrage parade on the evening prior to Wilson's presidential inauguration in March 1913. NAWSA and suffrage leadership selected Alice Paul to organize a parade of such scale that it would attract significant press coverage. Paul was one of the most prominent figures in women's suffrage movement of the early twentieth century. Before age thirty, she had participated in the militant branch of the British suffrage movement, endured a hunger strike and being forcibly fed, had been arrested and imprisoned, and was now organizing the parade. Many historians situate Paul within a radical feminist tradition.[55] Her relationship to black suffragists and support for equal rights for African Americans, however, complicates how to historicize Paul's activism. Differing accounts exist of her attitudes and behaviors toward black suffragists prior to, during, and after the parade. During the planning stages, Paul and her organizing committee imagined a political spectacle in which costumes, floats, banners, dynamic speakers, and ornate programs would convey the importance of women's suffrage and the political power of suffragists and suffrage supporters.

On Monday, March 3, 1913, clad in a white cape and astride a white horse, lawyer Inez Milholland led the great woman suffrage parade down Pennsylvania Avenue in the nation's capital. Behind her stretched a long line of marchers and participants: nine bands, four mounted brigades, three heralds, about twenty-four floats, and more than five thousand supporters.[56] The spectacular vision became a reality. The parade proved to be a historically significant event that made suffragists more visible to the national body politic.

NAWSA discussed the role of African American women prior to the event. In a letter dated January 15, 1913, Paul noted to Alice Blackwell, editor of the *Woman's Journal*, that "as far as I can see we must have a white procession, or a negro procession or no procession at all."[57] As a Quaker, Paul seemingly struggled with how to manage the staunch, racist opposition within NAWSA and in the nation's capital.[58] Notably, a specific racially charged incident occurred in D.C. months before the planned march. On December 24, 1912, Nathaniel Green, a black man, brutally attacked and raped a white woman government clerk near the Capitol.[59] The case inflamed existing racial tensions in the city, and a heightened sense of the possibility of retaliatory violence pervaded. According to a Mary Walton's *A Woman's Crusade: Alice Paul and the Battle for the Ballot*, Paul confided in Blackwell that she worried that many if not a majority of white marchers will refuse to participate if negroes in any number formed part of the parade.[60] Fearing the opposition of white southern suffragists, Alice Paul attempted to evade direction questions about black women's participation. On February 15, 1913, she received a letter from Nellie Quander, the graduate advisor of Alpha Kappa Alpha Sorority Inc. at Howard University, inquiring about participation in the suffrage parade.[61] Paul did not respond to Quander until February 23. Paul's response included an invitation for Quander to come to her office "to decide on the best place for your section."[62] No record exists attesting to whether this meeting occurred. Prominent African American suffragists such as Ida B. Wells perceived Paul's inaction as intentional evasiveness and unequivocally denounced the possible exclusion of colored delegations. "Southern women," Wells asserted, "have tried to evade the question time and again by giving some excuse or other every time it has been brought up. If the Illinois women do not take a stand now in this great democratic parade, then the colored women are lost."[63] In her personal recollections, Paul explained that she reached a compromise with Terrell and the National Association of Colored Women in which black women suffragists would march in the rear of the procession in a separate section. From actual photographs taken at the parade, it appears that Paul's recollection is more accurate, because black women are largely invisible in images of state and occupational delegations.

The hypervisibility of white feminine spectacle as political strategy attracted most of the mainstream media attention, as coverage of the march focused almost exclusively on the theatrics white suffragists employed.[64] The *Chicago Tribune* reported on the exhaustion and unnerving of Helen Keller.[65] The *Washington Post* detailed ambulances attempting to aid injured people at the march over the course of six hours.[66] According to an article written by Mary Walton about the parade on its centennial, violence commenced almost immediately after the parade. "Men, many of them drunk, spit at the marchers and grabbed their clothing, hurled insults and lighted cigarettes, snatched banners and tried to climb floats. Police did little to keep order."[67] Despite the "chaos" and attempts to thwart the parade's progress, the *New York Times* piece on the march ultimately described the pageant as "one of the most impressively beautiful spectacles ever staged in this country."[68] The reporting in major white newspapers conveyed much of what Paul and NAWSA intended—the violent responses of "ignorant men" to suffrage, bringing national awareness to this new chapter in suffrage activism.

The official order of the parade procession was detailed in the "Suffrage March Line." The first section of the procession was occupied by women from countries that enfranchised women. Following the international section were the "Pioneers" of the women's suffrage movement. Pioneers were suffragists who had participated in decades of suffrage activism. The Pioneers section was a whites-only delegation. Despite NAWSA's acknowledgment of black women's participation in the suffrage movement for several decades, black women pioneers were excluded from marching in this revered delegation of "activist" women. The occupational and state delegations marched behind the Pioneers. The final group on the Suffrage March Line consisted of male suffragists. According to a NAWSA diagram, floats and bands brought up the rear of the parade. Particular delegations of black suffragists, men and women, were absent from the processional order and did not appear on NAWSA's depiction of the Suffrage March Line. The invisibility of black suffragists on this representation of the parade processional spoke volumes about the relationship between black and white suffragists and the NAWSA vision of suffrage.

Despite attempts to limit the visibility of African American women at the parade, a few black women suffragists "snuck in" and marched with state and occupational delegations. Ida B. Wells-Barnett, a strong proponent of universal suffrage and founder of the Alpha Suffrage Club of Chicago, vehemently protested segregation in the parade. Founded in 1913 by Wells, the Alpha Suffrage Club of Chicago worked exclusively for woman's suffrage. Prior to the march, the Illinois delegation insisted that Wells march in a separate, colored delegation. Wells refused to march, if not with her state.[69] In defiance, Wells joined the Illinois Delegation during the march, literally inserting herself and, by extension, black women into white suffragists' political culture. While not obviously visible in the images, other black women participated in the parade or looked on as spectators. Contrasting with the spectacle-like political performances of white suffragists at the parade, black women performed political respectability using bodily adornment.

Figure 5.1: Women's suffrage procession, National Women's Suffrage Association, March 3, 1913. Postcard Collection, Historical Society of Washington D.C.

Figure 5.2: Women's suffrage procession; protestors demanding a constitutional amendment, March 3, 1913. Postcard Collection, Historical Society of Washington, D.C.

The experience of the founding members of Delta Sigma Theta Sorority Inc. at the March 1913 parade exemplifies how black Washington suffragists negotiated the political terrain created by NAWSA for the parade.[70] Only two months after their formation at Howard on January 13, 1913, with the guidance of honorary member Mary Church Terrell, the sorority's founders agreed that participating in the parade would be their first public act.[71] They collectively affirmed that black women needed the right to vote for protection, equality, and advancement. Twenty-two women marched along with Terrell under a Delta Sigma Theta Sorority banner. Dressed in attire similar to that in the sketch of Terrell in the *Colored American* in February 1900, this group of black women, newspapers reported, presented images of modern suffragists who mobilized around respectable femininity to garner respect for their political activism. Subjected to racism from opponents of woman's suffrage and from parade organizers, participants, and spectators, the women of Delta Sigma Theta Sorority strategically articulated a black female presence that countered damaging racial and gender ideologies. These women could not engage in the theatrics employed by their white suffragists counterparts, yet their visibility came through their ability to epitomize black feminine propriety in how they adorned their bodies for civil disobedience.

Terrell, members of Delta Sigma Theta, and smaller, unidentified "delegations" of black marchers from Washington assembled in a racially segregated area. After congregating, these women marched toward the rear of the procession and encountered hostility from spectators and fellow parade participants alike.[72] Their relegation to the periphery of the parade caused Terrell to reevaluate her involvement with NAWSA. Several years after the parade, she "conclude[ed] that, if [Paul] and other white suffragist leaders could get the Anthony Amendment through without enfranchising African American women, they would do so."[73] This question circulated among most black suffragists, but particularly among the black Washington women who participated in the March 1913 parade. Their experiences with the white women's suffrage movement at this event further distanced African American women's political activism from that of their white women counterparts.[74] White women could transgress the boundaries of feminine propriety and public "respectability" in their political culture without contributing to racialized discourses of inherent inferiority.[75] The rigidity of interracial stereotypes about the lasciviousness and wildness of black women, coupled with historical perceptions touted in the black press of African American women suffragists as "masculine," unattractive, and unfashionable, created context in which African American women engaged politics of adornment and bodily aesthetics to claim a distinct space within New Negro activism. Black women structured a political culture that simultaneously encompassed their engagement with racial uplift and advancement. White women could not escape gender ideologies that privileged particular notions of appropriate political behavior for women. Their racial identity, however, allowed them to create exclusionary boundaries for political activism.

Notwithstanding the racism black women in Washington endured during their involvement in the parade of March 1913 and in subsequent interracial protests and organizations, Washington's African American suffragists continued to fight for suffrage, often independently from the white women's suffrage movement.[76] They also fought against racism within the white women's suffrage movement. Looking back on the parade, participant and Delta Sigma Theta founder Florence Toms noted, "We marched that day in order that women might come into their own, because we believed that women not only needed an education, but they needed a broader horizon in which they may use that education. And the right to vote would give them that privilege."[77] Toms's reflection on the event captured a widely held sentiment that propelled New Negro women's suffrage activism before, during, and after the March parade. Toms's statement also captured the New Negro women's ethos extant among Howard women in the early twentieth century. "Coming into their own" meant etching out space for black women to aspire and to achieve. Racism and sexism could not destroy black women's political culture. Black women from Howard University participating in the parade in the face of racist spectators and participants signaled an emergent audaciousness. The hostile racial climate of the nation's capital on parade day, more heightened than usual because of the rape of Adelaide Grant, proved to be a testing ground for a new generation of local African American women suffragists. Their performance of fashionable and "respectable" black femininity positioned this small group of Howard women and Terrell as the face of this new era of African American women's political activism in the nation's capital.

Conclusion

Based on their particular experiences with prevailing racial and gender ideologies as well as existing political and cultural currents, black women developed a distinct political culture. Working within the parameters of a black women's culture of respectability, these women strategically invested in a politics of appearance that connected to their public political behavior.[78] New Negro women suffragists addressed the social conditions that African Americans confronted, but they also wanted to have their own voice as African American women, within the national body politic. With greater access to mass media outlets such as newspapers and other periodicals, New Negro suffragists capitalized upon a longstanding strategy in black women's activism to situate themselves as modern activists. In the October 24, 1915, edition of the *Afro-American*, Lucy Diggs Slowe publicly commented on the connections between the National Association for the Advancement of Colored

People (NAACP) and the suffrage movement. Slowe proclaimed, "[The NAACP] was in favor of universal suffrage because it could not support the one without supporting the other. It knows only too well that the voteless group in any republic is a helpless one. To a large extent the Negro in this republic is voteless, and therefore helpless."[79] Slowe, although not at Howard when she made this statement, echoed the widespread sentiment of the Howard women who marched in the suffrage parade in Washington. When she arrived at Howard in 1922 as the dean of women, Slowe walked into a campus greatly affected by the historic act of Terrell and the twenty-two founders of Delta Sigma Theta. The desire of Nellie Quander to have Howard women such as members of Alpha Kappa Alpha Sorority participate in the march, in spite of Paul's evasiveness and potential harm, mirrored a fearlessness entrenched in a strategic performance of feminine propriety.

Noting the utility of the politics of respectability as they pertained to personal aesthetics, black women marching in the March 1913 suffrage parade used aesthetic tropes of respectable femininity to insert themselves into political activism. Although their white women counterparts engaged in theatrics and other forms of pageantry to make themselves more visible in the national political arena, black women performed respectability to attain greater visibility through embodying the antithesis of myths about their character and lack of political savvy. Existing stereotypes about black women positioned their bodies, their expressive practices, and their styling choices within the realm of spectacle without having to employ theatrics. Whereas white women suffragists moved more toward the use of spectacle in the early twentieth century, African American women suffragists in Washington chose to perform ladyhood to claim a distinct space within the twentieth century women's suffrage movement.[80] White women suffragists, particularly those inspired by New Woman cultural currents, embraced the use of spectacle and theatrics to visualize a burgeoning political consciousness that began to think of ladyhood as restrictive and oppressive.[81] For white women, the Washington suffrage march represented a departure from ladyhood and a rejection of feminine propriety. Christine Stansell, in *City of Women: Sex and Class in New York, 1789–1860*, thoroughly discusses how white women mobilized around rejecting "bourgeois female decorum" using dress and manner. This new era of white women's suffrage activism tapped into this legacy of women decidedly existing outside of ladyhood. Conversely, black women lacked access to the protected status of ladyhood and its accompanying privileges. Ladyhood had racially specific meanings. For white women suffragists and women's rights activists, ladyhood signaled the policing of their bodies and the relegation of their bodies to private and semi-private spheres. African American women suffragists from Howard University in 1913, however, claimed and inhabited ladyhood. They recognized ladyhood as a powerful performative strategy that could transform public perceptions of black women's political capital. These women did not have white or male privilege. They confronted the harsh historical reality of exclusion from discourses of ladyhood. The performance and articulation of female decorum served a similar purpose to that of white women suffragists rejecting what they viewed as a protected/regulated/policed status.

The political articulations of black women such as the founding members of Delta Sigma Theta Sorority who participated in the suffrage parade also garnered the support of leading African American political outlets. African American male editors of the premier newspapers of Washington such as the *Colored American* trumpeted the arrival of a modern black political woman and presented this political ideal as a "splendid representation" of African American progress.[82] In Washington the African American media placed Terrell at the center of New Negro women's political culture. Her national and emergent international status bolstered their positioning of her as one of the most important black women political celebrities. Her words, fashion, and hairstyles coexisted as integral components to her success as a black woman political activist. In Terrell, black women in Washington had a prototype for a modern "political" woman; they, along with Slowe, recognized the importance of performing ladyhood both as a liberatory act and as a strategy for distinguishing themselves from their New Woman counterparts and for solidifying alliances with New Negro men.[83]

Whereas the black press honed in on "respectable" black political women as representatives of this new era of political activism, white press outlets such as the *New York Times*, the *Chicago Tribune*, and the *Washington Herald* reported on the pageantry and spectacular political performances of white women suffragists during large-scale protests such as the suffrage parade. The *New York Times'* description of the parade as "one of the most impressively beautiful spectacles staged in this country" failed to capture the marked exclusion of black women or the nonspectacle of the small delegation of African American women marching. The *Washington Herald*, although also reporting on injured marchers, spoke of the use of pageantry and spectacle as well. The white press viewed the theatrics of white women suffragists as attempts to reinvigorate a fledgling national movement. White newspapers acknowledged a distinct shift in the strategies of white women suffragists. Similar to the black press's coverage of women's suffrage activism of the early twentieth century, white newspapers proclaimed a new era in women's political activism.

This new era became evident through the fashion, styling, and politics of appearance women suffragists adopted. Both black and white women created political cultures in which aesthetics and representational politics were integral. For New Negro women in Washington, the ability to present themselves as cultured, fashionable, and respectable through their dress and hairstyle choices carried significant political weight. Politicizing respectability had a history in African American women's activism prior to the New Negro era but became solidified as a primary tactic during the late nineteenth and early twentieth centuries.[84] The demand for respect for women's broadened influence in the public sphere propelled black women's use of the performative feminine propriety during the New Negro era. Black clubwomen also used politics of respectability to counter prevailing racialized gender stereotypes of black women; New Negro women employed these politics to embed themselves more fully in contemporaneous political movements. Performing "ladyhood" offered an aesthetic path to becoming visible and viable within New Negro political culture. As "splendid" representations of themselves, New Negro women in Washington both contributed to an evolving political discourse and created a localized political culture authored by black women, one that connected them to a national vision of equality for African American women.

Notes

1. Rosalyn Terborg-Penn, *African American Women in the Struggle for the Vote, 1850–1920* (Bloomington: Indiana University Press, 1998), 31–106.

2. Ibid., 31–80.

3. *Colored American*, February 17, 1900.

4. Mary Church Terrell, "The Progress of Colored Women," speech to the National American Woman Suffrage Association Convention, Washington, D.C., February 18, 1898. Available at http://antislavery.eserver.org/legacies/the-progress-of-colored-women; Anna Julia Cooper, *Voice from the South* (London: Oxford University Press, 1990).

5. Terborg-Penn, *African American Women*, 51–80.

6. Kate Masur, An *Example for All the Land: Emancipation and the Struggle over Equality in Washington, D.C.* (Chapel Hill, NC: University of North Carolina Press, 2012), 127–73. Masur discusses at length the complicated terrain of suffrage activism in the nation's capital.

7. Elsa Barkley Brown, "To Catch the Vision of Freedom: Reconstructing Southern Black Women's Political History, 1865–1880." In Gordon, Collier-Thomas, Bracey, Avakian, and Berkman, *African American Women and the Vote*, 66–99.

8. Ibid., 86–87.

9. Ann D. Gordon, Bettye Collier-Thomas, John H. Bracey, Arlene V. Avakian, and Joyce A. Berkman, eds. *African American Women and the Vote, 1837–1965* (Boston: University of Massachusetts Press, 1997); Terborg-Penn, *African American Women*; Gerda Lerner, *Black Women in White America: A Documentary History* (New York: Vintage, 1997); Deborah Gray White, *Too Heavy a Load: Black Women in Defense of Themselves, 1894–1994* (New York: Norton, 1999); Marjorie Spruill Wheeler, *One Woman, One Vote: Rediscovering the Women's Suffrage Movement* (Troutdale, Ore.: NewSage Press, 1995); Lisa G. Materson, *For the Freedom of Her Race: Black Women and Electoral Politics in Illinois, 1877–1932* (Chapel Hill: University of North Carolina Press, 2009).

10. Terborg-Penn, *African American Women*, 4–7.

11. *African American Women and the Vote, 1837–1965* (Gordon, Collier-Thomas, Bracey, Avakian, and Berkman, eds.) loosely periodizes African American women's suffrage

activism. Two of the periods framed by the editors of this collection and in the extant scholarship on black women's suffrage activism are 1870–1896 and 1896–1935. These years are central to my temporal conceptualization of the New Negro era.

12. Darlene Clark Hine and Kathleen Thompson, *A Shining Thread of Hope: The History of Black Women in America* (New York: Broadway, 1998), 29.

13. Alexander Keyssar, *The Right to Vote: The Contested History of Democracy in the United States* (New York: Basic, 2009), 2.

14. *Dred Scott v. Sandford*, 60 U.S. 393, 573 (1856), Justice Benjamin R. Curtis, dissenting.

15. John Hancock, *Essays on the Elective Franchise; or, Who Has the Right to Vote?* (Philadelphia: Merrihew, 1865), 23.

16. Keyssar, *Right to Vote*, 2.

17. Leon E. Litwack, "The Emancipation of the Negro Abolitionist," in *African-American Activism Before the Civil War*, edited by Patrick Rael (New York: Routledge, 2008).

18. "The Second United States Census," 1800. See https://www.archives.gov/research/ census/african-american/slavery-in-dc-1800–1860.pdf.

19. Ibid.

20. Daniel A. Payne, *A History of the African Methodist Episcopal Church* (Chapel Hill: University of North Carolina Press, 2001).

21. Letitia W. Brown, *Free Negroes in the District of Columbia, 1790–1846* (New York: Oxford University Press, 1972).

22. Dorothy Sterling, ed., *Turning the World Upside Down: The Anti-Slavery Convention of American Women, Held in New York City, May 9–12, 1837* (New York: Coalition of Publishers for Employment, 1987), 12.

23. Ibid.

24. Ibid.

25. Carol Faulkner, *Women's Radical Reconstruction: The Freedmen's Aid Movement* (Philadelphia: University of Pennsylvania Press, 2004); Jean Fagan Yellin and John C. Van Horne, eds., *The Abolitionist Sisterhood: Women's Political Culture in Antebellum America* (Ithaca, N.Y.: Cornell University Press, 1994); Ellen C. DuBois and Vicki L. Ruiz, eds., *Unequal Sisters: A Multicultural Reader in U.S. Women's History* (New York: Routledge, 2000).

26. Elizabeth Cady Stanton, "Resolutions and Debate," First Annual Meeting of the American Equal Rights Association, New York, May 10, 1867.

27. Ibid.

28. Bettye Collier-Thomas, "Frances Ellen Watkins Harper," in Gordon, Collier-Thomas, Bracey, Avakian, and Berkman, *African American Women and the Vote*, 50.

29. Ibid., 50–51.

30. Nell Irvin Painter, *Sojourner Truth: A Life, a Symbol* (New York: Norton, 1996); Faulkner, *Women's Radical Reconstruction*; Terborg-Penn, *African American Women*.

31. Hine and Thompson, *Shining Thread of Hope*, 157.

32. Masur, "Reconstructing the Nation's Capital"; Nancy Bercaw, *Race, Rights, and the Politics of Household in the Delta, 1861–1875* (Gainesville: University Press of Florida, 2003).

33. Terborg-Penn, *African American Women*; Ellen C. DuBois, *Feminism and Suffrage: The Emergence of an Independent Women's Movement in America, 1848–1869* (Ithaca, N.Y.: Cornell University Press, 1978); Louise M. Newman, *White Women's Rights: The Racial Origins of Femi-*

nism in the United States (New York: Oxford University Press, 1999); Paula Giddings, *When and Where I Enter: The Impact of Black Women on Race and Sex in America* (New York: Bantam, 1984); Glenda Gilmore, *Gender and Jim Crow: Women and the Politics of White Supremacy in North Carolina, 1896–1920* (Chapel Hill: University of North Carolina Press, 1996); James E. McPherson, *The Struggle for Equality* (Princeton, N.J.: Princeton University Press, 1964); Laura F. Edwards, *Gendered Strife and Confusion: The Political Culture of Reconstruction* (Urbana: University of Illinois Press, 1997); White, *Too Heavy a Load*; Jacqueline Jones, *Labor of Love, Labor of Sorrow: Black Women, Work, and the Family from Slavery to the Present* (New York: Basic, 1985).

34. Masur, "Reconstructing the Nation's Capital," 127–73.

35. Allan J. Johnston, *Surviving Freedom: The Black Community of Washington, D.C. 1860–1880* (New York: Garland, 1993), 216.

36. Masur, 127–73.

37. Johnston, *Surviving Freedom*.

38. Hine and Thompson, *Shining Thread of Hope*, 165–212.

39. Cynthia Neverdon-Morton, "Advancement of the Race," 121.

40. Giddings, *When and Where I Enter*, 120.

41. *The Colored American*, February 17, 1900.

42. Kate Dossett, *Bridging Race Divides: Black Nationalism, Feminism and Integration in the United States, 1896–1935* (Gainesville: University Press of Florida, 2008).

43. *Colored American*, February 17, 1900.

44. Ibid.

45. Ibid.

46. Mary C. Terrell, "The Justice of Woman Suffrage," speech to the Biennial Session of the National American Suffrage Association, Washington, D.C., February 1900.

47. Salamishah Tillet, *Sites of Slavery: Citizenship and Racial Democracy in the Post–Civil Rights Imagination* (Durham, N.C.: Duke University Press, 2012), 11.

48. Ibid.

49. Patricia Hill Collins, *Black Feminist Thought: Knowledge, Consciousness, and the Politics of Empowerment* (New York: Routledge, 2008), 67–91. Collins discusses at length the formation and perpetuation of race/gender myths about black women. She defines them as controlling images. She also discusses how African American women contest these tropes.

50. Annelise Orlick, *Rethinking American Women's Activism* (New York: Routledge, 2014), 1–28; Katherine H. Adams and Michael L. Keene, *Alice Paul and the American Suffrage Campaign* (Urbana: University of Illinois Press, 2008); Christine A. Lunardini, *From Equal Suffrage to Equal Rights: Alice Paul and the National Woman's Party, 1910–1928* (New York: New York University Press, 1986); Doris Stevens and Carol O'Hare, *Jailed for Freedom: American Women Win the Vote* (Troutdale, Ore.: NewSage, 1995); Eleanor Clift, *Founding Sisters and the Nineteenth Amendment* (Hoboken, N.J.: Wiley, 2003); Inez H. Irwin, *Story of Alice Paul and the National Woman's Party* (Fairfax, Va.: Denlinger's, 1977).

51. Charlotte J. Rich, *Transcending the New Woman: Multiethnic Narratives of the Progressive Era* (Columbia: University of Missouri Press, 2009), 1–36. Rich identifies the "New Woman" across ethnic communities as a cultural and literary ideal rooted in desires for autonomy.

52. Jean Matthews, *The Rise of the New Woman: The Women's Movement in America, 1875–1930* (New York: Dee, 2004), 131.

53. Angela Y. Davis, *Women, Race, and Class* (New York: Random House, 1981), 114–44.

54. Ibid.

55. Adams and Keene, *Alice Paul*, 1–20.

56. *New York Times*, March 4, 1913.

57. Letter from Alice Paul to Alice Blackwell, January 15, 1913, National Woman's Party Papers, Library of Congress, box I:1, reel 1, February 12, 1891–February 5, 1913.

58. Mary Walton, *A Woman's Crusade: Alice Paul and The Battle for the Ballot* (New York: Palgrave Macmillan, 2010), 63–65.

59. Ibid., 63.

60. Ibid., 64.

61. Letter from Nellie Quander to Alice Paul, February 15, 1913, NWPP.

62. Letter from Alice Paul to Nellie Quander, February 23, NWPP.

63. Wanda A. Hendricks, "Ida B. Wells-Barnett and the Alpha Suffrage Club of Chicago," in Wheeler, *One Woman, One Vote*, 268–69.

64. *New York Times*, March 4, 1913; *Washington Post*, March 4, 1913; *Chicago Tribune*, March 4, 1913.

65. *Chicago Tribune*, March 4, 1913.

66. *Washington Post*, March 4, 1913.

67. Mary Walton, "The Day the Deltas Marched into History," *Washington Post*, March 1, 2013.

68. *New York Times*, March 4, 1913.

69. Hendricks, "Ida B. Wells-Barnett," 270.

70. Delta Sigma Theta Sorority Inc. was founded at Howard University on January 13, 1913 by twenty-two Howard women.

71. Walton, "Deltas Marched."

72. Ibid.

73. Terborg-Penn, *African American Women*.

74. Ibid., 1–12, 107–35. Terborg-Penn details the fractured relationship between white and black women suffragists at various points in the suffrage movement. The tensions reached a breaking point after the parade on March 3, 1913.

75. Collins, *Black Feminist Thought*, 67–91.

76. Terborg-Penn, *African American Women*, 107–66.

77. Florence Toms, "The Founders' Greeting," *The Delta*, May 1963, 18.

78. Tiffany M. Gill, *Beauty Shop Politics: African American Women's Activism in the Beauty Industry* (Urbana: University of Illinois Press, 2010), 36. Gill discusses how black women operationalized a politics of appearance through their engagement in beauty culture.

79. Carol L. L. Miller and Anne S. Pruitt-Logan, *Faithful to the Task at Hand: The Life of Lucy Diggs Slowe* (New York: SUNY Press, 2012), 44.

80. Linda K. Kerber and Jane Sherron De Hart, eds. *Women's America: Refocusing the Past* (New York: Oxford University Press, 2004); Ida B. Wells-Barnett and Jacqueline Jones Royster, *Southern Horrors and Other Writings: The Anti-Lynching Campaign of Ida B. Wells,*

1892–1900 (Boston: Bedford, 1997); Giddings, *When and Where I Enter*; Gilmore, *Gender and Jim Crow*; Christine Stansell, *City of Women: Sex and Class in New York, 1789–1860* (Urbana: University of Illinois Press, 1986); Jones, *Labor of Love*.

81. Walton, *Woman's Crusade*.

82. *Colored American*, February 17, 1900.

83. Matthews, *Rise of the New Woman*, 132.

84. The work of Higginbotham, Wolcott, and Hunter are particularly salient to understanding how black women used and transformed politics of respectability.

From
Marching Together: Women of the Brotherhood of Sleeping Car Porters,
by Melinda Chateauvert (1998)

6

"IT WAS THE WOMEN WHO MADE THE UNION"

Organizing the Brotherhood

MELINDA CHATEAUVERT

The men who founded the International Brotherhood of Sleeping Car Porters and Maids (BSCP) announced their vision for the union in its name: an international organization representing African American men and women in the labor movement. They sought to represent sleeping car workers in the United States, Canada, and Mexico. Similar to the Order of Sleeping Car Conductors, the BSCP avoided using "Pullman," establishing its independence from the company. And in the early years, the organization included women by name.[1]

Despite the explicit inclusion of porters and maids in the union's name, organizers stressed the goal of black manhood. At the Brotherhood's first public meeting on August 25, 1925, leaders announced, "Inaugurating the greatest movement in the History of the Negro. . . . A Call for only red-blooded he-men. . . . Pullman Porters only invited . . . August 25, 1925."[2] Pullman maids were not invited.

President Randolph's gendered rhetoric of race, his demand for black manhood rights, facilitated the construction of specific union roles for women and men. But during the union's early years the precise definition of these roles was ambiguous. While Brotherhood men looked to the "New Negro" as their model of manhood, some women drew on the image of the New Negro Woman, who stood for women's equality in the struggle for racial and economic justice. Drawing on the feminist icons of the Harlem Renaissance, they challenged women's customary work assignments, demanding the right to organize alongside men. They knocked on doors, collected union dues, addressed mass meetings, and argued over members' unfair discharge claims with Pullman management. Many tested traditional divisions of labor, rejecting the notion that women should play feminized roles to complement the brothers' manhood.[3]

The boldness of these New Negro Women made other porters' wives uneasy. Such promiscuous activities risked the respectability they sought to achieve through the Brotherhood. These women preferred to organize among other women, providing distaff support to the men. While they upheld the gendered division of union labor, the Women's Economic Councils successfully enlarged the accepted range of women's activities. With considerable acumen, these early auxiliaries exploited women's traditional role as fundraisers and made themselves essential to the union's financial stability. Their social events raised thousands of dollars for the BSCP and taught other women the benefits of trade unionism. These contradictory definitions of female respectability underlay many of the debates over women's place in the Brotherhood.

During the first years of organizing, the BSCP drew porters and maids, husbands and wives, trade unionists and middle-class reformers into the campaign. Drawing on his experiences as a labor organizer and magazine publisher, Randolph orchestrated a national campaign to raise money, establish local Brotherhood divisions and Women's Economic Councils, and to propagandize the movement, but his primary concern was fundraising. Rather than financing the entire drive from workers' empty pockets, he asked wealthy liberal patrons and progressive organizations for donations, utilizing his networks in the Socialist Party and his wife's networks among Harlem's upper class. A large grant from the American Fund for Public Service allowed Randolph to send "every porter" a six-month subscription of The Messenger, which became the union's official paper.[4]

New York porter-organizers Ashley L. Totten, William H. DesVerney, Frank Crosswaith, and Roy Lancaster established contacts with Pullman porters in other cities. Randolph and the men toured the country, whenever money was available, and sometimes when it was not. When money could be raised for a one-way ticket anywhere, one of the men would be on his way. Once there, the Brotherhood held mass meetings and "labor education institutes" or conferences at which local trade unionists, community leaders, and other supporters spoke on trade unionism to the working-class African American audiences. At each stop, organizers set up BSCP locals and Women's Economic Councils to continue organizing porters and wives in the city. After raising additional money through initiation fees, dues, and general appeals, the organizers would leave for the next city.

Brotherhood mass meetings welcomed maids, wives, and other porters' relatives, and substantial numbers of African American working people interested in trade unionism. Union leaders' decision to rely on public mass meetings as a principle organizing strategy served two purposes. Large meetings made it difficult for Pullman Company informants to identify the porters and maids who attended.

Equally important, such forums provided labor education to the African American community at large.

Local members arranged these meetings according to Randolph's carefully written instructions, such as those sent to Roy Lancaster for an upcoming labor institute in New York City. Randolph wrote: "I hope you will hit hard at the meetings in New York as I feel they ought to be a huge success if enough energy is put behind them. I would get the cooperation of the Intercollegiate Association from Mrs. Louise Jackson Johnson and Miss [Elizabeth] McDonald [sic: MacDougald]. [Messenger columnist George] Schuyler knows Miss McDonald. She is quite an active young woman. I would also enlist some of the moving spirits down town."[5] Outside major cities, wives often secured the meeting hall, distributed notices, and contacted porters' families to urge their attendance, while the wife of the local president usually held a dinner party in honor of Randolph and local supporters. With money tight and hotels open to African American guests uncommon, Randolph slept in his hostess's spare room more often than he wanted to recall.[6]

Mass meetings often featured the union's national leaders, who displayed a range of styles. Chicago organizer Milton P. Webster or New York porter-organizer Ashley L. Totten "would rough up the crowd, make people uneasy and agitated." Randolph followed "with the eloquent oratorical style he had honed as a Shakespearian actor: smoothing, other-worldly." The contrasting styles of these men fit perfectly together; as historian Greg LeRoy characterized them, "It was like a hell-fire Baptist preacher bringing on the Pope."[7]

Pullman Company informants also attended these meetings. The Brotherhood's iron-clad oath of secrecy protected members against these spies. Rank-and-file members did not speak about their experiences. Instead, Randolph and community leaders served as the main speakers in order to protect pro-union employees and their families from Pullman retaliation. Sometimes the widow or wife of a Brotherhood porter spoke, explaining the benefits of unionization for families. But this was risky too since the company could revoke the pension she collected.[8]

Other platform guests included the minister of the church where the meeting was held, a spokesperson from organized labor (typically white), and a spokeswoman from a women's club or a social service organization such as a settlement house, the Phyllis Wheatley Club, or Young Women's Christian Association. The broad representation from local officials and organizations gave the union credibility and helped reassure members. Speakers also donated money from their own organizations to the Brotherhood and raised money from the crowd by passing the hat.

The union's mass meetings attracted large numbers of women, both wives and maids, despite the male-only emphasis of the Brotherhood's inaugural meeting. BSCP membership rolls show that maids paid dues from the very beginning.

Women joined with the same enthusiasm as the men, and faced the same consequences for their actions. Company service records clearly stated which maids were "disloyal." Ada V. Dillon was fired in 1929 for violating Pullman's loyalty rule. In later years the Brotherhood honored her, along with maids Josephine Puckett of Chicago and Tinie Upton of Los Angeles, among the men who lost their jobs during the union struggle.[9]

Organizing women workers into a predominantly male union posed particular problems for female trade unionists. Frances Albrier described some of the difficulties she had organizing other maids in the mid-1920s:

[ALBRIER]: The maids joined the union with the brothers, the porters throughout the United States—South, East, and West—that was maids and Pullman porters on the Pullman cars. . . . There weren't many maids out here that sympathized with the union. They weren't brought up under that militancy and they didn't have the background that I had—going through [high] school at Tuskegee and [graduating from] Howard. Our responsibility was trying to educate the black public and the black women on these things. They didn't understand the economics; they only understood the need for the job.

[INTERVIEWER]: You had a privileged job—no question about it. I guess any woman who had it would feel so—would feel that she had a privileged job, especially if she's also supporting a family.

[ALBRIER]: Yes. A great many maids in the East didn't support the union. They were too busy. Some did. Some gave contributions but they didn't join because they were afraid their names would be known if they had a card belonging to the union. They let the men do it.[10]

Albrier's analysis of maids' attitudes about unionization reveals the competing definitions of female respectability for New Negro Women. Like men, women feared retaliation, a reminder of the lack of decent job opportunities for African American women. Second, she confirms that because of their breadwinning and domestic responsibilities, those who were female heads of households had very little time to participate in labor unions. And third, Albrier suggests that some maids believed unions were for men; women might donate money to the Brotherhood, but only permanent male workers needed a union. The Brotherhood's manhood rhetoric appealed to maids' sense of racial solidarity, affirming their distaste of Pullman paternalism. Although aware that, as women, they had specific problems, they defined their job grievances primarily as racial discrimination.

Albrier believed the Brotherhood could offer women significant benefits and job protection, and from extant membership records in Chicago and Oakland it appears that many other Pullman maids agreed. Furloughs, pay cuts, and the hiring of Asian replacements spurred the women's interest; between 1929 and 1930, twenty-two women paid initiation fees. During the dozen years of the Brother-hood's struggle for recognition, forty-three maids, of about one hundred working in Chicago, paid union dues. The level of women's participation, then, was equal to men's.[11]

Pullman maids had as many different backgrounds as they had reasons for going into service. There was no living male member of Rosa Broyles's family; she was the breadwinner for her family of five generations, including her maternal grand-mother of 110 years. A few maids were married to porters; they often continued to work after marriage and after childbirth. Others, like some porters, worked for Pullman only briefly, until they earned enough money to do something else. Per-haps like Albrier, some tired of their old jobs and thought they might see a bit of the world.[12]

A canvass of maids' service record cards provides a glimpse into their lives and Pullman careers. Almost all of these women began working for the Pullman Company between 1920 and 1925. Most were in their late twenties to early thir-ties; the median age of newly hired maids was thirty-one. Marital status could be determined for about half of the women. Twenty-two married either before or during their Pullman service, two were divorced; only two were given an honorific "Miss." None of the records surveyed indicated children, although other evidence clearly shows that several maids were mothers.[13]

Some women may have hesitated to join the BSCP because of male leaders' antipathy toward their participation. As men, porters embraced the distinctly masculine culture of traveling men and the railroad brotherhoods. On the road, or at home, local Brotherhood headquarters, PPBA lodges, and even crowded Pull-man sleeping quarters encouraged fraternization with local and foreign men telling tales, playing cards, and drinking and talking about women. The Oakland BSCP office shared space with a pool hall, owned and managed by local organizer C. L. Dellums. In Chicago, organizer Milton P. Webster, a cigar-chomping, Republican wardheeler, had little use for women, unless they commanded party posts. His "elegant wife" Elizabeth, although active in club and social service, did not belong to the BSCP women's organization because he wanted her to "stay home" raising their three children. Webster's hostility towards women's participation, coupled with the union's rhetorical stress on black manhood, posed barriers to these po-tential Brotherhood members.[14]

Nonetheless, in the midst of an alienating masculine culture, many African American working women saw the union as a solution to their problems. The participation of Chicago maid Josephine Puckett as well as the prominence of white and African American women trade unionists may have further encour-aged their support. For some, the Women's Economic Council may have offered a female-controlled refuge from the male-dominated union hall, even when the council focused on domestic, rather than workplace, concerns.[15]

Tinie Upton, the wife of Los Angeles Brotherhood President Charles L. Upton, joined the union as a Pullman maid, the local's first woman member. She was soon fired. "During the heated campaign for the organization, she worked faithfully and brilliantly in the enrollment of both porters and maids. In fact so successful was her work that the management called her into the office and discharged her for union activities. This move on the part of the management only served to spur her on in her valiant fight for economic freedom."[16] Though dismissed, she exercised her right as a former Pullman worker and remained a Brotherhood member. In 1935 she even ran for a position in the 200-member Los Angeles local, but lost to a younger man.[17]

Porters and maids devised methods to keep their union membership secret. Frances Albrier, running out of San Francisco, paid her dues at the end of the line. "I paid my dues in New Orleans," Albrier recalled. "I didn't pay it out here [in Oakland] because they couldn't see my name on a list. A lot of them did in other cities." The strategy of paying union dues in a foreign city can be confirmed in the Chicago local's rolls. Several of those entries indicate the names of Chicago residents who paid, for example, in New York and Tacoma, Washington.[18]

The Pullman Company used maids as well as porters to spy on the union. The "Porter Growls" column warned of one maid who kept management aware of union activities.

> All hail the power of Miss Capitola Mynard [sic] a Pullman maid operating on the Golden Arrow Limited, Penn. Terminal District, who is alleged to be helping the Pullman Company bring distress to the home and families of porters by reporting them to the superintendent because they asked her to join the union. Some who know her while in Chicago wonder if she would be as active for the company, if porters were white men? If the report is true, it would be well to watch the maid.[19]

The "growling" columnist's attack on Minyard linked her support of the company with allegations that she dated white men. Thus Minyard was doubly suspect: disloyal to the economic advancement of the race and disloyal to African American men. Pullman however rewarded Minyard for her loyalty by promoting her to Maid Instructress.[20]

Pullman threatened union maids by hiring Chinese women to work on the Pacific Coast lines. These women tended to be much younger than African American women, hired at age twenty-two. But few remained long in Pullman service, quitting, on average, after eighteen months. The company hired the greatest majority of Chinese women between June 1, 1928, and December 31, 1929, the eighteen months immediately following the Brotherhood's strike threats. At least one African American maid "took exception" to their hiring and promptly quit.[21]

Pullman also used more subtle reprisals to prevent unionization. After the stock market crash in 1928, the company furloughed thousands of employees, including many maids who were indefinitely furloughed. The crew cuts were due, in part, to the changing needs of passengers. Manicurists were expensive incidental luxuries when business travel decreased with the economic downturn. When needed, porters could help mothers traveling with children. Maids had been in more demand when lady passengers needed assistance with their Victorian-era clothing. The only other jobs open to African American women in the Pullman Company were as laundry workers or car cleaners, jobs furloughed maids took willingly as unemployment figures mounted. The company tried to keep only those workers whom it believed were loyal, but many Brotherhood members remained on the job. Conversely, at least four Chicago maids fired for disloyalty could not be located on the local's membership rolls.[22]

In the mid-twenties, while the economy boomed and jobs were plentiful, the Brotherhood's victory seemed imminent. Membership soared, peaking at 4,632 porters and maids by 1928. "The men are flocking in," reported local secretaries all over the country. The New York local grew rapidly under Randolph's direction, drawing together over one thousand sleeping car workers from the region's four railroad terminals and yards. The BSCP represented the first race-controlled labor union, explaining perhaps why membership in Northwestern cities such as Seattle and Spokane, Washington, and Portland, Oregon, remained high, even during the union's "dark years."[23]

In Chicago, the headquarters of the Pullman Company, winning the support of porters and maids was critical to the Brotherhood's success. The city was the heart of the nation's transportation system, with five railroad lines operating out of the city's four stations. More than a third of Pullman's African American passenger car force lived on the city's south side. Under the leadership of Milton P. Webster, membership in Chicago rivaled the New York local, ranging from an estimated 1,150 peak in 1927 to a low of 250 in 1933. To gain the trust of these men and women, the union relied on the efforts of porters and maids, community leaders, trade unionists, religious leaders, and clubwomen.[24]

In Chicago and elsewhere, the Brotherhood drew on the support of many prominent African American clubwomen and white trade union women. These national leaders and neighborhood agitators worked to change black community opinion in favor of the union. Clubwomen provided introductions to male and female leaders, especially ministers, and arranged for Randolph to speak to their organizations, allowing their names to be used in public endorsements.

Ida B. Wells-Barnett, the nation's leading radical Race Woman, endorsed the Brotherhood in December 1925. Randolph gladly accepted Wells-Barnett's invitation to her home to speak to the Woman's Forum. Wells-Barnett also tried to secure the endorsement of the city's African American Republicans, but ran into the Pullman Company. She had originally planned to hold a reception for Randolph at the prestigious Appomattox Club, but its members, who had ties with Pullman, opposed her use of the building. The club's founder and first president, *Conservator* publisher Julius Avendorph, had worked as a messenger to Pullman Company president, Robert Lincoln.[25]

Randolph spoke to the Woman's Forum in December 1925. The club's endorsement of the BSCP introduced Randolph to other prominent Chicago clubwomen, such as Irene McCoy Gaines, then the Industrial Secretary of the Chicago YWCA Negro branch and president of the Illinois Federation of Republican Colored Women's Clubs. Wells-Barnett and Gaines converted "leading society women" to the Brotherhood and worked with the Chicago Citizens' Committee to raise funds and seek new endorsements. Gaines spoke regularly at Brotherhood mass meetings and affairs. Mary Church Terrell of Washington, D.C., former president of the National Association of Colored Women's Clubs, and prominent in Republican circles, announced her support in January 1928; then "she went with Brotherhood officials to call on President [Calvin] Coolidge, at which President Randolph presented the case of the Pullman porters and maids."[26]

In New York, Lucille Randolph seems to have persuaded her good friend A'lelia Walker to donate money to the union. The daughter of Madame C. J. Walker, founder of the black hair care empire, A'lelia was Harlem's leading socialite, with whom Lucille founded the Gothamite Debutantes Association, the first group for introducing young women to Harlem society. Lucille Randolph also organized her fellow Walker salon operators to donate prizes for the Brotherhood's beauty contests. Her 135th Street salon served as a distribution center for The Messenger, thus acquainting other Harlem women with the union.[27]

African American trade union women, although few in number, also announced their support for the porters. Gertrude Elise MacDougald Ayers was the vice-principal of P.S. 89, the highest ranking African American woman in the New York City school system and an American Federation of Teachers organizer. Maida Springer [Kemp], another Harlem labor organizer and BSCP supporter, perhaps began her lifelong friendship with Randolph at this time. Randolph editorialized the endorsement of "a capable young woman, Miss Floria Pinkney, graduate of Brookwood Labor College," who became the first African American woman organizer for the International Ladies' Garment Workers' Union. In Chicago, Neva Ryan, founder of the Domestic Workers' Union, endorsed the union as did Irene Goins, who organized Chicago's African American meatpackers and their families.[28] As part of the small world of black labor organizers, these women recognized the need to support each other's work. At the same time, porters' wives often worked in these trades, thus further strengthening the bonds.

White settlement house workers also voiced their support for the African American union. Mary McDowell, head of the Department of Charities at the University of Chicago, former Hull House resident, and Chicago Women's Trade Union League official, was an early proponent. McDowell did her own bit to organize sleeping car workers. She claimed that whenever she rode a Pullman car she "buttonholed" the porter about his Brotherhood membership, encouraging him to join. She continued to support the union and "never missed a Brotherhood mass meeting." Randolph credited McDowell for one of his favorite expressions: "Negroes are beginning to write their own economic contract."[29]

McDowell persuaded her colleagues to support the Brotherhood. Mary Anderson, Director of the U.S. Women's Bureau, accepted Randolph's invitation to speak to the 1929 Brotherhood convention, after McDowell interceded. From that time, Anderson spoke regularly to BSCP women. Lillian Herstein of the Chicago American Federation of Teachers spoke at several meetings; later, as director of the Chicago WPA Worker's Education Program, Herstein developed programs on consumers' cooperatives for the Ladies' Auxiliary.[30]

Among other white progressive and labor women, supporting the Brotherhood appears to have become a trend. In San Francisco, Charlotte Anne Whitney, a prominent socialite turned prodigal socialist, wrote letters on behalf of the union. In New York City, Elizabeth Gurley Flynn of the American Fund for Public Service, veteran leader of both the Lawrence, Massachusetts, and Patterson, New Jersey, textile mill strikes, and chair of the International Labor Defense, appeared at several BSCP mass meetings.[31]

Prominent society women enrolled in the Brotherhood's Citizen's Committees in Oakland, Chicago, New York City, St. Louis, and Boston. Los Angeles Brotherhood organizer and real estate broker George S. Grant wrote that these committees were "formed from among the most prominent individuals in each community who can be persuaded to support the Brotherhood." Committee membership included prominent local and some national leaders; many were also members of the National Association for the Advancement of Colored People. The New York Citizens' Committee of One Hundred on behalf of the Pullman Porters and Maids was chaired by attorney Henry T. Hunt, former member of the United States Railroad Labor Board. The committee pledged to assist in "establishing the right of self-organization [by] Pullman Porters and Maids" and "to stimulate public interest in favor of a living wage for the porters and maids."[32]

Several members of the Citizens' Committees may have endorsed the Brotherhood because they were part of a progressive network of mutually endorsing reformers; the union was another group in the long list of causes they supported. The New York list provides a fascinating glimpse of the networks to which Randolph had access. Socialists, progressives, feminists, and labor leaders all appear on the list, as well as ministers, professors, artists, and philanthropists; of the one hundred listed, twenty-two were women. As a public relations tactic, the Citizens' Committee gave the Brotherhood the stamp of legitimacy and helped to secure foundation funds and other donations.[33]

Yet society leaders and intellectuals did little to convince potential rank-and-file workers to join the BSCP. They may have known that E. R. A. Seligman was a distingushed economics professor at Columbia, but he did not hire Pullman porters; that was for the company to decide. Porters' wives had similar reasons to be skeptical. They perhaps suspected that white women such as Lillian Wald, Frieda Kirchwey, Florence Kelley, Harriot Stanton Blatch, Mary Dreier, Fannie Hurst, Helen Phelps Stokes, and Mary Simkhovitch, socialists though they may be, were more likely to hire African American women for domestic work than join them on the front lines in a struggle for the economic advancement of the race. None of these women was ever a platform guest for a BSCP mass meeting; their politics permitted them to endorse the movement, but their privileges of class and race did not require interaction with its members.

Nor did African American society women regularly attend the BSCP's labor institutes and meetings, except to give advice from "on high." Irene McCoy Gaines, for example, instructed a Chicago women's meeting to "seek culture." Mary Church Terrell did not include the Washington Women's Economic Council in local club activities. Even among the wives of the BSCP national organizers, only Walter (Mrs. C. L.) Dellums actively participated in the Oakland local's activities. Lucille Randolph, Elizabeth Webster, and Hazel Smith had their own circles of social service and club friends and did not belong to their local Women's Economic Councils. Historian Deborah Gray White argues such divisions were "the cost of club work, the price of black feminism," that encouraged class prejudice among African American women. Thus, rather than ally with the traditional leadership class of the African American community, Brotherhood women and men sought partnerships with trade unionists, white and black, in common cause against capital.[34]

The Women's Economic Councils of the BSCP sought to convert the porters' wives and female relatives into dedicated trade unionists. This was no easy task, for, despite intra-racial class prejudice, tradition demanded that African American working women look to clubwomen for leadership. Yet in the 1920s many began to question the dominance of this Republican class, as new political leaders and organizations arose. One example of this new attitude was Marcus Garvey's Universal Negro Improvement Association (UNIA), which attracted thousands of working-class and immigrant African Americans, but there were smaller revolts. In Washington, D.C., for example, Rosina Corrothers Tucker founded the Northeast

Women's Club in the early 1920s, "to do something constructive" for the community; the club provided clothing, shoes, and carfare to needy students, sent children to summer camp, and lobbied for better city services for the neighborhood.[35]

The Brotherhood of Sleeping Car Porters tapped these sentiments, advocating trade unionism as the solution to the race problem. But Randolph's view of the Brotherhood recognized the need for a distaff organization. Thus, in October 1925, just six weeks after the inaugural meeting of the BSCP, Randolph organized the first Women's Economic Council in New York City. This group, originally called the Hesperus Club, immediately began fundraising, sponsoring the union's first Christmas dance in December 1925 at "the aging but still majestic Rockland Palace (the old Manhattan Casino)." The dance was so popular that it became an annual event. The following year it featured a bobbed hair contest, with entrants from twelve hair culturists, including Madame C. J. Walker's own salon, and judges from the society press.[36]

The Hesperus Club was the first ladies' auxiliary; others soon followed. Wherever Randolph or Ashley Totten organized a Brotherhood local, they also set up a women's group. At the beginning, councils formed under a variety of local names. The Ever Ready Club of Philadelphia announced, "We, the women who are the essential body of everything, are doing our best to make the votes go over big and with huge success." The Chicago Colored Women's Economic Council, founded May 6, 1926, brought together forty-five women, under the leadership of Jessie Bonds, the daughter of Pullman Porter William Puckett and Pullman Maid Josephine Puckett. By 1926, eleven cities boasted women's groups: New York, Chicago, Washington, D.C., Boston, St. Paul, Minneapolis, Oakland, Los Angeles, Denver, Omaha, and Salt Lake City, the principal northern terminals for Pullman operations.[37]

Any African American woman could join the Economic Council, whether or not she had a relative working for the Pullman Company. Special efforts to recruit porters' wives were made because they might convince their husbands and families to support trade unionism. Randolph also recognized that wives' control of the household budget played a considerable role in whether husbands paid their dues regularly. Council women visited the homes of porters and maids spreading the Brotherhood message, proselytizing, like a band of trade union missionaries. Their tactics fooled company detectives. Sleeping car workers were out for days, sometimes weeks at a time while their families were left to "hold the fort." Pullman did not suspect that a coffee klatsch of wives would gather to discuss unionization. Literature could be left with the family for all members to read. Men could leave their dues for the organizer to collect, or as sometimes happened, the wife would pay her husband's dues without his knowledge. As Rosina Tucker recalled,

> There were some men who were willing to join the organization but who were prevented from doing so by their apprehensive wives. On the other hand, there were

many men whose wives were eager for them to join but who balked for fear of losing their jobs. There were some women who put their husbands' names on the rolls and paid their dues for years. If I dare say so, it was the women who made the union in those early days. The men were afraid, though with good reason.[38]

The fear that Pullman would retaliate against union supporters, male or female, required the Brotherhood to extend its oath of secrecy to council members.

Leadership of the Women's Economic Council was a matter of concern to the men. To ensure the continued operation of these groups, Randolph advised: "Success in organizing the council will depend largely upon the character and personality of the individual secured as head or President of the Council. The aims should be to get as strong and popular a woman as possible, provided such person can also be interested enthusiastically in the work of assisting the Brotherhood of Sleeping Car Porters."[39] But Randolph did not require these female leaders to work exclusively with other women, leaving open the possibility that some would attempt to establish a gender-integrated movement. In Los Angeles, the dynamic Mattie Mae Stafford and George Grant worked with porters, maids, family members, and community members, with slight discrimination between the sexes. Grant's proposed "Cooperation Plan," outlining the organizational work of the Brotherhood, demonstrated a remarkable degree of gender integration.[40]

Rosina Tucker challenged sex segregation by working primarily with male union officials as the BSCP's Washington liaison, even though her official title was President of the Women's Economic Council. With President Randolph's consent, she also successfully argued porters' unfair discharge claims to Pullman officials, a task normally reserved for the highest union officials.[41]

Lucy Bledsoe Gilmore, president of the Colored Women's Economic Council, often spoke to Brotherhood mass meetings in St. Louis. In 1927 she spoke to a large audience, where Pullman supervisor-informant J. A. Koupal reported her address to company officials. Two hundred and fifty people, three-fourths of whom were women, attended. "Mrs. Gilmore got up and started out in her usual florid style" which aroused "the baser element," reported Koupal. Her husband, I. C. Gilmore, had been furloughed ten months because he supported the Brotherhood. "If we never have another bite to eat we will still fight for the Brotherhood," said Gilmore. "I am like a rubber ball, the harder you throw me, the higher I bounce."[42]

The $72.50 per month wages her husband had earned was too little to be missed, according to Gilmore, but the principle angered her greatly. "In slave time we could assemble in our own cabins and confer with each other and not be bothered by their masters." According to Koupal, "she became very violent in her denunciation of the officials of the Company" almost creating "a riot right in the church." Attacked, Koupal minced no words, describing Gilmore's betrayal of, and ingratitude toward, the company: "I am sure that the Anarchistic method displayed by . . . Totten, and

Mrs. Gilmore, (who is a second Emma Goldman) will [do] more to convince the porters . . . than anything else that has been done."[43] Lucy Gilmore raised money in the same manner that African American religious leaders raised money. She challenged the assembly to give money while BSCP officers passed around the donation basket. Gilmore frequently "took a very active part in the meeting, took up a collection, calling on the men to give a dollar a piece for the good cause."

"That hoorah manner of hers seems to catch the fancy of the men and cause them to respond more liberally to the request for money," reported Pullman's informer. At another meeting, she "wanted . . . eighteen men to have five dollars ready for the collection, said she had two already paid." Gilmore then identified and scolded the Pullman spy: "'Mr. Koupal keeps hanging around and he must want to do something for us.' She addressed me personally then and said, 'Mr. Koupal, we want five dollars from you.'" Koupal did not say whether he gave her five dollars.[44]

The company retaliated against Mrs. Gilmore. As the widow of one porter and the wife of another, Supervisor A. V. Burr had allowed her to collect insurance premiums at the railroad yard. He revoked her privileges, thus denying her a livelihood. But the BSCP might have also lost its income: it seems likely that Lucy Gilmore used her yard privileges to collect union dues as well as insurance premiums from Brotherhood men and women.

Such subterfuges were not uncommon, according to Greg LeRoy, who found that in Chicago, Milton P. Webster acted as the union's public organizer, while John C. Mills, secretly a member of the BSCP, served as a porter-representative for the Employee Representation Plan. William and Josephine Puckett, a porter and maid, seemed to have split organizing duties, too, with their daughter leading the council. This pattern of organizing appears to have been repeated in other cities. To contact the Louisville, Kentucky, local, Randolph wrote Anna R. Hughes, "the source of information." Rosina Tucker, the wife of a Pullman porter, acted as BSCP's Washington, D.C., secret contact, although *The Messenger* listed Peter A. Anthony as the union's organizer. In 1930, "Mrs. Olds" worked as secretary of the St. Paul, Minnesota, division with Frank Boyd.[45] In New Orleans, Oneida M. Brown served as secretary, although whether her membership in the BSCP was based on occupation or family is unclear. It is likely that she also had another Brotherhood member organizing secretly in the city.

Tucker explained how the union's iron-clad oath of secrecy allowed women to play a central role in organizing the Brotherhood:

Public meetings [in which porters could speak] were out of the question. Any overt involvement by anyone employed by the Pullman Company was suicide. So it devolved upon the wives of the porters to do most of the organizational work.

Fortunately, most of the porters, or so it seemed, had very fine wives who were dedicated as much or more than their husbands to the formation of the union. I was asked to act as liaison between Mr. Randolph and the Washington division. Material was sent to me and I personally disseminate[d] it to the men. I kept in touch with what was going on, because it was dangerous for them to let it be known even to each other that they were members or had expressed any interest in the Brotherhood. One never knew for sure who the informers were. I was responsible for collecting dues and sending them on to New York. I visited the families of the porters and personally explained to them what the union meant and what benefits it could bring. I suppose I visited over three hundred porters in Washington, telling them the advantages of their being members, and letting them know just what progress was being made, what difficulties were being encountered, and how the other men were responding.[46]

Tucker's description of this secret organizing substantiates the pattern discovered in Chicago and that may have been used elsewhere. A BSCP man or woman served as the public representative, while another union supporter operated behind the scenes. The Brotherhood story says that "men were fired for simply being seen on the same side of the street as a Brotherhood organizer."[47] By using two organizers, the union misled Pullman Company informants.

Women such as Frances Albrier, Lucy Gilmore, and Rosina Tucker are examples of the New Negro Women who joined the Brotherhood of Sleeping Car Porters. They plunged into the organizing campaign, convincing both women and men to join the union. Their activities defied gender stereotypes, demonstrating that women had more to offer the union than their adoring support. And because they were New Negro Women, they believed they could work in mixed-sex groups and maintain their respectability. Yet many porters' wives were unwilling to challenge the traditional division of union labor, maintaining that women should provide the conventional feminine support that complemented their husbands' quest for manhood. To show their support for the BSCP, these women drew on their experience as fundraisers for charities and churches.

The Women's Economic Councils proved economically resourceful supporters of the fledgling union. When Brotherhood men recalled women's contributions, they stressed women's fundraising abilities. This was no small matter; rents had to be paid, organizers needed to travel, and propaganda must be printed. Indeed, when Ada V. Dillon and Sara Harper described the New York City Council's early activities, money was most prominent: "In the early dark days of the Brotherhood, when we did not know where our next dollar was coming from to carry on the work, the women just rolled up their sleeves and went to work to raise money to help with the organization's expenses. They had dinners at their homes Saturday nights until the Brotherhood could raise enough money to have a place of their own. Mrs. Carrie Love, then a maid on the Pennsylvania Road, and Mrs. Frank Crosswaith, served many Saturday night dinners at their homes."[48]

To raise money for the BSCP, the women sponsored public dances and parties at which they sold refreshments and homemade food. In St. Louis, Ruth Harris of the Citizens' Committee worked with the council to give a very successful dance. "Many tickets were bought by people who do not dance, just to assist and encourage Miss Harris and her co-workers in the splendid work they were doing for our group." The Chicago women "gave their first monthly entertainment on Saturday . . . at the Barrett Music School where some two hundred Brotherhood members and wives passed a very enjoyable evening."[49]

Bid whist tournaments, the card game that Pullman porters claim to have invented, and similar group card parties were also a popular form of fundraising. Working with the Brotherhood, the women helped to organize raffles, boat rides, and picnics. The union sponsored a gift book campaign; when the person sold every item in his or her book, "a beautiful and useful gift" awaited.[50]

For a short while, the women even helped pay a mortgage for the BSCP's headquarters at 238 West 136th Street. The house was apparently used for offices, as a recreation hall, and as a boarding house for foreign porters. In Oakland, Walter (Mrs. C. L.) Dellums helped operate a similiar house for foreign porters and maids; while the Los Angeles Council was asked to "assume the responsibility of paying the house rent each month." The wives of Brotherhood officers often ran the local office while their husbands were on the road.[51]

The Brotherhood story venerated the fundraising work of the Women's Economic Councils while ignoring challenges to the sexual division of union labor. This collective history even rewrote women's role in the Brotherhood. Ada Dillon is remembered as a member of the New York Women's Economic Council, even though she lost her job as a Pullman maid due to her union activities. Similarly, the BSCP's official version praises Rosina Tucker for convincing wives to support the union, but neglects her door-to-door organizing work. Grounded in the ideology of black manhood, the Brotherhood story celebrated women whose activities complemented rather than those who challenged sex segregation.

Black manhood encouraged women to guard their respectability. The councils sought respect for their trade union by sponsoring fundraising events similar to African American women's clubs. Other women sought to distinguish themselves from the traditional leadership class, causing tension as they sought to emulate the New Negro Woman. Pullman maids such as Albrier believed trade unionism was respectable. She willingly solicited her fellow workers, male and female, even though she believed herself more effective among the women. Lucy Gilmore collected insurance premiums (and perhaps union dues) in the St. Louis yards, while serving as president of the Women's Economic Council. In New York City however, Katherine Lassiter, a porter's widow, apparently confined herself to organizing women, choosing a traditional role of union wife.

Geography, Albrier and Tucker both contended, made a difference in organizing women and the risks they were willing to take for the union. In the East, wives and maids were too busy to get involved, or too scared, and although eastern women contributed money, it was women on the West Coast who joined and fought. "In the West," Tucker believed, "women had suffrage long before our southern women and were therefore more accustomed to political matters." On the other hand, Albrier thought maids in the West were not as militant as those in the East because they had less exposure to trade unionism. The conflicting perceptions result, in part, from each woman's organizing agenda. Tucker equated women's interest in the union with suffrage and politics, while Albrier described women's interests in the union as economic. Yet they agreed that one could be both a lady and a trade unionist.[52]

Brotherhood wives provided both traditional and nontraditional support to the union. The councils brought women together in common cause to fight for their homes, their families, their men, and their own respectability as wives. They organized and financed Brotherhood activities, planned mass meetings, spoke out at rallies, and then went home to serve dinner to visiting organizers. All of these interests encouraged women to join the movement for economic justice. Their efforts secured the strength of the Brotherhood of Sleeping Car Porters in its struggle for a contract.

Notes

1. William H. Harris, *Keeping the Faith: A. Philip Randolph, Milton P. Webster, and the Brotherhood of Sleeping Car Porters, 1925–37* (Urbana: University of Illinois Press, 1977, 1991), 35; CLD to Mike Patino, Feb. 18, 1937, UCB/CLD Box 6. In their 1937 contract talks the BSCP agreed it would not represent porters in Mexico. Unionization of the Canadian porters began in 1941 (see chapter 5.)

2. Handbill, n.d. in "Propaganda: Bills, Poster, Stickers, etc.," PCOP Box 267.

3. Amy Jacques Garvey coined the term New Negro Woman. See Mark D. Mathews, "'Our Women and What They Think': Amy Jacques Garvey and *The Negro World*," *Black Scholar* (May/June 1979): 5.

4. Harris, *Keeping the Faith*, 36–38; Brailsford Brazeal, *The Brotherhood of Sleeping Car Porters: Its Origin and Development* (New York: Harper and Brothers, 1946), 19–20.

5. APR to Lancaster, Aug. 3, 1927, LC/APR Box 7; Pauli Murray, *Song in a Weary Throat: An American Pilgrimage* (New York: Harper & Row, 1987), 85–86; "Activities of the Month," *Messenger* 11 (1928): 40.

6. RCT, "My Life As I Have Lived It," [ca. 1980], RCTP; MPW to CLD, Sept. 5, 1941, UCB/CLD Box 3.

7. Greg LeRoy, "The Founding Heart of A. Philip Randolph's Union: Milton P. Webster and Chicago's Pullman Porters Organize, 1925–1927," *Labor's Heritage* 3 (July 1991): 37.

8. Harris, *Keeping the Faith*, 55–56; RCT, "My Life," RCPT.

9. Maids Service Records Box, PCOP; *Black Worker* (Jan. 1938): 3; (Sept. 1938): suppl. 4; (Aug. 1936): 8.

10. Frances Mary Albrier, *Frances Mary Albrier: Determined Advocate for Racial Equality*, interview conducted by Malca Chall. Women in Politics Oral History Project (Berkeley: Regional Oral History Office, Bancroft Library, University of California, 1979), 80–81.

11. Brazeal, *The Brotherhood*, 221–23; Chicago Membership Rolls, CHS/BSCP Box 44A.

12. "Five Generations, Eldest 110, in Pullman Maid's Family" *Pullman News* 5 (August 1926): 112.

13. In looking for clues about marital status I did not use honorific titles alone, since Pullman did not always show maids this respect. When an employee, for example, requested leave to care for an injured husband, I assumed she was married. A total of 620 service cards for 573 African American maids and 47 Chinese maids were located at the Newberry Library. Cards providing the most data on African American workers were pulled, for a total of fifty-seven records. Of these, twenty-eight were from the five Chicago districts; five from Pennsylvania Terminal; five from New York districts; eleven from San Francisco and Los Angeles combined; and seven altogether from Boston, Washington, D.C., New Orleans, and Memphis.

14. Jack Santino, *Miles of Smiles, Years of Struggle: Stories of Black Pullman Porters* (Urbana: University of Illinois Press, 1989), 131–41; Harold F. Gosnell, *Negro Politicians: The Rise of Negro Politics in Chicago* (Chicago: University of Chicago Press, 1935; reprint, 1967), 204; LeRoy, "Founding Heart," 22–25. According to a fellow unionist, Oscar Soares, president of the Los Angeles BSCP Division also forbid his wife from participating in the union (see Charles Upton to CLD, Oct. 15, 1939, UCB/CLD Box 5); Dellums instructed that a reception for Randolph have "no women whatever," CLD to W. B. Holland, Nov. 6, 1939, UCB/CLD Box 30; also ALT to CLD Oct. 21, 1939, UCB/CLD Box 3; RCT, "My Life," reported similar attitudes among rank-and-file union men. On the other hand, the invitation to the Thirteenth Annual Winter Dance in New York read, "Two fellows always waiting to dance with one girl," and pictured a porter and maid holding hands, UCB/CLD Box 24.

15. Alice Kessler-Harris, "Where Are the Organized Women Workers?" *FS* 3 (1975): 92–110. Cleanliness and women's use of the union hall was frequently an issue, see for example, Charles Upton to CLD, Mar. 17, 1939, and Charles Upton to CLD, June 20, 1939, UCB/CLD Box 5; Ardella Nutall, Elma Patrick, Lucilla (?) S. Shaw, and Willa B. Parker, to CLD, Feb. 25, 1949, UCB/CLD Box 8.

16. *Black Worker* (Aug. 1936): 7.

17. Ibid.; Brazeal, *The Brotherhood*, 222. In 1939, Upton became a charter member of the Los Angeles Ladies' Auxiliary and served on the Auxiliary Executive Board. The BSCP pensioned her in 1941, CLD to APR, Feb. 2, 1942 and Feb. 24, 1942, all in LC/APR Box 61; Charles Upton to CLD, June 26, 1936, UCB/CLD Box 30; Letitia Murray to CLD, July 1, 1939, UCB/CLD Box 5.

18. Albrier, *Determined Advocate*, 80–81; membership list, Oakland BSCP Division, n.d., but ca. June 1928, UCB/CLD Box 23; Chicago Brotherhood Division Membership Book, CHS/BSCP Box 44; see also EJB, "Some of the Hardships Encountered by the BSCP in the St. Louis District in the Early Days of Organizational Program by the then Field Organizer, E. J. Bradley," Jan. 2, 1947, CHS/BSCP Box 10.

19. "Porter Growls," *Black Worker* (June 1930): 3.

20. Maids Service Records. Minyard was hired by the ACL in December 1939 as a maid from the New York district. She joined the BSCP in 1951 when the railroads became a closed shop industry. That same year, the Atlantic Coast Line suspended its maid service; Minyard joined the class grievance filed by the BSCP on the maids' behalf. See chapter 10, and Randolph's correspondence with the ACL LC/APR Box 13, and miscellaneous materials in LC/BSCP Box 80.

21. The service records of all forty-seven Chinese maids were studied. Eleven worked less than two months, while one worked for twelve years. [Name withheld] of the San Francisco district resigned January 15, 1929, after five years of service on the Overland Limited, -PCOP, Maids Box; see also "Records of Grievance of Maid Y. J. Drye," UCB/CLD, Container 12.

22. EJB, "Some of My Early Experiences Organizing Pullman Porters in St. Louis," n.d. (ca. 1949–50), LC/APR Box 10; Brotherhood Membership books, CHS/BSCP. The two "disloyal" maids were from the St. Louis and San Francisco districts, where membership records are not extant. No employment record was located for Upton.

23. William H. Harris, "Federal Intervention into Racial Discrimination: The Fair Employment Practice Committee and the West Coast Shipping Yards during World War II," *Labor History* 22 (1981): 325–47. BSCP membership in Seattle remained high even in 1933, when nationally the union had lost 85 percent of its members in five years (Brazeal, *The Brotherhood*, 221–22); see also "Minutes," Ladies Auxiliary, Seattle, Oct. 21, 1937, UCB/CLD Box 9.

24. "Souvenir Program, BSCP Silver Jubilee Anniversary and Seventh Biennial Convention," Sept. 10, 1950, RCTP; St. Clair Drake and Horace R. Cayton, *Black Metropolis: A Study of Negro Life in A Northern City,* rev. and enl. ed. (New York: Harcourt, Brace, and World, 1962), 235–36. The Chicago local had 2,496 members in 1943 (Brazeal, *The Brotherhood,* 222).

25. This group consisted of "teachers, business and professional women whose purpose is to study and discuss the important questions of the day and their relation to our particular group," "S.W.O., Monday, Dec. 21, 1925," LC/APR Box 7; see also MPW to APR, Mar. 5, 1928, and MPW to APR, Mar. 9, 1928, both in CHS/BSCP Box 3. LeRoy, "Founding Heart," 25, notes Avendorph's role in the club. However, Allan G. Spear, *Black Chicago: The Making of a Negro Ghetto, 1890–1920* (Chicago: University of Chicago Press, 1967), gives Avendorph (who died in 1912) as the founder of the *Conservator,* not the *Defender.* Spear also promotes Avendorph to Lincoln's assistant, rather than his more probable job as messenger.

26. "The Truth About the BSCP," *Messenger* 9 (1926): 37; MPW to APR, Jan. 4, 1928; Program, BSCP Labor Conference, Jan. 23, 1928; BSCP to "Friend," Feb. 2–5, 1928, all in CHS/BSCP Box 3; Program, "Towards Greater Economic Security for the Negro Worker," Mar. 21, 1932, CHS/BSCP Box 4; "Negro Women Turn Attention to Problems of Labor," *Black Worker* (Mar. 1932), in LC/APR Box 54; *Messenger* 10 (1927): 358.

27. Souvenir Program, First Annual Brotherhood Ball, Dec. 3, 1926, LC/APR Box 54; A. Sagitarrius, "Bobbed Hair Contest," *The Messenger* 10 (Jan. 1927): 29; "Activities of the Brotherhood," *Messenger* 11 (1928): 64; "Concerning the New York Citizens' Committee of One Hundred," n.d. (ca. 1927), LC/APR Box 54.

28. Kemp interviewed Randolph for the Columbia University Oral History Project, 1965; "Colored Women Dressmakers Organizing," *The Black Worker* 1 (Dec. 15, 1930): 3; *Domestic Worker* 1:1 (May 1938): 1; LC/APR Box 54; Phyllis Palmer, *Domesticity and Dirt: Housewives and Domestic Servants in the United States, 1920–1945* (Philadelphia: Temple University Press, 1989); James R. Barrett, *Work and Community in the Jungle: Chicago's Packinghouse Workers, 1894–1922* (Urbana: University of Illinois Press, 1987).

29. MPW, "Sidelights on the National Negro Labor Conference," *Black Worker* (Mar. 1930): 1; *Messenger* 8 (1926): 370; APR to MPW, Mar. 7, 1928, and Program, Second Annual Negro Labor Conference, Feb. 3–5, 1929, both in CHS/BSCP Box 3; Program, National Negro Labor Conference, Second Annual Session, Jan. 19–23, 1931, CHS/BSCP Box 4; Barrett, *Work and Community,* 85–86, 141–45, 222–23.

30. Lillian Herstein, *Report of the Proceedings of the First National Convention of the Ladies Auxiliary . . . Held at Chicago, Ill., Sept. 24 to 27, 1938,* 39–43, CHS/BSCP Box 27; "Miss Mary Anderson to Address National Negro Confab," press release, Nov. 15, 1929, UCB/CLD Box 23; MPW to Mary Anderson, Feb. 5, 1930; RCT to Mary Anderson, Nov. 19, 1936; Program, BSCP Labor Mass Meeting, Dec. 6–11, 1936, Washington, D.C.; all in -NARA/W Box 52.

31. Charlotte Anne Whitney to D. J. Jones, Oct. 22, 1927, UCB/BSCP Box 393; "Brotherhood Anniversary," *Messenger* 9 (1926): 265; Helen C. Camp, "Elizabeth Gurley Flynn," s.v., *Notable American Women.* Flynn joined the Communist Party in 1926, before Randolph broke with it over the National Negro Labor Congress. In 1948, Flynn's name (along with Irene McCoy Gaines and Charlotte Hawkins Brown) on a Hull House program to "Salute to Chicago's Women Citizens," brought Randolph's strictest "suggestion" that Ladies Auxiliary International President Halena Wilson not participate (APR to HW, Jan. 26, 1948, LC/BSCP Box 75).

32. "Citizens Committee," *Messenger* 11 (1928): 90; "Concerning the New York Citizens Committee."

33. "Concerning the New York Citizens Committee." Among those listed were Rev. Lloyd Imes, William H. Baldwin, Morris Hillquit, Mary Simkhovitch, Arthur B. Spingarn, Dr. Norman Thomas, Prof. Franz Boas, Dr. W. E. B. Du Bois, Harriot Stanton Blatch, Heywood Broun, Dr. Henry Sloane Coffin, Prof. John Dewey, Mary E. Dreier, Fannie Hurst, Freda Kirchwey, Eugene O'Neill, William L. Patterson, Anita L. Pollitzer, Rev. A. Clayton Powell Sr., Paul Robeson, Ernestine Rose, Prof. E. R. A. Seligman, Helen Phelps Stokes, Samuel Untermyer, Oswald Garrison Villard, Lillian Wald, Walter White, and Leo Wolman (Harris, *Keeping the Faith,* 35–38).

34. Deborah Gray White, "The Cost of Club Work, the Price of Black Feminism," in Nancy A. Hewitt and Suzanne Lebsock, eds., *Visible Women: New Essays on American History* (Urbana: University of Illinois Press, 1993), 247–69.

35. RCT, "My Life."

36. David Levering Lewis, *When Harlem Was in Vogue* (1979; reprint, New York: Oxford University Press, 1981), 106; Souvenir Scrapbook, Second Annual Ball, [1926], LC/APR Box 54; *Messenger* 10 (1927): 29.

37. "Souvenir Program" [1926]; *Black Worker* (July 1935): 2; APR, "The Brotherhood's Anniversary," *Messenger* 8 (1926): 265.

38. RCT, "My Life"; APR to MPW, May 29, 1927, CHS/BSCP Box 2.

39. "Cooperation Plan of the Women's Economic Council," SCH/BSCP 87–53 Box 1.

40. APR to "Brother," Oct. 25, 1929, and "Group Plan of Organization" (ca. Oct. 25, 1929), UCB/CLD Box 9; APR to MPW, Aug. 10, 1928, CHS/BSCP Box 3; for more on the plan see chapter 4.

41. RCT, "My Life"; ALT to APR Aug. 29, 1935, LC/APR Box 1; Festival of American Folklife, 1983 and 1984, recordings of retired sleeping car porters, SI/OFP; see also CLD to C. Beridon, Feb. 18, 1938, UCB/CLD Box 6: "No, the sisters cannot vote in the Brotherhood election and . . . the porters cannot participate in the Auxiliary election."

42. J. A. Koupal to A. V. Burr, memo, Sept. 19, 1927, "Propaganda," -PCOP; "St. Louis," *Messenger* 10 (1927): 335. Gilmore is not mentioned in T. D. McNeal's or E. J. Bradley's version of the division history, LC/APR Box 10, although she is mentioned in contemporary reports.

43. J. A. Koupal to A. V. Burr, Sept. 19, 1927, -PCOP.

44. Ibid.

45. LeRoy, "Founding Heart," 37; *Black Worker* (Feb. 1930): 2; (Aug. 1930): 2; (Mar. 1938): 2; RCT, "My Life"; "Souvenir Program."

46. RCT, "My Life."

47. Ibid.; EJB, "Some of My Early Experiences"; "Souvenir Program."

48. Ada Dillon and Sara Harper, "New York Local Organized Oct. 1925," LC/BSCP Box 74.

49. *Messenger* 11 (1928): 16, and 10 (Dec. 1927): 358; also MPW to APR, Mar. 28, 1927, CHS/BSCP Box 2.

50. "Women's Economic Council of Los Angeles," *Messenger* 11 (Jan. 1928): 15; Santino, *Miles of Smiles*, 2; *Messenger* 10 (Dec. 1927): 359.

51. Chicago *Defender*, Dec. 12, 1928, cited in Sterling D. Spero and Abram L. Harris, *The Black Worker: The Negro and the Labor Movement* (1931; reprint, New York: Antheneum, 1969), 457; APR to MPW, Oct. 4, 1928, CHS/BSCP Box 3; APR to CLD, Feb. 14, 1940, UCB/CLD, Box 4; MPW to APR, Mar. 15, 1928, CHS/BSCP Box 3; see also MPW to APR, Sept. 4, 1928, CHS/BSCP Box 3; APR to Robert Linton, May 12, 1932, CHS/BSCP Box 4. The rented Chicago headquarters were used for offices, overnight sleeping quarters, and a recreation hall. APR to MPW, June 26, 1928, and MPW to APR, Oct. 1, 1928, CHS/BSCP Box 3; MPW to Moore, Mar. 4, 1929, and MPW to Moore, Feb. 18, 1929, UCB/BSCP Box 393; "Souvenir Program"; CLD to W. B. Holland, Apr. 5, 1935, UCB/CLD Box 5.

52. Albrier, *Determined Advocate*, 80–81; RCT, "My Life"; Naomi DesVerney, "Speech Made at Second Anniversary in New York City" *Messenger* 11 (1928): 40.

From
Nursing Civil Rights: Gender and Race in the Army Nurse Corps,
by Charissa J. Threat (2015)

7

NURSE OR SOLDIER?

White Male Nurses and World War II
(Excerpt)

CHARISSA J. THREAT

So that the man who stands ready to meet his country's call, shall, in
his hour of need, have the best that nursing care can give.
—Edith Aynes, *American Journal of Nursing*, May 1940

Male Nurses and National Nursing Associations

In the United States, women dominated the occupation of nursing almost exclusively from its infancy. Since schools of nursing that trained men were rare and
often associated with mental hospitals, the public knew almost nothing about men
in nursing. The newly organized professional associations all but ignored male
nurses. In 1897, a group of nurses in North America formed the Nurses' Associated
Alumnae of the United States and Canada. In 1911 the U.S. nurses renamed their
organization the American Nurses' Association (ANA). As with most nurse training schools that developed following Reconstruction, professional associations
like the ANA reflected the evolution of the profession during the late nineteenth
century. Following many of the tenets touted by Florence Nightingale, the ANA
promoted the profession as properly and naturally occupied by women.[1]

Membership requirements and the organization's bylaws barred male nurses
early in the ANA's history and reflected a gendered perspective on caregiving.[2] For
example, until 1930 members were not only required to be graduates of training
schools and members of their state associations, but their training had to include
"practical experience in caring for men, women, and children."[3] This phrasing

meant that male nurses did not qualify for membership. While the curriculum for men and women in nursing schools shared a great deal in common, male nurses were excluded from training in the pediatric and obstetrics/gynecological fields. They received instead training in urology and psychiatry.[4] This meant that men had little to no contact with either women or children and led some women nurses to view the men nurses as less skilled or competent practitioners. In 1924 male nurse Kenneth T. Crummer lamented that "the man who nursed was often frowned upon as an imposter, not a nurse, but an attendant or orderly of limited training."[5] This attitude led to a belief that male nurses were unworthy of professional recognition: one observer noted that men who nursed had no "representation in [professional] associations." The failure of professional nurse associations to "recognize the same need and protection for the man nurse in our profession" was a failure of professional organizations to fulfill their obligations to support and protect all nurses, the observer concluded.[6] Even as male nurses trained at some of the same institutions as female nurses or under the same educational tenets, the inability to participate in professional associations underscored the assumption that men nurses' limited job prospects defined a role somewhere between a trained nurse and a nurse's assistant. The opposite proved true for African American female nurses. Until the second decade of the twentieth century, African American women had little problem joining the American Nurses' Association. Race played an indirect factor only in determining which female nurses had access to membership in the ANA. They could gain professional recognition in the ANA in multiple ways.

Early in the ANA's history, membership required the affiliation with alumnae, state, or local nursing associations; therefore, a number of African American female nurses could and did join the ranks of the ANA. In 1916, however, as part of the reorganization of the ANA, the association changed its membership rules to stipulate that members must hold membership in their state associations. This barred most African American women from the organization, especially those who lived and worked in states that refused them membership in the nurse associations.[7] In contrast, male nurses, who would otherwise qualify for membership because of their connection to state associations, had little recourse to challenge bylaw requirements that excluded men from the ANA. Male nurses had no representatives among the ANA leadership; nurse training was firmly set against male nurse education in obstetrics or gynecology, while the 1916 changes to the ANA's bylaws defined membership requirements through training in these subjects and membership in state nursing associations. Unwittingly or not, the American Nurses' Association relied on both gendered and racialized conventions in determining whom it recognized as nurses in the first several decades of the twentieth century. As a result, until the ANA again amended its bylaws, the professional organization excluded a sizable majority of African American female nurses and all male nurses.[8]

The *American Journal of Nursing* deliberated on the position of men nurses in the profession several times in the years before the American Nurses' Association changed its bylaws to include them. As the voice of national nursing news—particularly two of the three national nursing organizations and dozens of state nursing associations—the *American Journal of Nursing* was, arguably, the most important forum for disseminating information to and about professional and student nurses.[9] Here, male nurses and their supporters found a platform from which to argue for professional recognition and to call attention to their perception of mistreatment by the wider profession. In a 1924 letter to the editor, a nurse identified only as M.H.R. remarked, "One of [the] wrongs still waiting our attention and action concerns the male nurses of our profession and the recognition and place to which they have a *right* in our nursing world and with the public."[10] The question of equal rights was not far from the minds of many American citizens in 1924, especially women. Only a year before, Alice Paul and the National Women's Party introduced the first Equal Rights Amendment (ERA) to Congress. Its central premise was equality of rights regardless of sex. Published in the same volume as M.H.R.'s letter, prominent nurse leader Lavinia L. Dock detailed her support of the ERA; citing its importance to the labor industry, she suggested that the ERA would guarantee "equal rights and opportunities for adult men and women without restriction or exclusion based on sex alone."[11] Dock's emphasis on the idea of equal rights in her letter to the editor focused not only on the inequities faced by women in the labor market—one for which she blamed custom and common law—but argued also that this inequity harmed both men and women and future labor conditions. Yet she did not refer to the unequal conditions faced by men in her own profession, which was, by custom and common practice, deemed the protected domain of women. M.H.R.'s emphatic demand that the profession "right this wrong," then, alludes to broader implications of disregarding male nurses in professional associations. While female nurses could and did understand the importance of equal rights among the sexes, especially for the economic future of the nursing occupation, they often ignored or missed how they enabled sex discrimination and the continued gendering of the profession. By perpetuating bias against male nurses, and by failing to recognize trained male nurses as their professional equals, the ANA and other national nursing associations failed in their obligations to promote and support professional nursing on behalf of all nurses.[12]

Proposed amendments to the bylaws of the ANA failed throughout the 1920s, but discussions about male nurses continued during the period.[13] In 1928, for example, Kenneth Crummer pointed out that male nurse education and the job opportunities for graduate male nurses had expanded faster in the previous ten years than at any point since the turn of the century.[14] Still, it was not until the late spring of 1930 that a proposed amendment to the membership bylaws came to a vote. Members voted at the biennial convention in Milwaukee to approve the following addition to its membership requirements: "The training for male nurses must include practical experience in caring for men, together with theoretical and practical instruction in medical, surgical and urological nursing."[15] It is important to note that this proposal was only an addition to existing membership requirements; it did not necessarily reflect an acceptance of equality between male and female nurses, but it did recognize that male nurses needed access to professional representation. Tacked on to existing membership language, it removed the constraints keeping male nurses from the organization but did not attempt to write a single inclusive membership bylaw. In the published news and highlights from the 1930 biennial convention, there was no indication that this amounted to a significant change for the organization. Instead, the proceedings' highlights contained copious notes about the fundraising activities of the association and its chapters. Male nurses were included quietly and without fanfare. The understated admission of male nurses reveals an important reality for men. Admission did little to change the fact that they were still very restricted in the opportunities to practice in the field, and their future was still uncertain when it came to professional treatment.

Although national professional membership became available to male nurses in 1930, their modest numbers did little to help alleviate the continued inequity they faced within nursing organizations and the vocation. According to census accounts in 1930, 5,452 men reported "trained nurse" as their occupation.[16] Until their addition to the ANA, they lacked any national unifying male body to fight and organize on their behalf. Instead, it was up to active male nurses in state nursing associations and nursing schools to lead the fight.[17] According to one male nurse activist, the "effort and achievement on the part of men and of those responsible for their leadership" was the only way to assure the "changing attitude of women in the nursing profession towards male nurses."[18] Still, whatever hopes male nurses had about greater opportunities because of their acceptance into such a large national nursing organization proved elusive. Unless the entire nursing profession altered its attitude and perceptions, little would change for men in nursing.

Male nurses were by no means the silent minority. They actively discussed and pursued job opportunities and recognition from a variety of nursing associations, educational institutions, and the United States government. In the mid-1930s, the *American Journal of Nursing* published a series of articles that examined the vocational and educational opportunities for male nurses. Written by nurses and doctors alike, the articles concluded that improvements in nursing education and work toward professionalization increased the number of men in the profession. Dr. J. Frederick Painton, for example, noted that "with the gradual progress of nursing from very humble beginnings to its present place among professions ... men, real men, are invading women's own profession and making good."[19] Yet the job opportunities or even advanced educational opportunities for male nurses remained few. Registered nurses Frederick Jones and Frances Witte complained of the scarcity of jobs for men nurses. This was the result of limited opportunities for advancement. "The time is at hand when the male student and graduate must have the same educational advantages as the young women, if we are to assure the community of safe and intelligent nursing," Witte writes.[20] Male nurse educational opportunities then were directly linked to vocational opportunities and recognition. Even in positions wherein male nurses were welcomed—in industrial nursing or mental hospitals—graduate trained male nurses faced competition from graduate female nurses with advanced training and untrained male nurses. Improving male nurse recognition and access to advanced or inclusive training remained the key to equality among the sexes in nursing.

LeRoy Craig, a graduate of the McLean Hospital School of Nursing for Men in Waverly, Massachusetts, became a leading advocate and activist for men in the nursing profession. In 1914 he accepted the position of directing the Pennsylvania Hospital School of Nursing for Men. Pennsylvania Hospital had a long tradition of training nurses; its school of nursing for women opened in 1875 and quickly became an innovator in the field. Its new school for men, with Craig at its helm, took a radical new approach to training male nurses. Unlike other schools of nursing that trained men, it consisted entirely of men. Its director, superintendents, instructors, and student body were all men. It was its "own organization, [had] a separate [governing] policy, its own ideals, and traditions." It was distinct from the School of Nursing for women.[21] This was unusual because male nurse training and education were traditionally conducted under female leadership. Even at schools that trained only men, women often served in leadership and oversight roles.

Men at the Pennsylvania Hospital School received training not only in psychiatric nursing but also as general nurses with genitourinary specialties. The idea was to improve the overall training of male nurses, thus producing more competent, well-rounded nurses who, as registered nurses, Frances Witte later suggested, would, "deepen [male nurses'] sense of social responsibility."[22] Furthermore, the education of male nurses by male nurses was groundbreaking. One male nurse commented that it was an "idea" from which "come ideals." It would produce a quality of men "who were capable and ready to serve where a woman, for various reasons, cannot." In short, several male nurse leaders believed that the right training and education of male nurses improved the condition and position of male nurses in civilian society and would extend to male nurses greater opportunities in industry and the military.[23] This training also demonstrated that men were capable enough to perform as professional nurses.

Following their acceptance in the ANA, Craig, along with male and female nurse activists, urged other nursing organizations to pursue similar recognition. They saw the American Red Cross as an obvious place to push for broader acceptance and employment of male nurses. The American Nurses' Association and American Red Cross had a long cooperative relationship; the ANA even worked with the Red Cross to create the Red Cross Nursing Service, the registry of nurses available for emergencies and service in the armed forces nurse corps. This established the ANA and Red Cross, along with the National League of Nursing Education (NLNE) and National Organization of Public Health Nursing (NOPHN), as the most prominent nursing groups directing nursing policies and the public's perception of nurse care in the United States.[24] In 1934 male nurse supporters asked the board of directors of the ANA to appeal to the National Committee on Red Cross Nursing Service to change its policy excluding men nurses from the service.[25] The Red Cross Nursing Service had not only served as the staffing organization for Army and Navy Nurse Corps since before World War I, but it had also provided a number of community health classes focused especially on the health and well-being of women and children.[26] The committee returned the following reply: "Inasmuch as the Red Cross Nursing Service is the reserve of the Army and Navy Nurse Corps which are composed of woman nurses and for which male nurses would not be accepted, no change be made in the present requirement . . . Furthermore . . . other types of Red Cross Nursing Services . . . being restrictive in nature, are not able to utilize other than woman nurses."[27] The Red Cross's response appeared to be practical for the kinds of services they provided. However, their decision overlooked how much their services might expand with the inclusion of men. The public health nursing aspect, for example, could expand to include male nurses for long-term, male-focused healthcare.

Given its primary focus on staffing the Army and Navy Nurse Corps, the Red Cross could do little to change its decision regarding male nurses. However, the organization's comments reflected not only the stereotype but also the public conviction that nursing, especially general nursing, was no place for men. More troubling and disappointing about the response of the Red Cross was the continuing insistence that male nurses, regardless of training or experience, should remain in very limited areas and jobs within the field of nursing. This included jobs in mental and psychiatric hospitals and jobs as private-duty nurses or in industrial nursing. Teaching courses in the care of the sick or working as public health nurses under the auspices of the Red Cross remained closed to men nurses. After men successfully gained membership in the American Nurses' Association, one can assume that the failure to change the policy of the Red Cross was a setback for those campaigning for full and fair recognition as nurses.

Nurses who aspired to service within the Army or Navy Nurse Corps first had to enroll in the Red Cross Nursing Service. The refusal of the Red Cross to change its policy with regard to male nurses in 1935 left little room for men to maneuver for a place within either nurse corps. Nevertheless, male nurses continued to appeal for change in the policies of the Red Cross concerning the employment of men. Nor did they stop applying pressure to the American Nurses' Association to take a more forceful role in supporting men in nursing. As U.S. entry into World War II became more likely in the closing years of the 1930s, male nurses, similar to African American female nurses, became another group that nursing leaders turned to in their attempt to coordinate nursing resources. This in turn provided men nurses the opportunity to draw attention to their cause. Near the end of 1939, the Red Cross reconsidered its policy concerning men and agreed to allow male nurses to register with the Red Cross Nursing Service. Registration with the service, however, was not meant to enroll men nurses for service in the Army or Navy Nurse Corps. It would organize "properly qualified male nurses, who if needed by the Army or Navy will serve . . . as technologists for service auxiliary to the Army and Navy Nurse Corps." These men, according to the announcement, would in the "event of national emergency . . . be eligible for enrollment in the Army as non-commissioned officers." While the requirements for male and female nurses wishing to apply to the nursing service were similar, the *American Journal of Nursing* reminded readers that federal law limited the job opportunities—at least in the military—for men nurses.[28] However, the Red Cross also continued to ignore male nurses for the other services it provided to local communities.

A 1940 recruitment appeal for nurses demonstrated that the Red Cross had not changed its opinion that nursing and women were synonymous. The informational insert in the *American Journal of Nursing* made no mention of male nurses; instead, it used feminine pronouns to describe nurses and to recruit women. This strengthened the argument of male nurses that as long as "nurse" remained defined as "she," men would occupy an inferior status to female nurses.[29] The continued emphasis on nursing as the natural function of women pointed to a larger societal understanding that caregiving was a biological function of women that translated to professional nursing as the apparent domain of women.[30] This recruitment plan, coupled with the Red Cross's limited acceptance of male nurses, suggests that allowing male nurses to register with the Red Cross Nursing Service was an organizational tactic used to help the Red Cross figure out how many male nurses were available for service in the event of an emergency. Although the Red Cross noted in April 1940 that changes to the nursing service had been underway for more than a year, and the threat of war had no basis in the decision, within months the major national nursing organizations in the United States organized the Nursing Council for National Defense with the purpose of planning the place of nurses in the nation's defense.[31]

Preparation for war allowed men in the American Nurses' Association to also take a stronger stance on pushing for male nurse recognition. This was in no small part due to the campaigning of male nurses and to the strong participation of men in their state nurses' associations. In the late 1930s, for example, district branches of the New York State Nurses' Association began forming Men Nurses' Committees to increase membership and the professional activities of male nurses throughout the state. They were able to sponsor men nurse sessions at state nursing conventions and eventually sessions and even a dinner at the American Nurses' Association's biennial convention. These statewide activities translated into increased publicity for male nurses at the national nursing level. As a result, the ANA created the Men Nurses' Section at their 1940 biennial convention in Philadelphia.[32] The section's job was to address the needs and issues that specifically affected male nurses. This included encouraging a better public understanding and acceptance of men in nursing and pushing for the use and recognition of male nurses within the Nurse Corps of the Armed Forces.[33] Beyond amending their membership requirements in 1930 and petitioning the Red Cross in 1935 on behalf of male nurses, this was the first major recognition by the ANA that the difficulties faced by male nurses needed special attention from the organization.[34]

One of the section's first duties with regard to expanding opportunities for male nurses was to publicize the American Red Cross's new program to enroll male nurses. In his 1940 article "Opportunities for Men Nurses," LeRoy Craig acknowledged that the Red Cross Nursing Service offered one possibility for men wishing to nurse with the federal government.[35] While not admission to the armed forces' nurse corps, Craig and other nurses noted that the status of male nurses in 1940 was much better than it had been in the previous two decades. In short, there was, at the very least, a recognition by the military and Red Cross that male nurses were vital to healthcare in the United States. However, did this signify a broadening attitude on the work and place of male graduate nurses, or was it a result of circumstance? Craig hoped that "in justice to men nurses they [male nurses] . . . be assured of duties, rank, and pay comparable to that granted other professional individuals." Would male nurses perceive serving as "medical technician or technologist" an acceptable alternative for service in the Army and Navy Nurse Corps?[36]

Male Nurses and the Nation's Defense

Several alumni and state nursing associations initially approved of the Red Cross Nursing Service Program. At the very minimum it was an opportunity for men nurses to gain some recognition in the military. Even this small concession was denied to a small group of nurses who sought recognition while serving in France during World War I.[37] Individually, however, most men dismissed the decision by the Red Cross to enroll male nurses for service as medical technicians; they viewed the program as an unsatisfactory resolution to the question of military service for men nurses. Sandy F. Mannino, for example, questioned the distinction in the acceptance of male nurses only as medical technicians when men and women received similar training, when men had membership in all the national nursing organizations, and when they were eligible for registration in every state.[38] Registered nurse Nathaniel Wooding echoed the same sentiment in a letter to the surgeon general's office: "Forty-seven schools of nursing [admit] men students" and "men candidates [met] the same qualifications as do women."[39] Over the course of six months following the initiation of the Nursing Service Program, male nurses struggled to convince the War Department, nursing leaders, and President Roosevelt that the use of male nurses as enlisted men and noncommissioned officers amounted not only to discrimination against men but also defeated the purpose of the nurse corps.[40] The basic law of the ANC, Edward F. Perreault wrote to the president, was an "antiquated law" that should be "repealed, and in its place get one which gives men and women nurses equal opportunity in the military service."[41] Whether in peace or wartime, these men argued, male nurses should be serving their country as nurses with the same privileges provided female nurses, not fighting to attain the right to do so.

In the fall of 1940, Congress passed and the president signed into law the first peacetime draft in United States history. The Selective Service Act mandated that every able-bodied man between the ages of twenty-one and thirty-five register for service in the U.S. military.[42] As part of their draft registration, men described their training and work capabilities in order to give the War Department an idea about how their skills would most benefit the military. The Red Cross informed male nurses that by registering with the Red Cross Nursing Service first, they would ensure that their extensive experience and training placed them into positions within the Medical Department. In a memo from the office of the surgeon general, the Army Medical Department listed the occupational specialties and accompanying serial numbers it recommended be assigned to the department when men were classified under the draft. This memo further noted that the Red Cross maintained a list of men identified under the occupation of medical technician (male nurse) and serial number 123. As a result, men who did not register with the Red Cross Nursing Service risked assignment outside the medical department in jobs that may have little to do with their nurse training. Furthermore, the group advised men that registering with the nursing service brought additional benefits. This included promotion to technical sergeant, if there were vacancies, and the eventual possibility of Officers' Candidate School after four months of training and service.[43]

This plan for the promotion of male nurses, however, proved problematic for several reasons. First, while many nursing leaders believed that the Red Cross and

War Department's plan for male nurses was the first step to eventual acceptance of men into the Army Nurse Corps, not all men registered with the Red Cross. Registration with the Red Cross, although encouraged, was voluntary, and many men were suspicious that the program offered men little in the way of equality with female nurses. In fact, some male nurses refused to register as a means of protest. In a letter to Senator Henry C. Lodge, Mitchell Blake angrily noted, "I have been criticized ... for not joining the Red Cross Service [but will not do so until] those of us who wished to devote our services can do so without reservation—and without doing the work of a hospital orderly."[44] Blake's terse remarks reveal the general sense of disgust that many male nurses felt at the blatant disregard for their training. Furthermore, in the summer before the bombing of Pearl Harbor, the Nursing Service counted only twenty-five men among their new enrollments.[45] Many male nurses believed that by not registering with the Red Cross Nursing Service, they had more control over where they would end up if drafted. Second, while male nurses wanted guarantees to advancement and possibly officer's status, the War Department stated that promotion would occur only if vacancies existed in particular ranks. This meant that registering with the Red Cross Nursing Service was no guarantee of better standing in the Army Medical Department or even assignment within it. Finally, because there was no guarantee of promotion for male nurses with nursing degrees or training, in some cases men with limited training as medics received promotion before men with civilian nursing degrees. If the War Department was so concerned with the best healthcare for their soldiers, why not allow men to join the ANC or, at the very least, as some suggested, form a sub-branch of the nurse corps focused on the specialties of male nurses? As a matter of fact, LeRoy Craig suggested the formation of a "reserve group of male nurses with psychiatric training with the rank of second lieutenant," the same rank initially given to female nurses. He believed that such a group would be able to address the psychological needs of soldiers and would provide some compensation to male nurses restricted from the nurse corps. However, he received little in the way of support from the surgeon general for his suggestion.[46]

The War Department and surgeon general's office responded to these suggestions by focusing on the impracticality of employing male nurses, an argument also used to limit African American female nurse participation. Replying to the American Nurses' Association's push to revoke the law that designated the ANC as a female institution and to include male nurses, Brigadier General Albert G. Love noted:

> I regret that this office cannot concur in your opinion. It would be impracticable to employ male nurses in time of peace since such employment could complicate unnecessarily the administrative problems. We feel that we have provided a satis-

factory and dignified position for such male nurses as may be employed during the military emergency. In addition, we feel sure that the Secretary of War would not approve the legislation suggested by you.[47]

The administrative issues to which Love and others referred centered on the impracticality of building separate housing and mess facilities and on the presumption that men nurses were soldiers first and nurses second.[48] Focusing on the "problems" involved in reversing the forty-year-old law mandating that only females work in the Army Nurse Corps, the surgeon general's office dismissed the subject of discrimination, which was in the forefront of the minds of many male nurses. Further, Love's assertion that the secretary of war would not approve of any changes to the current law and arrangement of the nurse corps suggests a genuine lack of support for any change. Love implied that to pursue such a course was unpatriotic and also in opposition to the war effort. Men and women each had a role, clearly delineated by sex; frontline activities were the responsibilities of men, while support and caregiving were the responsibilities of women.

This perspective on gender difference in the context of wartime recruitment raised uncomfortable questions about the responsibilities and obligations of male nurses in war mobilization before and after the bombing of Pearl Harbor in December 1941. Were they nurses or soldiers? Where did male nurses serve their country best, as civilians or in the military? According to Richard Musser, graduate male nurses best served their country doing their job for American soldiers. They, Musser argued, "expect to assume their part of the country's defense with the rest of the men ... [but] their proper place in national defense is denied them."[49] This duty remained out of their reach because nursing—as the Red Cross recruitment campaign revealed—remained a female occupation. "Male" and "nurse" did not belong together. Overcoming this dichotomy was an ongoing struggle for male nurses, one that a particular nurse training school attempted to address two decades before the war by advertising their school as an institution that produced "men who think straight and see straight, who are capable and ready to serve where women, for various reasons, cannot."[50] The undertone in comments such as this stressed the difficulties male nurses faced in their chosen profession, especially during wartime. Already facing unfair treatment because of their sex, they had to persuade the American public of the importance, legitimacy and, to a large degree, the "manliness" of men nurses. While men nurses and their supporters could agree that assigning eligible men to military duty outside the nurse corps was a poor use of the workforce, some argued that the men nurses should be recruited instead to civilian hospitals to supplement the shortage of female nurses entering military service.

The Men Nurses' Section of the American Nurses' Association pushed this belief further by suggesting that the experience and training of male nurses should classify them as "necessary men" in war labor plans. Necessary men were those designated by the War Department as exempt from Selective Service because of the nature of their job. A man qualified for the classification if he met one of the following conditions: "he cannot be replaced satisfactorily because of a shortage of persons with his qualifications or skill in such an activity," or "his removal would cause a material loss of effectiveness in such activity." Furthermore, a necessary man was one in "any industry, business, employment, agricultural pursuit, governmental service, or . . . in training or preparation therefore, the maintenance of which is essential to the national health, safety, or interest in the sense that a serious interruption or delay in such activity is likely to impede the National Defense Program." According to nursing leaders, based on the War Department's own criteria, male nurses were "necessary men." The removal of male nurses from nursing schools by drafting them could have detrimental consequences for the future of nursing and impeded the ability of male nurses to do their jobs, thereby affecting national health.[51] If the military did not want them in the nurse corps, they were certainly essential in civilian hospitals. The surgeon general's office did not, however, agree with this assessment and responded that nothing in the Selective Service Act defined "male nurses as an occupational group."[52]

The National Nursing Council for War Service (NNCWS) bolstered the claim that men nurses could provide a valuable service to civilian life if the War Department had no intention of employing them as nurses.[53] Male nurses could be recruited, the council argued, to serve in civilian hospitals to replace the female nurses who joined the military or were recruited to care for American soldiers once they returned to the United States. The suggestion that men nurses support the war effort in this way was reminiscent of the strategy used to recruit women into the military and war industries.[54] While the public remained uncomfortable with and perhaps even suspicious of male nurses, the National Nursing Council for War Service argued that their labor was critical to the health of the civilian population and to the continuation of nursing programs.[55] Regardless of the NNCWS's comments, many men nurses understood that until the War Department changed its opinion on the use of them within the ANC, they could achieve no hope of parity in their civilian lives or the nursing profession. This understanding placed white male nurses in an unusual position; they found that their sex hindered their success in nursing even while they tried to serve their county. In this way, white male nurses, very much like African American female nurses—albeit for different reasons—saw military service as the first step in resolving claims of discrimination.

Very little changed for male nurses in the first two-and-a-half years of the war; with few exceptions, public discourse about nursing remained focused on the recruitment of women while the military judiciously avoided appeals from male nurses. Male nurse advocates, who included among their ranks the American

Nurses' Association and the American Medical Association, were baffled about how to change the War Department's, surgeon general's, and Congress's opinion of trained male nurses.[56] Frustrated, male nurse R. A. Chiniok wrote: "I hope somebody can show the Washington legislators whereby the folly of the forty year law banning us out of the rights in Army Nursing."[57] The War Department, however, faithfully replied to all queries that during wartime male nurses "are not normally used by the Medical Department in times of peace," but they are used in accordance with provisions of the Selective Service Act: as medical technicians and orderlies.[58] Even without the provisions of the Selective Service Act to support their position, the War Department and surgeon general had a recent and ongoing tradition by which to set the example concerning the successful employment of male nurses in the U.S. military.

The U.S. Navy's special need for shipboard medical service led it down a path that produced male medical personnel with pharmaceutical, nursing, and general medical capabilities. In 1917 the U.S. Navy established the Pharmacist's Mate School. Here, men received instruction in a variety of subjects, including nursing and general healthcare, in preparation for duty with the hospital corps. As part of the hospital corps, pharmacist mates helped maintain the health of naval personnel and aided in the sick and disabled. In contrast to the women of the Navy Nurse Corps, however, these men also performed all manner of scientific work, became public health officers, served as independent medical officers on ships, drilled and instructed recruits, and assisted in clerical work. In other words, beyond their medical education, the pharmacist's mates received training in all aspects of military life. The pharmacist's mate was the epitome of the masculine nurse, one that removed almost all of the feminine traits of caregiving. By 1927 the Pharmacist's Mate School claimed for itself the title of "largest school for male nurses in the world." The fact that two states, California and Virginia, allowed graduates of the school to register as nurses supported this claim. The War Department and surgeon general then could and did use the U.S. Navy pharmacist's mate as an example on how to use men nurses in the current conflict in both the hospital corps and the army medical corps and avoid the charge of work discrimination. In doing so, however, they disregarded two points of contention among trained professional nurses: their education and their nursing experience before entering military service.[59] Moreover, the War Department's acceptance of female nurses as officers in the nurse corps and male nurses as privates in the Medical Department further provoked a sense of discrimination and lack of fair play among men nurses. It was made glaringly obvious to male nurses that neither their experience nor their education could ever overcome the fact that they were not women and therefore had no place in the ANC.

Col. Florence A. Blanchfield, chief of the Army Nurse Corps in 1943, argued that the corps would not be a satisfactory place for men within the military. "Our standing is not as good and in some respects not as secure," she wrote John Welch of the New York State Nurses' Association. Female nurse officers only carried a rank "relative" to the regular Army, without many of the same benefits as commissioned officers.[60] Historically, the matter of rank plagued the nurses' place in the military. When the ANC was founded in 1901 as part of the Army Reorganization Act, the act made no reference to either the rank or status of nurses. At the turn of the century, Congress and army leadership were reluctant to assign official rank or status to women in the military, even if they were nurses. Therefore, the only stipulations that defined the job and organization of the ANC were that the nurse corps would consist of a "superintendent, chief nurses, nurses, and reserve nurses." The surgeon general approved the appointment of the nurses to serve for three years. From the beginning, this vague definition presented problems for the ANC, especially the question of rank. Lack of clearly defined status and rank with the U.S. Army exposed nurses to abuse and unfair treatment not only from the Army Medical Department but also from the military establishment as a whole. As a result, by the end of World War I the army could no longer ignore the question of rank.[61]

Nurses and their supporters demanded equality in the form of official recognition in the U.S. Army. In June 1920 Congress reluctantly agreed, and President Wilson signed a bill that provided army nurses with "relative rank," or rank comparable to other officers. But even this came with limitations; the secretary of war defined exactly what relative rank meant for army nurses. Army nurses would be accorded the same respect and protection as other commissioned officers, including the right to wear the insignia of their grade and the privilege of salute, but would be denied the right to command, for example.[62] By 1943 the only change to this status was a 1942 bill that finally gave nurses pay commensurate with that of other commissioned officers. Even then, nurses were not entitled to be spoken to by rank but were supposed to be addressed as "nurse," according to Blanchfield. Therefore, incorporating male nurses into the ANC would have provided men with an empty title and only a temporary place in the military.[63] The underlying implication from this situation was that male nurses would want the same benefits granted to men in other positions in the military. The desired status would include the security of access to benefits to support their families, retirement, and career advancement. These discussions reveal how men's service alongside women in a female-gendered occupation could potentially create unacceptable inequalities between men and women in the nurse corps and among men in other military services. "No doubt men with relative rank would be more conscious of this difference in status than women are," Blanchfield surmised. In order to avoid this uncomfortable situation, the Medical Department assured male nurses that it kept them out of the nurse corps and assigned them to positions with the regular army in the "best interest of registered male nurses."[64]

A long tradition of gender segregation in nursing complicated the integration of men. Interestingly, the Medical Department and Colonel Blanchfield's assertion that male nurses needed protection from unequal treatment in the ANC highlights the hypocrisy of the treatment of female nurse officers who received rank comparable only to commissioned male officers. In effect, the army denied women the full benefits and security of military service; accepting male nurses into the ANC would require that the army acknowledge this discrepancy and thereby be forced, perhaps, to consider equal treatment for women. By focusing on the reasons that male nurses should be denied entry into the ANC, army representatives shifted the spotlight away from gender inequality, but this did not diminish male nurses' hopes that the need for nurses would supersede gender discrimination.

The National Nursing Council for War Service (NNCWS) demonstrated the difficult nature of the male nurse campaign for ANC membership. African American female nurses secured an advantage when the NNCWS made their integration campaign a priority after mid-1943. Seeing African American women as a logical, but also severely underused, source of nursing power, the NNCWS took an active role in ending discriminatory quotas and treatment of black nurses. After researching the treatment of black nurses the year before, in early 1945 the NNCWS published its report, which revealed the damage done to the war effort and to the health and safety of American soldiers by neglecting to use African American female nurses more fully within the nurse corps.[65] The report claimed that a more inclusive use of eight thousand available African American female nurses would alleviate any shortage of nurses. Yet, not surprisingly, the report ignored the use of male nurses to meet nursing needs. This oversight reflected the differences in support and strategies that white male nurses and African American female nurses used in their integration campaigns. African American female nurses, with the help of the NNCWS, relied not only on the rhetoric of women's natural affinity to nursing to make their case, but they also looked to a well-organized advocacy group in the National Association of Colored Graduate Nurses that had long fostered connections to civil rights groups, politicians, and philanthropists. The report concluded that increasing the number of African American nurses would "demonstrate that as American men, regardless of race, creed, or color are fighting for democracy, American women are being given the opportunity, equally without discrimination, to care for them when ill or wounded."[66] Male nurses, in contrast, had only the Men Nurses' Sections in their State Nursing Associations, the newly formed

Men Nurses' Section of the ANA, a few select politicians, individual nurses, and the lingering hope that legislation would change their predicament.

The Men Nurses' Section of the American Nurses' Association acted to publicize and campaign on behalf of male nurses. In December 1943, the section published an article in the *American Journal of Nursing*, which revealed that at least 320 graduate male nurses were serving with the armed forces in 1943 and another two thousand were available for service. While "a large proportion of the men nurses . . . [could have been] assigned to services where their nursing experience [could] be used," they were not, and therefore the "nursing and medical service has lost these men nurses who could have made a valuable contribution." Placing this article alongside the NNCWS's report, the failure to mention male nurses in the report is significant for two reasons. First, the number of male nurses in the armed forces was just ten less than the number of African American female nurses serving in the nurse corps, and yet the council seemingly ignored that the recruitment of men into the ANC could help reduce the nursing shortages that they argued harmed American soldiers. Second, the NNCWS's report failed to highlight that nearly 50 percent of the nursing shortage—based on the number of African American female and white male nurses available—would disappear with the use of both these groups. The goal of the Men's Section article was to "secure as much information as possible . . . [which] will be extremely useful when and if legislation is introduced"; however, the NNCWS's failure to use this information in its report just a year after the information on male nurses was published is telling. The NNCWS and its report portrayed nursing as a quintessentially female profession, even in the face of nursing shortages.[67]

[. . .]

Shifting attitudes regarding race and gender relations marked World War II even while many Americans continued to embrace traditional values. While the exigencies of war refashioned women's duties in the workforce, albeit temporarily in some cases, they did not alter all responsibilities and obligations gendered as male or female. The result was that although the possibility of drafting female nurses helped to end race restrictions in the ANC, but not race discrimination, it also perpetuated discrimination against male nurses in both the military and civilian society. For male nurses, gender became the important factor in determining who was best suited to provide care to America's fighting men. Frances Bolton's response to a male nurse underscored the general belief that the admission of male nurses to the ANC would overturn the gender norms of the profession: "The Army Nurse Corps was created as a 'female' Corps, and there is very strong feelings that it would be exceedingly unfortunate to change that fundamental ruling, not because men can't nurse well and are not really desperately needed in some of the specialties, but rather because men as a whole do better with women nurses than men."[68] Repeatedly, when faced with questions about male nurses, the War Department reiterated traditional beliefs about gender roles—even when faced with desperate nursing shortages.

Nevertheless, the debates about men nurses and the gender restrictions within the Army Nurse Corps did not fade away. Nursing shortages persisted and continued to be a problem for the nurse corps and for civilian society. They remained tied to a larger discussion about discrimination and equality in the postwar period. Cold War fears and a growing civil rights campaign forced the armed forces to refashion its fighting force; it addressed not only race, but also gender roles in its attempt to meet the challenges it faced in its fight to defend democracy. While the question about whether soldiers worried about the race or sex of the nurse providing care was provocative, it did not change the fact that, in the end, the sex of the nurse did matter to some people. Both the military and civilian society at large ultimately supported the idea that nursing was the responsibility of women, not men. Sex, rather than race, proved to be the overriding determinant of who could nurse during World War II.

Notes

1. The first organization dedicated to nursing education was the American Society of Superintendents of Training Schools for Nurses, founded in 1893; in 1912, they were renamed the National League for Nursing Education. This was one of three national nursing organizations that dominated the profession in the first half of the twentieth century. The other two organizations were the American Nurses' Association and the National Organization for Public Health Nursing, founded in 1912. ANA membership requirements originally focused on alumnae associations, not individual nurses. When the group changed its name in 1910, they became open to individual membership, but only by those who belonged to alumnae associations. Susan M. Reverby, *Ordered to Care: The Dilemma of American Nursing, 1850–1945* (Cambridge University Press, 1987), 123–24.

2. No direct discussion about male nurses appears to have taken place regarding the ANA's bylaws; however, the qualifications for membership limited the inclusion of male nurses.

3. "Amendments to the By-Laws," *American Journal of Nursing* 30, no. 4 (April 1930): 508.

4. According to Bruce Mericle, even at the same nursing school, women and men received different instruction at the end of the nineteenth century. This meant the women were kept from receiving instruction in urology in the same way men were kept from obstetrics. However, by all accounts, because women received more general nurse training, they probably had more contact with patients in these areas than male nurses did with obstetrics. The Mills School of Nursing for Men did not offer a course in obstetrics until 1957. Mericle, "Male as Psychiatric Nurse," *Journal of Psychosocial Nursing* 21, no. 11 (1983), 30–31; and Chad E. O'Lynn and Russell E. Tranbarger, eds., *Men in Nursing: History, Challenges, and Opportunity* (New York: Springer, 2007), 44–46.

5. Kenneth T. Crummer, "A School of Nursing for Men," *American Journal of Nursing* 24, no. 6 (March 1924): 459.

6. M.H.R., "Male Nurses in our Profession," *American Journal of Nursing* 24, no. 10 (July 1924): 837.

7. "Proceedings from the Nineteenth Annual Convention of the American Nurses' Association," *American Journal of Nursing* 16, no. 9 (June 1916): 787–957; and American Nurses' Association, "Basic Historical Review," American Nurses' Association, available at http://nursingworld.org/FunctionalMenuCategories/AboutANA/History/BasicHistoricalReview.pdf (accessed on August 20, 2014); and O'Lynn and Tranbarger, *Men in Nursing*, 28–29.

8. As late as 1940, the ANA continued to deliberate their membership requirements concerning African American nurses. At that time, the only black nurse members who did not belong to their state associations were alumnae members of the Freedman's Hospital in Washington, D.C., because the association was a member of the ANA before the 1916 bylaw changes. To compensate for this problem, the National League of Nursing Education changed its membership laws in 1940 to accept black nurses who belonged to the National Association of Colored Graduate Nurses. "The Philadelphia Biennial," *American Journal of Nursing* 40, no. 6 (June 1940): 677 and 684.

9. For most of its existence, the *American Journal of Nursing* was the organ for the American Nurses' Association, the National League of Nursing Education, and the majority of state nursing associations.

10. Emphasis added. M.H.R., "Male Nurses," 837.

11. Lavinia L. Dock, "Equal Rights," *American Journal of Nursing* 24, no. 10 (July 1924): 843.

12. Kenneth T. Crummer, "Male Nurses: A Survey of the Present-Day Situation of Graduate Male Nurses," *American Journal of Nursing* 28, no. 5 (May 1928): 467–69.

13. M.H.R.'s letter to the editor noted that an amendment was submitted to the national association to substitute genitourinary training for men for obstetrical and children's training for women as a requirement for membership. This amendment failed to bring "graduate male nurses into active membership." It would be another six years before male nurses would achieve national professional recognition from the ANA. M.H.R., "Male Nurses," 837.

14. Crummer suggested that the reason for this expansion was a combination of improvements in nurse education, younger nurse students than in previous years, and different attitudes among male nurses and about male nurse occupation opportunities. Crummer, "Male Nurses," 467.

15. "Amendments to the By-Laws," 508.

16. "The Census Looks at Nurses," *American Journal of Nursing* 40, no. 2 (February 1940): 136.

17. Unlike the National Association of Colored Graduate Nurses, who by the mid-1930s had revamped their organization to launch a full-scale campaign to fight black nurse discrimination, male nurses in the United States lacked a national "male nurse" body to proceed with such an undertaking and were instead left with few prominent and outspo-

ken male nurses to call attention to the cause. Furthermore, until the late 1930s, no state association had a separate committee or section dedicated to male nurses; branches of the New York State Nurse Associations began organizing "men nurse sections" in the late 1930s.

18. Crummer, "Male Nurses," 468.

19. J. Frederick Painton, "The Outlook in Male Nursing," *American Journal of Nursing* 37, no. 3 (March 1937): 281.

20. Frances W. Witte, "Opportunities in Graduate Education for Men Nurses," *American Journal of Nursing* 34, no. 2 (February 1934): 135; and Frederick W. Jones, "Vocational Opportunities for Men Nurses," *American Journal of Nursing* 34, no. 2 (February 1934): 131–33.

21. Crummer, "School of Nursing," 457.

22. Witte, "Opportunities," 135.

23. Crummer, "School of Nursing," 457–58; and LeRoy Craig, "Opportunities for Male Nurses," *American Journal of Nursing* 40, no. 6 (June 1940): 666–70.

24. The NLNE worked directly with the ANA (and vice versa) to promote and direct the field of professional nursing in the United States.

25. A state association with a high number of men nurses asked the board of directors for the ANA to solicit the Red Cross to change its policies excluding men.

26. The Red Cross Nursing Service was established in 1909 with the help of Jane Delano, the superintendent of the Army Nurse Corps. Its purpose was to develop a reserve for the Army Nurse Corps and to augment local nursing services in times of emergency or disaster. The Red Cross Nursing Service also provided a variety of basic aid classes to women in local communities. Virginia Dunbar and Gertrude S. Banfield, "Red Cross Nursing Service Contemplates Changes in Enrolment Plan," *American Journal of Nursing* 46, no. 2 (February 1946): 82; and Jane A. Delano, "Red Cross Work," *American Journal of Nursing* 9, no. 8 (May 1909): 582–83.

27. "No Male Red Cross Nurses," *American Journal of Nursing* 35, no. 4 (April 1935): 388.

28. Some men felt insulted by the nursing service's concession to male nurses. In light of the nursing service's limited use of male nurses, they refused to register with the Red Cross, pointing out that they had more control over their professional lives and more opportunity in the private sector if they did not register. "Red Cross Enrolls Men Nurses as Technologists," *American Journal of Nursing* 40, no. 4 (April 1940): 453; Craig, "Opportunities for Male Nurses," 670; and "Male Nurses and the Armed Forces," *American Journal of Nursing* 43, no. 12 (December 1943): 1066–69.

29. Crummer, "School of Nursing," 459.

30. "What Can We Do Now?" *American Journal of Nursing* 40, no. 7 (July 1940): 795; see also "Red Cross Nursing and the Army," *American Journal of Nursing* 40, no. 7 (July 1940): 791–94.

31. "Nursing Council on National Defense," *American Journal of Nursing* 40, no. 9 (September 1940): 1013.

32. Several state nursing associations followed suit and formed their own Men Nurse Sections in the six months following the biennial convention. This included Massachu-

setts, Pennsylvania, and Tennessee, to name a few. "The Philadelphia Biennial," *American Journal of Nursing* 40, no. 6 (June 1940): 678; and "News about Nursing," *American Journal of Nursing* 40, no. 12 (December 1940): 1404–38.

33. "Nursing in Democracy," *American Journal of Nursing* 40, no. 6 (June 1940): 671–72; and O'Lynn and Tranbarger, *Men in Nursing,* 29.

34. Patrick Clerkin from Central Islip State Hospital in New York was elected as the temporary first chair of the section; by 1942, LeRoy Craig had become the chair of the Men Nurses' Section. See Threat, *Nursing Civil Rights,* Appendix B. In the 1940 ANA census, the organization noted that there were roughly eight thousand male nurses in the United States. Of these, two thousand were active graduate and three thousand were student male nurses available for military service. "The Philadelphia Biennial," *AJN,* 678.

35. While Craig noted that qualified male nurses could join the military as noncommissioned officers, the reality proved different. In most cases, male nurses entered the service as privates or ensigns and only later, after months of service, moved to a higher rank. Craig, "Opportunities for Male Nurses," 70.

36. Medical technicians in the army, also known as medics, were privates in the Medical Department. Their rank placed them in the position under female nurses in the ANC. Both doctors and nurses supervised them. After a number of months of service and provided a vacancy existed, medics could eventually obtain the rank of technical sergeant. Given that female nurses entered the military as officers, male nurses did not view this proposal as a welcome opportunity. "Male Nurses," 1066–69.

37. According to a memo written by Hon. Charles B. Smith, dated April 13, 1918, a group of seven male nurses located at Base Hospital 25 in France petitioned the Army Medical Corps to be classified as nurses instead of orderlies. This request was denied but reveals that World War II was not the first time male nurses attempted to integrate the ANC; it was during World War II that their campaign was considerably larger, more organized, and much more public. "Proud to Serve: The Evolution of Male Army Nurse Corps Officers," available at http://history.amedd.army.mil/ancwebsite/articles/malenurses.html (accessed August 20, 2014).

38. Sandy F. Mannino to Franklin D. Roosevelt, June 13, 1940, ANCA, OSG, box 110.

39. Nathaniel H. Wooding to Col. Albert G. Love, July 5, 1940, ANCA, OSG, box 110.

40. Between June and December 1940, the Office of the Surgeon General received or forwarded a number of letters concerning the position of male nurses within the army. About a dozen of these were included as basic information on the topic, beginning with a letter from Joseph O'Connell to President Roosevelt, December 18, 1940, ANCA, OSG, box 110.

41. Edward F. Perreault to Franklin D. Roosevelt, October 10, 1940, ANCA, OSG, box 110.

42. Once the United States entered the war, age limits were expanded to require men between ages eighteen and forty-five to register with their local draft board. Those men of age excluded from the draft included conscientious objectors and men labeled as "necessary" to the work they were already doing in the civilian or government service sector. Interestingly enough, according to historian Timothy Stewart-Winter a large number

of conscientious objectors were classified as I-A-O. This meant that they objected only to combatant service and "typically served as medics . . . in the military." My focus here is on graduate trained nurses, however, and for this reason will not discuss the I-A-O medic as part of the conversation. Timothy Stewart-Winter, "Not a Soldier, Not a Slacker: Conscientious Objectors and Male Citizenship in the United States during the Second World War," *Gender and History* 19, no. 3 (November 2007): 519–42.

43. Col. Albert G. Love to Lt. Col. Herbert Holdridge, October 2, 1940, ANCA, OSG, box 110; "Male Nurses and the Armed Services," 1066; and "Male Nurse," ANCA, OSG, box 110.

44. Mitchell Blake to Sen. Henry C. Lodge, December 7, 1940, ANCA, OSG, box 110.

45. "Red Cross Nursing Service Enrollments," *American Journal of Nursing* 41, no. 12 (December 1941): 1452.

46. LeRoy Craig to Col. Albert G. Love, July 6, 1940, ANCA, OSG, box 110.

47. American Nurses' Association, "Re Status of Male Nurses in the Army and Navy," January 13, 1942, from document "Resume of Actions Taken by American Nurses' Association with Regard to Securing Recognition of Male Nurses Serving in the Armed Forces," January 9, 1943, ANCA, OSG, box 110.

48. Love rarely defined what he meant by "administrative problems" but did allude to it in a memo he typed on behalf of the surgeon general. Here, he suggests that managing the nurse corps, including basic efforts like housing, would be impossible with the inclusion of male nurses. Furthermore, unlike female nurses who were appointed to one job, male service members were expected to be flexible and able to perform whatever duties were needed of them to support the mission of the army. Memo located with Joseph P. D. O'Connell to President Roosevelt, December 18, 1940, ANCA, OSG, box 110; Henry L. Stimson to Robert R. Reynolds, April 5, 1944, *Records of the War Department*, RG 165, NARA, box 181.

49. H. Richard Musser, "Nurse or Soldier," *American Journal of Nursing* 41, no. 12 (December 1941): 1449.

50. American Nurses' Association, "Service of Male Nurses during War," 1942, ANCA, OSG, box 110, pp. 1–3.

51. American Nurses' Association, "Service of Male Nurses," 11.

52. Nathaniel H. Wooding to Col. Albert G. Love, September 7, 1940; and Col. Albert G. Love to Nathaniel H. Wooding, October 1, 1940, ANCA, OSG, box 110. Nathaniel H. Wooding, "Nursing Is an Essential Occupation," *American Journal of Nursing* 41, no. 7 (July 1941): 838.

53. The National Nursing Council for War Service was established in 1940 as the Nursing Council for National Defense and changed its name in 1942. The group helped coordinate nursing resources with representatives from nursing organizations, nursing schools, and the U.S. military, providing guidance and support on nursing during World War II.

54. Maureen Honey, *Creating Rosie the Riveter: Class, Gender, and Propaganda during WWII* (Amherst: University of Massachusetts Press, 1984); and Leila Rupp, *Mobilizing Women*

for War: German and American Propaganda, 1939–1945 (Princeton, N.J.: Princeton University Press, 1978).

55. American Nurses' Association, "Service of Male Nurses," 1–3.

56. American Nurses' Association, "Resume of Actions," 1–4; and John K. Welch to Col. Florence A. Blanchfield, July 24, 1943, ANCA, OSG, box 110.

57. R. A. Chiniok to Lt. Cuppy, December 6, 1943, France P. Bolton Papers, Western Reserve Historical Society, Cleveland, Ohio, folder 140 [hereinafter WRHS].

58. "Male Nurses," [1943?], ANCA, OSG, box 110; Williams, *Gender Differences at Work*, 40–42.

59. J. Beatrice Bowman, "The Pharmacist's Mates' School," *American Journal of Nursing* 27, no. 7 (July 1927): 523–27; and Miriam M. Bryan to Frances P. Bolton, February 19, 1945, Frances P. Bolton Papers, WRHS, folder 140.

60. "Relative rank" allowed a woman in this still-auxiliary group to receive pay commensurate with that of commissioned officers of the same rank, but not all other rights and privileges. Col. Florence A. Blanchfield to John K. Welch, August 6, 1943, ANCA, OSG, box 110.

61. Sarnecky, *History*, 50–51 and 56–57.

62. Ibid., 146–47.

63. Blanchfield to Welch, August 6, 1943; and "Male Nurses," 1943, ANCA, OSG, box 110.

64. Leslie, Capt. C. J. to John Livingstone, April 1, 1943, "Ref. to Men Joining the ANC," ANCA, OSG, box 110.

65. See Threat, *Nursing Civil Rights*, Appendix A; see also Threat, *Nursing Civil Rights*, chapter 2.

66. National Association for Colored Graduate Nurses and the National Nursing Council for War Service, February 21, 1945, *Facts about Negro Nurses and the War* (New York: NACGN and NNCWS Headquarters, 1945) OSG, ANCA, box 108.

67. Nursing estimates suggested that there were about eight thousand male nurses practicing during the war; however, only about two thousand of them were qualified for military service. Further, the 320 male nurses serving with the armed forces in 1943 worked in a variety of areas, not all of which were the Medical Department. "Male Nurses and the Armed Services," 1067.

68. Frances P. Bolton to Dan Wacks, February 17, 1945, Frances P. Bolton Papers, WRHS, folder 140.

From
Beauty Shop Politics: African American Women's Activism in the Beauty Industry,
by Tiffany M. Gill (2010)

8

"BLACK BEAUTICIANS WERE VERY IMPORTANT"

Southern Beauty Activists and the Modern Black Freedom Struggle

TIFFANY M. GILL

In 1964, after a sit-in at a Woolworth lunch counter where she had food and drink, not to mention racial epithets, hurled at her, civil rights freedom fighter Anne Moody made a curious sojourn to a place she knew her embattled body and spirit could be refreshed and replenished, a place that stood in stark contrast to the Wool-worth counter, a place of safety, refuge, and community support. Her quest did not take her to a local church. As Moody recalls in her canonical memoir, *Coming of Age in Mississippi*, "I stopped in at a beauty shop across the street from the NAACP office. . . . The hairdresser took one look at me and said, 'My land, you were in the sit-in, huh?' 'Yes,' I answered. 'Do you have time to wash my hair and style it?' 'Right away,' she said, and she meant right away. There were other ladies already waiting, but they seemed glad to let me go ahead of them. The hairdresser was real nice. She even took my stockings off and washed my hair while my legs were drying."[1]

Moody's desire to get clean after being doused with ketchup and mustard during the sit-in is not surprising. However, her request to have her hair not only washed but also styled, combined with her description of the gentle pampering by the hairdresser and the deference shown to her by the other clients, highlights that beauty salons functioned as places where black women could rebound from their direct confrontations with Jim Crow segregation. Photographer and scholar Deborah Willis, the daughter of a beautician who spent much of her childhood in her mother's home-based salon, had similar recollections: "Often . . . domestics . . . would leave work and come to our house to be beautiful for church. . . . [They] shared stories about humiliating encounters."[2] Indeed, beauty salons, particularly those in the Jim Crow South, functioned as asylums for black women ravaged by the effects of segregation and served as incubators of black women's leadership and platforms from which to agitate for social and political change.

While activism was already deeply entrenched in the professional culture of beauticians by the 1960s, the political climate of the modern black freedom struggle gave their access to community space and intimate role in black women's lives greater significance. Black beauty culturists in this period were keenly aware of the economic autonomy their profession afforded them, the unique institutional space they controlled, and the access they had to black women within their communities. They were instrumental in developing the political infrastructure for African American women's involvement in the civil rights movement, which was for the most part under black female control and under the radar, hidden from whites unsympathetic to the cause of racial justice.

Beauty Activism in Professional Organizations

Continuing a tradition of political engagement dating back to the organization's founding, the National Beauty Culturists' League should be in the pantheon of civil rights organizations. At the league's 1948 convention in Washington, D.C., President Cordelia Greene Johnson explained that "the time had come for [beauticians] to take an active part in the fight for civil rights." Johnson further exhorted beauty operators to "refrain from the old time practice of gossiping with their customers about petty problems about their neighbors' private lives and rather talk about vital civil rights issues that confront the race."[3] On the one hand, Johnson's comments seem to ignore the long and rich activist history of the organization. However, what is most significant is that Johnson understood that her organization needed to acknowledge and be included in the shift happening in postwar black activism.[4] In 1955, the theme of the NBCL's annual convention was "Beauticians United for New Responsibilities." Maude Gaston, a politically active beautician from New York, led a panel titled "Beauticians United for Political Action," where she and other beauticians already active in political organizing discussed ways for beauticians to harness their political power. That fall, based in large part on deliberations of the 1955 convention, Cordelia Greene Johnson issued a letter to President Dwight D. Eisenhower on behalf of the league expressing their outrage over the murder of Emmett Till in Mississippi. Johnson stated that the NBCL had "supported and cooperated with this administration in every way" but explained that the organization was "deeply concerned about the welfare and civil rights of Negroes in America" and pressed Eisenhower to take bolder steps on behalf of civil rights.

By 1957, beauticians were seen as such a formidable force that Martin Luther King Jr. accepted the invitation to be the keynote speaker at NBCL's convention that summer. King was in high demand that year, receiving three honorary degrees, the NAACP's prestigious Spingarn Medal, and his first ever *Time* magazine cover. His address, "The Role of Beauticians in the Contemporary Struggle for Freedom," was well received and he was awarded the organization's Civil Rights Award.[5] Katie Whickham, who assumed the presidency of the NBCL that year, asked King to address the convention again in 1958. Citing a "long standing commitment in another section of the country," King declined the invitation but went on in a letter to talk about his work in the then-nascent Southern Christian Leadership Conference (SCLC). He asked Whickham if she would instead give veteran civil rights leader Ella Baker a chance to make a statement concerning the voter registration efforts of the SCLC to bring together the "vast wealth of latent potential" that existed among beauticians.[6] Whickham welcomed Baker's involvement, and the two became political allies. Baker, recognizing the NBCL's ability to reach women, later recommended that Whickham become the first female SCLC staff officer. Openly dissatisfied with the lack of women in leadership positions, Baker lobbied extensively to get more on the executive staff. She was successful in 1959, when she proudly announced Whickham's election as assistant secretary: "[I]n keeping with the expressed need to involve more women in the movement, we believe that Mrs. Whickham will bring new strength to our efforts. The National Beauty Culturists' League, Inc. of which she is president, has strong local and state units throughout the South, and voter registration is a major emphasis to its program."[7] However, Whickham's appointment did not have a sustained impact on the SCLC's gender imbalance, as her tenure did not last long, which was common with the organization's female appointees.[8] Although she was only on staff for just over a year, she remained dedicated to political activism throughout her life. Her legacy included an invitation by Vice President Richard Nixon to serve on the President's Committee on Government Contracts, an appointment as a Civil Defense consultant during the Kennedy administration, and an invitation by President Lyndon Baines Johnson to participate in a conference after the passage of the Civil Rights Act of 1964 called "To Fulfill These Rights."[9]

Whickham also was recognized by Louis Martin, a newspaper executive who served as the deputy chairman of the Democratic National Committee from 1961 to 1969, the first African American to hold that post. When trying to figure out a way to extend President Lyndon Baines Johnson's appeal in the 1964 election by "activat[ing] those below the level of the middle-class," he approached Marjorie Stewart Joyner and Katie Whickham to get beauticians in their respective organizations involved in the campaign to elect President Johnson.[10] He found beauticians to be among his most ardent grassroots organizers and explained, "There were some people that were active, some people were interested, some weren't. But where you found a beauty operator who was interested, you really had a jewel."[11]

Marjorie Stewart Joyner was certainly one of those jewels and had already been active in political campaigns before she was approached by Martin. Just four years after she led a group of beauticians on their first European excursion, she chose "Your Ballot, Ticket to Freedom" as the theme of the United Beauty School Owners and Teachers Association 1958 national convention. Later that year, after meeting a young senator with presidential aspirations, John F. Kennedy, she articulated UBSOTA's goals: "We aim to make every shop owner and every beautician a missionary to mobilize all the Negro women they come in contact with to make voting next to God and cleanliness."[12] The organization continued to advocate for voting rights, galvanizing black women to vote and support Democratic candidates.[13]

While organizations such as the NBCL and UBSOTA inspired beauticians on the national level, grassroots leaders in state organizations and local beauty shops took Whickham and Joyner's admonitions to heart in unprecedented ways. A flurry of state level organizing emerged in the 1930s and 1940s in response to new state regulation and licensing. Nowhere was this growth in state beauty organizations more evident than in the South.[14] One of the most active of these groups was the Mississippi Independent Beautician Association (MIBA), which started in April 1941 after a local beauty school organized to create an award-winning float in the annual Delta Cotton Makers Jubilee parade in Greenville. Seeing the successful float as an indication of the beauticians' latent potential, Clemmie Todd, along with her sister, laid the foundation for the MIBA. In July 1941, eighty beauticians from forty-two cities and towns across the state gathered in Greenville and, according to the association's historian, Evelyn Stegall, "blindly, but enthusiastically set up plans, made laws and by-laws and divided the state into seven districts." In just over a year, the organization boasted more than five hundred members.[15]

By July 1954 the association was formidable enough that their annual convention, held in Clarksdale, garnered front page news coverage in the *Jackson Advocate*, the state's oldest black newspaper. The headline proclaimed, "State Beauticians Praise Supreme Court Decision; Group Urged to Resist Any Form of Continued Segregation." The Supreme Court decision referenced was the landmark *Brown v. Board of Education,* which had declared segregation on account of race in public schools unconstitutional just a few months earlier. White political officials in Mississippi, such as Senator James Eastland, called the decision a "monstrous crime," while Governor Hugh L. White plainly and emphatically stated, "We're not going to pay any attention to the Supreme Court decision. We don't think it would have any effect on us down here at all."[16] Members of MIBA, on the other hand, issued a "Declaration of Principles" that was boldly printed in the *Advocate*:

> We, the members of the Mississippi Independent Beauticians Association in annual convention assembled in Clarksdale, Miss., July 11–14, hereby make the following declaration of principles:

That we go on record as highly endorsing the decision of the United States Supreme Court in outlawing segregation in public schools.

For generations the system of public school provided for Negroes in Mississippi has most assuredly generated a feeling of inferiority as to our status in the community which has a bearing on our hearts and minds.

Now that the United States Supreme Court has declared the practice of segregation in public schools as being unconstitutional we can look forward to our children enjoying in the future the same human rights as children of any other race—the best in public education—hoping they will not have to endure the untold sufferings of their forebears.

We are encouraging the beauticians of Mississippi to cooperate with public school officials when called upon, only to implement the ruling handed down by the high court of the land calling for complete integration, however, under no circumstances will we cooperate with any group which has its objective the perpetuation of segregation in any form—voluntarily or otherwise.[17]

While the members of the MIBA were certainly positioning themselves against whites in their state who were determined to maintain segregation at all costs, a stance that could put their organization, indeed their very lives, in peril, the statement is more accurately understood as an activist call to those within the black community to continue the fight for civil rights. The declaration's publication in the black press, along with African American beauticians' well-established position in black communities, meant that they were not just responding to white supremacy but also were at the forefront of inspiring an activist agenda among the black readers of the *Advocate*. Furthermore, the statement that MIBA would not work with any groups that voluntarily or passively supported segregation is certainly directed toward African Americans who were not willing to engage in the inevitable battle to uphold the Supreme Court's ruling.

In many ways, the different approaches of the national and state organizations reflect Charles Payne's analysis of the community organizing tradition versus the community mobilizing tradition of civil rights activism.[18] While the beautician's organizations on the national level strengthened black women's role in large-scale and national campaigns and events, state organizations focused on activating those within their communities, particularly those who were already a part of local organizations or professional associations, to engage in social change. State organizations were able to speak to the needs and fears of their local communities with accuracy and insight. Beauticians who were organized on the city level in Durham, North Carolina, for example, were perhaps even more in tune with the dynamics in their communities and more vocal about their intolerance for those African Americans who were unwilling to engage in civil rights activism. They reserved their harshest criticism for black male leaders; ministers, seemingly the most praised members of the civil rights community, were often the recipients of their disapproval. Although ministers and beauticians shared an admirable professional position in terms of flexible hours, a stable salary, an all-black clientele, and a nontraditional work environment, beauticians in Durham did not feel as though ministers took advantage of those occupational benefits. When the *Carolina Times* asked its readers if Durham ministers should take a more active part in the civic life of the city, members of the local Cosmetologist Club were among the most vocal critics, contrasting their own activism with the perceived apathy of the ministers.[19]

On the local level, beauticians such as Ruby Parks Blackburn of Atlanta demonstrated the ability to advocate for improvements in their communities while helping their own businesses. Born in Rockdale, Georgia, in 1901, Blackburn received her training at the Apex Beauty School after spending a few years as a domestic worker. In 1932, she opened a beauty shop on Simpson Road in Atlanta and founded the TIC (To Improve Conditions) Club, an all-female organization that over the years of Blackburn's presidency tackled everything from environmental racism to neighborhood beautification. TIC played an important role in getting an additional junior high school for Atlanta's black residents and establishing a day nursery for working mothers.[20]

Although Blackburn became a successful beautician, she never forgot the poor conditions she worked under as a domestic servant.[21] During World War II she established the Atlanta Cultural League and Training Center for Domestic Workers, an organization whose objective was to make domestic workers more employable. However, beyond simply training better laborers, the organization also had a strong civic and political mission. In the postwar period she tackled issues like political enfranchisement and bus desegregation through the local NAACP which honored her for her efforts in their voter registration drives. In 1951, she formed the Georgia League of Negro Women Voters and worked diligently to overcome obstacles in registering black female voters.[22]

Of all of her efforts, she was best known for her work to get bus service extended to black neighborhoods.[23] In 1953, she and another local businesswoman, Irene Sims Hendrix, brought suit against the Dixie Hills Bus Line for not providing "proper and adequate transportation" to black neighborhoods. After being threatened by a boycott, Dixie Hills responded by extending their service and schedule. Blackburn and Hendrix were undoubtedly interested in getting their clients and customers unfettered access to their establishments, but they used this personal agenda to benefit those in their race who were dependent upon public transportation.[24]

While national, state, and local organizations gave beauticians a place to develop their collective leadership, the beauty salon was the site where most of the civil rights activities came to life. The black beauty salon in the Jim Crow South was a unique place, replete with ironies and contradictions. In fact, the paradoxical nature of the beauty shop is what gave it its political power. A salon visit was a personal and intimate experience occurring in the midst of a social context. While the focus is on the client and having her hairstyling needs met, the beautician wields a considerable amount of power as an arbiter of good taste and proper behavior. The grooming that occurs within a salon, which for black women during most of the twentieth century entailed an elaborate process of hair cleansing, conditioning, and oiling of the hair and scalp followed by the pulling of the hair through the teeth of a steel comb heated over an open flame, was at once pampering and torturous. Salons themselves served as places of rest for black female bodies, a luxury for women who often spent their days laboring for white families and their evenings caring for the needs of their own households. Feminist scholar bell hooks remembers the beauty parlors of her youth as places "where one did not need to meet the demands of children or men. It was the one hour some folk would spend 'off their feet,' a soothing, restful time of meditation and silence."[25] However, these same salons were often sites of twelve-hour days of grueling labor for the beauticians who worked there.

Beauty salons, particularly those in the South, conflated homespace and workspace. Linking the rhetoric of the 1950s that emphasized women's domestic duties with the very real financial needs of African American families, beauticians opened salons in their homes so that they could earn a living without disrupting their domestic duties. For example, Coazell Frazier, owner of Cozy's Beauty Nook in St. Helena, South Carolina, opened her salon in her home so that she could care for her ailing mother.[26] Similarly, Bernice Caldwell of Charlotte, North Carolina, "fixed a shop on her sun porch," allowing her to care for her children while earning a living.[27]

Furthermore, a beautician's success was based on her ability to convince her client that her services were not a luxury to be indulged in sporadically but a necessity that required consistent upkeep. Indeed, a trip to the hair salon to receive the standard "press and curl" was a specialized process that required regular visits to the salon. By the 1940s, African Americans became the largest per capita consumers of cosmetic and hair preparations, and this growth increased throughout the civil rights movement.[28] Indeed, in this time of heightened political activity, the practice of straightening or pressing one's hair, linked to white beauty standards in previous decades, had become so deeply entrenched in black women's lives that there was little discussion over its meaning. Older public debates over whether straightened hair detracted from racial consciousness had largely been abandoned. Indeed, by the 1950s, beauticians were well known and respected for supporting causes to dismantle racism and used their activism to minimize discussions concerning the conflation of hair straightening with a white beauty aesthetic.

However, by the early 1960s, there were changes in the services offered in salons. Beauty culturists who were accustomed to doing a press and curl as their standard repertoire were now faced with learning how to use chemical straighteners and even learning to style wigs. Rose Morgan openly discussed having to shift with the times when, in 1962, the wig craze took off. Morgan opened a wig salon and explained that her operators were now trained to administer "both the older thermal, or 'heat' method of straightening hair and the newer chemical hair relaxing processes." She also diversified her line of services by offering manicuring, make-up application, and massage therapy. In addition, she added a charm school for children and adults on the premises.[29]

In the 1950s and 1960s, hair that was styled to release or straighten the curl pattern was the only acceptable way for African American women to wear their hair. For whites to see black women with their hair in its natural state was considered feeding into negative stereotypes of black women as unruly and undeserving of respectable treatment. As Maxine Leeds Craig points out, "Grooming was a weapon in the battle to defeat racist depictions of blacks."[30] Photographs of those who engaged in the early civil rights movement depict well-groomed women with fashionably straightened and styled hair.[31] The instructions given to Vivian Malone and James Hood to "dress modestly, neatly . . . as if you were going to church" when they attempted to register for classes at the previously segregated University of Alabama in 1963 would have meant for Malone, at least, that her hair be freshly pressed.[32] A legacy of the era of racial uplift in which notions of respectability governed the actions and presentation of black bodies, African Americans in the modern civil rights movement linked grooming to racial progress and political acceptance. Beauty product manufacturers such as the Madam C. J. Walker Company, which once had avoided any reference to hair straightening and advertised their products by invoking racial pride and economic opportunity, now openly advocated straightened hair as the only acceptable way for a black woman to wear her hair.[33]

Beauticians, therefore, had to walk a fine line in salons: they had to create a relaxing environment in the midst of smoking hot combs, chemical creams, and pulled hair; they had to create a sense of community in the midst of gossip and rigid beauty standards; they had to sustain a politicized environment in the midst of the frivolity of hair care. To that end, they relied heavily upon their roles as counselors and confidants. Many beauticians, such as Christiana Pitts of Raleigh, North Carolina, felt this was a natural outgrowth of her personality and explained, "I always did love people. . . . So I was just at hand being a counselor too. Not in an aggressive way, not trying to make anybody do anything, but ending up 'cause they wanted to ask me, not just for hair but kind of counseling on living."[34] Others, such as Margaret Williams Neal of Wilmington, North Carolina, understood that her clients not only visited her for physical beautification but also desired, perhaps even expected, her to care about their nonbeauty needs. She remembered that hairstyling was not the only reason women came to her Wilmington, North Carolina, salon, noting that "women would come by just to chat—an elderly woman would sit there to feel better since she lived alone."[35] A beautician, she further explains, "is the one that you are there with them and you sit in there and they can talk to you and you'll listen and that's what they want."[36] African American women in the Jim Crow era visited beauty salons for more than grooming; they looked to these sites as places of safety and empowerment. It is no surprise, then, that black women and those wishing to reach them would look to their beauty shops as key institutions in the fight against segregation.

Cora McLeod, a Durham beautician and member of the Cosmetologists' Club, "remembered that the NAACP often visited her shop during the 1950s and 1960s with fliers urging people to become involved in civil rights activity."[37] Similarly, organizers who wanted to get information out about the election of Lyndon Baines Johnson in 1964 also turned to beauty shops to distribute campaign literature to blacks. Louis Martin, who expanded the work he did with beauticians' organizations to include local beauty shops, explained that "the most significant thing about the 1964 vote thing was we had to figure out how to reach the rank-and-file blacks without necessarily paying dues to local wheels that wanted money. You had to bribe them to give out your literature." He said that he stumbled upon an "inspired idea" when in five states he put materials in "every beauty shop. . . . The material was there. They didn't have to pass it out. It was just sitting there and the people would come in and see it. The politicians couldn't figure out what happened. . . . But we shipped it in and that really worked. We got out a bigger vote in the states in which that operated."[38] These efforts on the part of the NAACP and the Democratic National Committee were not dependent upon a savvy beautician, but the mere availability of a space frequented by a varied group of African American women that was hidden from those with a competing agenda. In other words, the black beauty salon was considered an important political institution for those interested in the furtherance of black civil rights.

However, not all beauty salons were involved in politically subversive activities. Still, even those salons that did not explicitly engage in political activities served as vital community institutions. For example, in Tippah County, Mississippi, Hazel Foster, a beautician, earned such a good living that she became the first person in the county (white or black) to own a telephone and was literally the center of the town's communication.[39] Communication often led to gossip and community divisions. Harriet Vail Wade, a beautician from New Bern, North Carolina, recounted the story of a woman in another salon who shampooed a client, put her under the hood dryer, and proceeded to talk about her on the phone. To the beautician's chagrin, the client heard every word and an argument ensued.[40] Wade noted that the best way to understand her salon was that it was a meeting place "for information like a newspaper is now or like television. People spoke of their accomplishments, bragged on their children, talked about how hard times were." Margaret Williams Neal says that while overtly political conversations did not take place in her salon, she did see beauticians having a role in their clients' lives beyond just spreading gossip: "We listen, we give advice. I guess you have to tell your problems to someone, and a beautician is the one that you are there with them and you sit in there and they can talk to you and you'll listen and that's what they want."[41] So whether functioning as a safe space or a contested space, it was a location that was unique in its ability to sustain community. For African American women in the Jim Crow era, excluded from the male-dominated spaces of the black church and the white-dominated spaces of formal political networks, the ability to gather in a place of pampering and self-care led to community activism.

The Consummate Beauty Activist

Of all of the civil rights programs initiated in the South, the one where beauticians were the most visible was in the Highlander Folk School's Citizenship Schools Program. Committed to interracial education and political action since the 1930s, the Highlander Folk School emerged at the "forefront of the drive to end racial segregation in the South, during the 1950s."[42] Starting in 1953, the Tennessee-based group led by Myles Horton began to turn its attention toward racial discrimination with a workshop titled "The Supreme Court's Decisions and the Public Schools." Highlander held workshops throughout the 1950s that drew those who would become movement figures, but the school's greatest contribution to the civil rights movement was the Citizenship Education Program it started in 1957.

In 1954, Esau Jenkins, the owner of a small bus line that transported people on the South Carolina Sea Islands to their jobs in Charleston, attended his first Highlander workshop and shared his experiences as a native of Johns Island, South Carolina. The South Carolina Sea Islands at the time had a population of four thousand people, 67 percent of whom were black, 90 percent of whom were illiterate. To complicate matters further, Sea Islanders primarily spoke a Gullah dialect and therefore had difficulty finding employment beyond the most menial jobs. Jenkins came to Highlander and described the local people's desire to vote as well as their extreme poverty and illiteracy. Septima Clark, a Charleston schoolteacher, also happened to be attending a workshop at Highlander in 1954, and she, Jenkins, and Horton began brainstorming about bringing workshops like the ones being held at

Highlander to the people of the Sea Islands. Highlander staff began making trips to Johns Island in November of that year.[43]

The following year, Septima Clark invited her cousin, Bernice Robinson, to attend a Highlander workshop with her in Tennessee that sought to connect local economic concerns to global developments. Robinson, a forty-one-year-old Charleston beautician, was struck most by the interracial living arrangement at the school, something she was not accustomed to in her hometown. Before she left the workshop, Robinson told her cousin that she would do anything to help the organization fulfill its mission. It is a promise Clark would ask her to make good on in just a few months, when she invited her to become the first teacher for Highlander's Citizenship Schools.

Bernice Robinson's life experiences prepared her for the role she was to play in the Citizenship Education Program. Born in Charleston, South Carolina, on February 7, 1914, during "the first time that they had had snow in maybe one hundred years," Robinson had a happy childhood. Although her family was not rich, her father, a bricklayer and tile setter, refused to say that they were poor.[44] Her soft-spoken mother was primarily a homemaker who took in sewing to supplement the family's income. While Robinson noted that white people were not talked about much in her home, she recounted that both her mother and father were adamant about preventing their children from working for whites: "The only thing that was ever discussed in my family in reference to the whites was that my mother said, 'Well, I don't ever want any girl of mine to do any domestic work or work in these white folk's kitchen.'" As a child, Robinson was raised to value economic self-sufficiency.

Early in her childhood, Robinson showed promise as a musician. After graduating from high school, her older sister, who had migrated to New York City, planned to enroll her in the prestigious Boston Conservatory of Music. Robinson went to New York City in the summer of 1931 to work with her sister in the garment industry and save money for school. Unfortunately, her sister became very ill and was forced to quit her job, so Robinson's plans for college were thwarted. Concerned for her future, Robinson returned to Charleston and sought financial security in a short marriage that brought her a daughter, Jacquelyn, but little else. Left with a child and little money, Robinson took a job as a maid at a hunting resort on one of the Sea Islands. "My mother cried when I did it," Robinson explained, "because she had never wanted any of her kids to work in a white person's place like that, but I was always a realist, and I knew that when you've got to do it, you do it and get it over with."[45] Though she defied her mother's wishes, Robinson understood domestic work was one of the few reliable ways for a black woman to make a living in the South.

After her failed marriage and her dead-end job as a maid, Robinson became increasingly frustrated with her lack of employment prospects, so in 1936, she, like so many others, migrated north to New York City. She began working again in a garment factory during the day and, in her own words, "at nights I went to school to learn beauty culture, and then on weekends I would work at beauty shops to get some experience."[46] Robinson found beauty work to be more consistent than laboring in a garment factory. She explains: "I made good money there—about thirty-five to forty-five dollars a week—and I probably would have stayed in that work, but the problem with that was that in a garment factory that salary was not *steady*. It was only steady for a period of time.... That's when I said, 'I need to get into something that's steady,' and I began to take courses in beauty work. And it really *was* steady." Beauty work proved for Robinson and other black women to be not only an escape from domestic labor but also a better labor alternative than the seasonal and volatile industrial labor since black women were often the last hired and the first fired in factories.[47]

Still, while beauty culture paid well and was steady, it was laborious. Robinson often had to work eighteen-hour days, causing family members in Charleston to be concerned about her health. The long hours seemed to get to Robinson as well. Soon after the start of World War II, she decided to move to Philadelphia, where her sister was living, and take the civil service examination. She qualified to work with the Philadelphia Signal Corps but did not like Philadelphia and subsequently returned to New York City. She again took the civil service examination and was sent to work with the Internal Revenue Service and subsequently the Veteran's Administration. In 1947, just as she was about to begin work with the Treasury Department making seventy-five dollars a week, she had to return to Charleston to care for her sick mother. She did not have plans to remain in Charleston for more than a few days, but her mother's condition worsened, and Robinson remained in Charleston until her own death.

Charleston, Robinson soon realized, did not present her with employment opportunities comparable to the ones she had in New York and Philadelphia. She was unable to get civil service work despite her experience and qualifications. The best she could get in Charleston was a job "working six days a week for an upholstery man making cushions for fifteen dollars a week." Robinson was not just appalled by the low wages in Charleston but also disturbed that she was unable to register to vote there, since that was something she was accustomed to in New York and Philadelphia. In New York City, as early as 1944, she even helped a black assemblyman mail cards and letters to his constituents. Indeed, the intersection of her economic necessity and political disappointments fueled the groundbreaking path that her life was soon to take.[48]

In 1950, Robinson returned to the profession that served her well in New York City during the Great Depression. She learned what many other black women trained in beauty work understood: Beauty work was not only depression proof but also migration proof and Jim Crow proof. In other words, it was something that a black woman could depend upon for a steady income whether she was in a Madam Walker salon on 145th Street in Harlem or in a back room off a kitchen in Charleston. Robinson explained that after her father died, her brothers built her a beauty shop in her Charleston home, where, she says, "I started making it all right."[49]

Robinson's economic self-sufficiency in turn fueled her political career in Charleston. Although Robinson had been a member of the Charleston branch of the NAACP since she returned to the city in 1947, it was in 1951 that the branch and even Robinson herself became a force to be reckoned with in the black freedom struggle. In fact, Robinson was instrumental in getting the number of NAACP members up from three hundred to over a thousand; she opened up her beauty shop as a meeting place to strategize about voter registration drives as well as to distribute NAACP literature. In the words of her interviewer, Elliot Wigginton, her salon became a "center for all sorts of subversive activity."[50] Robinson says of her involvement in voter registration, "It got to the point where we were working so hard getting people to register to vote, that I would leave people under the dryer to take others down to the registration office to get them registered. I would say, 'If you get too hot under there, just cut her off and come out!'" According to Robinson, she realized the importance of voter registration based on her experience in New York. "When I lived in New York I was able to vote . . . and then when I came home I couldn't vote," she explained. "So as soon as the decision was handed down then I was ready, gung ho, to get out there and help other people get registered."[51]

Robinson also attributed her extensive involvement with voting rights and other civil rights campaigns directly to the economic autonomy she enjoyed as a beautician: "I didn't have to worry about losing my job or anything because I wasn't a schoolteacher or a case worker with the Department of Social Services or connected with anything I might be fired from." Robinson knew about this first-hand since her cousin Septima Clark was a schoolteacher who failed to have her contract renewed just before she was scheduled to retire and subsequently lost all her pension benefits due to her civil rights involvement.[52] Clark was not alone. In 1955, in response to the *Brown* decision, the South Carolina legislature passed a law making it illegal for city and state employees to belong to the NAACP. The South Carolina state NAACP, of which Robinson served as a branch secretary, saw its membership drop as a result of these pressures. In 1954, there were 7,889 card carrying members; by 1957, the number had dropped to 2,202.[53] Robinson noted that the measures taken by the legislature had created "quite a lot of fear among teachers and other public employees whom we have depended upon for years."[54] She further lamented that "that's the way it was all over the South. The whites would chop you down in a minute if you were dependent on them for a job." But

Robinson explained her own situation: "I had my own business, supplied by black supply houses, so I didn't have to worry. Many people did."[55] She felt so beyond reproach that she told her customers, many of whom were teachers, nurses, and domestic workers, to have their NAACP membership cards sent to her house so that their white mailman would not see them and subsequently tell their employers. However, once Robinson became involved with Highlander's Citizenship Schools, she did lose friends who feared reprisals for associating with her. When an article was published about the Citizenship Schools in a white Charleston paper, Robinson was ostracized from her card group and ignored by neighborhood friends who thought her activities were too radical.[56]

By the end of 1956, Robinson's civil rights work was so impressive that Septima Clark suggested to Myles Horton that Robinson was best qualified to be the first teacher for Highlander's Citizenship School. After two decades working primarily in the labor movement, in 1953 the Highlander staff launched a series of workshops that focused on community desegregation. With the assistance of Clark and Esau Jenkins, a Citizenship Schools project developed on the South Carolina Sea Islands. The ultimate goal was to teach black adults to read and write and to prepare them to register to vote. After finding a location, they needed to find a suitable teacher. Black schoolteachers were eliminated immediately, even though, as Katherine Mellen Charron notes, Clark herself, a lifelong educator, saw the Citizenship Education Program as an extension of the work black schoolteachers had been doing since the turn of the century. Still, Clark's difficulties trying to mobilize and organize teachers who were dependent upon the state for their livelihood, in addition to her concern that formal educators would be too curriculum driven and too far removed from the lives of their illiterate Johns Island pupils, led Clark to her cousin, Bernice Robinson. The ever-stubborn Myles Horton eventually concurred.[57]

On January 7, 1957, Robinson stood before her first class of eleven women and three men at the Johns Island Citizenship School in an old dilapidated school building purchased by Highlander. Even though Clark, the seasoned educator, was involved in the selection process for a teacher, it was Robinson who, in the words of Horton, "developed the [educational] methods used by the Citizenship Schools."[58] Robinson established a pedagogical approach based on the needs of the students and told them on the first day, "I'm really not going to be your teacher. We're going to work together and teach each other." She also engaged them as active participants in the learning process, asking them what they wanted to accomplish in the class. The students, the majority of whom were completely illiterate and the remainder only partially literate, explained that they wanted to write their names, read the Bible, fill out a money order, and fill out blanks when ordering from a catalog. In addition, Robinson mimeographed sections of the South Carolina election laws, and many of the students mastered the text and learned basic literacy skills over the two month session. By February of the next year, eight of the fourteen students with at least five months of classes were able to read the required paragraph in the state constitution and sign their names in order to receive their voter registration certificates.[59]

Witnessing the success of the Johns Island School, others were soon added in neighboring regions. Beautician and activist Marylee Davis of North Charleston, who had also attended workshops at Highlander, asked for help in starting a school in her neighborhood and offered her beauty parlor as a meeting place.[60] Robinson served as the teacher for the twelve women enrolled in the school, most of whom were domestic workers. Davis, an integral part of the North Charleston community, was intimately acquainted with the conditions plaguing her neighborhood and wanted the students to not only learn to read the required passage for voter registration but also learn how to navigate local political hierarchies to get better roads and other community improvements.

Based on the success in South Carolina, Horton, Clark, and Robinson sought to expand the program to Tennessee, Alabama, and Georgia and realized that beauticians were best equipped to further Highlander's Citizenship Schools' goals. In December 1960, Clark, who had assumed the role of director of education, convened a meeting specifically for "members of the beauticians' profession only" at Highlander's headquarters in Monteagle, Tennessee, to be held January 15–16, 1961. The workshop, "New Leadership Responsibilities," was convened, according to Clark, because the "Highlander Folk School has been impressed with the leadership possibilities among beauticians." She continued in an appeal letter sent to beauticians in the three states: "This is one of the professions which offer to its members great freedom for leadership in community action. We also see it as offering opportunities especially suitable for *professional* women who also want to be active in the struggle for justice in the South."[61]

While Clark understood that women like teachers in the typical middle-class professions were not the best option for Citizenship Schools teachers, she knew that she had to appeal to the professional identity of beauticians to encourage their participation. In his autobiography, Myles Horton explained the strategic importance of gathering beauticians as leaders in civil rights initiatives due to their unique status in their communities. "A black beautician, unlike a white beautician, was at that time a person of some status in the community," he explained. "They were entrepreneurs, they were small business women, you know, respected, they were usually better educated than other people, and most of all they were independent."[62] While beauticians had an elevated status, were small-business women, and were usually better educated, they, unlike teachers, did not have a separation from or a patronizing relationship to the black masses. Because of segregation,

Figure 8.1: Bernice Robinson (standing left) and Septima Clark (standing right) facilitate a teacher training workshop. Used with permission from the Wisconsin Historical Society (WHi-41508).

they were indebted to the black community for a client base and were never far removed from their respective communities.

Moreover, black female beauticians had a degree of independence relative to other blacks—especially black women—whose occupations were usually under the watchful eye of whites. Throughout the Jim Crow years, black women worked primarily as domestics, doing work that was often isolating and constantly supervised, clearly not offering a site to organize collective resistance. Even black professional women, like schoolteachers within segregated school systems, faced constraints due to their dependence upon white-run school boards and city councils. Beauticians worked within black female-owned establishments, were supplied by black manufacturers, and were patronized by black female clients within segregated communities.

On January 15, 1961, fifty-two beauticians from several counties in Tennessee and Alabama met for two days at Highlander's headquarters.[63] Many were given scholarships to attend and carpooled to Monteagle. While on the two-hundred-acre farm nestled in the Cumberland Mountains, they participated in workshops led by Horton, Robinson, and a beauty shop owner named Johnnie Mae Fowler, who was already active in her community in Winchester, Tennessee. Fowler's presentation, "The Beauty Salon: A Center of Communication and Influence," delineated key areas where beauticians could be an asset to the civil rights movement. She envisioned beauticians providing leadership in efforts to see that the *Browder v. Gayle* decision to desegregate buses and train stations was a reality in their communities. "We think the beautician should step out front and our people will see us doing this [*sic*] things without fear," she stated. What beauticians should be doing, Fowler said, was "sitting on buses on a first come first served basis." She also explained that beauticians "can help a lot by discussing this [desegregation of public transportation] in their salons." Beauty salons, according to Fowler, should be the primary place for the community to gather and obtain information. She encouraged the beauticians to not only open their businesses for civic meetings, PTA groups, and other social organizations but also to keep abreast of local happenings, like the schedule for school board meetings, so that they could share the information with their clients.

The meetings inspired the beauticians in attendance to act immediately to impact their communities. Just one day after the adjournment of the gathering, the women, under the leadership of Eva Bowman, former state inspector and examiner for the Tennessee Cosmetology Board and main contact person for the Highlander meeting, announced the formation a board of directors, who would be responsible for implementing what was to be called the Volunteer Health Center in Fayette County, Tennessee. The board was comprised solely of beauticians who attended the workshops. The center was to benefit twenty sharecropping families evicted by white landowners in retaliation for a series of events that started in 1959 with the conviction by an all-white jury of a black man who was accused of killing a white man. Local black leaders filed a suit under the Civil Rights Act of 1957, citing their omission from jury pools based on being prevented from registering to vote. The African Americans won their case, and led by gas station owner John McFerren and his beautician wife, Viola, they organized voter registration drives in the county. Despite widespread intimidation tactics and an escalation of tension in Fayette County, more than twelve hundred African Americans voted in the November 1960 elections. As a result, white landowners evicted black sharecroppers en masse, and those with no where else to go were invited to set up tents on the property of an independent black landowner, Sheppard Towles, forming what residents called "Tent City."[64]

The inhabitants of Tent City had many needs, including food, clothing, and security. Inspired by their recent trip to Highlander, beauticians thought they were best able to tend to the health of Tent City's inhabitants. The beauticians demonstrated a complex understanding of citizenship rights and education; while they were brought to Highlander under the auspices of the traditional Citizenship Education Program, they forced Highlander to expand the meaning of citizenship to addressing issues concerning the immediate needs of their communities such as health care. Clark and Robinson supported these efforts even in their capacities as director of education and field director, respectively, but the onus was on Bowman and the beauticians on the board of directors to execute the plans for the center.

At their initial meeting held in January 1961, the beauticians outlined a comprehensive plan: They were to purchase a tent and floor along with heating and lighting facilities, propose a trip to Tent City for the state beauticians' organizations from Alabama and Tennessee to view the needs up close and enlist them in fundraising efforts, and contact doctors and nurses to establish the medical program. That nurses and doctors were not the ones to initiate this program demonstrated just how much more beauticians were connected to the needs of the poor and those who were living out the often difficult backlash of exercising citizenship rights.[65]

Things were promising—at first. In February, beauticians met at Highlander for a second time and agreed to place donation boxes for Tent City in their shops, donate the money earned from one client's hairdo each week, and encourage those within their professional networks to do the same. In March, more than three hundred beauticians from Chattanooga pledged their support and donated money to the center, and plans were made to break ground on an actual building in late April. This shift from putting up a tent to erecting a building for the center led to confusion and greatly undermined the project. Clark, the seasoned leader and pragmatist, directed Bowman in a letter to "buy a tent and get to work on the things needed in the community now. Then later push the county to get a building and maintain a clinic or integrate the one they have."[66] Unfortunately, the beauticians' dreams for a health center were never fully realized, and after living in tents for over two years, the residents of Tent City began moving into new, affordable homes.[67]

Despite the failure of beauticians to provide a health facility for the residents of Tent City, the Highlander Folk School continued to partner with beauticians. In the midst of the Tent City debacle, another "New Leadership Responsibilities" workshop exclusively for beauticians was held at Highlander in late October 1962. An announcement explained that the purpose of the meeting was "to find the things which need to be done in a community that cannot be done by City, State, or Federal employees." The flier also addressed the question "Why beauticians?" by affirming, "Beauticians can speak out openly and can publicly promote the cause for justice and equality in the South," in ways that others could not.[68] In March 1963, beauticians attended a demonstration at Highlander on "How to Use a Voting Machine," so that they could share the information with their clients when they returned home.

Beauticians and beauty shops proved to be so effective in part because they were so hidden. It took whites in the Charleston area a while to find out about the schools Bernice Robinson had started. Otis Perkins, a reporter from the *Charleston News and Courier,* was surprised that schools had been conducted for three years before the white community discovered anything about them.[69] Similarly, Robinson, despite being an essential part of Highlander, was not well known among those who were trying to destroy its operations. In 1961, Highlander's Tennessee facility was raided by the Grundy county police department, and everyone on site was charged with possession of whisky. While most of the charges did not stick, Horton's deed to the property was declared void at the circuit court. The case went up to the Tennessee Supreme Court, which upheld the decision and revoked Highlander's tax exempt status. As a result, by the summer of 1961, Highlander was beginning a process of ending its involvement with the Citizenship Schools and handing its administration over to the Southern Christian Leadership Conference. Still, anyone with ties to Highlander was closely watched by the Tennessee authorities. For example, the *Chattanooga Free Press* ran an article in May 1961 vilifying Septima Clark for taking the Peace Corps examination in Chattanooga. The "second Negro woman" who accompanied Clark was unknown to reporters, but based on a photograph printed in the newspaper, she was Robinson. In fact, the reporter was surprised that they knew so little about "the second Negro woman," especially since she gave the Highlander Folk School as her address.[70] Despite Robinson's activism, she and indeed all the beauticians in the movement always seemed to operate below the radar, exactly where Horton and other movement leaders thought they were most useful to the cause.

When administration of the Citizenship Education Program was handed over to SCLC, the project's leaders, including Andrew Young, continued to rely upon the independence of beauticians, though Young marginalized their input—and indeed women's input in general.[71] Young explained that when he could not locate a black leader within the community, he and his team would go to the beauty parlor in addition to male-owned barbershops and funeral homes to find economically independent black leaders.[72] While beauticians were not targeted exclusively under SCLC's administration of the program as they were with Highlander, one emerged as a leader in the Citizenship Schools in the volatile region of Clarksdale, Mississippi. Clarksdale had an active NAACP that mounted a successful boycott against white-owned businesses for their discriminatory hiring practices, poor service, and segregated practices. However, the town also had a particularly repressive chief of police who attempted to suppress black resistance through violence and intimidation. The law also turned a blind eye toward violence inflicted upon African Americans by racist whites. For example, Vera Pigee, a beautician who had served her local NAACP as branch secretary and youth branch organizer, was beaten by a gas station attendant in 1963 when she attempted to use the whites-only bathroom. As with most of the violence inflicted upon African Americans, the police turned a blind eye to the white assailants and even joined them in the terrorizing of black communities.

In spite of, or perhaps because of, such difficulties, African Americans in Clarksdale were eager for Citizenship Schools, and Pigee was eager to be involved with establishing the program.[73] Pigee, known for wearing hats and encouraging her clients to engage in the freedom struggle from the beauty shop she operated attached to her home, attended a Citizenship Education Workshop in 1961 and impressed the staff so much that they pegged her to be a supervisor of the schools in her region. Just four years later, she could boast of twenty Citizenship Schools, and in 1965 alone, of registering more than one hundred voters, no small task in such a volatile region. Andrew Young admitted that while male leaders were at the forefront of the movement, it was women like Pigee who really "ran the operations."[74] Her economic independence was crucial in a repressive place like Clarksdale, and while that did not prevent her getting beaten, she never had to fear losing her job.

In fact, Clarksdale's chief of police, Ben C. Collins, interrogated both Vera Pigee and her husband Paul concerning their civil rights activities at their respective places of employment. When Collins questioned Paul Pigee, a laborer at North Delta Compress, a cotton compression and warehouse facility, he asked him, "Do you want this job?" and spoke to his foreman about Pigee's work hours and performance. After Paul refused to denounce the civil rights activities of his family, the chief turned to his manager and stated, "I know you are going to fire him." When the manager replied that he had no cause to terminate Pigee, Collins replied, "Cause? Don't you know that his wife is the most aggressive leader of the NAACP in Clarksdale?" But the manager stood his ground and asserted Pigee's exemplary work performance.[75] When Collins confronted Vera Pigee, there was no manager or foreman with whom to deal. Instead, he asked about her customers, and Vera refused to divulge their names, explaining, "I pay city, county, and state taxes to operate a legitimate business. You have moved in with *your* secretary and made your office in *my* beauty shop. Now I am asking both of you to leave. If I ever need your service I will call you." While neither Paul nor Vera Pigee lost their jobs as a result of Collins's actions, Collin's use of workplace intimidation is telling. Vera Pigee felt empowered enough to withhold her clients' names and expel the staunch segregationist from her salon because she held ownership of her labor. Her husband was perhaps equally willing to stand up to Collins, but his economic stability was dependent upon a thankfully supportive employer.

Conclusion

When remembering the Highlander Folk School, Myles Horton marveled at the role of beauticians in the Citizenship Education Program: "They thought that I was bringing these beauticians together to talk about straightening hair or whatever . . . they do, [but] I was just using them because they were community leaders and they were independent. . . . We used beauticians' shops all over the South to distribute Highlander literature on integration."[76]

In many ways, Horton's statement illuminates the key issues surrounding the unique ways beauticians merged their profession with the politics of the civil rights movement. They were, for the most part, highly regarded in their communities and strove to be among the best women of the race. However, because of segregation and their indebtedness to the black community for a client base, beauty culturists were never far removed from their respective communities.

While women like Ruby Blackburn, Bernice Robinson, and Vera Pigee were undoubtedly activists, they were still businesswomen. Septima Clark said of a beautician who was involved in the Highlander Folk School's Citizenship Schools Program that "she wished to see her street and that section improved in order to preserve and advance her economic investment." Still, Clark was quick to add that the beautician was ultimately "more interested in doing something for the people who were suffering" than in advancing her own business.[77] Beauticians demonstrated that they could look after their own economic needs and the needs of their communities simultaneously, perhaps better than any other group of black businesspeople.

Moreover, beauticians had a degree of independence relative to other blacks—especially black women—whose occupations were usually under the watchful eye of whites. During the years of the freedom struggle, Southern black women worked primarily as domestics, doing work that was often isolating and constantly supervised, clearly not offering a site to organize collective resistance. Even black professional women, such as schoolteachers within segregated school systems, faced constraints due to their dependence upon white-run school boards and city councils. Beauticians worked within black female-owned establishments, were supplied by black manufacturers, and were patronized by black female clients within segregated communities. They took advantage of the benefits of their economic independence and the heightened political activity of the 1950s and 60s to take risks without fears of reprisals, something they had done for most of the twentieth century.

Notes

1. Anne Moody, *Coming of Age in Mississippi* (1968; reprint, New York: Delta Trade Paperbacks, 2004), 293.

2. Christina Royster-Hemby, "Reflected in the Lens," *Baltimore City Paper*, 30 March 2005, http://www.citypaper.com/arts/prinready.asp?id=9785/ (accessed December 15, 2005).

3. National Beauty Culturists League, *Daily Bulletin*, 11 August 1948, Series 18, Box 7 Folder 3, Records of the National Council of Negro Women, National Beauty Culturists League, MMBCH.

4. For a larger discussion of the nature and scope of postwar black women's activism, see Martha Biondi, *To Stand and Fight: The Struggle for Civil Rights in Postwar New York City* (Cambridge: Harvard University Press, 2003); Megan Taylor Shockley, *"We, Too, Are Americans": African American Women in Detroit and Richmond, 1945–1954* (Urbana: University of Illinois Press, 2004); Gretchen Lemke-Santangelo, *Abiding Women: African American Mi-*

grant Women and the East Bay Community (Chapel Hill: University of North Carolina Press, 1996); Shockley, "We, Too, Are Americans"; Christina Greene, *Our Separate Ways: Women and the Black Freedom Movement in Durham, North Carolina* (Chapel Hill: University of North Carolina Press, 2005); and Laurie Green, *Battling the Plantation Mentality: Memphis and the Black Freedom Struggle* (Chapel Hill: University of North Carolina Press, 2007).

5. Convention information is derived from Vernice Mark, *The National Beauty Culturists' League, Inc.*, 2nd ed. (Detroit: Harlo Press, 1994), 36.

6. Martin Luther King to Katie Whickham, 7 July 1958, in Martin Luther King Jr., Peter Halloran, and Clayborne Carson, eds., *The Papers of Martin Luther King, Jr.*, vol. 4, *Symbol of the Movement* (Berkeley and Los Angeles: University of California Press, 1992).

7. Quoted in Belinda Robnett, *How Long? How Long? African American Women and the Struggle for Civil Rights* (New York: Oxford University Press, 1997), 93.

8. See Robnett's discussion of the gender politics of the SCLC in ibid., 93.

9. Mark, *National Beauty Culturists' League*, 288–289.

10. Louis Martin, interviewed by Michael L. Gillette, 12 June 1986, Internet copy, Lyndon Baines Johnson Library, University of Texas, Austin. For more information on Louis Martin see, Alex Poinsett, *Walking with the Presidents: Louis Martin and the Rising of Black Political Power* (New York: Rowan and Littlefield, 2000).

11. Martin interviewed by Gillette.

12. "So This Is Washington," *Chicago Defender*, 24 May 1958.

13. Ethel L. Payne to MSJ, 11 January 1958, MSJP.

14. South Carolina Beauticians Club (1936), North Carolina State Beauticians and Cosmetologists Association (1939), the Orange Blossom Cosmetologist Association of Florida (1939), Arkansas Beauticians Association (1940), Mississippi Independent Beautician Association (1941), Tennessee State Beauticians Association (1956), Texas State Association and Beauty Culturists League (1942), Virginia State Beauticians Association (1943), Alabama Modern Beauticians (1944), Georgia State Beauty Culturists' League (1946), Louisiana State Beauticians Association (1946). See Mark, *National Beauty Culturists' League*.

15. Mark, *National Beauty Culturist's League*, 158–163.

16. Quoted in Davidson M. Douglas, *Reading, Writing, and Race: The Desegregation of Charlotte Public Schools* (Chapel Hill: University of North Carolina Press, 1995), 26.

17. "State Beauticians Praise Supreme Court Decision; Group Urged to Resist Any Form of Continued Segregation," *Jackson Advocate*, 24 July 1954, 1.

18. See Charles Payne, *I've Got the Light of Freedom: The Organizing Tradition in the Mississippi Civil Rights Movement*, 2nd ed. (Berkeley and Los Angeles: University of California Press, 2007).

19. See *Carolina Times*, 22 August 1950, 22.

20. See undated letter, Box 4, Ruby Parks Blackburn Papers, Auburn Avenue Research Library on African American Culture and History, Atlanta (hereafter cited as RPBP).

21. See appointment books and receipts from Blackburn's beauty salon, RPBP.

22. Kathryn Nasstrom, "Women, the Civil Rights Movement, and the Politics of Historical Memory, 1946–1973" (Ph.D. diss., University of North Carolina- Chapel Hill, 1993), 71.

23. For more on the segregated housing and public transportation system in Atlanta during the early years of Jim Crow, see Hunter, *To 'Joy My Freedom;* for the postwar period, see Gary Pomerantz, *Where Peachtree Meets Sweet Auburn: A Saga of Race and Family* (New York: Penguin Books, 1997); Herman "Skip" Mason, *Politics, Civil Rights and Law in Black Atlanta, 1870–1970* (Charleston: Arcadia Publishing, 2000).

24. See Georgia Public Service Commission vs. Dixie Hills Bus Lines, 6 October 1953; and J. C. Steinmetz to Ruby Blackburn, 14 October 1953, both in RPBP; Mason, *Politics, Civil Right and Law*, 49–54.

25. bell hooks, *Bone Black: Memories of Girlhood* (New York: Henry Holt, 1996), 112.

26. Coazell Frazier, interviewed by Tunga White, St. Helena, S.C., 7 August 1994, BTV.

27. Bernice Toy Caldwell, interviewed by Leslie Brown, Charlotte, N.C., 7 June 1993, BTV.

28. Robert Weems, *Desegregating the Dollar: African American Consumerism in the Twentieth Century* (New York: New York University Press, 1998), 34.

29. "Integration Comes to the Beauty Business," *Ebony*, August 1966.

30. Maxine Leeds Craig, *Ain't I a Beauty Queen: Black Women, Beauty, and the Politics of Race* (New York: Oxford University Press, 2002), 35.

31. For collections of photographs of the civil rights movement, see Bruce Davidson, *Time of Change: Civil Rights Photographers, 1961–1965* (Los Angeles: St. Ann's Press, 2002); Herbert Randall, *Faces of Freedom Summer* (Tuscaloosa: University of Alabama Press, 2001); Manning Marable and Leith Mullings, *Freedom: A Photographic History of the African American Struggle* (London: Phaidon, 2002); Steven Kasher, *The Civil Rights Movement: A Photographic History, 1954–1968* (New York: Abbeyville Press, 1996); Cecil Williams, *Freedom and Justice: Four Decades of the Civil Rights Struggle as Seen By a Black Photographer of the Deep South* (Macon, Ga.: Mercer University Press, 1995).

32. Marisa Chappell, Jenny Hutchinson, and Brian Ward, "'Dress modestly, neatly . . . as if you were going to church': Respectability, Class and Gender in the Montgomery Bus Boycott and the Early Civil Rights Movement," in *Gender and the Civil Rights Movement*, ed. Peter Ling and Sharon Monteith (New Brunswick, N.J.: Rutgers University Press, 2004), 96n1.

33. See Madam C. J. Walker Company Advertisements in the 1960s in black publications like *Ebony* as well as in the Madam C. J. Walker Papers at the Indiana Historical Society, Indianapolis.

34. Pitts quoted in Rhonda Mawhood, "Tales to Curl Your Hair: African Americans Beauty Parlors in Jim Crow Durham" (unpublished seminar paper, Duke University, 1993, author's possession), 17.

35. Margaret Williams Neal, interviewed by Rhonda Mawhood, Charlotte, N.C., 19 July 1993, BTV.

36. Ibid.

37. Greene, *Our Separate Ways*, 32.

38. Martin interviewed by Gillette.

39. Julie Ann Willet, *Permanent Waves: The Making of the American Beauty Shop* (New York: New York University Press, 2000), 150.

40. Harriet Vail Wade interviewed by Rhonda Mawhood, Wilmington, N.C., 1 August 1993, BTV.

41. Neal interviewed by Mawhood.

42. John M. Glen, *Highlander: No Ordinary School*, 2nd ed. (Knoxville: University of Tennessee Press, 1996), 154.

43. John M. Glen, introduction to Glen, *Highlander*.

44. All direct quotes from Bernice Robinson's life have been taken from typed, unedited interview: Bernice Robinson, interviewed by Sue Thrasher and Elliot Wiggington, Charleston, S.C., 9 November 1980, Box 1, Folder 5, Avery Research Center, College of Charleston, Charleston, S.C.

45. Ibid.

46. Ibid.

47. For a larger discussion of black women's precarious situation with factory work, see Jacqueline Jones, *Labor of Love, Labor of Sorrow: Black Women, Work, and the Family from Slavery to the Present* (New York: Basic Books, 1985).

48. On the resiliency of the black beauty market, see A'Lelia Bundles, *On Her Own Ground: The Life and Times of Madam C. J. Walker* (New York: Scribner Books, 2001); and Juliet E. K. Walker, *The History of Black Business in America: Capitalism, Race, and Entrepreneurship* (New York: Macmillian Reference Library, 1998).

49. Robinson interview by Thrasher and Wiggington.

50. Elliot Wigginton, ed., *Refuse to Stand Silently By: An Oral History of Grassroots Social Activism in America, 1921–1964* (New York: Doubleday Books, 1991).

51. Robinson quoted in LaVerne Grant, "Contributions of African-American Women to Nonformal Education During the Civil Rights Movement, 1955–1965" (Ed.D. diss., Pennsylvania State University, 1990), 46.

52. For more information on the life of Septima Clark, see Septima Clark, *Echo in My Soul* (New York: E. P. Dutton, 1962); Cynthia Stokes Brown, *Refuse to Stand Silently By: Septima Clark and the Civil Rights Movement* (Navarro, Calif.: Wild Trees Press, 1986); and Katherine Mellen Charron, "Teaching Citizenship: Septima Poinsette Clark and the Transformation of the African American Freedom Struggle" (Ph.D. diss., Yale University, 2005).

53. R. Scott Baker, "Ambiguous Legacies: The NAACP's Legal Campaign Against Segregation in Charleston, SC, 1935–1975" (Ph.D. diss., Columbia University, 1993), 180.

54. Bernice Robinson to Lucille Black, 28 January 1956, in *Papers of the NAACP, Selected Branch Files, 1956–1965* (Bethesda, Md.: University Publications of America, 1991).

55. Robinson interview by Thrasher and Wiggington.

56. Sandra Brenneman Oldendorf, "Highlander Folk School and the South Carolina Sea Island Citizenship Schools: Implications for the Social Studies" (Ph.D. diss., University of Kentucky, 1987).

57. For a larger analysis of the hesitancy of African American schoolteachers to get involved in civil rights activities, see Charron, "Teaching Citizenship," 345–348. For an analysis of Clark's reasons not to use teachers, see 479.

58. Cynthia Stokes Brown, *Ready from Within: Septima Clark and the Civil Rights Movement* (California: Wild Tree Press, 1986), 51; Myles Horton, *The Long Haul: An Autobiography* (New York: Doubleday Books, 1990), 105.

59. See Charron, "Teaching Citizenship," 480–484.

60. Glen, *Highlander*, 197; Charron, "Teaching Citizenship," 487.

61. See "Announcing a workshop on New Leadership Responsibilities" and Septima Clark to beauticians in Tennessee, Alabama, and Georgia, 12 December 1960, Box 80, Folder 10, Highlander Folk School Papers, Social Action Collection, Wisconsin Historical Society, Madison (hereafter cited as HFSP); emphasis added.

62. Horton quoted in Aldon Morris, *The Origins of the Civil Rights Movement*: Black Communities Organizing for Change (New York: Free Press, 1984), 145.

63. A press release dated 17 January 1961 claims the attendance of "fifty-two women beauticians from Tennessee and Alabama," but the sign in sheets reflect thirty-four women and one male beautician. I find it interesting that the press release ignored the presence of the man. See MSS 265, Box 80, Folder 10, HFSP.

64. Charron, "Teaching Citizenship," 514–515.

65. See untitled press release, 17 January 17 1961, and Notes from the Board of Directors meeting, 16 January 1961, MSS 265, Box 80, Folder 10, HFSP.

66. Septima Clark to Eva Bowman, n.d., Box 38, Folder 6; Bowman to Co-workers, 19 April 1961, Box 38, Folder 6 (HFSP); quotation from handwritten note Clark to Bowman, n.d., Box 38, Folder 6 (HFSP).

67. Charron, "Teaching Citizenship," 518.

68. Announcement of Workshop for Beauticians on "New Leadership Responsibilities," 28–29 October 1962, Box 80, Folder 10, HFSP.

69. Oldendorf, "Highlander Folk School," 67.

70. For more information about the raid on Highlander and its legal battles, see Glen, *Highlander*; Horton, *Long Haul*; Aimee Isgrig Horton, *The Highlander Folk School: A History of its Major Programs, 1939–1961* (Brooklyn, N.Y.: Carlson Publishing, 1989). See "Highlander School's Septima Clark Among Seven Taking Peace Corps Test," *Chattanooga Free Press*, 29 May 1961, clipping in Clark/Robinson Papers, Folder 5, Avery Research Center, College of Charleston, Charleston, S.C.

71. For a larger discussion of the SCLC, namely, its gender politics, see Robnett, *How Long? How Long?*

72. Young quoted in Mellon, "Teaching Citizenship," 536.

73. For a larger discussion of the situation in Clarksdale with regard to resistance and repression, see Annelieke Dirks, "Between Threat and Reality: The National Association for the Advancement of Colored People and the Emergence of Armed Self-Defense in Clarksdale and Natchez, Mississippi, 1960–1965," *Journal for the Study of Radicalism* 1, no. 1 (2007): 71–98.

74. For more on Pigee, see Françoise Nicole Hamlin, "Vera Mae Pigee (1925-): Mothering the Movement," in *Mississippi Women: Their Histories, Their Lives*, ed. Martha Swain, Elizabeth Anne Payne, Marjorie Spruill, and Susan Ditto (Athens: University of Georgia Press, 2003), 281–93; Charron, "Teaching Citizenship," 557–5588; and Vera Pigee, *The Struggle of Struggles* (Detroit: Harlo Press, 1975).

75. Pigee, *Struggle of Struggles*, 99–100.

76. Morris's interview with Myles Horton in *Origins of the Civil Rights Movement*, 145.

77. Clark, *Echo in My Soul*, 161.

From
Radical Sisters: Second-Wave Feminism and Black Liberation in Washington, D.C.,
by Anne M. Valk (2010)

9

ORGANIZING FOR REPRODUCTIVE CONTROL

ANNE M. VALK

Women's access to safe and legal abortions and, more broadly, their right to freely decide when to become mothers, emerged as a central organizing issue for women in Washington in the late 1960s and early 1970s. Joining in a movement for reproductive control, activists from across Washington's liberal and radical political spectrum fought to secure legal, safe, and affordable abortion and contraception and to end involuntary sterilization. The D.C. Women's Liberation Movement and welfare rights activists, along with NOW, the Young Socialist Alliance, and other groups, united behind the movement's basic objectives. The reproductive rights coalitions that activists formed represented a rare instance of cross-racial, cross-class organizing around explicitly defined women's issues during this era. But even when women agreed that securing access to abortion and reproductive rights were central to women's liberation, activists visualized the barriers that restricted women's choices in distinct ways and they emphasized different approaches to political change. Through the campaigns and coalitions they formed, activists continually redefined the meaning of reproductive rights and connected their demands for reproductive control to movements for economic justice, black liberation, and women's liberation.[1]

Alice Wolfson, who moved to Washington in 1969, quickly became a central figure in the local fight to secure women's reproductive freedom. Along with other members of the DCWLM, Wolfson sought collective solutions to the health problems women experienced. A pediatric audiologist who was married to a physician, Wolfson brought personal and professional insight to the group's discussion of

America's health care system. DCWLM members formed a women's health group where participants discussed their shared frustrations with the medical system. Many felt anger at the dismissive and condescending way physicians treated them and stifled in attempts to control their own health care. Matters related to fertility topped their list of grievances. At the time, no states allowed women unrestricted access to abortion, although the District's laws were some of the most liberal in the country, sanctioning so-called therapeutic abortions in order to preserve a woman's health and life. But even under these conditions, Washington women felt powerless and many had risked death to obtain illegal abortions or suffered side effects from ineffective or dangerous contraception. Without access to safe and legal forms of birth control, many DCWLM members struggled to make their own decisions about motherhood.[2]

In September 1969, participants in the DCWLM health group paired with members of the Citywide Welfare Association (CWA) to fight for improved medical resources. Specifically, they pressed to change the abortion practices of the city's only public hospital, the primary medical facility serving the District's poor residents. The women accused D.C. General Hospital of practicing economic discrimination by adhering to excessively restrictive criteria when determining women's eligibility for abortions. In contrast, more expensive private hospitals interpreted the city's abortion law more broadly and approved more women's requests for the procedure. The coalition attempted to meet with city health officials to discuss D.C. General's policies; after they were turned away, they responded by picketing the Public Health Department and staging a sit-in at officials' offices. These protests subsequently spun in several directions: legal action to force equitable compliance with the city's abortion statutes, public hearings on the issue of reproductive rights, and demonstrations during congressional hearings about the safety of birth control pills.

Within a year, campaigns for reproductive rights and safe abortions achieved greater prominence, pulling in liberal feminists, welfare activists, representatives of family planning organizations, and black liberation proponents. Throughout, Alice Wolfson made pivotal contributions: she organized picket lines, forced her way into meetings and Senate hearings, appeared on national television and radio shows, and published critiques of the medical profession. Wolfson's outrage grew along with her medical expertise and as she learned the ways that race and class differences affected women's ability to control their fertility.[3]

The pressure that Wolfson and other activists brought to bear changed how the District's laws were implemented even before the *Roe v. Wade* ruling granted women's right to choose to undergo an abortion.[4] *Roe,* the high court's 1973 decision, represented an important victory by making abortion legal, safer, and more widely available. The significant impact of *Roe* obscured, however, the broader issues that shaped how women articulated a reproductive rights agenda, including the challenge to define reproductive rights and to develop strategies to address a broad array of women's health concerns at the local level. Wolfson and other DCWLM members viewed women's control of their fertility—which they initially defined primarily as unrestricted access to abortion and safe, effective birth control—as a necessary component for women's liberation and they acted to ensure that such rights could be exercised. But through their attempts to secure these rights, and especially as a result of collaboration with other activists, women's liberationists expanded their conception of what reproductive freedom meant. In addition, through campaigns that lasted for more than a decade, feminists came to understand that poverty, racism, and sexism imposed multiple barriers to women's rights. Securing a legal right to abortion was vital to the movement, but activists discovered that this right alone would not ensure all women's control over their reproductive lives. Instead, feminists and their allies integrated the fight for improved health care for women, the battle for safe contraception, freedom from sterilization abuse, and the assertion of all women's right to bear children into the movement to secure women's right to reproductive control.[5]

Fighting for Women's and Community Control

Medical innovations, legal decrees, and federal government programs in the 1960s expanded the resources that made it possible for women to control their fertility. This shift began in 1960 when the U.S. government approved sales of oral contraceptives—the birth control pill—to U.S. consumers following a short period of testing on a small population of uninformed women in Puerto Rico. U.S. drug manufacturers rushed to market the pill and within five years of its introduction to U.S. consumers, the oral contraceptive became the leading method of birth control, attesting to women's desire for dependable and easy-to-use forms of birth control. The market for the new oral contraceptives widened further in 1965 when a Supreme Court decision, *Griswold v. Connecticut,* held that laws banning the use of contraception by married couples violated Americans' constitutional right to marital privacy.[6]

The *Griswold* ruling and the availability of the birth control pill provided new tools for public and private agencies that offered family planning services. The Metropolitan Washington chapter of Planned Parenthood, which had operated two family planning clinics in the city since the 1930s, augmented its educational programs and health services by distributing contraceptive devices, typically birth control pills and diaphragms, to married women. More than promoting sexual equality, Planned Parenthood staff were committed to strengthening communities by promoting wanted children, healthy women, and stable families. Ophelia Egypt, a black social worker who ran a Planned Parenthood clinic in southeast

D.C., encouraged residents' involvement in the administration of the facility's programs. African American women who lived near the clinic developed clubs for parents, distributed birth control information, and lobbied the city government to create maternity centers at the city's public hospital. Thus, the clinic encouraged community participation and control over family planning initiatives.[7]

With Planned Parenthood's assistance, Washington's Department of Public Health began to distribute contraceptive materials and information in 1964, using federal funds to provide free birth control for low-income women at the D.C. General Hospital and five health clinics located across the city. The funds came at the urging of Senator Robert Byrd, chair of the Senate subcommittee on D.C. Appropriations, who had pushed District health officials to dispense contraceptive information to welfare applicants.[8] Planned Parenthood staff assisted this initiative by training public health workers, physicians, and caseworkers to direct eligible women to the new services. Like the federal and city governments, Planned Parenthood staff agreed that birth control was critical in the battle against poverty. "To fight poverty without birth control is to fight with one arm tied behind your back," declared the executive director of the Washington group.[9] Senator Byrd even more directly saw birth control as a tool for decreasing poverty and cleaning up the city's black neighborhoods. According to the senator, birth control use would decrease illegitimacy and improve "parental responsibility," thereby lessening welfare caseloads and juvenile delinquency. But if illegitimacy in black families went unchecked, Byrd warned, "the burden of crime, riots and dole will ultimately become unbearable."[10]

The distribution of oral contraception, backed by the *Griswold* ruling, potentially increased family autonomy over fertility, but other actions threatened to lessen the control exercised by poor women. Namely, after 1965, the federal government began to sponsor family planning programs in the United States through War on Poverty initiatives. That year, for example, the federal government created the Medicaid program, a form of health insurance for low-income families. As part of the domestic War on Poverty, the Office of Economic Opportunity turned its attention to the role that birth control could play in alleviating poverty within the United States, an initiative that differed from previous efforts to fund family planning programs outside the country through the Agency for International Development (AID). The OEO authorized the establishment and funding of family planning clinics as part of its community programs and, although OEO regulations specified that participation in family planning programs was voluntary, participation was also limited to women who were single or separated from their husbands. Amendments to the Social Security Act enacted in 1967 went further by requiring states to establish family planning programs, and permitted them to distribute grants to private agencies, including Planned Parenthood, that engaged in this mission.[11]

By yoking family planning to the fight against poverty, the federal government ensured wider availability of birth control within poor communities and implied that participation in antipoverty programs required women to use contraception. The connection of family planning and antipoverty measures also promoted differential standards of morality for poor unmarried women, for whom contraception was deemed socially responsible, and unmarried women whose financial means disqualified them from publicly funded programs and, hence, from legal contraceptive use. Because African American women of all income levels utilized public family planning services at greater rates than did white women—whether they were run by hospitals, family planning agencies like Planned Parenthood, or as part of other public health clinics—they experienced greater vulnerability to the priorities and regulations established by federal funders.[12] Indeed, federal funds were seldom available for family planning programs without some strings attached, and power dynamics created by racism and poverty compounded the pressure on poor women.[13]

Surgical sterilization represented the most egregious form of coercion in the federally funded family planning effort, with welfare recipients and poor women of color undergoing the procedure at much higher rates than in the general population. An estimated 100,000–150,000 poor women, nearly 50 percent of them African American, were sterilized annually in the early 1970s under the auspices of Medicaid or other federally funded welfare programs. Thousands of Native American women, by some counts as many as one quarter of women of childbearing age, were operated on without their knowledge or consent. Whatever their racial and ethnic background, women who depended on publicly funded health services possessed little recourse when physicians or social workers used deception or force to limit their fertility. Staff at one city hospital, for example, informed the head of a Washington welfare rights group that if she wanted an abortion she would have to submit to permanent sterilization; refusal would have sent her looking for other, more dangerous, ways to terminate her pregnancy. Other women consented to abortions after being threatened with loss of their welfare benefits, or were sterilized without giving their consent. By contrast, women who did not depend on welfare or Medicaid often struggled to find doctors willing to sterilize them at their request.[14]

The coercive uses of birth control and sterilization among black and poor women convinced many Americans that the government's family planning initiative was driven by racist intentions. Activists adopted the term "genocide" to describe what they perceived as the U.S. government's deliberate attempt to make birth control an instrument to promote a capitalist, imperialist mission in the world and white supremacy at home. In the summer of 1969, shortly before the DCWLM-CWA protests at the public hospital, Marilyn Salzman Webb, the journalist and member of the DCWLM, had published an article criticizing the worldwide population-control efforts of the Nixon administration. Webb accused the administration of backing family planning initiatives in order to curtail population growth in the Third World. Nixon and his associates, linking high population density with high rates of poverty, had justified these policies as an attempt to diminish poverty across the globe. But Webb countered that poorly distributed resources, rather than overpopulation, caused poverty in developing nations in Africa and elsewhere. Instead of fighting deprivation, aid to birth control programs promoted U.S. economic and political hegemony around the globe, Webb argued, while the federal government justified population control at home as a means to prevent social disorder. "Housing, education, ecology, and, indeed, our 'democratic' form of government would be threatened if babies continue to be born at the current rate in the U.S., particularly, it would seem, poor or black babies," Webb concluded.[15]

To Webb and other activists, tests of oral contraceptives on unsuspecting Puerto Rican women, incidents of U.S. welfare recipients sterilized without their knowledge or consent, and the prolific distribution of birth control in the Third World all added up to a targeted effort by the U.S. government to reduce population growth among selected groups. That these efforts concentrated on populations in places where mass movements were challenging the power of colonial or antidemocratic regimes seemed more than a coincidence. Family planning agencies including Planned Parenthood also came under suspicion for operating as an agent of the state rather than as a vehicle for women's liberation.[16]

Whether or not Webb accurately interpreted the U.S. government's motives, such ideas gained popularity at the end of the 1960s, especially among those activists who became outspoken critics of the alleged racist motivations behind government expenditures and policies.[17] An article in the Nation of Islam's official paper, *Muhammad Speaks,* argued that although sterilization clinics claimed to be "aiding the indigent," the obvious intention was "surgical genocide, as effective in a long term sense as Nazi Germany's gas chambers and with the same objective." Similarly, in 1969, the *Black Panther* newspaper described birth control as "nothing more than part and parcel of the anti-human practices of the fascist racist and U.S. government and their genocidal war effort."[18] The Nation of Islam and the Black Panther Party encouraged supporters of racial liberation to resist the government's genocidal efforts by increasing the size of their families. Promoting large families under patriarchal control, the *Black Panther* paper in January 1969 instructed black men to "educate your woman to stop taking those [birth control] pills. You and your woman—replenish the earth with healthy Black warriors." In other words, female activists could support the black freedom movement, and protect the African American community, by heeding male authority and rearing large families.[19]

The Nation of Islam and the Black Panther Party did not represent the perspectives of all African American activists—and the Black Panther Party's position on this issue even changed over time, eventually advocating birth control as an important tool for women's liberation.[20] Other black activists supported family planning programs and considered birth control vital to personal and family well-being. New York State Representative Shirley Chisholm, the first black woman elected to Congress, objected to any form of pressure that resulted in "compulsory pregnancy." Speaking in D.C. in 1970 at a conference at the Howard University College of Medicine, Chisholm advocated safe and sanitary abortions for women who wanted them. In addition to stressing the need for women's control of their reproductive decisions, she highlighted the risks that criminal abortions posed. Citing 80 percent of maternal deaths that resulted from illegal abortions, Chisholm asked "What could be more like genocide than that?"[21]

Bobby McMahan, Elizabeth Perry, and Beverly Crawford, members of the D.C. Family Rights Welfare Organization, also prioritized poor women's need for contraceptive access over the government's motives. Testifying in early 1970, when Congress considered legislation expanding the federal government's family planning and population research activities, they announced the welfare organization's support for an expansion in federal programs. Speaking as poor black welfare recipients, the three women conceded that many people in their community ascribed to the argument that the federal government hoped to reduce the African American population through its efforts. But they also backed family planning as a right that should be available to all women. "We think," McMahan testified, that "any woman, rich or poor, black or white, who wants to plan how many children she wants, and when she wants them, should have access to a comprehensive family planning service. . . . If the woman is pregnant and wants an abortion, we think she is entitled to have one."[22]

Suspicions about family planning were exacerbated as the legal structure that restricted abortion access began to fall. The increase in government-funded birth control programs, occurring at the same time that challenges to abortion laws grew, left many activists fearful that women might become more vulnerable to outside interventions. Among the most important figures in dismantling the city's abortion laws was Milan Vuitch, a physician who opposed the city's restrictions on where and why abortions could be performed. Vuitch refused to operate his medical practice in a secretive manner and, instead, allowed advocates to openly disseminate his name to women who wanted abortions. Arrested for his activities in 1968, Vuitch challenged the city's laws in court, arguing that the provision allowing abortions to protect a woman's health should apply also to her mental health.

A year later, in November 1969, a judge from the U.S. District Court of the District of Columbia ruled that the D.C. law was unconstitutionally vague in describing when abortion was warranted, making it difficult for physicians, hospitals, and law enforcement to determine if violations had occurred. Only a month earlier, a California judge similarly had found that state's abortion law to be unconstitutionally vague. In D.C., where only Congress held the power to amend the laws, the judge called for consistent application of the existing regulation. "It is legally proper and indeed imperative," the ruling stated, "that uniform medical abortion services be provided all segments of the population, the poor as well as the rich. Principles of equal protection under our Constitution require that policies in our public hospitals be liberalized immediately."[23] The U.S. attorney general's office appealed the decision to the Supreme Court, but in the interim, the ruling in *Vuitch* set aside the old law and created grounds for the city to implement new guidelines for Washington hospitals to follow.

Women's Coalition for Health and Abortion Rights

By invalidating the terms of D.C.'s restrictive abortion law and by urging the establishment of new regulations to ensure equal access, the *Vuitch* decision promised to increase the number of legal abortions performed in the city. This prospect alarmed city officials and public health administrators. But abortion supporters seized new opportunities to shape public policy as a tool for women's liberation and community empowerment.

Women affiliated with the DCWLM and the CWA introduced a new phase of the city's reproductive rights movement when they organized protests at the D.C. General Hospital in September 1969. Their campaigns transformed both the style and substance of the abortion movement. Calling for free medical care and abortion on demand, these activists exploited the ambiguity in the city's abortion laws to create a women-centered movement for birth control and abortion that relied on arguments and tactics earlier honed by welfare rights, antipoverty, feminist, and civil rights movements. Using mass protest and direct action strategies to pressure officials to change public policy, their pickets at the hospital represented the first mass demonstration against the city's abortion laws. By framing abortion within the context of women's quest for liberation and as part of a push for quality health care, they highlighted economic issues that determined women's ability to act in accordance with the city's laws. Yet the coalition brought into the open the differing views of women's liberationists and welfare activists regarding the connection between reproductive rights and women's liberation.

Members of the city's welfare rights organizations had not specifically tackled the lack of abortion access before the fall of 1969. But the problematic health care available to poor women and children had prompted Washington welfare activists to campaign against one hospital that refused to accept Medicaid payments despite its location in a primarily low-income area of Washington.[24] Members of the CWA also had prodded Congress in 1968 to improve health care access when setting the city's budget appropriations. In addition to following up on an issue of concern to its members, the CWA's attack on D.C. General in 1969 reflected that group's view that poor mothers were entitled to privacy, authority over their family, and autonomous decisions about motherhood.

For the DCWLM, the campaign at D.C. General represented both a continuation of previous activities and a new direction. In 1968, in the context of discussing women's health, members of the DCWLM had highlighted difficulties caused by limited information about and access to birth control and abortion. In addition, women's liberationists who counseled women who contacted their office seeking assistance in obtaining abortions heard stories about abortions occurring under terrifying, humiliating, and expensive circumstances. The most egregious abuses occurred when poor women went to D.C. General Hospital seeking safe and legal abortions, only to be turned away without adequate explanation and without time to pursue other options. Denied the opportunity to find a physician who agreed to perform a legal abortion, such women could bear unwanted children, try home remedies to induce abortions, or patronize the network of underground abortionists who often conducted the procedure in dangerous conditions and charged exorbitant fees.[25]

Alarmed by the accounts of women who had applied for abortions at the public hospital, members of the CWA and the DCWLM united to protest what they considered arbitrary and unfair implementation of Washington's abortion laws by D.C. General. Whereas physicians affiliated with the city's private hospitals might charge as much as $600 for an abortion, D.C. General charged little for services to low-income patients. But despite making abortions available at minimal cost, the hospital's rigorous policy for determining eligibility disqualified most women. In order to meet D.C. General's criteria, an applicant had to undergo evaluation by one of the General Hospital's four staff obstetricians and two other specialists who agreed that carrying a pregnancy would threaten her life or health. This policy disadvantaged women without the time and money to undergo the multiple examinations, denying them the ability to choose the doctors who examined them and to present their own rationales for their decisions. Even with the necessary documentation, the hospital inexplicably turned away women only to have them return for emergency care after they had tried other means to induce abortion. In addition, some D.C. General physicians insisted that poor women follow up abortions with sterilization, forcing them to relinquish the possibility of future children.[26]

Not surprisingly, disparate access carried significant consequences for women. In 1967, D.C. General doctors performed eight therapeutic abortions. Only doctors at Washington's four Catholic hospitals conducted fewer, whereas staff at two of Washington's private hospitals performed an average of 170 procedures each month.[27] The public hospital's policies failed to deter desperate women, however, and more than 500 women every year sought treatment at the facility for complications resulting from illegal and self-induced abortions. In 1969 alone, according to a report issued by the D.C. City Council, the hospital admitted more than 900 women who fell ill after incomplete or illegal abortions. By conducting so few abortions, therefore, the public hospital actually exacerbated women's health and reproductive problems and increased its caseload.[28]

When two women were inexplicably refused abortions by the hospital, despite having met D.C. General's criteria, DCWLM and CWA members requested conferences with public health department and hospital officials to discuss D.C. General's abortion policy. After the administrators refused to meet, the women picketed the hospital. Gathering in front of the main entrance, more than twenty women called out for "free abortions on demand" and "free medical care for all."[29] The next day, thirty women and children barged into the office of the director of public health, who oversaw policies at D.C. General Hospital, staging a sit-in until he agreed to form a committee to recommend policy changes that would bring the hospital into line with the regulations imposed by other facilities. Once established, this committee included six members of the women's liberation group, three members of the CWA, and a slightly greater number of medical professionals and administrators. After meeting several times over the following months, the Department of Public Health's committee on abortion asked the health director to give D.C. General administrators permission to authorize all abortions unless medically harmful to the patient. The only objections to the recommendation came from a Catholic priest and physician who ran the obstetrics unit at Georgetown University's hospital.[30]

Throughout the fall, women activists also attempted to participate in hearings of a task force to study health resources in the city. The District's mayor, Walter Washington, had established the task force to reorganize the city's health department, designating a subcommittee to investigate conditions at the hospitals. When the subcommittee convened two days of closed hearings to gather information about D.C. General, welfare rights and women's liberation activists showed up and refused to leave the sessions until they expressed their grievances. Charging the task force with inappropriate secrecy, they argued that residents familiar with conditions at the hospital should be allowed to relate their experiences to the committee. Furthermore, they objected that male doctors rather than the women who depended on the hospital made up the majority of the task force members. Without input from residents who used public health facilities, and especially without adequate representation by women, activists feared the task force would downplay the serious health crisis facing the city. Disrupting the hearings by shouting out comments and questions, they demanded that the subcommittee address high mortality rates among infants and women in childbirth. Under pressure from the publicity created by the activists, the subcommittee chair invited the women to participate in future meetings, and the mayor appointed two CWA members to the group. In its report to the mayor, the task force concluded, "In the District of Columbia, legal abortions are almost totally unavailable to poor women because of the restrictive policy followed by D.C. General Hospital." Based on such evidence, the task force recommended that the mayor order the hospital to eliminate all restrictions and extend abortions to women upon request.[31]

The impact of the collaborative activities undertaken by the DCWLM and CWA can be measured in several ways. The tactics employed by the activists—picket lines, rallies, sit-ins—represented the continuation of methods previously used effectively by black liberation and welfare rights activists and expanded the repertoire of women's liberationists. In addition to asserting women's right to participate in policy setting, the coalition combated the silence typically surrounding abortion. Rather than treating abortion as a matter for discussion within the privacy of bedrooms or the confines of doctors' and clergy's offices, the welfare rights and women's liberation activists framed abortion as a woman's political due. Taking the issue to the public, welfare rights and women's liberation activists acted on their belief that shame—at poverty, welfare dependency, past mistreatment by physicians, or sexual activity outside of marriage—contributed to women's oppression. Coalition members overcame their own shame when publicly associating themselves with the movement and they hoped that their boldness would empower other women to join their movement.

Within welfare rights and women's liberation groups, the coalition provided an opportunity to act on critically important issues. Neither the CWA nor the DC-WLM, however, intended to make the fight for improved health care and abortion access their primary focus. Instead, they viewed the hospital campaigns as one aspect of their ongoing struggles to win welfare rights and women's liberation, respectively. Only four days before the protests at D.C. General, welfare rights activists had picketed the welfare department demanding money for back-to-school clothing. During the fall, as DCWLM members fought to gain inclusion on the mayoral task force and met repeatedly with the Department of Public Health's committee on abortion, other women's liberationists took part in the WITCH protest at the Justice Department.[32] Even when joining to protest the hospital and the city's health care practices, welfare rights activists and women's liberationists established points of commonality but retained their larger—and separate—goals and activities.

In some ways, too, the coalition actually accentuated the different views of motherhood and fertility control held by DCWLM and CWA. To women's liberationists such as Alice Wolfson, free abortion on demand constituted a key element of women's liberation, a goal that also required eradicating sexism from the medical system and the larger society. Wolfson explained, "Freedom for women means the freedom for other forms of life work and identity than just the family."[33] In a similar vein, DCWLM member and journalist Judith Coburn maintained, "Women's liberation must fight to change society to allow women to make their own reproductive choices and whether or not to choose other careers than housewife and mother. For married women, this means round-the-clock day care centers at the place of work. For men, it means sharing equally the responsibilities of children, household, and conception."[34] Coburn's and Wolfson's statements suggested that DCWLM participants perceived women's roles as wife and mother as repressive, serving the interests of capitalism and patriarchy. In contrast, welfare rights activists embraced the identity of mother as a potential source of power and authority—when women possessed resources adequate to ensure the security of their families. But women's liberationists aimed to relieve pressures on women to marry and become mothers. With convenient and inexpensive access to abortion and birth control, they believed, women could freely make decisions about motherhood and achieve an essential step toward liberation.

Along with their concern for removing obstacles that prevented women's self-determination in reproductive areas, Wolfson and other women's liberationists viewed the problem of abortion access as a symbol of women's lack of control over their health care decisions. Doctors and hospital officials held inordinate power to determine the outcome of a pregnancy, but many, according to DCWLM activists, lacked compassion for women patients. One DCWLM publication, "Women and Health," reported that the doctor who headed the obstetrics/gynecology unit at D.C. General Hospital had allegedly stated that his staff avoided performing abortions because the procedure was "too boring." Believing such attitudes pervaded the medical field, women's liberationists concluded that widespread changes in the medical profession must accompany the movement to grant women's reproductive freedom.[35] Men vastly outnumbered women in the medical profession and business interests exerted too much sway over health care, feminists believed. Driven by the quest for profit, medical researchers who were funded by drug companies subjected women to new birth control pills before the risks had been sufficiently determined and information widely conveyed to consumers. Planned Parenthood contributed to the problem by funding contraceptive research and distributing unsafe birth control devices. Making abortion in particular and medical care in general freely available would eliminate the profit motive that resulted in a lack of excellent medical care for all Americans, especially those with little money.

Indeed, DCWLM argued, even middle-class women lacked adequate health care because quality medical treatment "requires a system that is not based on profit for hospitals, doctors, drug industries, and private insurance companies. Health care must be seen as a national responsibility and it must be approached with a system of preventive as well as curative medicine." Thus, according to feminists, the battle for reproductive rights should be pursued as part of an effort to transform the country's health care system.[36]

Like women's liberationists, welfare rights activists understood that health care professionals exerted an extraordinary influence over women's reproduction. In contrast to the DCWLM, however, members of the CWA perceived that poverty and the structure of the welfare system posed the greatest obstacle to their reproductive control. The principle that women's receipt of public assistance funds should not restrict maternal rights was central to the welfare rights movement. Similarly, receipt of welfare or Medicaid did not prove a woman's qualifications as a mother. But women's economic status and the public assistance system limited how they could exercise their rights as mothers, affecting how well they could provide for their children's material needs and often forcing them to choose not to have or raise children. Within a political context where poor African American women were targeted as the reason for numerous social ills, the distinction between voluntary restrictions on contraception and coercion was ambiguous. Welfare activist Etta Horn characterized this situation as genocide: the medical system and, especially, the D.C. Department of Public Health, forced women into the abortion underground, while social workers at the welfare agency scared public aid recipients into using birth control. Furthermore, Horn argued, the ill health that had driven many women out of the labor force and onto public aid exacerbated the hazardous side effects of oral contraceptives. Whatever the political or economic motives that led public health workers and welfare caseworkers to discourage recipients' fertility, welfare activists insisted that impoverished women possessed the right to regulate their reproductive lives. As welfare activist Bobby McMahan put it, all women had the right to decide if and when they wanted children. Politicians might believe that welfare recipients demonstrated less concern for their families' well being than did more affluent Americans, but McMahan argued the reverse. "Poor people care just as much as the rich, if not more, about the welfare of their children. Poor people don't want their children to be destined to poverty."[37]

Thus, although members of all of the concerned groups agreed that restrictions on reproductive choice should be eliminated and that women must exercise reproductive control, they understood the problems in different ways. Women's liberationists emphasized the demand to terminate pregnancies, while welfare activists stressed the right to bear children. This difference in perspective did not make feminists' and welfare activists' demands incompatible, but did reflect how women's class and race backgrounds affected their experiences. Furthermore, the different perspectives represented by the two organizations limited their continued collaboration. White women in DCWLM acknowledged that the CWA taught them a lot about the conditions poor black women faced, especially how the government used reproductive control to conduct political and racial genocide. Yet DCWLM also conceded that it never "adequately resolve[d] the question of abortions as a means of genocide in the black community vs. the need for sanitary, free abortions for all, especially poor and black women. . . . We realized that we should not isolate the abortion issue from an overall demand to women's right to control our bodies, but this was not easy to carry out in practice and much of our work failed to get beyond these problems."[38]

These different emphases were accompanied by differences in approach. Whereas the CWA had called for legislative reforms that would restructure public assistance to better meet the needs of the country's poor, the DCWLM had prioritized changing culture over reforming laws or policies. Transforming consciousness about the existence of women's oppression, they reasoned, constituted one step toward a revolution that would bring equality to society, but reformist approaches would fall short of liberating women. The DCWLM's denunciation of reform may explain why Etta Horn contended that the coalition had not "really gotten together to work on abortion reform."[39] But the DCWLM gave pragmatic realities—including the predicaments women faced and the opportunities to influence public policy during a critical period—priority over their political ideals. As they described it in a pamphlet, organizing for abortion access required the group to "walk a fine line between continual struggle for ultimate freedoms and meeting some real and immediate needs at each step along the way." The fight to gain abortion rights, which they believed would address the urgent problems of illness and death caused by illegal abortions, could provide some short-term benefits until complete social and economic upheaval brought about women's true liberation.[40]

After women gained seats on the official policy-making boards of the city council and health department, the CWA and DCWLM sought new means to expand women's reproductive control. Moving away from the singular focus on abortion access, welfare rights and women's liberation activists both turned to push for reproductive freedom and safety by addressing women's need for safe birth control and to eliminate the particular pressures to terminate or avoid pregnancy that poor women endured. In general, despite their desire for more revolutionary change, DCWLM members focused on health care and abortion reform by way of the courts and Congress and consistently offered counseling to individual women. Simultaneously, welfare rights activists maintained their efforts to educate feminists about poor women's experiences and to highlight the coercive uses of birth control and abortion. Both groups continued to stress the disparities that marked women's ability to control their reproduction and to search for opportunities to express their demands and analyses to new audiences.

In the spring of 1970, DCWLM joined a suit to challenge D.C. General Hospital's criteria for determining women's eligibility for abortion. In response to the *Vuitch* ruling, D.C. General began to accept psychiatric evidence in order to assess women's mental health, but imposed stricter standards of evidence than private facilities in the city. As a result, the hospital lagged far behind other facilities in the terms of the numbers of abortions its staff performed, and women who seemingly met the hospital's criteria still found themselves inexplicably turned away.[41] A class action suit brought by the ACLU, which the DCWLM supported, tried to clarify the hospital's procedures and compel the facility to grant abortions without delay to eligible women. The suit clearly followed up on the DCWLM-CWA coalition's earlier efforts to make abortion available to low-income women on grounds similar to those available to patients able to pay for medical care, as demonstrated in a statement that the DCWLM issued opposing abortion, contraception, or sterilization used to oppress specific groups of people and affirming women's right to terminate unwanted pregnancies and to have children if and when they wanted them.[42]

Other DCWLM members acted on their concerns about the potentially harmful effects of birth control pills. After ten years of availability to U.S. consumers, research data on the detrimental physical and mental health complications of oral contraceptives suggested a need for further medical research. In 1969 and early 1970, the Senate's Small Business Subcommittee on Monopoly, headed by Senator Gaylord Nelson, convened hearings on the pill's safety. The DCWLM's Health Committee members had discussed their own experiences with the unpleasant side effects of oral contraception. Interested in learning more, Alice Wolfson and other DCWLM members decided to attend the Senate's hearings. As they sat in the chambers, they grew outraged at the voluminous evidence linking oral contraception to cancer and numerous other dangers. In addition, they objected to the absence of women researchers on the speakers' list and to the congressional committee's failure to solicit testimony from women who had used the pill.[43] Members returned to the hearing room the next day and brought the proceedings to a standstill by shouting out questions and comments from the floor. Their disruption halted the hearings, garnered national publicity, and won DCWLM an audience with Senator Nelson. After listening to their concerns, Nelson agreed to add "qualified" women to the witness list—researchers and women who had experienced severe complications as a result of the pill—but he refused to let DCWLM members question witnesses.[44]

The protests compounded radical feminists' distrust of the political system and of the efficacy of reform as a tool for women's liberation. DCWLM members' misgivings expanded further when, shortly after the Nelson subcommittee's hearings closed, the FDA weakened rather than strengthened the safety warning on oral contraceptive packages. Wolfson and other members of the DCWLM reacted with a sit-in at the office of Health, Education, and Welfare Secretary Robert Finch to protest the inadequate safety warnings and to demand that more explicit language be included in package inserts. The new FDA policy, according to Alice Wolfson, reflected the government's disregard for women's lives and health. The lesson from these encounters, Wolfson concluded, was that "if we are ever to have control over the institutions which govern our lives, women must band together and refuse to recognize a government policy that puts profit over people."[45]

As part of repudiating government authority in health care matters, in March 1970, the DCWLM organized their own hearings about the pill. More than 100 women gathered in a church to listen to personal testimony about women's health problems caused by taking oral contraception. One speaker accused drug manufacturers, advertisers, and physicians of prescribing and promoting oral contraception in order to turn a profit. "They never thought about what the pill would do to us women . . . it is genocide on Black people, poor whites, and women."[46] Other speakers warned of the many health problems associated with birth control—serious medical ailments that made its use ill-advised for women with some preexisting conditions. Among these groups were the many welfare recipients who, suffering from poor health that pushed them out of the job market, risked death if they used oral contraception. In alarm, Etta Horn insisted that better regulations should allow women to "decide what is done with their bodies." The hearings and publications that activists produced carried no official weight, but they contributed to the reproductive health movement by creating a forum for women to share their experiences, listen to research data detailing contraceptive risks, and create a public record of their concerns.[47]

Expanding the Fight

Between 1970 and 1973, welfare rights activists, radical feminists, and other women and men organized countless rallies and public meetings where they demanded women's control of their own fertility and improved health care for women. Across the country, state abortion laws toppled in response to suits brought by activists and reforms enacted by legislatures. New York led the way, passing legislation in early 1970 that made abortion legal during the first six months of gestation. Hawaii and Maryland quickly followed suit. For advocates of abortion rights, these state-level victories—and their sometimes insecure status—justified continued activity to overturn restrictive laws elsewhere. Abortion rights supporters also began to fight for legal repeal on the federal level, mounting a national campaign that would overlap state-level efforts.

In D.C., women's access to abortion expanded while public officials responded to popular pressure and tried to standardize the conditions under which abortions could be performed locally. Between the summer of 1970 and the fall of 1972, a series of public hearings demonstrated the degree of popular support for abortion access and convinced the city council to further extend the requirements determining when abortions could be legally performed.[48] In 1971, the council passed regulations allowing physicians to perform abortions at offices and clinics licensed for that purpose.[49] That same year, the Supreme Court ruled in the *Vuitch* case that the city's abortion law was constitutional, a decision that reversed the earlier judgment, but nonetheless accepted the argument that abortion for mental health purposes could be accommodated within the language of the law.[50]

The new *Vuitch* ruling and the city council's decision authorizing abortions in clinics and licensed physicians' offices made abortion services more widely available. By the fall of 1971, women could obtain abortions at four clinics located in the hospitals or independently run by reproductive health organizations. Four other organizations joined the DCWLM to provide information, referrals, and counseling about abortion. Planned Parenthood expanded services at its downtown clinic, offering pregnancy testing, abortion counseling, and prenatal adoption referrals. However, access to abortion continued to be uneven, with some hospitals and clinics refusing to grant abortions to women under twenty-one years of age without parental approval or to married women who did not have the consent of their husbands (even if the couple had separated). Women's ability to get abortions also varied depending on their economic resources, a condition Planned Parenthood tried to rectify by arranging loans for women who could not afford abortion services even at the $200 rate offered by most clinics.[51]

With the expanded visibility and legitimacy conveyed by the city council and Supreme Court actions, greater numbers of people were drawn into the local abortion rights movement, including representatives of organizations that previously had avoided taking a public stance on the controversial topic. More than in earlier campaigns for women's liberation or welfare rights, activists chose coalitions as the main vehicle for organizing activities and building public awareness about the need to expand abortion rights. The existence of three coalitions, formed in 1971, showed that winning women's reproductive rights represented a goal that united women who otherwise held distinct organizational affiliations and advocated contrasting views about women's liberation and social change. At the same time, the impulse to form three distinct coalitions, rather than one single umbrella organization, suggested the limits of unity and the difficulty of bringing together women with differing political philosophies and priorities to fight for reproductive rights. Alliances emerged, and folded, on the basis of participants' ability to develop consensus and compromise on tactics and priorities.

Typically, abortion rights coalitions framed their agenda around issues that seemingly all women shared rather than around demands that could be associated with particular groups of women. In the context of the growing national reproductive rights movement, this meant equating abortion rights with women's legal rights, and asserting abortion rights as the primary means to secure women's reproductive control. Articulating the right to legal abortion as the central demand of Washington's alliances, however, caused abortion supporters to downplay other barriers that restrained women's access to freedom of choice, including disparities in interpretation of the District's relatively liberal laws, and the problems of coercion that poor women of color experienced.

The difficulty that one new coalition, the Metropolitan Abortion Alliance (MAA), experienced in developing activities and sustaining consensus exemplified the challenges of linking activists with distinct ideas about women's liberation. The MAA formed in the spring of 1971 and included members of the DCWLM; representatives from the D.C. chapters of the Young Socialist Alliance (YSA), NOW, and FEW; members of a George Washington University women's liberation group; and supporters of Planned Parenthood and Zero Population Growth. The MAA initially agreed to promote three demands: (1) women's control over their own bodies; (2) free and safe abortions on demand, without involuntary sterilization; (3) and safe contraception for any woman who sought it.

Within months of reaching consensus on this agenda, divisions emerged over the strategy of arguing for abortion rights. NOW and YSA prioritized repeal as a goal, pushing to overturn restrictive abortion laws. In contrast, other members concluded that in D.C., where laws were relatively permissive, the worst abuses stemmed from poor women's inability to procure abortions in a safe, legal, and affordable manner.[52] Originally, the MAA had planned to publicize the "oppressive abortion policies" that denied women's control of their bodies by demonstrating in front of D.C. General. Harkening back to the DCWLM-CWA coalition's activities, this event would highlight the plight of the city's poor African American women. But at the last minute, YSA members relocated the rally to Lafayette Park, across Pennsylvania Avenue from the White House, a site that promised greater exposure and symbolically linked the MAA to a national cause. But the move symbolized a shift in attention away from local conditions to the national front, with legal repeal taking precedence over issues of access and implementation. In addition, the emphasis on repeal hinted at the MAA's attempt to articulate abortion rights as a demand all women shared, even those who might not identify with the problems of access that poor women experienced.[53]

Nonetheless, the Lafayette Park rally reflected the breadth and depth of the abortion movement on a national scale. Nationally known and local feminist speakers inspired the crowd with information about ongoing efforts to fight for abortion rights across the country. Jeannie Reynolds of the MAA and the local NOW chapter explained that two local groups were bringing legal suits using two different tactics: one challenging the tax-exempt status of the Roman Catholic Church because of its lobbying activities opposing the abortion movement, the other seeking to declare the city's abortion statute unconstitutional. A law student reminded the crowd that free abortion on demand would prevent the deaths of poor women who died as a result of having sought illegal abortions. Tina Hobson, the wife of former CORE director Julius Hobson and a representative of FEW, asserted that the meager benefits available to federal employees limited women's reproductive freedom by denying maternity leave and failing to make day care available. Finally, a high school student spoke of the difficulties faced by young women who became pregnant.[54]

About 200 people attended the rally in Lafayette Park, a turnout that disappointed organizers, but still exceeded numbers present at previous abortion rights demonstrations in the city.[55] The rally also solidified many activists' support for the focus on legal repeal and mass demonstrations as strategies to secure abortion rights. Jeannie Reynolds encouraged NOW's members to look beyond the small crowds at the Lafayette Park rally and commit to an ongoing fight. NOW should continue to participate in abortion rights demonstrations, Reynolds argued, and should create ways to organize the "energy and interest" evidenced by its members.[56] Another activist appealed to readers of *off our backs* to get serious about supporting "the most important issue in the movement." Calling on women to mobilize into "an organized fighting force," she argued that "sit-ins, protests, demonstrations of all kinds and more rallys [sic] are necessary to build sisterhood and an unshakable solidarity."[57]

The MAA disbanded shortly after the Lafayette Park rally, done in by conflict over strategy and focus. Another coalition, spearheaded by the local branch of the Women's National Abortion Action Coalition (WONAAC) soon took its place. The D.C. chapter of WONAAC formed in the summer of 1971, fighting to repeal abortion laws across the country and challenging local abortion practices. WONAAC was founded by YSA members who considered abortion of "central importance because as long as women are denied the right to control their own bodies, they cannot control their lives. At some time in her life, virtually every woman feels the threat of an unwanted pregnancy, and thus every woman has a stake in repealing the abortion laws." Strategically, the YSA argued that the abortion movement should abandon the earlier call for "free abortion on demand," a slogan that focused attention on medical services, and instead focus on women's legal right to abortion. The issue of abortion law repeal could form the center of a nationwide campaign with the participation of masses of women who might feed into a larger movement to transform America's political system.[58]

In keeping with YSA's philosophy, WONAAC primarily organized mass pro-tests in support of repealing abortion laws. The group's position attracted many adherents, including the local chapters of NOW and FEW. By the fall of 1971, WO-NAAC had become the most visible abortion rights organization in the city. The D.C. branch joined a class action suit to protest the waiting period proposed by the city council and held public gatherings where women spoke from firsthand expe-rience about back-alley abortions, sterilization, and local abortion regulations.[59] In November 1971, it coordinated the first national abortion rights demonstra-tion in Washington, bringing more than two thousand activists to the Capitol and inspiring antiabortion activists to hurriedly put together a competing protest for the same day. WONAAC's agenda also called for an end to forced sterilization and the elimination of restrictive contraceptive laws, arguing that "restrictive abortion laws provide the basis of legalized murder of thousands of women. Involuntary sterilizations are the price poor women are often forced to pay in order to obtain safe, legal abortions." But these demands were always secondary to the fight for abortion law repeal and never became the focus of WONAAC's campaigns.[60]

Prominent local figures, including Bobby McMahan from the NWRO and Mary Treadwell, formerly of SNCC and now an executive director of Pride, Inc., publicly supported WONAAC. For African American women like Treadwell and McMa-han, the coalition offered a place to join the fight for abortion law repeal but still advance a distinct perspective. WONAAC formed a Black Woman's Task Force and in Washington, black women's abortion groups were organized at American University and Howard University. These groups simultaneously provided affilia-tion with WONAAC, but also conveyed recognition that African American women faced particular dilemmas in the quest for reproductive control.[61]

Indeed, Mary Treadwell kept African American women's distinct concerns at the forefront when she spoke at a press conference that WONAAC organized in October 1971 to announce the founding of its Black Women's Task Force. Treadwell argued that racism in America convinced her of the necessity of abortion law re-peal. "The legislators of this country are overwhelmingly white and overwhelm-ingly male," Treadwell pointed out. "While rejecting legalized abortion," she argued, "these very men sit in hypocritical splendor and refuse to provide an adequate guaranteed annual income for these children born to women without financial and social access to safe abortion. While rejecting legalized abortion, these very men refuse to fund quality, inexpensive prenatal and post-natal care to women without access to abortion . . . [and] refuse to fund quality education and training for the children of women without access to abortions."[62] In addition to highlighting the ways that racism and poverty limited women's reproductive control, Treadwell addressed black liberation activists on the issue of genocide. She argued that African Americans needed to understand that compulsory pregnancy, whether coerced by the government or by liberation activists, denied women's rights and damaged black communities. "Black women," she insisted, "particularly need this personal freedom to be able to fulfill themselves sexually without fear of conception. The outside pressures of this society wreak enough havoc within the black home and the black unit. It is unspeakable that legislated, racist pressures should accompany the black woman to her bedroom and creep insidiously into the center of her bed."[63]

Unlike Treadwell, other abortion supporters rejected WONAAC's approach. The organization's affiliation with the YSA led members of the DCWLM to question the sincerity of WONAAC's support for feminist demands and its role in the dissolution of the MAA. This distrust stemmed from the presence of men in socialist groups and from feminists' perception that WONAAC's attempts to organize women actually masked an effort to enlarge the socialist movement. In addition to suspicion about WONAAC's motives, some former participants in the MAA argued that YSA's single-issue focus on abortion law repeal would not lead to women's liberation.[64] Accusing WONAAC of pandering to the status quo by focusing on repeal, these former MAA members charged that making abortion legal would not make it accessible. "As long as hospitals and clinics can charge exorbitant rates and set their own policies . . . [WONAAC's] so-called 'right-to-choose' will be out of reach of poor women, especially Black and Latin American women."[65] WONAAC's approach also angered Healthwitches, a group with ties to the DCWLM that offered abortion counseling and referrals. Healthwitches objected that WONAAC's single-issue focus on abortion would not lead toward the larger goal of women's liberation; instead, the group anticipated that the movement would disintegrate after that goal was won. In addition, they noted that repealing abortion laws would not make abortions affordable to poor women or give women more control over their bodies. Poor women would still find abortions out of reach and "there would only be one more surgical experience available to us in impersonal hospitals and clinics." A better approach, the Healthwitches insisted, would incorporate the fight for abortion access into a movement to create alternatives to abortion (free prenatal care, free childbirth) and extend health care to every member of society.[66]

Reproductive Rights after *Roe v. Wade*

The 1973 Supreme Court decision upholding women's access to abortion on the grounds of privacy changed the nature of the movement for reproductive rights. The decision affirmed the legality of women's right to choose abortion during the first trimester of pregnancy. An article in *off our backs* called the decision a "significant first start in a continuing struggle for the right to choose." By making abortion legally accessible, the ruling represented a significant victory. But the terms on which *Roe* articulated women's legal right to abortion—in consultation with their doctors, during the first three months of pregnancy, and on the basis of their right to privacy—left ample room for opponents to limit the scope of the ruling. In addition, *Roe* did not secure women's access to abortion free from economic want, nor did the decision address other obstacles that prevented women's reproductive freedom, including the practice of involuntary sterilization.[67]

Antiabortion forces mobilized in response to *Roe,* seeking ways to roll back the rights it recognized. Within a year of the ruling, ten antiabortion bills and two constitutional amendments had been introduced in Congress. Many locales simply resisted compliance with the ruling or restricted the conditions under which abortions were available.[68] Regulations that exploited economic inequalities proved especially effective. The Bartlett Amendment was introduced in 1974 as part of the annual appropriations bill for the Departments of Labor and Health, Education, and Welfare. Under the amendment, none of the money allocated to HEW could be used to pay for or to promote abortions. More specifically, the amendment sought to ban the use of Medicaid payment for abortions, to restrict abortion counseling by any agency that received federal funds, and to prohibit medical schools that received funds from HEW to teach abortion techniques. Congress reconsidered the bill every year until it passed in 1976 under the sponsorship of Senator Henry Hyde.[69]

Opinion polls attested that a vast majority of D.C. residents supported legal abortion rights, some of whom mobilized to prevent Congress from further limiting abortion or declaring the procedure unconstitutional. Others, such as women formally affiliated with DCWLM's counseling service, continued to offer information and referrals to local women.[70] But activists put little emphasis on building alliances and coordinating mass protests. Instead, local feminist organizations used their publications to disseminate information about attacks on abortion rights and the deaths of poor women who could not obtain legal abortions. *Off our backs* reported regularly on congressional and state-level campaigns to restrict the scope of *Roe,* and NOW's newsletter urged readers to let elected officials know that they opposed new limitations. Members of the local NOW chapter used their location in the capital as a base while Congress deliberated restrictive abortion laws, organizing petitions and letter-writing campaigns, testifying at hearings, and lobbying elected officials from critical states. D.C. NOW members were deliberate in their strategies, picking ways to register their opposition that would depict feminists in a favorable light. As one NOW member explained, "Our tactics have to be different from the past. We should be in contrast to Right to Life. We want to show Congress that we have thought this out, that we're not a fringe group. Fanaticism

... [is] not appreciated on the Hill. Instead, we ask Congress to look at the pros and cons rationally." But although NOW and other feminists' tactics were meant to appeal to elected officials by emphasizing publicity through feminist publications and by minimizing the use of mass protests, activists ensured that smaller numbers of women knew about or cared to join campaigns to fight the Bartlett and Hyde amendments.[71]

Moreover, activists painted the attack on abortion rights in this later period as solely a danger to poor women of color rather than the first shot in a campaign intended to deprive all women of reproductive rights. African American women moved to the forefront of the movement against the proposed amendments, revealing their particular stake in maintaining the right to abortion. In the fall of 1974, "black middle-class Washington women" in the newly formed National Black Feminist Organization lobbied members of Congress against the Bartlett Amendment. They were occasionally joined by representatives of the NWRO. Telling reporters that because most of the Washington residents who received Medicaid benefits were black women, the women argued that they had "to fight for our sisters." The *Washington Afro-American,* which had paid little attention to the topic of abortion before 1973, now spoke against the Bartlett Amendment on the grounds that it discriminated against the poor. Warning that the amendment would send many poor black women "back to the bootleggers and hustlers who promise a complete abortion, no ill effects and no infections," the paper applauded the "ladies" who got out to lobby against the amendment.[72]

Mary Treadwell remained an outspoken advocate for abortion rights and black liberation. In 1975, she testified in Congress against the proposed constitutional amendment to prohibit abortion. As she had argued earlier, Treadwell indicated that abortion was essential to the well-being of black women and children. In order to provide secure, loving homes for children, poor black women needed access to safe, affordable, and legal abortions and better family planning services so they could avoid unwanted pregnancies.[73] Treadwell emphasized these same themes in a letter to the *Washington Star* in 1977. The Hyde Amendment would force women to seek abortions in "the back alleys of our country." Berating opponents, she reasoned, "If just one fourth of the financial resources and fervor which are being used by those who are against abortion had been directed to a working pro-life situation," many African American women would be spared death and young people promised a future free from want.[74]

Despite the energetic efforts of Treadwell and other black women activists, the assault on abortion rights moved forward. Indeed, the tactics and arguments that feminists and other supporters of abortion rights used probably mattered little in the face of the mounting antiabortion movement and increasing conservatism of the times. The approaches taken by abortion supporters in Washington in the years after *Roe* provide evidence, however, of the exceptional nature of the coalitions that formed to press for reproductive rights between 1970 and 1973. Before the *Roe* decision, many feminists saw the reproductive rights campaign as an opportunity to broaden the movement's base by drawing in women who had rejected feminism for ideological or political reasons. Concentrating on reproduction and, by extension, women's health, motherhood, and families, feminists had articulated concerns that presumably all women shared regardless of race, economic means, or sexual identity. The presumed overlap between women's reproductive and health care struggles provided an impetus for white feminists to form alliances, reaching out to welfare rights and black liberation activists. In Washington, African American women and welfare rights recipients had responded affirmatively, publicly supporting reproductive rights and linking that movement to campaigns for economic justice and black liberation. But the victory that *Roe* conveyed, although limited, broke the fragile alliances that formed to support abortion rights and relieved activists from the difficult work of coalescing.

The associations that African American women perceived between poverty, racism, and women's lack of reproductive control provided the motivation to protest the Bartlett and Hyde amendments and other attempts to restrict women's access to abortion. Feeling a sense of connection to the struggles of their "sisters," Treadwell and other African American women stressed the life-and-death issues at stake in abortion debates and brought necessary attention to the lives of poor African American women. Black women's activism also challenged white feminists' supposition of women's commonality by reminding the public about the different circumstances under which women lived and organized politically. By emphasizing poverty and the quality of life in black communities, these activists sidestepped charges that abortion and other forms of birth control endangered African American solidarity and liberation. Positioning themselves squarely on the side of black liberation, they commanded awareness for the distinctive rights due to African American women.

Notes

1. New scholarship on black women's organizations and nationalist groups such as the Young Lords Party has challenged the view that all women of color opposed abortion and contraception on the grounds that these forms of population control represented federally orchestrated forms of genocide. Jennifer A. Nelson, *Women of Color and the Reproductive Rights Movement* (New York: New York University Press, 2003); M. Rivka Polatnick, "Diversity in Women's Liberation Ideology: How a Black and a White Group of the 1960s Viewed Motherhood," *Signs* 21 (Spring 1996), 679–706; Jael Silliman et al., *Undivided Rights: Women of Color Organize for Reproductive Justice* (Boston: South End Press, 2004).

2. Mary Wiegers, "Women's Lib: 'Only Active Radicals in Town,'" *Washington Post,* 11 March 1970, B3.

3. Alice J. Wolfson, "Clenched Fist, Open Heart," in *The Feminist Memoir Project: Voices from Women's Liberation,* edited by Rachel Blau DuPlessis and Ann Snitow, 268–83 (New York: Three Rivers Press, 1998).

4. *Roe* was followed in 1973 by *Doe v. Dalton,* a Supreme Court ruling striking down restrictive laws specifying eligibility requirements. For background on the struggle for abortion rights, see Leslie J. Reagan, *When Abortion Was a Crime: Women, Medicine, and Law in the United States, 1867–1973* (Berkeley: University of California Press, 1997); David Garrow, *Liberty and Sexuality: The Right to Privacy and the Making of Roe v. Wade* (New York: MacMillan, 1994); Marlene Gerber Fried, ed., *From Abortion to Reproductive Freedom: Transforming a Movement* (Boston: South End Press, 1990).

5. Jennifer A. Nelson also argues that women of color were critical to transforming feminists' approach to abortion, although she dates their influence to the late 1970s. Nelson, *Women of Color and the Reproductive Rights Movement.*

6. In 1972, the Court extended the right to contraception to unmarried men and women in its *Eisenstadt v. Baird* decision. On the popularity of the birth control pill, see William D. Mosher, *Trends in Contraceptive Practice: United States, 1965–76,* DHHS Publication No. (PHS) 82–1986 (Hyattsville, Md.: National Center for Health Statistics, 1982), 11.

7. "Family Planning," Folder 3, Box 10, Ophelia Egypt Papers, Moorland-Spingarn Research Center, Howard University.

8. Cornelia Ball, "Byrd Backs Birth Control," *Washington Daily News,* 15 October 1963; William Grigg, "Birth Control Study Started by District," *Washington Star,* 16 October 1963, both in Birth Control 1965–1969 Article File, MLK Library, Washington, D.C.

9. 1964 Year-End Report, PPFA Records, Sophia Smith Collection, Smith College.

10. "Byrd Urges Birth Control for Slum-Area Negroes," *Washington Post,* 17 August 1967, Birth Control Article File, MLK Library.

11. The history of U.S.-sponsored family planning initiatives is covered by Donald T. Critchlow, "Birth Control, Population Control, and Family Planning: An Overview," *Journal of Policy History* 7 (1995): 1–21; James Reed, *The Birth Control Movement and American Society: From Private Vice to Public Virtue* (Princeton, N.J.: Princeton University Press, 1984).

12. National Center for Health Statistics, *Utilization of Family Planning Services by Currently Married Women 15–44 Years of Age,* DHEW Publication No. (PHS) 78–1977 (Hyattsville, Md.: U.S. Department of Health, Education, and Welfare Public Health Service, 1977), 20–21.

13. See assorted articles from Birth Control Article File, MLK Library.

14. Calvin Zon, "In Memory of Sisters Murdered By Abortion," *Washington Star,* 8 May 1972, Abortion, 1972–1978 Article File, MLK Library; Nelson, *Women of Color and the Reproductive Rights Movement,* 64–70; Lawrence, "Indian Health Service and the Sterilization of Native American Women."

15. Marilyn Salzman Webb, "Nixon on Birth Control: A Hard Pill to Swallow," *Guardian,* 23 August 1969, 10.

16. "Who Says Too Many?" *off our backs,* Health Supplement, Summer 1971, 24–25; Judith Coburn, "Off the Pill?" *Ramparts,* June 1970, 46–49.

17. These arguments are covered in Nelson, *Women of Color and the Reproductive Rights Movement*; Angela Y. Davis, *Women, Race, and Class* (New York: Vintage Books, 1983); Loretta J. Ross, "African American Women and Abortion," in *Abortion Wars: A Half Century of Struggle, 1950–2000,* edited by Rickie Solinger, 161–207 (Berkeley: University of California Press, 1998).

18. *Muhammad Speaks* and *Black Panther* quoted in Nelson, *Women of Color and the Reproductive Rights Movement,* 85.

19. Evette Pearson, "White America Today," *Black Panther,* 4 January 1969, reprinted in Foner, *Black Panthers Speak,* 26; Judi Douglas, "Birth Control," *Black Panther,* 7 February 1970, 7.

20. Nelson, *Women of Color and the Reproductive Rights Movement,* 85–86.

21. Sally Quinn, "Abortions in the City," *Washington Post,* 25 March 1970, B3. Another report on this conference appears in Box 1, Hearing Files, 1967–1974, Records of the City Council, National Archives.

22. Bobby McMahan testimony, Committee on Labor and Human Resources, U.S. Senate, *Family Planning and Population Research* (Washington, D.C.: Government Printing Office, 1970), 276–80.

23. Judge Gesell, who made the ruling, may have been influenced by his wife, who sat on the board of the city's Planned Parenthood Association chapter in 1964–65. Only spotty records of the PPA chapter are available, making it difficult to determine whether she still served on the association's board when her husband ruled in the Vuitch case. Minutes, Board of Trustees, PPAF Papers, Sophia Smith Collection; Lader, *Abortion II,* 1–17; *United States of America v. Milan Vuitch,* 305 F. Supp. 1032 (1969).

24. The CWA established a Health Group, although it is unclear what activities the group undertook. Press release issued by D.C. Citywide Alliance, 5 November 1968, Box 2083, NWRO Papers, Moorland-Spingarn Research Center, Howard University.

25. Wolfson, "Clenched Fist," 270–71; "Washington Women's Liberation Project Groups," Fall 1969, Folder 21, Carton 1, Charlotte Bunch Papers, Schlesinger Library, Radcliffe Institute, Harvard University; Marilyn Salzman Webb, "A Hard Rain's Gonna Fall," *WIN Magazine* 6 (January 1970): 4–6.

26. Meeting the conditions for therapeutic abortion did not guarantee that women would receive the procedure, as in the case of two women reportedly turned away by D.C. General in August 1969, despite having obtained the proper certification. Myra MacPherson, "Abortion Protest Stymied," *Washington Post,* 9 September 1969, B1–B2.

27. "Abortions at D.C. General Hospital," *off our backs,* 27 February 1970, 4. Historian Leslie Reagan similarly has argued that the enforcement of abortion laws in the 1950s and 1960s led to the emergence of a system wherein white women with private health insurance were most likely to receive therapeutic abortions in private hospitals, while poor, African American, and Latina women were more likely to seek criminal abortions. Reagan, *When Abortion Was a Crime,* 193.

28. The 1967 figures used by abortion proponents ranged from 500 to more than 800 women who received treatment at D.C. General for complications from illegal abortions.

In contrast, official figures compiled by the D.C. Department of Public Health show a total of forty-two deaths from abortions between 1960 and 1967 and a sharp increase in the number of therapeutic abortions performed at four Washington hospitals between 1959 and 1969. "Statement by Washington Women's Liberation to the Mayor's Task Force on Public Health Goals" and "Committee on Abortions Meeting," Folder 42, Carton 2, Addenda, Bunch Papers. Other reports present different numbers but reveal the same trend of extremely low numbers of therapeutic abortions completed at D.C. General relative to the higher numbers of women who sought treatment there after illegal abortions. Statement by Alyce C. Gullattee in *Report of the City Council's Health and Welfare Committee on Abortions in the District of Columbia, October 1970* (Washington, D.C.: Government of the District of Columbia City Council, 1970); Donald Hirzel, "Court Turns Down Plea for Abortion," *Washington Evening Star,* 7 March 1970, Abortion Article File, MLK Library.

29. Irma Moore, "Hearings Set on State of D.C. General," *Washington Post,* 11 September 1969, A26; Stuart Auerbach, "Hospital Employees Join Doctors' Protest," *Washington Post,* 17 September 1969, C3; Carl Bernstein, "Hospital Needs Told at Probe," *Washington Post,* 18 September 1969, B2.

30. "Committee on Abortions Meeting," minutes, 23 September 1969, Folder 42, Carton 2, Bunch Papers.

31. Richard E. Prince, "Panel Backs Abortions at D.C. General," *Washington Post,* 4 December 1969, Abortion Article File, MLK Library; Sidney Lippman, "Mayor's Unit Asks Abortions at D.C. General," *Washington Daily News,* 2 December 1969, 5.

32. "School Clothing for Welfare Children," *NWRO/Welfare Fighter,* September 1969, 7; Malcolm Kovacs, "'Witch' at the Justice Department," *Quicksilver Times,* 1–11 October 1969, 4.

33. Washington, D.C., Women's Liberation, "'It's Alright Ma (I'm Only Bleeding),'" Folder 41, Carton 2, Bunch Papers.

34. Judith Coburn, "Off the Pill?" *Ramparts* 8, no. 12 (June 1970): 49.

35. Alice Wolfson, "Women and Health," Folder 42, Carton 2, Bunch Papers.

36. "'It's Alright Ma'"; Webb, "Hard Rain's Gonna Fall," 4; Coburn, "Off the Pill?" Women in Chicago went a step further and created their own abortion service. Laura Kaplan, *The Story of Jane: The Legendary Underground Feminist Abortion Service* (New York: Pantheon Books, 1995).

37. "Washington Women's Liberation Statement on Birth Control Pills," Appendix X, U.S. Congress, Senate, Committee on Small Business, Subcommittee on Monopoly, *Competitive Problems in the Drug Industry,* 2nd Session, Pt. 17 (Washington, D.C.: Government Printing Office, 1970); Malcolm Kovacs, "The Pill Hearings," *D.C. Gazette,* 23 March 1970, 6–7; Committee on Labor and Human Resources, Senate, *Family Planning and Population Research* (Washington, D.C.: Government Printing Office, 1970), 277.

38. Bunch, "Ourstory, Herstory: A Working Paper on the D.C. Women's Liberation Movement, 1968–1971," Sharon Deevey Papers, Columbus Ohio.

39. "Horning In," *off our backs,* 14 December 1970, 6.

40. "'It's Alright Ma.'"

41. Peter Osnos, "D.C. General Is Sued Again over Abortion," *Washington Post,* 30 April 1970, A1–A2; Mary Ann Kuhn, "Mother at 14 Decries Hospital," *Washington Daily News,* 30

April 1970, 26; Peter Osnos, "Woman Testifies in Private for Abortion at D.C. General," *Washington Post,* 10 March 1970, A1, A8; Peter Osnos, "Abortion Pleas Is Rejected, Appeal Set," *Washington Post,* 12 March 1970, A1, A14; Peter Osnos, "Mental Health Abortion Ordered at D.C. General," *Washington Post,* 13 March 1970, A1, A11.

42. District of Columbia Health and Welfare Council, "Position Paper on Abortion," 27 July 1970, Subject Files, Box 10, City Council Papers, Gelman Library, George Washington University; "Health Crisis Breaks in D.C.: Systemic Conditions Are Showing Up," Folder 42, Carton 2, Bunch Papers. For information on the collective action suit, see "Contempt for Women," *off our backs,* 19 March 1970, 4; and front-page *Washington Post* articles, March 10–13, 1970.

43. Stuart Auerbach, "Women Disrupt Hearing on the Pill," *Washington Post,* 24 January 1970, B1, B3; Regina Sigal, "Politics of the Pill," *off our backs,* 27 February 1970, 3.

44. Judith Coburn, "Off the Pill?" *Village Voice,* 5 February 1970, 14–15; Wolfson, "Clenched Fist, Open Heart," in DuPlessis and Snitow, *Feminist Memoir Project,* 271.

45. Alice J.Wolfson and Philip E. Wolfson, "The Food and Drug Administration and the Pill," *Social Policy* 1 (September-October 1970): 52–53; Alice Wolfson, "More on the Pill," *off our backs,* 19 March 1970, 6.

46. Nancy Beezley, "How Safe the Pill?" *Quicksilver Times,* 3–13 April 1970, 8.

47. Women's liberation and welfare activists' testimony eventually became part of the official record of the Senate hearings. Washington Women's Liberation Statement on Birth Control Pills, *Competitive Problems in the Drug Industry,* 7283–85; Alex Ward, "Women Hold Own Hearing on Pill," *Washington Post,* 8 March 1970, L7; "Women Hold Their Own," *off our backs,* 19 March 1970, 3.

48. Accounts of these hearings appear in Alex Ward, "Repeal of Abortion Laws Urged," *Washington Post,* 27 June 1970, B1; *Report of the City Council's Health and Welfare Committee on Abortions in the District of Columbia;* Hearing Files, 1967–1974, Box 1, Records of the City Council, RG351, National Archives; D.C. Health and Welfare Council, "Position Paper on Abortion," 27 July 1970, Abortion Subject File, Box 10, City Council Files, GWU.

49. "Records of 22 October 1971 Hearing Regarding the Proposed Licensing of Abortion Clinics," Box 1, Records of the City Council, Hearing Files, 1967–1974, National Archives. In 1972, the City Council instituted a twenty-four-hour waiting period, but proabortion groups sued to stop the implementation. WONAAC to Dr. Henry Robinson, Chair, Health and Welfare Committee of the D.C. City Council, 14 July 1972, Abortion Subject Files, Box 10, City Council Papers, GWU; Ron Taylor, "D.C. City Council Backs New Abortion Rules," *Washington Post,* 12 July 1972, C1; "D.C. Is Upheld on Enforcement of Abortion Law," *Washington Post,* 21 October 1972, A3.

50. *U.S. v. Vuitch,* 402 U.S. 62 (1971).

51. "Rules for Abortion," *Washington Post,* 21 March 1972, A18; "Abortion Law Repeal Gathers Speed," *NOW Acts* 3 (Winter 1970): 16; "Clinics: An Answer to Hospital Overcrowding?" *NOW Acts* 4 (Spring 1971): 9–10; *Vocal Majority* 2 (June 1971): 24; "Abortion Clinic to Open at Washington Hospital," *Washington Daily News,* 15 January 1971; "Abortion Clinic to Open Downtown," *Washington Daily News,* 25 March 1971; Ned Scharff, "I Was Just So Grateful," *Washington Star,* 17 October 1971, Abortion Article File, MLK Library;

News Notes: Planned Parenthood of Metropolitan Washington, D.C. 21 (Fall 1971), Folder 10, Box 16, Egypt Papers.

52. "MAA: The Metropolitan Abortion Alliance," *Vocal Majority* 2 (March 1971): 7; "D.C. Women Campaign for Free Abortions," *Washington Daily News,* 16 April 1971, 4.

53. "D.C. Women Campaign for Free Abortions," *Washington Daily News,* 16 April 1971, 4; Jean Powell, "Women Don't Agree," *Washington Evening Star,* 28 July 1971, Abortion 1971 Article File, MLK Library; MAA Position Paper, Women's Ephemera Collection, Abortion—Metropolitan Abortion Alliance Folder, Northwestern University.

54. "If Men Could Get Pregnant, Abortion Would Be a Sacrament," *off our backs,* 24 June 1971, 20; Joy Billington, "NOW to Challenge All," *Washington Star,* 27 April 1971, Abortion Article File, MLK Library.

55. "Another Reaction," *off our backs,* 24 June 1971, 20; Jeannie Reynolds, "Metropolitan Abortion Alliance Rally," *Vocal Majority* 2 (June 1971): 23.

56. Jeannie Reynolds, "Abortion Committee Proposed," *Vocal Majority* 2 (July 1971): 7.

57. Gail Martens, "Another Reaction," *off our backs,* 24 June 1971, 20.

58. Elizabeth Barnes, "Panel Foresees Mass Women's Movement," *The Militant,* 16 January 1970, 8; Jaquith, "Issues before the Abortion Movement," in Jenness, *Feminism and Socialism.*

59. Toba Singer, "Suit Contests D.C. Abortion Statutes," *The Militant,* 4 October 1972, 16; "Abortion Law Change Hit," *Washington Star,* 16 July 1972; Calvin Zon, "In Memory of Sisters Murdered by Abortion," *Washington Star,* 8 May 1972, Abortion, 1972–1978 Article File, MLK Library.

60. *WONAAC Newsletter,* 21 October 1971, 4; "Women for Abortion Action," *D.C. Gazette,* 15 December 1971; "Women March on Washington," *Space City!* 16 December 1971, 11; Caroline Lund, "Nov. 20 Spurs Int'l. Abortion Struggle," *The Militant,* 3 December 1971, 4–5; John Mathews and Jacqueline Trescott, "Abortion—2 Points of View," *Washington Evening Star,* 21 November 1971, A3; "November 20th—Some Reporting, Some Diatribe, Some Analysis," *off our backs,* 12 December 1971, 16; Scrapbook, Reel 2, WONAAC Papers.

61. "Black Women," *WONAAC Newsletter,* 21 October 1971, 13.

62. Mary Treadwell, "Black Women," *WONAAC Newsletter,* 21 October 1971, 7. A variation of this article appeared as "Is Abortion Black Genocide?" in *Family Planning Perspectives* 4 (January 1972): 4–5 and in Treadwell's testimony before Congress, Committee of the Judiciary, Subcommittee on Constitutional Amendments, *Abortion,* Pt. 4 (Washington, D.C.: Government Printing Office, 1975), 683–85.

63. Committee of the Judiciary, *Abortion,* 684–85.

64. Varda One, "Women's Liberation Where Are You Going?" *Everywoman,* February 1971, 16–18; Caroline Lund, "Red-Baiting and Women's Liberation," *The Militant,* 13 November 1970, 9; Caroline Lund, "Issues in Female Liberation Split," *The Militant,* 5 February 1971, 14, 22.

65. Jean Powell, "Women Don't Agree," *Washington Star,* 28 July 1971, Abortion Article File, MLK Library; "Bringing Abortion Home," *off our backs,* October 1971, 10; "A House Divided," *off our backs,* October 1971, 11; "November 20th—Some Reporting, Some Diatribe, Some Analysis."

66. "November 20—Some Reporting, Some Diatribe, Some Analysis"; Karlyn Barker, "Divisions Slow Women's Lib Drive," *Washington Post*, 14 November 1971, D1, D6.

67. Carol Edelson, "Supreme Court Abortion Ruling," *off our backs*, 31 March 1971, 4; Adele Clark and Alice Wolfson, "Class, Race, and Reproductive Rights," *Socialist Review* 78 (November-December 1984): 110–20.

68. The Buckley Amendment proposed to expand the definition of "person" in the Constitution to apply to all human beings, including their unborn offspring. The Helms Amendment proposed to prohibit abortion from the time of conception, without exception.

69. The amendment that passed in 1976 allowed Medicaid payments for abortion in cases to protect a mother's life. Lawsuits challenging the amendment were immediately filed by health care providers and abortion rights groups.

70. According to a 1975 survey of Washington, D.C., residents conducted by the Bureau of Social Science Research, 77 percent agreed that decisions about abortions should be left to a woman and her doctor. Support among white respondents (78 percent) was somewhat higher than support among nonwhite respondents (69 percent). Jay Mathews, "Abortion, Homosexual Rights Backed," *Washington Post*, 8 August 1975, C1, C3; D.C. Women's Health and Abortion Information Project, "Abortion: A Woman's Right to Choose," Women's Ephemera Collection, Abortion—Washington Area Women's Center Folder, Northwestern University.

71. Mary Bailey, "Senate Abortion Hearings: Do They Really Hear," *off our backs*, 31 May 1974, 6; "Memorial," *off our backs* 7 (December 1977): 9; Folder 48, Box 1970, NOW Papers, Schlesinger Library; "Since the Supreme Court Decision on Abortion," *Vocal Majority* 4 (June 1973): 5, 7.

72. Elizabeth Becker, "Abortion Recipients Attack Proposed Ban on Medicaid Help," *Washington Post*, 20 October 1974, B7; Lillian Wiggins, "Bartlett Amendment Discriminatory to the Poor," *Washington Afro-American*, 5 October 1974, 4.

73. Committee of the Judiciary, *Abortion*, Pt. 4, 683–94, 698–706.

74. Mary Treadwell Barry, "The Poor's Right to Abortion," letter to the editor, *Washington Star*, 18 June 1977, A6.

From
*Lost in the USA: American Identity from the Promise Keepers
to the Million Mom March,*
by Deborah Gray White (2017)

10

THINGS FALL APART; THE LGBT CENTER HOLDS

(Excerpt)

DEBORAH GRAY WHITE

Special Rights

The 1990s were remarkable for America's intolerance *but* growing tolerance for sexual minorities. In many ways the decade-long struggle between the forces of acceptance and rejection determined the nature, structure, and platform of the turn-of-century 2000 Millennium March.

The election of Democrat Bill Clinton in 1992 seemed to be the dawn of a new era. Under the leadership of Ronald Reagan and then George H. W. Bush (1980–88; 1988–92), Republicans had at first ignored, and then underfunded, HIV/AIDS research. Their traditional-values platforms demonized sexual minorities along with racial and ethnic minorities and feminists. Clinton was a breath of fresh air. Unlike his predecessors, he seemed comfortable with lgbts, held public discussions with them, and could talk about their issues without flinching or seeming embarrassed. The fact that he made gays in the military, an AIDS czar, lifting the travel ban on people with HIV, and appointing sexual minorities to high-level offices campaign issues was a remarkable shift that suggested that lgbts would have a friend in the White House.

But Clinton was a disappointment. His "Don't Ask, Don't Tell" compromise, as opposed to an outright end to the ban on gays in the military, was seen by most sexual minorities as "institutionalized bigotry."[1] He never lifted the travel ban on people with HIV but rather signed a bill into law that instituted stricter provisions on travel. Additionally, he did not break with the H. W. Bush policy of keeping

Haitians infected with HIV detained at Guantanamo Bay until a federal judge ruled that the detention was unconstitutional. No one with HIV/AIDS expertise was appointed to Hillary Clinton's health-care panel, and the person he belatedly appointed as AIDS czar, Kristine Gebbie, was considered by many to be inexperienced. His failure to even be in Washington, DC, the weekend of the 1993 march was seen by some as evidence of his abandonment. Said former San Francisco supervisor Harry Britt, "Our success in the '90s will not depend on Bill Clinton but on how assertive we are."[2]

Two anti-lgbt state referendums, Measure 9 in Oregon and Amendment 2 in Colorado, made Britt's prediction more than just rhetoric. Removed from federal jurisdiction, these state referendums were intended to prevent sexual minorities from being considered a protected class of citizens, a status that would have given them legal protection against discrimination and hate crimes. The Oregon measure failed with 56.4 percent voting against to the 53.5 percent who voted for it. But the Colorado Amendment 2 passed by a margin of six percentage votes, with 47 percent of voters voting against and 53 percent voting for the amendment. The language used by the respective states was very different and suggests the two-pronged approach of lgbt enemies.

The measure in Oregon represented the tactic intended to provoke moral outrage. It prevented all governments and school boards from using their money or property to promote homosexuality, pedophilia, sadism, or masochism. All levels of government, including public education systems, had to set a standard that recognized those behaviors as "abnormal, wrong, unnatural and perverse" and that were to be "discouraged and avoided." These ideas were exemplary of those put forth by the evangelical Right. Take, for example, the teachings of Minneapolis trial attorney Roger Magnuson. At a 1992 gathering of the conservative organization Concerned Women for America (CWA), he spoke authoritatively about homosexuals who "testify to the regular consumption of human waste and fecal matter." When his audience shuddered he reassured them that their reaction was proper: "Homophobia is the natural revulsion normal people feel in the face of sexual perversion," he said.[3] Beverly LaHaye, founder and president of CWA, thought likewise. She believed that "homosexuals want their depraved 'values' to become our children's values." Because she thought that "homosexuals expect society to embrace their immoral way of life" and "are looking for new recruits,"[4] she gave proponents of the Oregon proposal free airtime on her syndicated radio show *Beverly LaHaye Live,* a Christian talk show that reached hundreds of thousands of listeners. In the case of the Colorado amendment, she flew to Denver and actively campaigned for its passage. In Colorado, the Local Prayer/Action chapters of CWA distributed hundreds of thousands of tabloid-style newsletters citing "facts" like

"Lesbians are now having babies, conceived by homosexual semen," and "Fact: Homosexuals are 12 times as likely as heterosexual teachers to molest children."[5]

As effective as was the morality-based campaign against homosexuals, another tactic proved more powerful in its ability to sway voter opinion. In 1991 LaHaye authored a document entitled "The Hidden Homosexual Agenda." In it she documented her version of the history of the "Homosexual Movement" from 1948 to the 1990s. By her account there "appeared to be an explosion from the closets" between 1968 and 1970, and from then on the gay movement assumed an unprecedented militancy. According to LaHaye, "homosexuals may differ" on many issues but "they have agreed on a specific agenda for the movement" by which they hope to obtain the ultimate goal of "total acceptance." That demand, said LaHaye, was that "Americans accept the homosexual community as a legitimate minority having the same legal status as married couples in society." Homosexuals are demanding, wrote LaHaye, total acceptance, not just tolerance. They have, she said, manipulated America's traditional values so that their values appear to be rights that the government and society must affirm. For LaHaye, and the many that she spoke for, sexual minorities were fighting for the *special* right to have their *values* accepted as rights. "This concept of sexual deviants being given special rights and privileges because of their sexual orientation, challenges, if not subverts the entire fabric of America's foundation," she declared. If homosexuals were designated a special class of people—like racial minorities had been—then their values, argued LaHaye, would be protected by law. Once that happened, the Judeo-Christian values at the core of American society would disintegrate; promiscuity, AIDS, and prejudice against heterosexuals would ensue; and classrooms across the nation would be inundated with homoerotic curricula that would ultimately recruit American youth into homosexual lifestyles. "The Hidden Homosexual Agenda" reviewed all of the legislative victories scored by lgbts and argued for the mobilization against a politics that enabled these special rights. Homosexuals, LaHaye's report maintained, already had "the same rights as heterosexuals." What they actually want, she said, "is to be granted special privileges to carry out their illicit practices to receive affirmation of being that legitimate minority."[6]

As argued by LaHaye and others, the "special rights" strategy became the linchpin in the Christian Right 1990s antigay campaign. Its effectiveness was demonstrated when Colorado's Amendment 2 passed. In contrast to Measure 9's highly moralistic language, Amendment 2 implicitly represented gays as people who wanted more rights than heterosexuals and the same rights as racial and ethnic minorities. The amendment stated that no homosexual, lesbian, or bisexual could lay claim to "minority status, quota preferences, protected status or claim of discrimination." Though proponents believed the language of Oregon's law—that homosexuality was abnormal, wrong, and perverse—the focus of Amendment 2 was on denying lgbts the same *civil rights* that had been given to minorities to redress previous discrimination.

Coming at a time when polls showed growing tolerance, even acceptance, of gays and lesbians, the "special rights" campaign was especially lethal. For example, a *USA Today* telephone poll of 1,065 adults taken on the eve of the '93 march showed that people polled were evenly split on giving gays the same coverage under civil rights laws as blacks and women, with 48 percent both opposed and in favor. Women were more supportive than men (56 percent to 35 percent) as were younger respondents between eighteen and twenty-nine (56 percent). There was also an increase in the number of people who believed that being gay was not a chosen lifestyle—the idea hawked by the Christian Right—but something one was born with. While only 31 percent thought homosexuality was genetic, this was up from 16 percent in 1983. Meanwhile, fewer people in 1993 than in 1983 thought that homosexuality was something that developed over time. In 1983, 25 percent of those polled thought that it developed over time, but this was down by eleven percentage points, to 14 percent, in 1993.[7]

No doubt the greater acceptance of lgbts was helped along by television. According to communications scholar Ron Becker, in the early 1990s competition from cable television forced the networks to seek edgier, more hip programing in order to appeal to the eighteen-to-forty-nine-year-old audience. "By 1995 there seemed to be little room on network TV for sentimentality, wholesomeness, or heartwarming narratives about the American family living in the heartland. Domestic dramas and family sitcoms were out of fashion and squeezed to the margins," argues Becker.[8] However, there *was* room for gay characters and gay-themed episodes, and as the 1990s progressed they increased exponentially, as did the subplots, jokes, and innuendos dependent on homosexuality. According to Becker, by the 1996–97 viewing season, thirty-three different queer characters were scattered across twenty-four different prime-time network programs.[9] The new programming reflected the changing taste of consumers who, being more exposed to a variety of cultures, drove an economy thirsty for a variety of new goods, information, and entertainments. It appealed to a new cohort that some would define as neoliberal—people who considered themselves fiscal conservative social liberals; people who appreciated or were at least open to cultural, racial, and gender differences; people who considered themselves cosmopolitan; people whose politics were centrist or left of center; people who were likely supporters of Bill Clinton.[10]

With the polls showing less repugnance toward sexual minorities and television programming normalizing them, the special rights tactic was timed to derail tolerance and acceptance. By pairing morality and civil rights in such a way as to make affirmation of lgbt civil rights look like approval of an immoral lifestyle, the strategy targeted all who were uncomfortable with unconventional sexual desire and gender identification. By arguing that homosexuals did not want the same civil rights as heterosexuals, but in fact wanted exceptional rights, the strategy made lgbts look extreme. For example, people like twenty-three-year-old Steven Doering from Toledo, Ohio, could not isolate the issue of civil rights from concerns about immorality. From Doering's perspective, the immoral gay lifestyle had nothing to do with civil rights: "It is just a lifestyle and it doesn't go along at all with normal morals.... I don't think they should have separate rights just because they're gay." On the other hand, those like forty-three-year-old Patricia Strausbaugh of Bowling Green, Ohio, were not swayed by the special rights argument. For her, individual civil rights existed independent of lifestyle. Comparing gays to women and African Americans, who similarly had demanded equal rights, Strausbaugh maintained: "I don't think they're asking for anything special just like the women's movement and the black movement didn't ask for anything special."[11] The special rights campaign was targeted at the Doerings of America, and there were many like him.

It was also geared to build a coalition between the Christian Right and minorities, especially African Americans.[12] Unlike the Promise Keepers, whose racial reconciliation did not evidence a political angle, Christian Right organizations like the Traditional Values Coalition and the Christian Coalition enlisted African American social conservatism and sensitivities about civil rights in their antigay political crusade. One needed only to hear the heterosexist rant of the Reverend James D. Sykes, pastor of the St. James African Methodist Episcopal Church of Tampa, Florida, to realize that the special rights campaign touched a nerve in black America. When the Ku Klux Klan marched against gays in 1991 in a town near Tampa, Florida, Sykes declared that "if I knew that was the only reason the Klan was marching, I'd march with them." Sykes's qualifying remark showed not only how clearly he understood the ironic implications of his philosophical alignment with this historically racist organization, but also how deep the lgbt rights issue cut in African America. Sykes vehemently opposed the NAACP's endorsement of the 1993 March on Washington for Lesbian, Gay and Bi Equal Rights and Liberation on two grounds. First, as we have seen, many African Americans, including many black lgbts, resented the parallels being drawn between the oppression endured by blacks and that endured by sexual minorities. Sykes's notion of the latter was of affluent, self-indulgent whites who were indifferent to racism. He claimed he was not against gays, only against "them trying to coattail on our civil rights movement." He resented even their use of the title "March on Washington," which for him evoked the iconic image of Martin Luther King framed by the columns of the Lincoln Memorial. But Sykes opposed lgbts on another level as well. Discarding the NAACP's political coalition-building, Sykes contended that "the National Association for the Advancement of *Colored* People" (Sykes's emphasis) has no business "jumping on the bandwagon with people who are immoral." Sykes thought it unfortunate that blacks did not have the clout to effect political change without lgbts, but he likened joining with them to making a deal with Satan. Said Sykes: "Martin Luther King and the others did not march down in Selma, Alabama, for no gays to be walking naked in the streets of Washington, D.C."[13]

If Sykes's opinion was the minority view in black America, the majority did not speak up. As previously explained, historically, African Americans have put distance between them and anything associated with sexual deviance. In 1993, when march organizers solicited marchers and supporters for their Washington demonstration, clergy from twelve predominantly African American denominations met in Cleveland, Ohio, and drafted a position paper opposing the march and a pending bill in Congress, the Civil Rights Act of 1993 (H.R. 431 of the One-Hundred-Third Congress), which proposed giving lgbts the status of a protected minority. The series of meetings began in March. The clergy, who met every week for about two months, represented approximately 28,000 active members. When they finished "The Black Church Position Statement on Homosexuality," they took it back to their respective congregations for opinion and input, whereupon 2,500 congregants signed a petition against the proposed civil rights legislation.[14] Basically, the fifteen-paragraph statement cited biblical teachings that explained homosexuality as immoral; cited psychological evidence that homosexuality was a chosen lifestyle that could, with therapy, be changed; and expressed opposition to the proposed civil rights legislation on the grounds that homosexuality was a choice but "race, ethnicity, and gender may be denied or discounted but they represent a reality that does not change." The report further stated that "homosexuality is an identity orientation that develops over time and is expressed through behavior and/or lifestyle. . . . Therefore it would be inconsistent, illogical, and immoral to equate an ontological issue (referring to what one is) with a behavior issue (what one does)."[15] The interdenominational Ohio group then shared "The Black Church Position Statement on Homosexuality" with African American clergy groups in Omaha; Pittsburgh; Kansas City, Missouri; and with black pastors of congregations affiliated with white denominations. Though this last group was asked not to sign off on the declaration because their congregations might not agree with the pastor's personal opinion, the overwhelming support for this manifesto affirmed white Christian Right organizations' perception that they had as much, if not more, to offer African Americans than the lgbt Left.

The 1993 video *Gay Rights, Special Rights: Inside the Homosexual Agenda* produced by the Traditional Values Coalition followed up on this assertion. While television coverage of the 1993 march contributed to the growing visibilization of lgbts, simultaneously inviting closeted gays to "out" themselves and join a vocal beloved community, *Gay Rights, Special Rights: Inside the Homosexual Agenda* took march footage and used it to demonstrate the Christian Right's perception of a perverted community. The forty-minute film not only recounts the evils that will befall America if lgbts are given minority status, but it employs a zero-sum game argument to convince minorities, especially blacks, that gains made by lgbts would diminish those won during the civil rights movements.[16]

This is done effectively by contrasting the African American 1963 March on Washington for Jobs and Freedom and the 1993 March on Washington for Lesbian, Gay and Bi Equal Rights and Liberation. Images of Martin Luther King and other dignitaries are contraposed with transvestite striptease scenes and same-sex kissing and dancing couples. Voice-overs and on-screen comments by Edwin Meese, Pat Robertson, and Trent Lott—who were known to feminists and civil rights advocates for their misogyny and racism—juxtapose "legitimate" minorities with "illegitimate" sexual minorities, who are cast as wealthy, educated, white professionals who had never been discriminated against, or denied the vote, or segregated from the rest of society. Lou Lopez, identified as a member of the Anaheim, California, school district, appears on screen to say that the "Hispanic community does not want to be compared to homosexuals," and Raymond Kwong, identified as president of the Chinese Family Alliance, says that "the government has no business putting its stamp of approval on a behavior-based group, let alone elevated to full minority status."

African Americans are featured more than other minorities and they echo Sykes in their outrage at the prospect of lgbts being granted minority status. Flanked by other African American women, Jan Rice, who is identified as being from the Committee of Public Affairs, says "there's just no comparison" between lgbts and minorities. Although lgbts never proposed taking rights away from blacks, Rice maintains that "for them to want protection under this law and to try to further beat down the minorities and further lessen their [minorities'] chances of equal protection and equal chances at jobs, I just think is ludicrous." The women surrounding her agree. So does African American Lester James of the Traditional Values Coalition. For him, the "high-handed" attempts of gays to gain minority status are "an offense to black America" and an attempt to "undermine and belittle the entire civil rights efforts of the 1960s." Cheryl Coleman, another African American, repeated the idea that lgbt rights threatened black rights. Identified as a public affairs representative, she claims that granting lgbts minority status would "completely neutralize the Civil Rights Act of 1964" because amending the civil rights bill would give anyone "with any type of central preference, which would include everyone," protection under the law. Seemingly oblivious of minority lgbts, and the fact that white conservatives used the same rationale to oppose affirmative action for minorities and women—that it would give the undeserving an unfair advantage over whites—Coleman presses her argument that special rights for lgbts would mean that "there would be no protection for minorities specifically."[17]

In sum, as the 1990s progressed, the special rights strategy gained currency across the nation. Not long after the 1993 march, the liberal advocacy group People for the American Way (PFAW) issued a statement about the religious Right proclaiming that "no argument in their rhetorical arsenal has yielded more mileage for their voter mobilization and fundraising than the 'special rights' message." So effective was this tactic that the PFAW thought it necessary to distribute a flyer listing pro-gay counterarguments to be used in debates with special rights advocates, debates pro-gays had to win if they were to prevail in 1994 when citizens in nine states would decide on ballot initiatives like those in Colorado and Oregon.[18] Meanwhile, around the same time, Ralph Reed, executive director of the Christian Coalition, proclaimed that "we are not going to concede the minority community to the political left anymore."[19] Citing polls that showed that on social and economic issues African Americans and Hispanics held opinions similar to his white constituency, Reed concluded that his and other Christian conservative groups found blacks and Hispanics fertile ground for recruitment. As outlined by Reed, the Christian Coalition planned to start with ballot initiatives in California, and if successful expand their recruitment. They planned to end the policy of renting their membership list only to white churches. Now they would expand their constituency by sending voter guides to "every black and Hispanic church that we can get on a list."[20]

Reed's comments and those of the People for the American Way illustrate the battle lines that were drawn in the early 1990s. The polls reflected more acceptance of sexual minorities, but the Colorado victory and the success of the special rights strategy showed that acceptance to be tenuous. Clearly, the latter two-thirds of the 1990s would be crucial for sexual minorities. They would have to convince straight Americans that they did not seek anything beyond what they were entitled to by virtue of their humanity and American citizenship. This was easier said than done because as external pressure mounted, internal divisions deepened.

The Millennium March of 2000

Writing in the *Nation*, sociologist Joshua Gamson described the Millennium March as "the first of its kind." The fourth mass lgbt march to be held in the nation's capital, Gamson was obviously not referring to the event's placement in the sequence of national marches. Rather, the march was a first because of the way it was organized and the acrimony it sparked. The "strangest and most revealing first," said Gamson, was the fact that "bands of lesbian, gay, bisexual and transgender activists are working as hard as they can to convince other lesbian, gay, bisexual and transgender people not to attend a national lesbian, gay, bisexual and transgender march on Washington."[21] The sparks that flew before, during, and after the march were a direct result of external pressure put on lgbts who were already splintering from within.

Those who protested the march and discouraged others from going were, generally speaking, queers, sex radicals, leftists, and people of color—people who put a premium on cultural, racial, and ethnic diversity. They were angry about a lot of things that mostly came under the heading of assimilationist politics. At the top of their long list of grievances was the top-down organizing by the Human Rights Campaign (HRC), the wealthiest gay lobby organization in the nation, and the similarly wealthy Universal Fellowship of Metropolitan Community Churches (UFMCC), a Christian denomination founded to minister to sexual minorities. Queer radical Tristan Taormino described the HRC as "one of the richest, most conservative, most powerful, and (among many activists) most despised gay and lesbian organizations in the country."[22] Sounding a similar note, historian John D'Emilio described the HRC's organizational culture as "a culture of arrogance."[23] "This was such a dramatic shift in how the other marches had been organized," said New Yorker Leslie Cagan, a coordinator of the 1987 March on Washington.[24] Previous marches had been organized by grassroots organizations that met locally and discussed whether a march was a good idea and then, collectively, set the march's purpose and agenda. By contrast, said black activist Barbara Smith, this march "was called by a few self-appointed white 'leaders' sitting in the Human Rights Campaign Office."[25]

Some protested the closed process by establishing the Ad Hoc Committee for an Open Process (AHC), whose members led the very public opposition to the march. Besides the secretive process, they objected to a national march that could potentially drain resources and energy away from the local and statewide ballot referendums where lgbt rights were on the line. They were also offended by the Christian-oriented name of the march, which carried no mention of gays, lesbians, transgenders, or bisexuals. Though no doubt influenced by the Reverend Troy Perry, founder of the UFMCC, who was apparently one of the "self-appointed white 'leaders' in the room" alluded to by Smith, for AHC member Bill Dobbs, the absence of a signifier was an affront. "It's a way to hide the identities," said Dobbs. "They are trying to water it down."[26] The Ad Hoc Committee for an Open Process also thought that the white-led HRC and the UFMCC were trying to expand their base at the expense of people of color and the overall heterogeneity of the movement. Said AHC member Diana Onley-Campbell, "A small group of people made the decision to have it, and those of us who are people of color, transgender and part of the leather community were excluded from that process." Accordingly, the AHC demanded that racial and ethnic minorities and labor activists have representatives from their organizations be put on the board.[27]

Another thorn was the crass commercialism. The complaints ranged from the preponderance of celebrities to too many corporate sponsors. Advertisements, including those of United Airlines, the Showtime network, and PlanetOut, a media and entertainment company catering to lgbts, were so prominent that Bill Dobbs thought the march was less a civil rights demonstration than "a marketing event"[28] For Billy Hileman, a cochair of the 1993 march, the fact that the United Airlines logo was above the stage of the march proved it belonged to United, and "is not obligated to the constituency it intends to speak for."[29] While Rick Garcia, a representative of a gay rights group called Equality Illinois, thought the Millennium March an apolitical "tchotchke sale on the Mall," a critic describing himself as a white Latin American said it amounted to "a fairly standard street festival with gay people in it."[30]

This critic also lamented the homogenized culture that was projected. There were no "leather daddies, trannies, drag queens and hard-core dykes, shirtless lesbians and people of color from all origins."[31] The crowd, he wrote, "consisted of mostly men, mostly white and mostly shirtless, mostly looking like every other mostly shirtless white man in the group, drinking expensive lemonade and having a fabulous time."[32] Seattle resident Christopher Smith, founder of Bigot Busters, an organization dedicated to defeating antigay initiatives, similarly opposed the erasure of lesbians and gays of color, queer radicals, and labor organizers. Speaking to ensure that "grassroots activists, glitter-haired drag queens, and leather-clad dykes" did not get shoved aside by "uptight Wall Street homo-brokers, ultra-cool lipstick lesbians, and overpriced political consultants," Smith protested the seeming new direction of the movement. "Supposedly, our issues now are forming stable relationships, supporting gays raising children, satisfying the desire to legally wed, and returning to the churches of our youth!" he claimed. Though he understood the politics behind the agenda—the need to defeat the special rights advocates— he nevertheless objected to an lgbt agenda that "screams the need for acceptance from **K**üche, **K**irche und **K**inder fundamentalists" (emphasis added).[33]

An ad published by the AHC and signed by 300 prominent activists summed up the concerns and objections of those troubled by the Millennium March. Much more was at stake, the ad claimed, than just the process of calling the march. The very soul of the movement was on the line, signers insisted. The fight was about the direction of the movement and whether it would be about freedom, justice, and equality for all: "This is about power and how it is wielded, manipulated and abused. Who sits at the table and who decides how the table is set." Arguing against the "normal" or assimilationist agenda of the HRC, the ad proclaimed:

> We want a movement that fights for the rights of each of us. Even if we do not fit into the corporate image of an "American family." That these national organizations project white Christian middle-class representations and set the agenda accordingly is nothing less than institutionalized racism. Claims to diversity mean nothing if the sexual is sanitized and no genuine effort is made to include the perspectives and leadership of lgbts from different races, classes, sexualities and genders.[34]

   Despite the uproar from march opponents, including the AHC, the march proceeded and drew record numbers to the Washington Mall on April 30. San Francisco state assemblywoman Carole Migden was probably right when she opined that most marchers were unconcerned about the power struggle among the leadership—the "inside baseball," as she put it—and that what determined attendance was whether supporters could afford to go, could get off work, and whether their friends were going.[35] In 2000 there were more "out" lgbts than ever before—a measure of the success of the visibilization tactic—and they were, like marchers before them, eager to demonstrate their existence, to quell feelings of isolation by being in a majority, and to be among those who were hopeful about the future. Evidence that marchers were aware of the damage done by the special rights strategy come from people like Pam Lessard of Melbourne, Florida, who proclaimed "we are the same," or like Adam May of Atlanta, who insisted that "we're only asking for the same rights as everyone else. . . . Depriving one person puts everyone at risk of losing."[36] If organizer Dianne Hardy-Garcia was right, there were more people from small- and medium-sized towns than at any previous national march, which to her signaled a truly national movement.[37]
   Ironically, while march opponents feared the loss of the movement's heterogeneity, marchers touted their own brand of diversity. One of the most interesting facts about the marchers was their celebration of a newfound freedom to be more than their sexuality, to be an individual who could project any number of identities. Tennis great Martina Navratilova, for example, said that being gay was an important part of who she was but it was not all of who she was. "That's just one part of me. I'm many, many things." This was part of her argument against special rights. If she became a spouse or a parent, she needed the legal rights to take care of her family. "This is not about special rights, it's only about equality," she maintained.[38] Like so many others, marcher Bruno Manning identified not just as gay but as a father. He wanted no more rights than any other family man because, he claimed, "we are a family at the same level as any . . . straight family and we deserve respect and recognition."[39] For some gays, region was the signifying identity. Jim McCarthy of Dayton, Ohio, proclaimed, "We're not just leather boys and drag queens. . . . A lot more of us are plain ol' boring Midwesterners."[40]
   As suggested by McCarthy, at the 2000 Millennium March, "boring" emerged as a badge of victory. Although many would hardly identify Dan Savage of Seattle, a writer of racy tales of homosexual life, as boring, he identified himself as such: "What's wrong with being boring?" he asked. "The vast majority of people are boring and stupid and cheap."[41] Savage was clearly mainstreaming himself and the movement, as was Jennifer Vanasco in a provocative piece titled "Boring Is Beautiful." Vanasco turned the argument against mainstreaming on its head by claiming it to be a radical response to anti-lgbts. Mainstreaming was radical because "it's

unexpected by homophobics, many of whom seem to think we hide pointed tails under our Gap jeans." What was radical about being boring, reasoned Vanasco, was the unprecedented ability to be so "when and where we want to . . . be our full awkward selves, instead of the selves pigeonholed by our sexual identities." Vanasco clearly understood the limitations of boring when she said that "it will get us our rights faster than outrageous—at least will get us white, middle-class rights." But Vanasco was willing to sacrifice others because, to her, boring was, as she put it, "comfortable." Once white, middle-class lgbts got the freedom to marry, adopt, and the legal ability to keep their jobs and apartments, they could, she said, perhaps "focus on other rights vital to our community, like equal pay for women, racial justice, protection against gender bias and education and job training for the poor." Sounding very much like post-black devotees who relished the freedom to express more than their racial identity, Vanasco claimed that "boring is rebellion" because for so long lgbts had fought fiercely for the right to be ordinary. In Vanasco's mind, the boring white middle class had finally emerged victorious.[42]

This was galling to nonassimilationists. Vanasco was obviously unaware of the role that "outrageous" had played in lgbt history. Many of those considered outrageous—the fairies, butches, cross-dressers, transvestites—had courageously carved out the lgbt rights and spaces that normals were now appropriating. Historically, the outrageous were the clarions. For decades they had brazenly announced lgbt existence while others hid their identity and secretly watched where and how the outrageous gathered.[43] The media's fascination with them had actually worked to the movement's advantage because the coverage of them exposed the community, an exposure that the closeted secretly took advantage of. The marches only heightened this exposure and visibilized this world that was legally bondaged and socially circumscribed. Now that the outrageous had successfully led the way in visibilizing the movement, assimilationists were stepping in and taking it over, leaving behind those who could not or would not blend in.

In short, the Millennium March was like an earthquake, sending the tools in the toolbox in different directions. The takeover of the march by the assimilationists was reminiscent of the kind of political expediency that captured the woman's suffrage, labor, and civil rights movements. Early in the century, Northern white suffragists argued against granting African American women the vote in order to win favor from Southern congressmen; at midcentury, labor and black civil rights organizations sacrificed leftists in order to appease anti-Communists. In each case, movement leaders sacrificed crucial constituencies in order to dilute opposition to their cause and win political favor. Now, under pressure from special rights proponents, assimilationists deemed it beneficial to showcase lgbt *sameness*—to show how un-American it was to deny white Americans who were willing to serve and die for America, who were gainfully employed, monogamous, consuming parents, the basic rights of citizenship. By emphasizing lgbt ordinariness and whiteness, assimilationists like Vanasco hoped to negate the charges of lgbt immorality and exceptionalness, and thereby dismantle the grounding arguments of fundamentalist homophobic thought. In doing so, they also alienated a substantial minority of their community.

The Center Holds

When the *New York Times* opinion piece that characterized the 1993 march as Ozzie and Harriet was published, an important caveat was added. The writer noted how understandable it was for gay Americans to fixate on "normalcy" given how they had been so demonized. But, said the writer, "it's a dangerous idea" to base full citizenship rights on how conventional or orderly or well-behaved people are. The measure of a just society is not how the Ozzie and Harriets are treated but whether the same full citizenship rights are given to those who don't look like the people next door.[44] Sociologist Margaret Cerullo and lesbian feminist civil rights activist Loree Cook-Daniels agreed. Their concerns were similar to those of the editorialist. They wanted freedom for the entire community, not just those who could be identified as respectable. In 1993, this seemed an open question; by the 2000 Millennium March, the question seemed to have been answered.

As had happened at all of the other marches/gatherings, multiple identities proved a stumbling block. This of course was profound since like Promise Keepers and African Americans, sexual minorities gathered on the basis of their identities. Being with others like themselves made them feel whole, happy, and fulfilled. National and local marches visibilized them in unimaginable ways and increased exponentially the numbers who lived open, unapologetic lives. But as Loree Cook-Daniels noted in 1993, the community itself was multicultured, economically layered, and racially and sexually diverse. All did not experience or serve the community the same way. It was ironic and yet predictable that the success of visibilization would divide and exclude rather than unite and harmonize. And it was tragic that sexual minorities could not offer the entire community to America and be accepted, and that their opponents used their multiple identities as a divide-and-conquer strategy.

The first years of the new century did in fact mark the expansion of lgbt rights. In June 2015, the Supreme Court made same-sex marriage legal across America, and same-sex couples gained all of the benefits of that status. In the first fifteen years of the new millennium, sexual minorities gained the right to adopt children, serve openly in the military, use antidiscrimination laws to work and live freely, and have the same rights to privacy as other Americans. These rights have made the lives of lgbts remarkably better. The community, such as it was and is, did fall apart, but clearly it did not disintegrate.

Notes

1. "Editorial, Jim Crow for Queers," *Outlines* 7, no. 3 (August 1993): 4, Shilts Papers, series 3, SFPL.

2. Quoted in "'Some of My Closest Advisors Are Gay' Syndrome, or Don't Be Fooled by Bill," in "Why I Hated the March on Washington" published by QUASH (Queers United Against Straight-acting Homosexuals) [ad-hoc newspaper], Ephemera Collection/Protests, etc./Marches on Washington, 1993, folder 2 of 2, San Francisco GLBT Historical Society.

3. Edward Cone and Lisa Scheer, "Queen of the Right," *Mirabella*, February 1993, 86, acc. #4511–001, box 4, Concerned Women for America folder, Suzzallo and Allen GLIC.

4. Memo from Concerned Women for America, n.d., acc. #4511–001, box 2, Concerned Women for America folder, Suzzallo and Allen GLIC.

5. Edward Cone and Lisa Scheer, "Queen of the Right," *Mirabella*, February 1993, 93, acc. #4511–001, box 4, Concerned Women for America folder, Suzzallo and Allen GLIC.

6. Beverly LaHaye, "The Hidden Homosexual Agenda," acc. #4511–001, box 4, Concerned Women for America 1991 folder, Suzzallo and Allen GLIC.

7. Robert Davis, "Rights Issue Still Divides," *USA Today*, April 26, 1993, 1A; Robert Davis, "Poll: Women More Tolerant," *USA Today*, April 26, 1993, 10A, acc. #4511–001, box 5, Clippings folder, Suzzallo and Allen GLIC.

8. Ron Becker, *Gay TV and Straight America* (New Brunswick, NJ: Rutgers University Press, 2006), 103.

9. Ibid., 1–3, 104.

10. Ibid., 108–35.

11. Robert Davis, "Rights Issue Still Divides" *USA Today*, April 26, 1993, 1A, acc. #4511–001, box 5, Clippings folder, Suzzallo and Allen GLIC.

12. See, for example, Ralph Z. Hallow, "Christian Coalition to Court Minorities," *Washington Times*, September 10, 1993, and Farai Chideya, "How the Right Stirs Black Homophobia," *Time*, October 18, 1993, acc. #4511–001, box 5, Clippings folder, Suzzallo and Allen GLIC.

13. All quotes from Eric Washington, "Freedom Rings: The Alliance between Blacks and Gays Is Threatened by Mutual Inscrutability," *Village Voice*, June 29, 1993, acc. #4511–001, box 5, Clippings folder, Suzzallo and Allen GLIC.

14. Edwards, "Religion," in Jarrett, *Impact of Macro Social Systems*, 237–38.

15. Ibid., 239–41.

16. *Gay Rights, Special Rights: Inside the Homosexual Agenda* (Hemet, CA: Traditional Values Coalition/Jeremiah Films, 1993). According to the film, which supports its claims with visuals and "expert" testimony, if special rights are granted to lgbts, the following will happen: homosexual teachers will teach a homosexual orthodoxy that will encourage their children to become homosexuals; boys will be co-opted so they won't want to be with boys, which will lead to the destruction of the family; taxpayers will have to pay for transvestite sex-change operations and artificial insemination for lesbians; churches who refuse to marry same-sexed couples will lose their tax-exempt status; private busi-

nesses will be forced to hire homosexuals; sexual practices like fisting, defecation, and sadomasochism will become the norm; AIDS will spread; children will be assaulted in parks; and the political power of gays will escalate while America degenerates into decay. Gays can be rehabilitated, and learn to be heterosexuals, says the narrator. Legislation is not the answer; neither are special rights. Only Christ can save this population, says the narrator. In Christ all things are possible, including the salvation of lgbts and the nation.

17. *Gay Rights, Special Rights*.

18. "Special Rights: A Code Word for Campaigns of Discrimination," flyer, People for the American Way Action Fund, acc. #4511–001, box 4, Gay Rights, Special Rights folder, Suzzallo and Allen GLIC.

19. Ralph Z. Hallow, "Christian Coalition to Court Minorities," *Washington Times*, September 10, 1993, Nation sec., acc. #4511–001, box 5, Clippings folder, Suzzallo and Allen GLIC.

20. Ibid.

21. Joshua Gamson, "Whose Millennium March?" *Nation*, March 30, 2000, 16.

22. Tristan Taormino, "Sex and Silence in D.C.," *Village Voice*, May 16, 2000, Hot Spot sec., 154.

23. Quoted in Gamson, "Whose Millennium March?" 16.

24. Ibid., 20.

25. Kim Diehl, "Here's the Movement, Let's Start Building" in *Colorlines*, November 2, 2000, accessed August 11, 2016, http://www.colorlines.com/articles/heres -movement-lets-start-building.

26. Richard Goldstein, "The Millennium March: A Gay March on Washington Spawns a Major Movement Rift," *Village Voice*, April 25, 2000.

27. "Gay Rights Activists' Millennium March on Washington," *ABC World News Tonight*, April 30, 2000.

28. Elaine Sciolino, "Gays Set to Flex Political Muscle in Today's Washington March," *Contra Costa* (CA) *Times*, April 30, 2000, News sec., A8.

29. Ann Scales, "Weekend Gay-Rights March Doesn't Sit Well with Some Grassroots Activists," *Boston Globe*, April 29, 2000, National/Foreign sec., A3.

30. Bob Morris, "The Age of Dissonance," *New York Times*, April 30, 2000, sec. 9, Style Desk, 1; "A Breakdown in the Instinct for Self-Preservation," SaddleSores.org, May 1, 2000.

31. "Mock Marriages Highlight Gay Rights Rally," *Pantagraph* (Bloomington, IL), April 30, 2000, News sec., A1; "Breakdown in the Instinct for Self-Preservation."

32. "Breakdown in the Instinct for Self-Preservation."

33. Christopher Smith, "Sparks Fly over National Gay Rally Plans," *Freedom Socialist* 20, no. 2 (July–September 1999).

34. The advertisement appeared in the September 18, 1998, issue of the *Washington Blade*, http://gaytoday.badpuppy.com/garchive/events/092298ev.htm, accessed July 13, 2016.

35. Marc Sandalow, "Millennium March: Gay Rally Bares Deep Divisions," *San Francisco Chronicle*, April 29, 2000.

36. Genaro C. Armas, "Mock Same-Sex Wedding Staged," Associated Press Online, April 30, 2000.

37. "A Gay Rights Movement in the New Millennium," *San Francisco Chronicle*, April 30, 2000, Editorial sec., 6.

38. Kyra Phillips and Miles O'Brien, "Supporters of Gay Rights March on Washington in Millennium March for Equality," CNN, April 30, 2000.

39. Brian Nelson and Kate Snow, "Thousands in Washington for Gay and Lesbian Rights," *CNN Worldview*, April 30, 2000.

40. Bob Dart, "Gay Activist Rally at Captiol," Cox News Service, April 30, 2000.

41. Edward Helmore, "College Football Hero Corey Johnson Came Out and No One Was Outraged," *Guardian* (U.S. edition) April 30, 2000.

42. Jennifer Vanasco, "Boring Is Beautiful," IGFCultureWatch.com, June 10, 2000.

43. See, for example, George Chauncey, *Gay New York: Gender, Urban Culture, and the Making of the Gay Male World, 1890–1940* (New York: Basic Books, 1994), 299; Elizabeth Lapovsky Kennedy and Madeline D. Davis, *Boots of Leather, Slippers of Gold: A History of a Lesbian Community* (New York: Routledge, 1993), 91–92, 374.

44. *New York Times*, April 27, 1993, Opinion sec., A20.

ORIGINAL PUBLICATIONS

Daina Ramey Berry. *"Swing the Sickle for the Harvest is Ripe": Gender and Slavery in Antebellum Georgia.* University of Illinois Press, 2007.

Melinda Chateauvert. *Marching Together: Women of the Brotherhood of Sleeping Car Porters.* University of Illinois Press, 1998.

Tiffany M. Gill. *Beauty Shop Politics: African American Women's Activism in the Beauty Industry.* University of Illinois Press, 2010.

Nancy A. Hewitt. *Southern Discomfort: Women's Activism in Tampa, Florida, 1880s–1920s.* University of Illinois Press, 2001.

Treva B. Lindsey. *Colored No More: Reinventing Black Womanhood in Washington, D.C.* University of Illinois Press, 2017.

Anne Firor Scott. *Natural Allies: Women's Associations in American History.* University of Illinois Press, 1992.

Charissa J. Threat. *Nursing Civil Rights: Gender and Race in the Army Nurse Corps.* University of Illinois Press, 2015.

Anne M. Valk. *Radical Sisters: Second-Wave Feminism and Black Liberation in Washington, D.C.* University of Illinois Press, 2010.

Lara Vapnek. *Breadwinners: Working Women and Economic Independence, 1865–1920.* University of Illinois Press, 2009.

Deborah Gray White. *Lost in the USA: American Identity from the Promise Keepers to the Million Mom March.* University of Illinois Press, 2017.

CONTRIBUTORS

DAINA RAMEY BERRY is Oliver H. Radkey Regents Professor of History and chairperson of the History Department at the University of Texas at Austin. She is also a Fellow of Walter Prescott Webb Chair in History and the George W. Littlefield Professorship in American History and the former associate dean of The Graduate School at the University of Texas at Austin. Her recent books include *The Price for Their Pound of Flesh: The Value of the Enslaved, from Womb to Grave, in the Building of a Nation* and, with Kali Nicole Gross, *A Black Women's History of the United States*.

MELINDA CHATEAUVERT is associate director of the Front Porch Research Strategy in New Orleans, Louisiana. She completed a Ph.D. in U.S. history at the University of Pennsylvania in 1992 and is the author of *Sex Workers Unite: A History of the Movement from Stonewall to SlutWalk*.

TIFFANY M. GILL is an associate professor of history at Rutgers University. She is an editor, with Keisha Blain, of *To Turn the Whole World Over: Black Women and Internationalism*.

NANCY A. HEWITT is distinguished professor emerita at Rutgers University and author most recently of *Radical Friend: Amy Kirby Post and Her Activist Worlds* and coauthor of *Exploring American Histories*, third edition.

TREVA B. LINDSEY is an associate professor of women's, gender, and sexuality studies at The Ohio State University. She has also contributed to Al Jazeera, *Cosmopolitan*,

HuffPost Live, *Complex* magazine, *The Marc Steiner Show*, and the *Left of Black* web series.

ANNE FIROR SCOTT (1921–2019) was the W. K. Boyd Professor of History Emerita at Duke University. She authored and coauthored numerous books; her first book was *The Southern Lady: From Pedestal to Politics, 1830–1930*. Scott received distinguished achievement awards from the Organization of American Historians and the American Historical Association. In 2012 she received the National Humanities Medal.

CHARISSA J. THREAT is an associate professor of history at Chapman University. Her published work has appeared in numerous journals and edited collections.

ANNE M. VALK is a professor of history at The Graduate Center of the City University of New York and director of the Center for Media and Learning's American Social History Project. She is the coauthor of *Living with Jim Crow: African American Women and Memories of the Segregated South* with Leslie Brown and coeditor of *U.S. Women's History: Untangling the Threads of Sisterhood* with Leslie Brown and Jacqueline Castledine.

LARA VAPNEK is a professor of history at St. John's University in Queens, New York. She is the author of *Elizabeth Gurley Flynn: Modern American Revolutionary*. Vapnek's articles appear in *Feminist Studies*, the *Journal of Women's History*, and *No Permanent Waves: Recasting Histories of U.S. Feminism*.

DEBORAH GRAY WHITE is Board of Governors Distinguished Professor of history and professor of women's and gender studies at Rutgers University. Her books include *Too Heavy a Load: Black Women in Defense of Themselves, 1894–1994*, *Let My People Go: African Americans 1804–1860*, and *Ar'n't I a Woman? Female Slaves in the Plantation South*.

INDEX

abortion. *See* reproductive control in Washington, D.C.

Acción, Facundo, 99–100

Adams, Abigail, 13

Ad Hoc Committee for an Open Process (AHC), 243–45

adoption, as LGBT right, 9, 246, 247

African American churches: enslaved preachers and, 43, 46–47; LGBT rights and, 239–40, 247; political activism in Washington, D.C. and, 115

Albrier, Frances, 141–42, 143, 151–53

alcohol: moral motherhood vs., 5; temperance and, 15, 19, 69, 79, 89, 120

Alcott, Louisa May, *Work*, 71, 73

American Equal Rights Association, 116–17

American Federation of Teachers (AFT), 145, 146

American Journal of Nursing, 160–62, 164, 173, 175n9

American Nurses' Association (ANA), 3; African American female nurses and, 159, 164, 167, 172, 175n8; equal rights among the sexes and, 160, 162, 172; gendered perspective on caregiving, 158–60, 163, 164, 168–69, 171–72; membership requirements, 158–63, 175n8, 175n13; Men Nurses' Section, 165, 168–69, 172–73, 176–77n32

American Red Cross, 163–65

American Social Science Association, 77

American Workman, 64, 70

Ames, Azel: *Sex in Industry*, 78

Anderson, Mary, 146

Andrews, Eliza: on slave families, 45

Anthony, Susan B.: and *The Revolution* (newspaper), 69–70, 73–75, 117; women's rights and, 76, 122, 129

Anti-Slavery Convention of American Women (1837), 115–16

Army Nurse Corps, 163–68, 170–74

Bagley, Sarah, 62

Baker, Ella, 182

Bartlett Amendment (1974), 226–28

beauty industry. *See* black beauty industry

Becker, Ron, 238

Beecher, Catharine, 64

Berry, Daina Ramey, 2, 7

Bigot Busters, 244

Binns, Arrie: on slave families, 44–45

birth control. *See* reproductive control in Washington, D.C.

bisexual rights. *See* LGBT rights

black beauty industry, 9, 180–204; civil rights movement and, 182–83, 185; communication within the community and, 188–89, 195–96; counselor and confidant role in, 186, 187–88, 200; Highlander Folk School Citizenship Schools Program and, 189–200; Jim Crow segregation and, 180–81, 185–88; Mississippi Independent Beautician Association (MIBA), 183–84; National Beauty Culturalists' League (NBCL), 181–83; straightening/pressing hair and, 145, 186–87; support for the Brotherhood of Sleeping Car Porters and Maids (BSCP), 145, 148; training for, 183, 191–92; United Beauty School Owners and Teachers Association (UBSOTA), 183; voting rights and, 182–83, 185, 191–92, 196–97; Madam C. J. Walker and, 145, 148, 187; wigs and, 187

Blackburn, Ruby Parks, 185, 200

Black Panther Party, 210–11

black Washington, D.C. women, 2, 6–7, 111–37; disenfranchisement of all Washingtonians (1874), 118–20; Jim Crow segregation, 111, 117–18; politics of appearance and bodily adornment, 111–13, 121–24, 127, 131–33; voting rights for black men and, 8, 112–19; voting rights for women and, 7, 8, 111–13, 118, 120–33; Women's Suffrage March (1913), 113, 124–33, 136n74. *See also* reproductive control in Washington, D.C.

Blackwell, Alice, 126

black women: alliances across identities and, 8–9; appearance and bodily adornment issues, 111–13, 121–24, 127, 131–33, 186–87; in the beauty industry (*see* black beauty industry); in the Brotherhood of Sleeping Car Porters and Maids (BSCP), 140–44, 150–53; and cigar-making in Florida, 86–89, 91, 98–100, 102–4, 106n4; cult of respectability and, 6; "domestic femininity" vs., 61; as domestic workers, 6, 64–65, 147, 185, 190, 200; female benevolent societies of, 15, 16, 18, 21, 23, 26; hair care products, 145, 186–87; Irish women within the idiom of blackness, 6; Jezebel trope and, 5; mammy trope and, 5; as nurses, 159, 164, 167, 172, 175n8; orga-

nizing separately from white women, 6–7; perceptions of white native-born women vs., 5–6, 7; Sapphire trope and, 5; in slave families (*see* slave families); in Washington, D.C. (*see* black Washington, D.C. women)

Blake, Mitchell, 167

Blanchfield, Florence A., 171–72

Boffin's Bower (Boston), 75–78

Bolton, Frances, 173

Boston Seaman's Aid Society, 17–18

Boston Working Women's League, 67–73

Bowman, Eva, 196

Brotherhood of Sleeping Car Porters and Maids (BSCP), 3–4, 138–57; Asian women and, 141–42, 143–44, 154n13, 155n21; black female union participation, 140–44, 150–53; Citizen's Committees, 145, 146–47, 152; expansion beyond New York, 138–44; funding sources, 139, 145–47, 149–53; The Messenger (union paper), 139, 145, 150; New Negro movement and, 138–39, 141–42, 152; Pullman company informants, 139–40, 143, 149–51; support by prominent African American and white women, 4, 139, 140, 144–53; women's auxiliaries, 139, 148; Women's Economic Councils, 3, 139, 142–43, 147–53

Browder v. Gale (1956), 195–96

Brown, Elsa Barkley, 112–13

Brown v. Board of Education (1954), 183–84, 192

BSCP. *See* Brotherhood of Sleeping Car Porters and Maids (BSCP)

Burke, Emily: on slave families, 42

Bush, George H. W., 235–36

Butler, Marshal: on slave families, 36–37, 39, 53

Byrd, Robert, 208

Caldwell, Bernice, 186

Callaway, Mariah: on slave families, 36, 38

Cambridge (Massachusetts) Female Humane Society, 19

Campa, José de la, 98

Capetillo, Luisa, 99–101, 106, 109n43

El Centro Asturiano (Florida mutual aid society), 86–87, 89

El Centro Español (Florida mutual aid society), 86–89

Cerullo, Margaret, 247

Chateauvert, Melinda, 3–4, 7–8

Chesterfield Female Benevolent Society (New Hampshire), 20

Chicago Women's Trade Union League, 146

Chisholm, Shirley, 211

Christian Coalition, 242

Christianity: enslaved preachers and, 43, 46–47; female benevolent societies and, 14–15, 23, 24, 28n2, 29n10; Second Great Awakening, 15, 29n10; slave families and, 37–38, 41–49. *See also* African American churches

cigar-making industry, 3, 8, 86–110; Cigar Makers' International Union (CMIU), 90–96, 98, 105, 107n12, 108n32; home-based work and, 97; Jim Crow segregation and, 86, 98, 103–4; mutual aid societies, 86–90, 101–5; readers, 99–100; role of women in the labor movement, 86, 90–102, 104–6; Socialist party and, 92–94, 98–99; strike of 1901, 90–91, 94; strike of 1910, 92–96, 97, 102–3, 108n32; tension between male and female workers, 97, 104–5

Cigar Manufacturers Association, 96

El Círculo Cubano (Florida mutual aid society), 86–87, 88, 89, 104

Citywide Welfare Association (CWA), 206, 209–10, 212–20, 230n24

Civil Rights Act (1957), 196

Civil Rights Act (1964), 182, 241

Civil Rights Act (1993), 240

civil rights movement: black beauty industry and, 180–200; domestic workers and, 185; education and, 183–84, 192; Highlander Folk School's Citizenship Schools Program, 189–200; March on Washington for Jobs and Freedom (1963), 241; schoolteachers and, 194–95, 200; voting rights and the black beauty industry, 182–83, 185

Civil War: female benevolent societies during and after, 65–66, 71–73, 74; labor movements following, 62, 66–80; racial segregation of the labor market following, 65

Claramunt, Teresa, 95

Clark, Septima, 189–98, 200

class. *See* social class

Clinton, Bill, 235, 236, 238

Clinton, Hillary, 236

Cobble, Dorothy Sue, 6

Coburn, Judith, 216

Cofer, Willis: on slave families, 38, 42, 53

Coleman, Cheryl, 241

Collins, Ben C., 199

Collins, Jennie: as abolitionist, 65, 71; Boffin's Bower (Boston), 75–78; Boston Working Women's League and, 67–72; as domestic servant, 62–64, 77; female benevolent societies and, 65–66, 74, 80; Garden Homestead movement and, 67–72; as labor movement activist, 74–78; *Nature's Aristocracy*, 75–78; as skilled garment maker, 64, 70–72; as textile worker, 60–62, 63; western migration and, 69–71

Colored American, The, 111–12, 121–24, 129, 132

Commission on Interracial Cooperation, 121

Concerned Women for America (CWA), 236–37

contraception. *See* reproductive control in Washington, D.C.

Cook-Daniels, Loree, 247

Coolidge, Calvin, 145

Cooper, Anna Julia, 112

Cott, Nancy: *Bonds of Womanhood,* 28

courtship, in slave families, 35–37

Craig, LeRoy, 162, 163, 165, 167, 177nn34–35

Craig, Maxine Leeds, 187

Crawford, Beverly, 211

Crenshaw, Kimberlé, 7

Crosswaith, Frank, 139

Crummer, Kenneth T., 159, 160–61, 175n14

CWA (Citywide Welfare Association), 206, 209–10, 212–20, 230n24

dance, among enslaved Americans, 47–49

Daniels, Elizabeth: Boston Working Women's League and, 67–73; Garden Homestead movement and, 67–72; western migration and, 69

Daughters of Africa (Philadelphia), 21

Davis, Marylee, 194

Davis, Paulina, 75

D.C. Family Rights Welfare Organization, 211

D.C. Women's Liberation Movement (DC-WLM), 205–7, 209–10, 212–22, 225–26

Degler, Carl, 5

DesVerney, William H., 139

Dillon, Ada V., 151, 152

Dock, Lavinia L., 160

Doe v. Dalton (1973), 229n4

domesticity: African American women vs. "domestic femininity," 61; female benevolent societies and, 13–14, 16, 17, 20; new domestic ideal for girls and women, 60–61

domestic workers: African American women as, 6, 64–65, 147, 185, 190, 200; black beauty industry as career escape for, 191; black beauty industry as support for, 186, 187–88, 200; former female white textile workers as, 62–64, 77, 80; Highlander's Citizenship Schools and, 193–200; Jim Crow segregation and, 195; sex work/prostitution preferred by, 63, 77; training for, 185; white ethnic/immigrant women as, 6, 63–65; working conditions of, 72–73, 78

Domestic Workers' Union, 145–46

Drumright, Ernest, 94–95

Easterling, J. F., 93

education and training: in the black beauty industry, 183, 191–92; *Brown v. Board of Education* (1952), 183–84, 192; civil rights movement and, 183–84, 192; for domestic workers, 185, 189–200; female benevolent societies and, 14–15, 16, 19, 20–22, 27, 32n52; Highlander Folk School's Citizenship Schools Program, 189–200; Howard University and the women's suffrage movement, 121, 122, 126, 129–32; and job opportunities for white male nurses, 159–64, 166, 170, 174n4; moral motherhood and, 5; voting rights and, 116–17, 119, 189–200

Egypt, Ophelia, 207–8

eight-hour day movement, 66–67, 75, 76, 80

Eisenhower, Dwight D., 181

Eisenstadt v. Baird (1972), 229n6

Elliott, S., 92–93

Equal Rights Amendment (ERA), 160

Equity Illinois, 244

family: adoption as LGBT right, 9, 246, 247; cigar worker mutual aid societies as support for, 86–90, 101–5; same-sex marriage as LGBT right, 9, 241, 246, 247; transformation of patriarchal gender and family

relations, 61. *See also* reproductive control in Washington, D.C.; slave families

Faulkner, Carol: *Women's Radical Reconstruction,* 117

La Federación Libre de los Trabajadores (FLT), 100–101

Federally Employed Women (FEW), 222–24

female benevolent societies, 13–32; benevolence/benevolent society, as terms, 14, 28n2; during the Civil War, 65–66, 74; cultural expectations for women and, 26–27, 32nn50–51; domestic activities and, 13–14, 16, 17, 20; education and mutual aid as goals of, 14–15, 16, 19, 20–22, 27, 32n52; free black women and, 15, 16, 18, 21, 23, 26; gossip and, 19–20, 30n25; growth of mixed-gender associations, 25–26; leadership effectiveness, 17–18, 27–28; origins in America, 13–15; orphans and, 15–17, 20–24; political dimension of, 27–28; post-Civil War, 71–73, 74; during the Revolutionary War, 13, 14; variations and spread of, 15–28; voluntary associations of men vs., 14–16, 24–26; western migration and, 23–24, 27; white women and, 16–28, 65–66, 70; "worthy"/"unworthy" poor and, 7, 14, 16–17, 18–19, 22, 30n15; written constitutions and records, 16, 18, 20, 21, 31n32

Female Benevolent Society (Lynn, Massachusetts), 20

Female Benevolent Society of St. Thomas (Philadelphia), 21

Female Bible and Charitable Society (Nashville), 22

Female Charitable Society (Morristown, New Jersey), 20

Female Charitable Society (Salem, Massachusetts), 20–21

Female Society for Relief of Indigent Women (Rhode Island), 19

feminism, feminist consciousness and female benevolent societies, 28

fertility. *See* reproductive control in Washington, D.C.

Fifteenth Amendment, 8, 112–19

Florida, cigar-making in. *See* cigar-making industry

Flynn, Elizabeth Gurley, 98–99, 146
Foster, Hazel, 188–89
Fowler, Johnnie Mae, 195–96
Frazier, Coazell, 186

Gabaccia, Donna, 6
Gaines, Irene McCoy, 145, 147
Gamson, Joshua, 242
Garcia, Rick, 244
Garden Homestead movement, 2, 67–72,
    78–79
garment industry. *See* white female textile/
    garment workers
Garvey, Marcus, 147
Gaston, Maude, 181
gay rights. *See* LGBT rights
Gay Rights, Special Rights (1993 video), 240–
    41, 248–49n16
Gebbie, Kristine, 236
General Federation of Women's Clubs, 4
Genovese, Eugene, 41
Georgia, slave families in. *See* slave families
Georgia League of Negro Women Voters, 185
Giddings, Paula, *When and Where I Enter*, 120
Gill, Tiffany M., 9
Gilmore, Lucy Bledsoe, 149–52
Graham, Isabella, 17, 27
Grant, Adelaide, 130
Grant, Ulysses S., 118
Greeley, Horace, 69
Green, Nathaniel, 126
Griswold v. Connecticut (1965), 207–8
Guerry, Goode M., 92–93

Hale, Sarah Josepha, 17–18
Hancock, John, 114
Harmon, Jane: on slave families, 47, 53
Harper, Frances Watkins, 118
Haywood, Big Bill, 91
Healthwitches, 225
Hendrix, Irene Sims, 185
Herstein, Lillian, 146
Hewitt, Nancy A., 3, 8, 28
Heywood, Ezra, 66
Higginbotham, Evelyn Brooks, 2
Highlander Folk School's Citizenship
    Schools Program, 189–200; Septima Clark
    and, 189–98, 200; raid and legal battle

(1961), 197–98, 204n70; Bernice Robinson
    and, 190–98, 200
Hine, Darlene Clark, 117–18
Hobson, Julius, 223
Hobson, Tina, 223
Homestead Act (1862): Garden Homestead
    movement and, 2, 67–72, 78–79; pas-
    sage, 67
homosexuality. *See* LGBT rights
Hood, James, 187
hooks, bell, 186
Horn, Etta, 217, 218, 220
Horton, Myles, 189–90, 193–95, 197–98, 199
Howard University, and the women's suf-
    frage movement, 121, 122, 126, 129–32
Human Rights Campaign (HRC), 243
Hunt, Henry T., 146
Hurley, Emma: on slave families, 39, 42,
    48–49
Hyde, Henry, 226
Hyde Amendment (1976), 226–28, 234n69

immigration: Asian women and the Brother-
    hood of Sleeping Car Porters and Maids
    (BSCP), 141–42, 143–44, 154n13, 155n21.
    See also white ethnic/immigrant women
Industrial Workers of the World (IWW),
    90–92, 98–99
International Brotherhood of Sleeping Car
    Porters and Maids. *See* Brotherhood of
    Sleeping Car Porters and Maids (BSCP)
International Ladies' Garment Workers
    Union (ILGWU), 145

Jenkins, Esau, 189–90, 193
Johnson, Cordelia Greene, 181
Johnson, Lyndon Baines, 182–83, 188
Johnson, Manuel: on slave families, 37–38
Johnson, Ryna, 39, 47, 57n81
Johnston, Allan: *Surviving Freedom*, 119
Jones, Frederick, 162
Joyner, Marjorie Stewart, 182–83

Kane, Louisa: on slave families, 50
Kemble, Frances: on slave families, 38, 44
Kennedy, John F., 182, 183
Kerber, Linda, 5, 13–14
King, Anna Page: on slave families, 51

King, Martin Luther, Jr., 181–82, 239–41
Knights of Labor, 67, 74
Kossovsky, Adele, 94, 98, 101
Ku Klux Klan, 239

labor movement: and the American Federation of Teachers (AFT), 145, 146; and the Boston Working Women's League, 67–73; in the cigar-making industry in Florida, 86, 88, 90–106, 107n12, 108n32; Domestic Workers' Union, 145–46; eight-hour day and, 66–67, 75–76, 80; female activists post-Civil War, 67–80; and the International Ladies' Garment Workers Union (ILGWU), 145; post-Civil War, 62, 66–80; ten-hour movement and, 62, 66, 78. *See also* Brotherhood of Sleeping Car Porters and Maids (BSCP)
Ladies Benevolent Society (Charleston), 21
Ladies Female Reform Association, 74
Ladies' Protection and Relief Society (San Francisco), 23–24, 27
LaHaye, Beverly, 236–37
Lancaster, Roy, 139
Latin women, 86–110; in the cigar-making industry labor movement, 86, 90–102, 107n12, 108n32; comparison with African American women, 86; mutual aid societies and, 86–90, 101–5; oral contraceptive research in Puerto Rico, 207, 210
Lebsock, Suzanne, *Free Women of Petersburg,* 25
Legare, J. D.: on slave families, 50–51
Leigh, Frances Butler, 45–46
LeRoy, Greg, 140
lesbian rights. *See* LGBT rights
LGBT rights, 235–50; adoption, 9, 246, 247; assimilationists vs. nonassimilationists, 242–47; coalition between Christian Right and minorities, 237–40, 247; Colorado Amendment 2, 236, 237–38, 242; equality in the military, 9, 235, 247; March on Washington for Gay and Lesbian Rights (1987), 243; March on Washington for Lesbian, Gay and Bi Equal Rights and Liberation (1993), 236, 239–44, 247; Millennium March (2000), 235, 242–47; nondiscrimination rights, 9, 246, 247; Oregon Measure 9, 236, 237–38, 242; privacy rights, 9, 247; same-sex marriage, 9, 241,

246, 247; "special rights" strategy, 235–42, 246–47, 248–49n16
Lindsey, Treva B., 2, 6–7
Litwack, Leon, 114
Lodge, Henry C., 167
Love, Albert G., 167–68, 178n48
Lowell, Francis Cabot, 62
Lowell, John, 62–64, 77
Lowell Female Labor Reform Association, 62, 66
L'Unione Italiana (Florida mutual aid society), 86–87, 89, 104
Lynn Fragment Society (Massachusetts), 20

MAA. *See* Metropolitan Abortion Alliance
Magnuson, Roger, 236–37
Malone, Vivian, 187
March on Washington for Gay and Lesbian Rights (1987), 243
March on Washington for Jobs and Freedom (1963), 241
March on Washington for Lesbian, Gay and Bi Equal Rights and Liberation (1993), 236, 239–44, 247
marriage: same-sex marriage as LGBT right, 9, 241, 246, 247; slave courtship and marriage, 35–40
Martin, Louis, 182–83, 188
Masur, Kate, 112, 118
Mather, Hannah, 14, 29n7
McCarthy, Jim, 245
McDowell, Mary, 146
McLean Hospital School of Nursing for Men (Massachusetts), 162
McLeod, Cora, 188
McMahan, Bobby, 211, 217, 224
Metropolitan Abortion Alliance (MAA), 222–23, 225
Michel, Louise, 95
Mickens, Jane: on slave families, 39, 45, 52
Migden, Carole, 245
Milholland, Inez, 126
military service: LGBT rights in, 9, 235, 247; white male nurses and, 163–74, 177–78n42
Millennium March (2000), 235, 242–47
Miller, Benton: on slave families, 37, 38, 40
Mills, John C., 150
Minyard, Capitola, 143, 155n20

Mississippi Independent Beautician Association (MIBA), 183–84

Moody, Anne: *Coming of Age in Mississippi,* 180

Mormons, female benevolent societies and, 23

Murray, Judith Sargent, 13–15

Musser, H. Richard, 168

National American Woman Suffrage Association (NAWSA), 118, 121, 122–23, 125–29

National Association for the Advancement of Colored People (NAACP), 130–31, 146, 181–82, 185, 188, 192–93, 198, 239–40

National Association of Colored Graduate Nurses, 172

National Association of Colored Women, 121, 122, 126

National Association of Colored Women's Clubs, 145

National Beauty Culturalists' League (NBCL), 181–83

National Black Feminist Organization, 227

National Labor Union, 66–67, 76

National League of Nursing Education (NLNE), 163

National Nursing Council for War Service (NNCWS), 169, 172, 173, 178n53

National Organization for Public Health Nursing, 174n1

National Organization of Public Health Nursing (NOPHN), 163

National Organization for Women (NOW), 205, 222–24, 226–27

National Woman Suffrage Association, 75

National Women's Party, 160

Nation of Islam, 210–11

Navratilova, Martina, 245

Navy Nurse Corps, 163–65, 170

Neal, Margaret Williams, 188, 189

Nelson, Gaylord, 219–20

Neverdon-Morton, Cynthia, 120

New England Labor Reform League, 66–67, 74–75, 77

New England Women's Club (NEWC), 63, 70, 71–73

New Negro era: competing definitions of female respectability and, 138–41; female bodily aesthetic discourses, 111–13, 121–24, 127, 131–33; model of manhood and sleeping car porters, 138–42, 152; tempo-

ral demarcations in, 113; women's suffrage activism, 111–13, 117, 120–33, 138–39

"New Woman" cultural movement, 106, 113, 124–25, 131–32

New York Widows' Society, 17, 27, 32n50

Nightingale, Florence, 158

Nixon, Richard, 182, 210

Norton, Mary Beth, 5

NOW. *See* National Organization for Women

Nurse Corps of the Armed Forces, 165

nursing. *See* white male nurses

Nursing Council for National Defense, 164–65

Olay, Maximiliano, 99–100

Order of Sleeping Car Conductors, 138

orphans, female benevolent societies and, 15–17, 20–24

Painter, Nell Irvin, *Sojourner Truth,* 117

Painton, J. Frederick, 161–62

Paul, Alice, 125–27, 129, 131, 160

Payne, Charles, 184

"pebbles" analogy (Spelman) for women's organizing in America, 1, 2, 4, 6, 9, 10n1

Pennsylvania Hospital School of Nursing for Men, 162

Penny, Virginia, *Think and Act,* 68, 69, 71

People for the American Way (PFAW), 242

Perkins, George, 91–92

Perkins, Otis, 197

Perry, Elizabeth, 211

Phelps, Aurora: Bethesda Laundry dedication, 79; Boston Working Women's League and, 67–72; Garden Homestead movement and, 67–72, 78–79

Phillips, Danielle Taylor, 6

Pigee, Paul, 199

Pigee, Vera, 198–99, 200

Pillsbury, Parker, 69–70

Pitts, Christiana, 187–88

Planned Parenthood, 207–10, 216, 221, 222, 230n23

political intersectionality (Crenshaw), 7

poverty: female benevolent/charity societies and, 15–22, 26–27; male voluntary associations and, 25–26; reproductive control in Washington, D.C. and, 206, 208–21, 228, 234n69

privacy: LGBT rights and, 9, 247; reproductive control and, 207, 213, 215, 225–26
Promise Keepers, 239, 247
prostitution: domestic service by white native-born women vs., 63, 77; moral motherhood vs., 5
Puckett, Josephine, 141, 142–43, 148, 150
Puckett, William, 148, 150
Puerto Rico: Florida cigar-makers from, 97, 99–101, 106; oral contraceptive research in, 207, 210
Pullman Company, 3–4, 138–53

Quander, Nellie, 126

Raleigh (North Carolina) Female Benevolent Society, 22
Randolph, A. Philip, 138–40, 144–51
Randolph, Lucille, 139, 145, 147
Reagan, Ronald, 235
Red Cross Nursing Service, 163–74, 176nn26–28
Reed, Ralph, 242
Regener, Hernan, 92
reproductive control in Washington, D.C., 8–9, 205–34; abortion, 8, 205–7, 209, 211–28, 234n69; birth control pills/oral contraceptives, 206–20, 228; black freedom movement and, 210–11; DCWLM/CWA coalition for health and abortion rights, 212–20; Medicaid coverage and, 208–9, 212–13, 217, 226, 227, 234; Planned Parenthood and, 207–10, 216, 221, 222, 230n23; protests at D.C. General Hospital, 206–16, 219, 230–31n28; surgical sterilization, 9, 205, 207, 209–10, 213, 219, 222, 224, 226; welfare rights and, 206, 208–21, 228, 234n69; women's liberation and, 205–7, 209–28
Revolution, The (newspaper), 69–70, 73–75, 117
Revolutionary War: female benevolent societies during, 13, 14; post-war abolishment of slavery in northern states, 114
Reynolds, Jeannie, 223
Rice, Jan, 241
Robinson, Bernice, 190–98, 200
Roe v. Wade (1973), 206–7, 225–26
Rogers, Henry: on slave families, 41, 52

Roosevelt, Franklin D., 166
Roosevelt, Theodore, 125
Rush, Benjamin, 27
Ryan, Neva, 145–46

Sanborn, Benjamin, 77
Sarraga, Belén, 95
Savage, Dan, 245
Scott, Anne Firor, 2, 3, 6–7
Second Great Awakening, 15, 29n10
Selective Service Act (1940), 166, 169–70, 177–78n42
settlement houses, support for the Brotherhood of Sleeping Car Porters and Maids (BSCP), 146
sexuality: metalanguage of, 7–8; and perceptions of black women, 4–7; rights of sexual minorities and, 9
Shepard, Robert, 46
Sineriz, A., 90–91
slave families, 33–59; abolition movement, 114–16; abroad marriages, 35, 39–40, 49, 54; courtship and mate selection, 35–37; defining slave families and communities, 34–35; family and community interaction, 52–53; Georgia Slave Code (1755) and, 52; male vs. female experience of slavery, 2, 116; marriage ceremonies, 37–40; matrifocal and extended family patterns, 35, 39–40, 49–51, 52, 54; mealtimes, 53; negative impact of slavery on, 33–34; religion and holidays, 37–38, 41–49; visitation passes and, 36, 39–40; working socials and interplantation events, 40–41
sleeping car porters and maids. *See* Brotherhood of Sleeping Car Porters and Maids (BSCP)
Slowe, Lucy Diggs, 130–31
Smith, Christopher, 244
Smith, Hazel, 147
social class: "leisure" of middle-class women and, 29n5; metalanguage of, 7–8; in mutual aid societies in Florida, 88–89; voting rights and, 121–24; white/wage slavery trope in uniting working class women, 8, 71–74; working-class union women vs. middle-class women, 3–4, 6, 66–80, 139–40, 144–53; working conditions of domestic workers and, 72–73, 78

socialism/Socialist party: cigar-makers and, 92–94, 98–99; sleeping car porters and, 139; Young Socialist Alliance and reproductive control, 222–25

Southern Christian Leadership Conference (SCLC), 182, 198

Spelman, Elizabeth: *The Inessential Woman,* 1, 9, 10n1; "pebbles" analogy for women's organizing in America, 1, 2, 4, 6, 9, 10n1

Stansell, Christine, *City of Women,* 131

Stanton, Elizabeth Cady: and *The Revolution* (newspaper), 69–70, 73–75, 117; women's rights and, 76, 116–17

Stegall, Evelyn, 183

sterilization. *See* reproductive control in Washington, D.C.

Sterling, Dorothy, 21

Stone, Lucy, 72

Stowe, Harriet Beecher, 29n35

suffrage. *See* voting rights

Sullivan, Ben: on slave families, 44, 47

Sykes, James D., 239–40, 241

Sylvis, William H., 66–67, 76

temperance, 15, 19, 69, 79, 89, 120

ten-hour movement, 62, 66, 78

Terborg-Penn, Rosalyn, *African American Women in the Struggle for the Vote, 1850–1920,* 117

Terrell, Mary Church: Brotherhood of Sleeping Car Porters and Maids (BSCP) and, 145, 147; women's suffrage and, 112, 119–20, 121–24, 126, 129, 131

textile industry. *See* white female textile/garment workers

Threat, Charissa J., 3

Till, Emmett, 181

Todd, Clemmie, 183

Toms, Florence, 130

Totten, Ashley L., 139, 140, 148, 149–50

training. *See* education and training

train porters and maids. *See* Brotherhood of Sleeping Car Porters and Maids (BSCP)

transgender/transsexual rights. *See* LGBT rights

Treadwell, Mary, 224–25, 227–28

Tresca, Carlo, 98–99

Truett, Julie Ann: on slave families, 49

Truth, Sojourner, 6, 116, 117

Tucker, Rosina, 148–53

Tyrell, William, 104

La Unión Martí-Maceo (Florida mutual aid society), 86–89, 91, 98–100, 104, 106n4

United Beauty School Owners and Teachers Association (UBSOTA), 183

Universal Fellowship of Metropolitan Community Churches (UFMCC), 243

Universal Negro Improvement Association (UNIA), 147

Upson, Neal, 46

Upton, Charles, 143

Upton, Tinie, 141, 143

U.S. Bureau of Labor Statistics, 96–97, 105, 108n33, 109–10n57

U.S. Immigration Commission, 96–97

U.S. Labor Department, *Woman and Child Wage-Earners in the United States,* 96

U.S. v. Vuitch (1971), 211–12, 219, 221, 230n23

Valk, Anne M., 3, 8–9

Vanasco, Jennifer, 245–46

Vapnek, Lara, 2–3, 8

voting rights: black beauty industry and, 182–83, 185, 191–92, 196–97; of black Washington, D.C. women and, 7, 8, 111–13, 118, 120–33; of cigar workers, 101; denial to free black people, 114; disenfranchisement of all Washingtonians (1874), 118–20; education and, 116–17, 119, 189–200; Fifteenth Amendment (1870, citizen right to vote), 8, 112–19; Highlander Citizenship Schools and, 193–94, 196–97; moral motherhood and, 5; National American Woman Suffrage Association (NAWSA), 118, 121, 122–23, 125–29; National Woman Suffrage Association, 75; in the New Negro era, 111–13, 117, 120–33, 138–39; *The Revolution* newspaper and, 69–70, 73–75, 117; universal suffrage movement, 112–19, 120–33; women in labor movements and, 153; women's suffrage movement, 111–13, 116–19, 120–33

Vuitch, Milan, 211–12, 219, 221, 230n23

Wade, Harriet Vail, 188–89

Walker, A'lelia, 145

Walker, Madame C. J., 145, 148, 187

Walton, Mary, 126–27
Washington, D.C.: African American churches and political activism, 115; disenfranchisement of all Washingtonians (1874), 118–20; enslaved population (1800), 114–15; March on Washington for Gay and Lesbian Rights (1987), 243; March on Washington for Jobs and Freedom (1963), 241; March on Washington for Lesbian, Gay, and Bi Equal Rights and Liberation (1993), 236, 239–44, 247; Millennium March (2000), 235, 242–47; reproductive control and (*see* reproductive control in Washington, D.C.); Women's Suffrage March (1913), 113, 124–33, 136n74. *See also* black Washington, D.C. women
Washington, Walter, 214
Webb, Marilyn Salzman, 209–10
Webster, Elizabeth, 147
Webster, Milton P., 140, 142, 144, 150
Wells-Barnett, Ida B., 126, 127, 145
western migration: female benevolent societies and, 23–24, 27; Garden Homesteads and, 69–71
Whickham, Katie, 182–83
White, Deborah Gray, 41
white ethnic/immigrant women: in the cigar-making industry labor movement, 94–98, 102–5; domestic service and, 6, 63–65; female benevolent societies and, 20; Irish women within the idiom of blackness and, 6. *See also* Latin women
white female textile/garment workers, 60–85; and the Boston Working Women's League, 67–73; earnings compared with male workers, 60–62, 63, 64, 68, 71–72, 76–77, 79; Garden Homestead movement, 2, 67–72, 78–79; language of white slavery and, 8, 71–74; post-Civil War labor movement and, 66–80; prostitution vs. domestic service and, 63, 77, 80; as skilled garment makers, 64, 65, 70–72; in Spain, 95; support for the Brotherhood of Sleeping Car Porters and Maids (BSCP), 146; ten-hour movement, 62, 66, 78
white male nurses, 158–79; American Nurses' Association (ANA) and, 158–63, 165, 168–69, 172–73, 176–77n32; Army

and Navy Nurse Corps and, 163–65; gendered perspective on caregiving, 158–60, 163, 164, 168–69, 171–72; as medical technicians and orderlies, 166, 167, 170, 177nn36–37; as pharmacist's mates, 170; Red Cross Nursing Service and, 163–74, 176nn26–28; Selective Service Act (1940) and, 166, 169–70, 177–78n42; state nursing associations and, 158–59, 165, 171, 172, 175–76n17; training and job opportunities, 159–64, 166, 170, 174n4; World War II and, 166–74
white native-born women: alliances across identities and, 8–9; female benevolent societies and (*see* female benevolent societies); Garden Homestead movement and, 2, 67–72; organizing separately from black women, 6–7; perceptions of black women vs., 5–6, 7; in the post-Civil War labor movement, 66–80; prostitution/sex work and, 63, 77; rejection of domestic service, 63, 77; republican motherhood and, 5; support for the Brotherhood of Sleeping Car Porters and Maids (BSCP), 144–52; as textile/garment workers (*see* white female textile/garment workers); westward migration and, 23–24, 27, 69–71; women's suffrage movement, 113, 116–19, 120–30, 132–33, 136n74. *See also* Latin women
"whiteness," concept of, 6, 83–84n63
Whitney, Charlotte Anne, 146
Wigginton, Elliot, 192
Willis, Adeline: on slave families, 37, 38–39, 52
Willis, Deborah, 180–81
Wilson, Woodrow, 104, 125, 171
Wing, Catherine, 41
Witte, Frances, 162
Wolfson, Alice, 205–7, 216, 220
women's club movement: General Federation of Women's Clubs, 4; National Association of Colored Women's Clubs, 145; New England Women's Club, 63, 70, 71–73
Women's Economic Councils, 3
Women's Homestead League, 78–79
Women's National Abortion Action Coalition (WONAAC), 223–25

World War I, Army and Navy Nurse Corps and, 163–64, 165, 171

World War II: male nurse recognition and, 164–74; rank of male vs. female nurses and, 167, 170–71, 179n60; Selective Service Act (1940), 166, 169–70, 177–78n42

Ybor, Ralph M., 103, 104

Ybor City Labor Temple (Florida), 88–89

Yglesias, Jose, 101–2, 109n50

Young, Andrew, 198, 199

Young Socialist Alliance (YSA), 222–25

Zero Population Growth (ZPG), 222

WOMEN, GENDER, AND SEXUALITY IN AMERICAN HISTORY

Women Doctors in Gilded-Age Washington: Race, Gender, and Professionalization
  Gloria Moldow
Friends and Sisters: Letters between Lucy Stone and Antoinette Brown Blackwell,
  1846–93   *Edited by Carol Lasser and Marlene Deahl Merrill*
Reform, Labor, and Feminism: Margaret Dreier Robins and the Women's Trade Union
  League   *Elizabeth Anne Payne*
Private Matters: American Attitudes toward Childbearing and Infant Nurture in the
  Urban North, 1800–1860   *Sylvia D. Hoffert*
Civil Wars: Women and the Crisis of Southern Nationalism   *George C. Rable*
I Came a Stranger: The Story of a Hull-House Girl   *Hilda Satt Polacheck;*
  edited by Dena J. Polacheck Epstein
Labor's Flaming Youth: Telephone Operators and Worker Militancy, 1878–1923
  Stephen H. Norwood
Winter Friends: Women Growing Old in the New Republic, 1785–1835   *Terri L. Premo*
Better Than Second Best: Love and Work in the Life of Helen Magill   *Glenn C. Altschuler*
Dishing It Out: Waitresses and Their Unions in the Twentieth Century   *Dorothy Sue Cobble*
Natural Allies: Women's Associations in American History   *Anne Firor Scott*
Beyond the Typewriter: Gender, Class, and the Origins of Modern American Office Work,
  1900–1930   *Sharon Hartman Strom*
The Challenge of Feminist Biography: Writing the Lives of Modern American
  Women   *Edited by Sara Alpern, Joyce Antler, Elisabeth Israels Perry, and Ingrid Winther Scobie*
Working Women of Collar City: Gender, Class, and Community in Troy, New York,
  1864–86   *Carole Turbin*
Radicals of the Worst Sort: Laboring Women in Lawrence, Massachusetts, 1860–1912
  Ardis Cameron
Visible Women: New Essays on American Activism   *Edited by Nancy A. Hewitt*
  and Suzanne Lebsock
Mother-Work: Women, Child Welfare, and the State, 1890–1930   *Molly Ladd-Taylor*
Babe: The Life and Legend of Babe Didrikson Zaharias   *Susan E. Cayleff*
Writing Out My Heart: Selections from the Journal of Frances E. Willard, 1855–96
  Edited by Carolyn De Swarte Gifford
U.S. Women in Struggle: A *Feminist Studies* Anthology   *Edited by Claire Goldberg Moses*
  and Heidi Hartmann
In a Generous Spirit: A First-Person Biography of Myra Page   *Christina Looper Baker*
Mining Cultures: Men, Women, and Leisure in Butte, 1914–41   *Mary Murphy*
Gendered Strife and Confusion: The Political Culture of Reconstruction   *Laura F. Edwards*
The Female Economy: The Millinery and Dressmaking Trades, 1860–1930   *Wendy Gamber*
Mistresses and Slaves: Plantation Women in South Carolina, 1830–80   *Marli F. Weiner*
A Hard Fight for We: Women's Transition from Slavery to Freedom in South Carolina
  Leslie A. Schwalm
The Common Ground of Womanhood: Class, Gender, and Working Girls' Clubs, 1884–1928
  Priscilla Murolo

Purifying America: Women, Cultural Reform, and Pro-Censorship Activism, 1873–1933
Alison M. Parker

Marching Together: Women of the Brotherhood of Sleeping Car Porters
Melinda Chateauvert

Creating the New Woman: The Rise of Southern Women's Progressive Culture in Texas,
1893–1918 *Judith N. McArthur*

The Business of Charity: The Woman's Exchange Movement, 1832–1900
Kathleen Waters Sander

The Power and Passion of M. Carey Thomas *Helen Lefkowitz Horowitz*

For Freedom's Sake: The Life of Fannie Lou Hamer *Chana Kai Lee*

Becoming Citizens: The Emergence and Development of the California Women's
Movement, 1880–1911 *Gayle Gullett*

Selected Letters of Lucretia Coffin Mott *Edited by Beverly Wilson Palmer
with the assistance of Holly Byers Ochoa and Carol Faulkner*

Women and the Republican Party, 1854–1924 *Melanie Susan Gustafson*

Southern Discomfort: Women's Activism in Tampa, Florida, 1880s–1920s *Nancy A. Hewitt*

The Making of "Mammy Pleasant": A Black Entrepreneur in Nineteenth-Century
San Francisco *Lynn M. Hudson*

Sex Radicals and the Quest for Women's Equality *Joanne E. Passet*

"We, Too, Are Americans": African American Women in Detroit and Richmond, 1940–54
Megan Taylor Shockley

The Road to Seneca Falls: Elizabeth Cady Stanton and the First Woman's Rights
Convention *Judith Wellman*

Reinventing Marriage: The Love and Work of Alice Freeman Palmer and
George Herbert Palmer *Lori Kenschaft*

Southern Single Blessedness: Unmarried Women in the Urban South, 1800–1865
Christine Jacobson Carter

Widows and Orphans First: The Family Economy and Social Welfare Policy, 1865–1939
S. J. Kleinberg

Habits of Compassion: Irish Catholic Nuns and the Origins of the Welfare System,
1830–1920 *Maureen Fitzgerald*

The Women's Joint Congressional Committee and the Politics of Maternalism, 1920–1930
Jan Doolittle Wilson

"Swing the Sickle for the Harvest Is Ripe": Gender and Slavery in Antebellum
Georgia *Daina Ramey Berry*

Christian Sisterhood, Race Relations, and the YWCA, 1906–46 *Nancy Marie Robertson*

Reading, Writing, and Segregation: A Century of Black Women Teachers in Nashville
Sonya Ramsey

Radical Sisters: Second-Wave Feminism and Black Liberation in Washington, D.C.
Anne M. Valk

Feminist Coalitions: Historical Perspectives on Second-Wave Feminism in the
United States *Edited by Stephanie Gilmore*

Breadwinners: Working Women and Economic Independence, 1865–1920 *Lara Vapnek*

Beauty Shop Politics: African American Women's Activism in the Beauty Industry
Tiffany M. Gill

Demanding Child Care: Women's Activism and the Politics of Welfare, 1940–1971
    Natalie M. Fousekis
Rape in Chicago: Race, Myth, and the Courts   Dawn Rae Flood
Black Women and Politics in New York City   Julie A. Gallagher
Cold War Progressives: Women's Interracial Organizing for Peace and Freedom
    Jacqueline Castledine
No Votes for Women: The New York State Anti-Suffrage Movement   Susan Goodier
Anna Howard Shaw: The Work of Woman Suffrage   Trisha Franzen
Nursing Civil Rights: Gender and Race in the Army Nurse Corps   Charissa J. Threat
Reverend Addie Wyatt: Faith and the Fight for Labor, Gender, and Racial Equality
    Marcia Walker-McWilliams
Lucretia Mott Speaks: The Essential Speeches   Edited by Christopher Densmore, Carol Faulkner,
    Nancy Hewitt, and Beverly Wilson Palmer
Lost in the USA: American Identity from the Promise Keepers to the
    Million Mom March   Deborah Gray White
Women against Abortion: Inside the Largest Moral Reform Movement of the
    Twentieth Century   Karissa Haugeberg
Colored No More: Reinventing Black Womanhood in Washington, D.C.   Treva B. Lindsey
Beyond Respectability: The Intellectual Thought of Race Women   Brittney C. Cooper
Leaders of Their Race: Educating Black and White Women in the New South   Sarah H. Case
Glory in Their Spirit: How Four Black Women Took On the Army during
    World War II   Sandy Bolzenius
Big Sister: Feminism, Conservatism, and Conspiracy in the Heartland   Erin M. Kempker
Reshaping Women's History: Voices of Nontraditional Women Historians
    Edited by Julie Gallagher and Barbara Winslow
All Our Trials: Prisons, Policing, and the Feminist Fight to End Violence   Emily L. Thuma
Sophonisba Breckinridge: Championing Women's Activism in Modern America
    Anya Jabour
Starring Women: Celebrity, Patriarchy, and American Theater, 1790–1850   Sara E. Lampert
Surviving Southampton: African American Women and Resistance in
    Nat Turner's Community   Vanessa M. Holden
Dressed for Freedom: The Fashionable Politics of American Feminism
    Einav Rabinovitch-Fox
Women's Activist Organizing in US History   Compiled by Dawn Durante

The University of Illinois Press
is a founding member of the
Association of University Presses.

———————————————————

University of Illinois Press
1325 South Oak Street
Champaign, IL 61820-6903
www.press.uillinois.edu